ISBN 978-1-334-31847-4
PIBN 10763343

Forgotten Books is a registered trademark of FB &c Ltd.
Copyright © 2017 FB &c Ltd.
FB &c Ltd, Dalton House, 60 Windsor Avenue, London, SW19 2RR.
Company number 08720141. Registered in England and Wales.

For support please visit www.forgottenbooks.com

English
Français
Deutsche
Italiano
Español
Português

www.forgottenbooks.com

Mythology Photography **Fiction**
Fishing Christianity **Art** Cooking
Essays Buddhism Freemasonry
Medicine **Biology** Music **Ancient
Egypt** Evolution Carpentry Physics
Dance Geology **Mathematics** Fitness
Shakespeare **Folklore** Yoga Marketing
Confidence Immortality Biographies
Poetry **Psychology** Witchcraft
Electronics Chemistry History **Law**
Accounting **Philosophy** Anthropology
Alchemy Drama Quantum Mechanics
Atheism Sexual Health **Ancient History**
Entrepreneurship Languages Sport
Paleontology Needlework Islam
Metaphysics Investment Archaeology
Parenting Statistics Criminology
Motivational

LETTERS

ON

IMPORTANT SUBJECTS,

Wrote from the Year 1618 to 1650.

By *JAMES HOWELL*, Efq; Clerk of the Privy-Council to King CHARLES I.

The TENTH EDITION.

Ut clavis portam, fic pandit epiftola pectus.

A B E R D E E N:

Printed and fold by F. DOUGLASS and W. MURRAY,
M,DCC,LIII.

PREFACE

BY THE

PUBLISHERS of this EDITION.

THE following LETTERS being of a miscellaneous nature, some of them are vastly more interesting than others. The author's reflexions on the government, manners, and then state of the countries through which he travelled, are judicious and entertaining: the many agreeable stories he relates to illustrate his subject, as most of them have a direct tendency to promote virtue and morality, cannot fail to please the reader.

THE beginning, procedure, and breaking off of the match betwixt CHARLES I. and the *Infanta* of *Spain*, is nowhere so fully treated of. The author was at the court of *Madrid* all the time it was on the tapis, and had good opportunities of being informed of all circumstances relating to it.

THE survey of the *Spanish* monarchy, the *United Provinces*, and the *Hanse* towns, is very agreeably wrote.

IT must be owned, the philosophy in severals of them is liable to objections; but it will be considered, they were wrote before philosophic knowledge attained to its present degree of perfection.

THE author had the misfortune to fall under the displeasure of the parliament towards the end of King CHARLES I's. reign, and was for several years confined in the *Fleet* prison, without ever being told for what offence. There he had sufficient leisure to reflect upon the then unhappy situation of his country; which is very affectingly

fectingly pointed out in several letters: the public distractions are traced to their original causes, and their con-
sequences very justly predicted.

WE hope the strain of piety and good humour which
runs through most of these letters, will recommend them
to many; and if the reader, sometimes meet with a word
or phrase *too free* 'tis hoped he will consider how difficult
it is to write on subjects of wit and humour without
sometimes falling into indecency of expression. It will no
doubt please him more to find, that 100 years ago,
gentlemen were not ashamed to be thought religious, than
it will disgust him to meet with a few exceptionable phra-
ses. ——Perhaps it may be necessary to make some apology for leaving out several poetical pieces, especially
those upon religious subjects; but it is universally allowed, that *English* poetry at the time these letters were
wrote, was far short of the elegance and perfection it
has now attained.

SINCE these LETTERS were first printed, several writers have obliged the public with remarks upon most parts
of *Europe*: in some of these, their towns, laws, cu-
stoms, &c. are more minutely described than was consi-
stent with the brevity of a letter. But these authors
have described the countries they treat of, as they were
of late; and we believe people will be well enough pleased
to know how they stood about 100 years ago. The style
is good for the time they were wrote.

WITH regard to the errors of former impressions, we
can honestly say we have corrected a great many: perhaps some have escaped us, but those we hope, are not
material.   F A-

FAMILIAR
LETTERS.

PART I.

LETTER I.

To Sir J. S. *at* Leeds *Caſtle.*

SIR,

IT was a quaint difference the antients did put betwixt a *letter*, and an *oration*, that the one ſhould be attired like a woman, the other like a man : the latter of the two is allowed large ſide robes, as long periods, parentheſis, ſimiles, examples, and other parts of rhetorical flouriſhes ; but a *letter* or *epiſtle* ſhould be ſhort-coated, and cloſely couched ; a hungerlin becomes a *letter* more handſomely than a gown. Indeed we ſhould write as we ſpeak ; and that's a true familiar letter which expreſſeth one's mind, as if he were diſcourſing with the party to whom he writes in ſuccinct and ſhort terms. The *tongue* and the *pen*, are both of them interpreters of the mind ; but I hold the *pen* to be the more faithful of the two : the *tongue, in udo poſita*, being ſeated in a moiſt ſlippery place, may fail and falter in her ſudden extemporal expreſſions ; but the *pen* having a greater advantage of premeditation, is not ſo ſubject to error, and leaves things behind it upon firm and authentic record. Now, letters though they be capable of any ſubject, yet commonly they are either *narratory, objurgatory, conſolatory, monitory,* or *congratulatory.* The firſt conſiſts of *relations,* the ſecond of *reprehenſions,* the third of *comfort,* the laſt two of *counſel* and *joy.* There are ſome who in lieu of letters write *homilies,* they preach when they ſhould epiſtolize ; there are others that turn them to tedious *tractats* : this is to make letters degenerate from their true nature. Some modern authors

A

there

there are, who have expofed their letters to the world ;
but moft of them, I mean among you *Latin* epiftolizers,
go freighted with mere *Bartholomew* ware, with trite
and trivial phrafes only, lifted with pedantic fhreds of
fchool-boy verfes. Others there are among our next
tranfmarine neighbours Eaftward, who write in their own
language, but their ftyle is fo foft and eafy, that their
letters may be faid to be like bodies of loofe flefh without finews, they have neither joints of art, nor *arteries* in
them ; they have a kind of fimpering and lank hectic
expreffions made up of a bombaft of words and finical affected complements only : I cannot well away with fuch
fleazy ftuff, with fuch cobweb compofitions, where there
is no ftrength of matter, nothing for the reader to carry
away with him, that may enlarge the notions of his foul :
one fhall hardly find an apothegm, example, fimily, or
any thing of philofophy, biftory, or folid knowledge, or
as much as one new *created* phrafe in a hundred of
them ; and to draw any obfervations out of them, were
as if one went about to diftil cream out of froth, infomuch, that it may be faid of them what was faid of the
eccho, *That fhe was a mere found and nothing elfe.*

I return you your *Balzac* by this bearer ; and when I
found thofe letters, wherein he is fo familiar with his
King, fo flat, and thofe to *Richelieu* fo puffed with
profane hyperboles, and larded up and down with fuch
grofs flatteries, with others befides, which he fends as
urinals up and down the world to look into his water,
for difcovery of the crazy condition of his body, I forbore him further. So I am

Your moft affectionate fervitor,

Weftminfter, July 25. 1625.   J. H.

LETTER II.

To my FATHER *upon my first going beyond Sea.*

S I R,

I Should be much wanting to myself, and to that obligation of duty, the Law of God, and his *handmaid* Nature hath impofed upon me, if I fhould not acquaint you with the courfe and quality of my affairs and fortunes, fpecially at this time, that I am upon the point of croffing the feas to eat my bread abroad. Nor is it the common relation of a fon that only induced me hereunto, but that moft indulgent and coftly care you have been pleafed, in fo extraordinary a manner, to have had of my breeding, though but one child of *fifteen*, by placing me in a choice methodical *fchool*, fo far diftant from your dwelling under a learned (though *lafhing*) mafter; and by tranfplanting me thence to *Oxford*, to be graduated; and fo holding me ftill up by the chin, until I could fwim without bladders. This patrimony of liberal education you have been pleafed to endue me withal, I now carry along with me abroad as a fure infeparable treafure; nor do I feel it any burden or incumbrance unto me at all: and what danger foever my perfon, or other things I have about me do incur, yet, I do not fear the lofing of this, either by fhipwreck or pirates at fea, nor by robbers, or fire, or any other cafuality afhore; and, at my return to *England*, I hope, at leaftwife I fhall do my endeavour, that you may find this patrimony improved fomewhat to your comfort.

The main of my employment is from that gallant Knight, Sir *Robert Manfell*, who, with my Lord of *Pembroke*, and divers other of the prime Lords of the Court, have got the fole patent of making all forts of glafs with pit-coal, only to fave thofe huge proportions of wood which were confumed formerly in the glafs-furnaces: and this bufinefs being of that nature, that the workmen are to be had from *Italy*, and the chief materials

A 2 from

from *Spain*, *France*, and other foreign countries, there is need of an Agent abroad for this ufe ; (and better then I have offered their fervice in this kind) fo that I believe I fhall have employment in all thefe countries before I return.

Had I continued ftill Steward of the glafs-houfe in *Broad-ftreet*, where Captain *Francis Bacon* hath fucceeded me, I fhould in a fhort time have melted away to nothing, amongft thofe hot *Venetians*, finding myfelf too green for fuch a charge ; therefore, it hath pleafed God to difpofe of me now to a condition more fuitable to my years, and that will, I hope, prove more advantageous to my future fortunes.

In this my peregrination, if I happen, by fome accident, to be difappointed of that allowance I am to fubfift by, I muft make my addrefs to you, for I have no other rendevouz to fly unto; but it fhall not be, unlefs in cafe of great indigence.

Touching the news of the time : Sir *George Villiers*, the new favourite, tapers up a-pace, and grows ftrong at Court: his predeceffor, the Earl of *Somerfet*, hath got a leafe of ninety years for his life, and fo hath his *articulate* lady, called fo, for articling againft the frigidity and impotence of her former Lord. She was afraid that *Cook* the Lord Chief Juftice (who had ufed extraordinary art and induftry in difcovering all the circumftances of the poifoning of *Overbury*) would have made white *broth* of them, but the *prerogative* kept them from the *pot :* yet the fubfervient inftruments, the leffer flies could not break thorough, but lay entangled in the cobweb. Amongft others, Mrs. *Turner*, the firft inventrefs of *yellow ftarch*, was executed in a cobweb lawn ruff of that colour, at *Tyburn*; and with her, I believe that *yellow ftarch*, which fo much disfigured our nation, and rendered them fo ridiculous and fantaftic, will receive its funeral. Sir *Gervas Elwaies* Lieutenant of the Tower, was made a notable example of juftice and terror to all officers of truft : for being acceffory, and that in a paffive way only to the murder, yet he was hanged on
Tower-

Tower-hill ; and the caveat is very remarkable which he gave upon the gallows, that, people fhould be very cautious how they make vows to heaven, for the breach of them feldom pafs without a judgment, whereof he was a moft ruthful example ; for being in the low-countries, and much given to gaming, he once made a folemn vow, (which he brake afterwards) that if he played above fuch a fum, *he might be hanged.* My Lord *(William)* of *Pembroke,* did a moft noble act like himfelf ; for the King having given him all Sir *Gervas Elwaies*'s eftate, which came to above 1000 l. *per an.* he freely beftowed it on the widow and her children.

The latter end of this week I am to go a fhip-board, and firft for the low-countries. I humbly pray your blef-fing may accompany me in thefe my travels by land and fea, with a continuance of your prayers, which will be as fo many good gales to blow me to fafe port ; for, I have been taught, *That the parents benedictions contribute very much, and have a kind of a prophetic virtue to make the child profperous.* In this opinion, I fhall ever reft

Your dutiful fon,

Lond. *March* 1. 1618. J. H.

LETTER III.

To Sir JAMES CROFTS, *Knight at St.* Ofith.

SIR,

I Could not fhake hands with *England,* without kiffing your hands alfo ; and becaufe, in regard of your diftance now from *London,* I cannot do it in perfon, I fend this paper for my deputy.

The news that keeps greateft noife here now, is the return of Sir *Walter Rawleigh* from his mine of gold in *Guinea,* the South parts of *America* ; which at firft was like to be fuch a hopeful boon voyage, but it feems that golden mine is proved a mere *chimera,* an imaginary airy

A 3 mine ;

mine ; and indeed, his Majefty had never any other conceit of it. But, what will not one in captivity (as Sir *Walter* was) promife to regain his freedom ? Who would not
promife, not only mines but mountains of gold for liberty ? And 'tis pity fuch a knowing well-weighed Knight
had not had a better fortune ; for the *Deftiny*, I mean
that brave fhip which he built himfelf of that name, that
carried him thither, is like to prove a *fatal* Deftiny to him,
and to fome of the reft of thofe gallant adventurers which
contributed for the fetting forth of thirteen fhips more,
who were moft of them his kinfmen and younger brothers, being led into the faid expedition by a general
conceit the world had of the wifdom of Sir *Walter Rawleigh* ; and many of thefe are like to make *fhipwreck* of
their eftates by this voyage. Sir *Walter* landed at *Plymouth*, whence he thought to make an efcape ; and fome
fay he hath tampered with his body by phyfick, to make
him look fickly, that he may be the more pitied, and
permitted to lie in his own houfe. Count *Gondamar* the
Spanifh Ambaffador fpeaks high language, and fending
lately to defire audience of his Majefty, he faid, he had but
one word to tell him : his Majefty wondering what might
be delivered in one word, when he came before him, he
faid only, *Pirates, Pirates, Pirates*, and fo departed.

It is true, that he protefted againft this voyage before,
and that it could not be but for fome predatory defign :
and, if it be as I hear, I fear it will go very ill with
Sir *Walter ;* and that *Gondamar* will never give him
over, till he hath his head off his fhoulders ; which may
quickly be done without any new arraignment, by virtue
of the old fentence that lies ftill dormant againft him,
which he could never get off by pardon, notwithftanding
that he mainly laboured in it before he went ; but his
Majefty could never be brought to it, for he faid, he
would keep this as a curb to hold him within the bounds
of his commiffion, and the good behaviour.

Gondamar cries out, that he hath broke the facred
peace betwixt the two kingdoms ; that he hath fired and
plundered *Santo Thoma*, a colony the *Spaniards* had
planted

planted with fo much blood, near under the *Line*, which made it prove fuch hot fervice unto him ; and where, befides others, he loft his eldeft fon in the action : and could they have preferved the magazine of *tobacco* only, befides other things in that town, fomething might have been had to countervail the charge of the voyage. *Gondamar* alledgeth further, that the enterprize of the mine failing, he propounded to the reft of his fleet to go and intercept fome of the plate-galleons, with other defigns which would have drawn after them apparent acts of hoftility, and fo demands juftice. Befides other difafters which fell out upon the dafhing of the firft defign, Captain *Renifh*, who was the main inftrument for difcovering of the mine, piftolled himfelf in a defperate mood of difcontent in his cabin, in the *Convertine*.

This return of Sir *Walter Rawleigh* from *Guinea*, puts me in mind of a facetious tale I read lately in *Italian*, for I have a little of that language already, how *Alphonfo* King of *Naples* fent a *Moor*, who had been his captive a long time, to *Barbary* with a confiderable fum of money to buy horfes, and to return by fuch a time. Now there was about the King a kind of *buffoon* or jefter, who had a table-book or journal, wherein he was ufed to regifter any abfurdity, or impertinence, or merry paffage that happened upon the Court. That day the *Moor* was difpatched for *Barbary*, the faid jefter waiting upon the King at fupper, the King called for his journal, and afked what he had obferved that day ; thereupon he produced his table-book, and amongft other things, he read how *Alphonfo* King of *Naples* had fent *Beltram* the *Moor*, who had been a long time his prifoner, to *Morocco* (his own country) with fo many thoufand crowns to buy horfes. The King afked him why he inferted that ? Becaufe, faid he, I think he will never come back to be a prifoner again, and fo you have loft both man and money : but if he do come, then your jeft is marred, fays the King : no Sir, *for if he return I will blot out your name, and put him in for a fool.*

The

The application is eafy and obvious : but the world
wonders extremely, that fo great a wife man as Sir *Walter Rawleigh* would return to caft himfelf upon fo inevitable a rock, as I fear he will; and much more, that fuch
choice men, and fo great a power of fhips fhould all come
home and do nothing.

The letter you fent to my father, I conveyed fafely
the laft week to *Wales*.   I am this week by God's help
for the *Netherlands*, and then I think for *France*.   If
in this my foreign employment I may be any way ferviceable unto you :   you know what power you have to difpofe of me, for I honour you in a very high degree, and
will live and die

Your humble and ready fervant,

Lond. March 28. 1618.   J. H.

L E T T E R IV.

To my Brother, after Dr. HOWEL, *and now Bifhop of*
Briftol, *from* Amfterdam.

BROTHER,

I Am newly landed at *Amfterdam*, and it is the firft
foreign earth I ever fet foot upon.   I was pitifully
fick all the voyage, for the weather was rough, and the
wind untoward;   and at   the mouth of the *Texel* we
were furprized by a furious tempeft, fo that the fhip was
like to fplit upon fome of thofe old ftumps of trees
wherewith that river is full; for in ages paft, as the
Skipper told me, there grew a fair forreft in that channel
where the *Texel* makes now her bed.   Having been fo
rocked and fhaken at fea, when I came alhore I began
to incline to *Copernicus* his opinion, which hath got fuch
a fway lately in the world, *viz.* that the earth, as well
as the reft of her fellow-elements, is in perpetual motion,
for fhe feemed fo to me a good while after I had landed.
He that obferves the fite and pofition of this country,
will

will never hereafter doubt the truth of that philofophical problem which keeps fo great a noife in the fchools, *viz.* that the fea is higher than the earth, becaufe, as I failed along thefe coafts, I vifibly found it true; for the ground here which is all betwixt marfh and moorifh, lies not only level, but, to the apparent fight of the eye, far lower than the fea, which made the Duke of *Alva* fay, that the inhabitants of this country were the neareft neighbours to hell (the great abyfs) of any people upon earth, becaufe they dwell loweft : moft of that ground they tread, is plucked as it were out of the very jaws of *Neptune*, who is afterwards pent out by high dikes, which are preferved with incredible charge, infomuch, that the chief *Dike-grave* here, is one of the greateft officers of truft in all the province, it being in his power, to turn the whole country into a falt lough when he lift, and fo to put *Hans* to fwim for his life, which makes it to be one of the chiefeft parts of his litany, *From the Sea, the Spaniard, and the Devil*, the Lord deliver me. I need not tell you who preferves him from the laft, but from the *Spaniard*, his beft friend is the fea itfelf, notwithftanding that he fears him as an enemy another way : for the fea ftretching himfelf here into divers arms, and meeting with fome of thofe frefh rivers that defcend from *Germany* to difgorge themfelves into him through thefe provinces, moft of thofe towns are thereby encompaffed with water, which by fluces they can contract or dilate as they lift : this makes their towns inacceffible, and out of the reach of cannon; fo that *water* may be faid to be one of their beft fences, otherwife I believe they had not been able to have born up fo long againft the gigantick power of *Spain*.

This city of *Amflerdam*, though fhe be a great ftaple of news, yet I can impart none unto you at this time, I will defer that till I come to the *Hague*.

I am lodged here at one Monfieur *Dela Cluze*, not far from the Exchange, to make an introduction into the *French* : becaufe I believe I fhall fteer my courfe hence next to the country where that language is fpoken; but

I think I ſhall ſojourn here about two months longer; therefore, I pray direct your letters accordingly, or any other you have for me. *one of the prime comforts of a traveller is to receive letters from his friends ; they beget new ſpirits in him, and preſent joyful objects to his fancy, when his mind is clouded ſometimes with the fogs of melancholy ;* therefore I pray make me happy as often as your conveniency will ſerve, with your's: you may ſend or deliver them to Capt. *Bacon* at the Glaſshouſe, who will ſee them ſafely ſent.

So my dear brother, I pray God bleſs us both, and ſend us after this large diſtance, a joyful meeting.

Your loving brother,

Amſterdam, April 1. 1617.   J. H.

LETTER V.

To DAN. CALDWALL, *Eſq; from* Amſterdam.

My dear DAN.

I Have made your friendſhip ſo neceſſary unto me for the contentment of my life, that happineſs itſelf would be but a kind of infelicity without it : it is as needful to me, as fire and water, as the very air I take in, and breathe out; it is to me not only *neceſſitudo* but *neceſſitas :* therefore I pray let me enjoy it in that fair proportion, that I deſire to return unto you by way of correſpondence and retaliation. Our firſt league of love, you know, was contracted among the muſes in *Oxford ;* for no ſooner was I *matriculated* to her, but I was *adopted* to you ; I became her *ſon*, and your *friend*, at one time : you know, I followed you then to *London,* where our love received *confirmation* in the *Temple,* and elſewhere. We are now far aſunder, for no leſs than a ſea ſevers us, and that no narrow one, but the *German* ocean : *diſtance ſometimes endears friendſhip, and abſence ſweeteneth it ; it much enhanceth the value of it, it*, *and makes it more precious.* Let this be verified in us; let that love which formerly ufed to be nourifhed by perfonal communication, and the lips, be now fed by letters; let the pen fupply the office of the tongue. Letters have a ftrong operation, they have a kind of art-like embraces to mingle fouls, and make them meet, though millions of paces afunder; by them we may converfe and know how it fares with each other, as it were by intercourfe of fpirits. Therefore, amongft your civil fpeculations, I pray let your thoughts fome-times reflect on me, (your abfent felf) and wrap thofe thoughts in paper, and fo fend them me over; I pro-mife you they fhall be very welcome; I fhall embrace and hug them with my beft affections.

Commend me to *Tom Bowyer*, and enjoin him the like: I pray, be no niggard in diftributing my love plen-tifully amongft our friends at the Inns of Court: let *Jack Toldervy* have my kind commends with this caveat, *That the pot which goes often to the water, comes home cracked at laft :* therefore, I hope he will be careful how he makes the *Fleece* in *Cornhill* his thorough fare too often. So may my dear *Daniel* live happy, and love his

Amfterdam, *April* 10. 1619.   J. H.

LETTER VI.

To my FATHER, *from* Amfterdam.

S I R,

I Am lately arrived in *Holland* in a good plight of health, and continue yet in this town of *Amfterdam*, a town, I believe, that there are few her fellows, being from a mean fifhing-dorp, come in a fhort revolution of time, by a monftrous increafe of commerce and naviga-tion, to be one of the greateft marts of *Europe*. It is admirable to fee what various forts of buildings, and fabrics are now here erecting everywhere, not in houfes
only,

only, but in whole ſtreets and ſuburbs: ſo that it is thought ſhe will in a ſhort time double her proportion in bigneſs.

.I am lodged in a *Frenchman*'s houſe, who is one of the deacons of our *Engliſh Browniſts* church here; it is not far from the ſynagogue of *Jews*, who have free and open exerciſe of their religion here. I believe in this ſtreet where I lodge, there be well near as many religions as there be houſes; for one neighbour knows not, nor cares not much what religion the other is of; ſo that the number of conventicles exceeds the number of churches here. And, let this country call itſelf as long as it will the *United* provinces one way, I am perſuaded in this point, there is no place ſo *diſunited*.

The dog and rag market is hard by, where every Sunday morning there is a kind of public mart for thoſe commodities, notwithſtanding their preciſe obſervance of the Sabbath.

Upon Saturday laſt I happened to be in a Gentleman's company, who ſhewed me, as I walked along in the ſtreets, a long bearded old *Jew* of the tribe of *Aaron*; when the other *Jews* met him, they fell down and kiſſed his foot: this was the Rabbi with whom our countryman *Broughton* had ſuch a diſpute.

This city, notwithſtanding her huge trade, is far inferior to *London* for populouſneſs; and this I infer out of their weekly bills of mortality, which come not at moſt but to fifty or thereabout; whereas in *London*, the ordinary number is betwixt two and three hundred, one week with another: nor are there ſuch wealthy men in this town as in *London*; for, by reaſon of the generality of commerce, the banks, adventures, the common ſhares and ſtocks which moſt have in the *Indian* and other companies, the wealth doth diffuſe itſelf here in a ſtrange kind of equality, not one of the Burghers being exceeding rich, or exceeding poor; inſomuch, that I believe our four and twenty Aldermen, may buy a hundred of the richeſt men in *Amſterdam*. It is a rare thing to meet with a beggar here, as rare as to ſee

a

a horfe, they fay, upon the ftreets of *Venice*, and this is held to be one of their beft pieces of government; for befides the ftrictnefs of their laws againft mendicants, they have hofpitals of all forts for young and old, both for the relief of the one, and the employment of the other; fo that there is no object here to exercife any act of charity upon. They are here very neat, tho' not fo magnificent in their buildings, efpecially in their frontifpieces and firft rooms; and for cleanlinefs, they may ferve for a pattern to all people. They will prefently drefs half a dozen difhes of meat without any noife or fhew at all: for if one goes to the kitchen, there will be fcarce appearance of any thing but a few covered pots upon a turf-fire, which is their prime fuel: after dinner they fall a fcouring of their pots, fo that the outfide will be as bright as the infide, and the kitchen fuddenly fo clean as if no meat had been dreffed there a month before: they have neither well nor fountain, or any fpring of frefh-water in or about this city, but their frefh-water is brought unto them by boats; befides, they have cifteros to receive the rain-water which they muft ufe; fo that my laundrefs bringing my linen to me one day, and I commending the whitenefs of them; fhe anfwered, that they muft needs be white and fair, for they were wafhed in *aqua cælefti*, meaning fky-water.

It were cheap living here, were it not for the morftrous excifes which are impofed upon all forts of commodities, both for belly and back; for the retailler pays the *State* almoft the one moiety as much as be paid for the commodity at firft; nor doth any murmur at it, becaufe it goes not to any favourite or private purfe, but to preferve them from the *Spaniard*, their common enemy as they term him; fo that the faying is truly verified here, *Defend me, and fpend me:* with this excife principally, they maintain all their armies by fea and land, with their garrifons at home and abroad, both here and in the *Indies*, and defray all public charges befides.

I fhall hence fhortly for *France*, and in my way take moft of the prime towns of *Holland* and *Zealand*, efpecially *Leyden*, (the Univerfity) where I fhall fojourn fome days. So humbly craving a continuance of your bleffing and prayers, I reft

Your dutiful fon,

May 1. 1619.   J. H.

L E T T E R VII.

To Dr. Thomas Prichard, *at* Jefus College *in* Oxford, *from* Leyden.

S I R,

IT is the Royal prerogative of love, not to be confined to that fmall local compafs which circumfcribes the body, but to make his fallies and progreffes abroad, to find out and enjoy his defired objeft, under what region foevei : nor is it the vaft gulph of *Neptune,* or any diftance of place, or difference of clime, can bar him of this privilege. I never found the experiment hereof fo fenfibly, nor felt the comfort of it fo much as fince I fhook hands with *England :* for, tho' you be in *Oxford,* and I at *Leyden ;* albeit you be upon an ifland, and I now upon the continent, (tho' the loweft part of *Europe*), yet thofe fwift poftillions my *thoughts* find you out daily, and bring you unto me. I behold you often in my chamber and in my bed ; you eat, you drink, you fit down, and walk with me, and my fantafy enjoys you often in my fleep, when all my fenfes are locked up, and my foul wanders up and down the world, fometimes thro' pleafant fields and gardens, fometimes thro' odd uncouth places, over mountains and broken confufed buildings. As my love to you doth thus exercife his power, fo I defire your's to me may not be idle, but roufed up fometimes to find me out, and fummon me to attend you in *Jefus College.*

I am now here in *Leyden*, the only academy befides *Franiker* of all the *United Provinces*. Here are nations of all forts, but the *Germans* fwarm more than any : to compare their *University* to yours, were to caft *New-Inn* in counterfcale with *Chrift-Church* college, or the alms-houfe on *Tower-hill* to *Sutton*'s hofpital. Here are no colleges at all God-wot (but one for the *Dutch*), nor fcarce the face of an *University*, only there are general fchools where the *fciences* are read by feveral Profeffors, but all the ftudents are *Oppidans :* a fmall time and lefs learning will fuffice to make one a *graduate ;* nor are thofe formalities of habits, and other decencies here, as with you, much lefs thofe exhibitions and fupport for fcholars, with other encouragements ; infomuch, that the *Oxonians* and *Cantabrigians.*——*Bona fi fua norint*, were they fenfible of their own felicity, are the happieft *Academians* on earth ; yet *Apollo* hath a ftrong influence here : and as *Cicero* faid of them of *Athens*, *Athenis pingue cœlum, tenuia ingenia : The Athenians had a thick air, and thin wits ;* fo I may fay of thefe *Lugdunenfians, They have a grofs air, but thin fubtle wits*, (fome of them): witnefs, elfe *Heinfius, Grotius, Arminius* and *Baudius :* of the two laft I was told a tale, that *Arminius* meeting *Baudius* one day difguifed with drink (wherewith he would be often), he told him, *Tu Baudi dedecorus noftram Academiam, & tu Armini noftram religionem.* Thou *Baudius* difgraceft our Univerfity, and thou *Arminius* our religion. The heaven here hath always fome cloud in his countenance ; and from this grofnefs and fpiffitude of air proceeds the flow nature of the inhabitants ; yet this flownefs is recompenfed with another benefit ; it makes them patient and conftant, as in all other actions, fo in their ftudies and fpeculations, tho' they ufe,

——*Craffus tranfire Dies, lucemque paluftrem.*

I pray, impart my love liberally amongft my friends in *Oxford*, and when you can make truce with your more

ferious

ferious meditations, beftow a thought drawn into a few lines, upon

Your

Leyden, May 30, 1619. **J. H.**

LETTER VIII.

To Sir JAMES CROFTS, *from the* Hague.

S I R,

THE fame obfervance that a father may challenge of his child, the like you may claim of me, in regard of the extraordinary care you have pleafed to have always fince I had the happinefs to know you, of the courfe of my fortunes.

I am newly come to the *Hague*, the Court of the fix (and almoft feven) *confederated* provinces; the Council of State with the Prince of *Orange*, makes his firm refidence here, unlefs he be upon a march, and in motion for fome defign abroad. This Prince (*Maurice*) was caft in a mould fuitable to the temper of this people: he is flow, and full of warinefs, and not without a mixture of fear; I do not mean pufillanimous, but politic fear. He is the moft conftant in the quotidian courfe and carriage of his life, of any that I ever heard or read of: for whofoever knows the cuftoms of the Prince of O-range, may tell what he is doing here every hour of the day, though he be in *Conftantinople*. In the morning he awaketh about fix in fummer, and feven in winter: the firft thing he doth, he fends one of his grooms or pages to fee how the wind fits, and he wears or leaves off his waiftcoat accordingly; then he is about an hour dreffing himfelf, and about a quarter of an hour in his clofet; then comes in the Secretary, and if he hath any private or public letters to write, or any other difpatches to make, he doth it before he ftirs from his chamber; then comes he abroad, and goes to his ftable if it be no fer-
mon-

mon-day, to fee fome of his gentlemen or pages (of whofe breeding he is very careful) ride the great horfe. He is very acceffible to any that hath bufinefs with him, and fheweth a winning kind of familiarity; for, he will fhake hands with the meaneft boor of the country, and he feldom hears any commander or gentleman with his hat on : he dines punctually about twelve, and his table is free for all comers, but none under the degree of a Captain fits down at it. After dinner he ftays in the room a good while, and then any one may accoft him, and tell his tale ; then he retires to his chamber, where he anfwers all *petitions* that were delivered him in the morning; and toward the evening, if he goes not to council, which is feldom, he goes either to make fome vifits or take the air abroad, and according to this conftant method he paffeth his life.

There are great ftirs like to arife betwixt the *Bohemians*, and the elected King the Emperor; they are come already to that height, that they confult of depofing him, and to chufe fome proteftant Prince to be their King ; fome talk of the Duke of *Saxony*, others of the *Palfegrave*. I believe the ftates here would rather be for the latter, in regard of conformity of religion, the other being a *Lutheran*.

I could not find in *Amfterdam* a large *Ortelius* in *French* to fend you, but from *Antwerp* I will not fail to ferve you.

So wifhing you all happinefs and health, and that the fun may make many progreffes more through the *Zodiac*, before thofe comely gray hairs of yours go to the grave, I reft

Your very humble fervant,

June 1619.   J. H.

LETTER IX.

To Captain FRANCIS BACON *at the Glass-house in* Broadstreet.

S I R,

MY last to you was from *Amsterdam*, since which time I have traversed the prime parts of the *United Provinces*, and am now in *Zealand*, which is much crest-fallen since the staple of *English* cloth was removed hence, as is *Flushing* also, her next neighbour, since the departure of the *English* garrison. A good intelligent gentleman told me the manner how *Flushing* and the *Brill*, our two cautionary towns here were redeemed, which was thus : the nine hundred and odd soldiers at *Flushing* and the *Rammakins* hard by, being many weeks without their pay, they borrowed divers sums of money of the States of this town ; who, finding no hopes of supply from *England*, advice was sent to the *States General* at the *Hague* ; they consulting with Sir *Ralph Winwood* our Ambassador, (who was a favourable instrument unto them in this business, as also in the match with the *Palsgrave*) sent instructions to the Lord *Caroon*, to acquaint the Earl of *Suffolk* (then Lord Treasurer) herewith ; and in case they could find no satisfaction there, to make his address to the King himself, which *Caroon* did. His Majesty being much incensed that his subjects and soldiers should starve for want of their pay in a foreign country, sent for the Lord Treasurer ; who drawing his Majesty aside, and telling how empty his exchequer was, his Majesty told the Ambassador, that if his masters the States would pay the money they owed him upon those towns, he would deliver them up. The Ambassador returning the next day to know whether his Majesty persisted in the same resolution, in regard that at his former audience he perceived him to be a little transported, his Majesty answered, that he knew the States of *Holland* to be his good friends and confederates both in point of re-

ligion

ligion and policy; therefore, he apprehended not the
leaft fear of any difference that fhould fall out between
them, in contemplation whereof, if they defired to have
their towns again, he would willingly furrender them.
Hereupon, the States made up the fum prefently; which
came in convenient time, for it ferved to defray the ex-
penceful progrefs he made to *Scotland* the fummer following. When that money was lent by Queen *Elizabeth*,
it was articled, that intereft fhould be paid upon intereft;
and befides, that for every gentleman who fhould lofe
life in the States fervice, they fhould make good five
pounds to the crown of *England*. All this his Majefty
remitted, and only took the principal: and, this was
done in requital of that princely entertainment and great
prefents which my Lady *Elizabeth* had received in divers
of their towns as fhe paffed to *Heydelberg*.

The bearer hereof is Signior *Antonio Miotti*, who was
mafter of a cryftal-glafs furnace here a long time; and as
I have it by good intelligence, he is one of the ableft and
moft knowing men for the guidance of a glafs-work in
chriftendom; therefore, according to my inftructions I
fend him over, and hope to have done Sir *Robert* good
fervice thereby. - So with my kind refpects unto you, and
my moft humble fervice where you know it is due, I
reft

Your obliged fervant,

June 6. 1619.   J. H.

L E T T E R X.

To Sir JAMES CROFTS. *Antwerp.*

S I R,

I Prefume that my laft to you from the *Hague* came
    fafe to hand. I am now come to a more chearful
country, and amongft a people fomewhat more vigorous
and metalled, being not fo heavy as the *Hollander*, or
homely

homely as they of *Zealand*. This goodly antient city
methinks looks like a difconfolate widow, or rather fome
fuperannuated virgin that hath loft her lover, being almoft quite bereft of that flourifhing commerce, wherewith, before the falling off the reft of the provinces from
Spain, fhe abounded to the envy of all other cities and
marts of *Europe*. There are few places this fide the
Alps better built and fo well ftreeted as this, and none
at all fo well girt with baftions and ramparts, which in
fome places are fo fpacious, that they ufually take the
air in coaches upon the very walls, which are beautified
with divers rows of trees and pleafant walks. The citadel here, though it be an addition to the ftatelinefs and
ftrength of the town, yet it ferves as a fhrewd curb unto her, which makes her chomp upon the bit, and fome
fometimes with anger, but fhe cannot help it. The tumults in *Bohemia* now grow hotter and hotter : they
write how the great council at *Prague* fell to fuch a
hurliburly, that fome of thofe Senators who adherred to
the Emperor were thrown out at the windows, where
fome were maimed, fome broke their necks. I am
fhortly to bid farewel to the *Netherlands*, and to bend
my courfe to *France*, where I fhall be moft ready to entertain any commands of yours. So may all health and
happinefs attend you, according to the wifhes of

Your obliged fervant,

July 5. 1619.

J. H.

LETTER XI.

To my FATHER, *from* Rouen.

SIR,

YOURS of the third of *Auguft* came fafe to hand
in an inclofed from my brother : you may make
eafy conjecture how welcome it was unto me, and to
what

what a height of comfort it raifed my fpirits, in regard it was the firft I received from you fince I croffed the feas, I humbly thank you for the bleffing you fent along with it.

I am now upon the fair continent of *France*, one of nature's choiceft mafter-pieces, one of *Ceres'* chiefeft barns of corn, one of *Bacchus's* prime wine cellars, and of *Neptune's* beft falt-pits ; a compleat felf-fufficient country, where there is rather a fuperfluity then defect of any thing, either for neceffity or pleafure, did *the policy of the country correfpond with the bounty of Nature, in the equal diftribution of the wealth among the inhabitants :* for, I think there is not upon the earth a richer country and poorer people. It is true, *England* hath a good repute abroad for her fertility, yet be our harvefts never fo kindly, and our crops never fo plentiful, we have every year commonly fome grain from thence, or from *Dantzick* and other places imported by the merchant ; befides, there be many more heaths, commons, bleak-barren hills, and wafte grounds in *England* by many degrees then I find here ; and I am forry *our* country of *Wales* fhould give more inftances hereof than any other part.

This province of *Normandy*, once an *appendix* to the crown of *England*, though it want wine, yet it yields the King as much defmeans as any of the reft : the lower *Norman* hath *cyder* for his common drink ; and I vifibly obferved that they are more plump and replete in their bodies, and of a clearer complexion then thofe that drink altogether wine. In this great city of *Rouen* there be many monuments of the *Englifh* yet extant. In the outfide of the higheft fteeple of the great church, there is the word G O D engraven in huge golden characters, every one almoft as long as myfelf to make them the more vifible. In this fteeple hangs alfo the greateft bell of chriftendom, called *d'Amboife* ; for it weighs near upon forty thoufand pound weight. There is alfo here St. *Oen*, the greateft Sanctuary in this city, founded by one of our compatriots as the name imports. This province is alfo fubject to *wardfhips*, and no other part of
France

France befides; but, whether the conqueror tranfported that law to *England* from hence, or whether he fent it over from *England* hither I cannot refolve you. There is a marvellous quick trade beaten in this town, becaufe of the great navigable river *Sequana* (the *Seine*) that runs hence to *Paris*, whereon there ftands a ftrange bridge that ebbs and flows, that rifeth and falls with the river, it being made of boats, whereon coaches and carts may pafs over as well as men : befides, this is the nearelt mercantile city that ftands betwixt *Paris* and the fea.

My laft unto you was from the *Low-Countries*, where I was in motion to and fro above four months ; but I fear it mifcarried in regard you make no mention of it in yours.

I begin more and more to have a fenfe of the fweet-nefs and advantage of foreign travel. I pray when you come to *London* find a time to vifit Sir *Robert*, and acknowledge his great favours unto me, and defire a continuance thereof according as I fhall endeavour to de-ferve them. So with my due and daily prayers for your health, and a fpeedy fuccefsful iffue of all your law bufi-nefs, I humbly crave your blefling, and reft

Your dutiful fon,

Septr. 7. 1619. J. H.

LETTER XII.

To Capt. FRANCIS BACON *from* Paris.

S I R,

I Received two of yours in *Rouen*, with the bills of ex-change therein inclofed, and according to your dire-ctions I fent you thofe things which you wrote for.

I am newly come to *Paris*, this huge magazine of men, the epitome of this large populous kingdom, and rendevouz of all foreigners. The ftructures here are in-differently fair, though the ftreets generally foul all the

four

four feafons of the year; which I impute firft, to the pofition of the city, being built upon an ifle, (the ifle of
France, made fo by the branching and ferpentine courfe
of the river of *Seine*) and having fome of her fuburbs
feated high, the filth runs down the channel and fettles
in many places within the body of the city, which lieth
upon a flat; as alfo for a world of coaches, carts, and
horfes of all forts, that go to and fro perpetually, fo that
fometimes one fhall meet with a ftop half a mile long of
thofe coaches, carts, and horfes, that can move neither
forward nor backward by reafon of fome fudden encounter
of others coming a crofs-way; fo that often times it will
be an hour or two before they can difentangle : in fuch
a ftop the great *Henry* was fo fatally flain by *Ravillac*.
Hence comes it to pafs that this town (for *Paris* is a
town, a *city*, and an *univerfity*) is always dirty, and 'tis
fuch a dirt, that by perpetual motion is beaten into fuch
a thick black unctious oil, that where it fticks no art can
wafh it off of fome colours, infomuch, that it may be no
improper comparifon to fay, that an ill name is like the
crot (the dirt) of *Paris*, which is indelible; befides the
ftain this dirt leaves, it alfo gives fo ftrong a fcent, that
it may be fmelt many miles off, if the wind be in one's
face as he comes from the frefh country. This may be
one caufe why the plague is always in fome corner or o-
ther of this vaft city, which may be called as once *Scythia*
was, *vagino populorum*, or (as mankind was called by a
great philofopher) a great mole-hill of ants : yet, I believe this city is not fo populous as fhe feems to be, for
her form being round, (as the whole kingdom is) the
paffengers wheel about, and meet oftner than they ufe to
do in the long continued ftreets of *London*, which makes
London appear lefs populous then fhe is indeed; fo that
London for length (though not for latitude) including
Weftminfter, exceeds *Paris*, and hath in *Michaelmas*
term more fouls moving within her in all places. 'Tis
under one hundred years that *Paris* is become fo fump-
tuous and ftrong in buildings; for her houfes were mean,
until a mine of white ftone was difcovered hard by,
which

which runs in a continued vein of earth, and is digged
out with cafe being foft, and is between a white clay and
chalk at firft, but being pullied up, with the open air it
receives a crufty kind of hardnefs, and fo becomes perfect free-ftone ; and before it is fent up from the pit,
they can reduce it to any form. Of this ftone, the
Louvre, the King's palace is built, which is a vaft fabric ;
for the gallery wants not much of an *Italian* mile in
length, and will eafily lodge 3000 men ; which fome
told me, was the end for which the laft King made it fo
big, that lying at the fag end of this great mutinous city,
if fhe perchance fhould rife, the King might pour out of
the *Louvre* fo many thoufand men unawares into the heart
of her.

I am lodged here hard by the *Baftile*, becaufe it is
furtheft off from thofe places where the *Englifh* refort ;
for I would go on to get a little language as foon as I
could. In my next, I fhall impart unto you what ftate-
news *France* affords in the interim, and always I am

Your humble fervant,.

Paris, March 30. 1620. J. H.

LETTER XIII.

To RICHARD ALTHAM *Efq; from* Paris.

Dear Sir,

LOVE is the marrow of friendfhip, and letters are the
elixir of love ; they are the beft fuel of affection,
and caft a fweeter *odour* than any franckincenfe can do :
fuch an *odour*, fuch an *aromatic* perfume your late *letter*
brought with it, proceeding from the fragrancy of thofe
dainty flowers of eloquence, which I found bloffoming
as it were in every line ; I mean thofe fweet expreffions
of love and wit, which in every period were interming-
led with fo much art, that they feemed to contend for
maftery which was the ftrongeft. I muft confefs, that you

put

put me to hard shifts to correspond with you in such exquisite strains and raptures of *love*, which were so lively, that I must needs judge them to proceed from the motions, from the *diastole* and *systole* of a heart truly affected. Certainly your heart did dictate every syllable you wrote, and guided your hand all along. Sir, give me leave to tell you, that not a dram, nor a dose, nor a scruple of this precious *love* of yours is lost, but is safely treasured up in my heart, and answered in like proportion to the full; mine to you is as cordial, it is passionate and perfect as *love* can be.

I thank you for the desire you have to know how it fares with me abroad. I thank God, I am perfectly well, and well contented with this wandering course of life a while: I never enjoyed my health better, but I was like to endanger it two nights ago; for being in some jovial company abroad, and coming late to our lodging, we were suddenly surprized by a crew of *filous* of night rogues, who drew upon us, and as we had exchanged some blows, it pleased God the *Chevalier du Guet*, an officer, who goes up and down the streets all night on horseback to prevent disorders, passed by, and so rescued us; but *Jack White* was hurt, and I had two thrusts in my cloke. There is never a night passeth, but some robbing or murder is committed in this town, so that it is not safe to go late anywhere, specially about the *Pont-Neuf*, the new-bridge, though *Henry the Great* himself lies centinel there in arms, upon a huge *Florentine* horse, and sits bare to every one that passeth; an improper posture methinks to a King on horseback. Not long since, one of the Secretaries of State (whereof there are here always four) having been invited to the suburbs of *St. Germains* to supper, left order with one of his lacqueys to bring him his horse about nine; it so happened, that a mischance befell the horse, which lamed him as he went a watering to the *Seine*, insomuch, that the Secretary was put to beat the hoof himself, and foot it home; but, as he was passing the *Pont-Neuf* with his lacquey carrying a torch before him, he might over-hear a noise of clashing

C or

of fwords, and fighting; and looking under their torch, and perceiving they were but two, he bad his lacquey go on; they had not made many paces, but two armed men with their piftols cocked, and fwords drawn, made puffing towards them, whereof one had a paper in his hand; which he faid, he had cafually took up in the ftreets, and the differences between them was about that paper; therefore, they defired the Secretary to read it, with a great deal of compliments; the Secretary took out his fpectacles, and fell a reading of the faid paper, whereof the fubftance was, *That it fhould be known to all men, that whofoever did pafs over that bridge after nine o'clock at night in winter, and ten in fummer, was to leave his cloke behind him, and in cafe of no cloke, his hat.* The Secretary ftarting at this, one of the comrades told him, that he thought that paper concerned him; fo they unmantled him of a new plufh cloke, and my Secretary was content to go home quietly, and *en cuerpo.* This makes me think often of the excellent nocturnal government of our city of *London,* where one may pafs and repafs fecurely all hours of the night, if he give good words to the watch. There is a gentle calmnefs through all *France,* and the King intends to make a progrefs to all the frontier towns of the kingdom, to fee how they are fortified. The favorite *Luines* ftrengtheneth himfelf more and more in his minionfhip; but he is much murmured at in regard the accefs of fuitors to him are fo difficult; which made a Lord of the land fay, that three of the hardeft things in the world were; *To quadrate a circle, to find out the philofopher's ftone, and to fpeak with the Duke of* Luines.

I have fent you by *Vacandary* the poft, the *French* bever and tweefes you write for: bever-hats are grown dearer of late, becaufe the *Jefuites* have got the *monopoly* of them from the King.

Farewel dear child of virtue and minion of the mufes, and continue to love

Yours,

Paris, May, 1. 1620.   J. H.

LET-

LETTER XIV.

To Sir JAMES CROFTS, *from* Paris.

SIR,

I Am to set forward this week for *Spain*, and if I can find no commodity of embarkation at *St. Malo's*, I must be forced to journey it all the way by land, and clammer up the huge *Pyreney-hills*, but I could not bid *Paris* adieu, till I had conveyed my true and constant respect to you by this letter. I was yesterday to wait upon Sir *Herbert Crofts* at *St. Germains*, where I met with a *French* gentleman, who amongst other curiosities which he pleased to shew me up and down *Paris*, brought me to that place where the late King was slain, and to that where the Marquis of *Ancre* was shot, and so made me a punctual relation of all the circumstances of those two acts, which in regard they were rare; and I believe two of the notablest accidents that ever happened in *France*, I thought it worth the labour to make you partaker of some part of his discourse.

France, as all christendom besides, (for there was then a truce betwixt *Spain* and the *Hollander*) was in a profound peace, and had continued so twenty years together. When *Henry* IV. fell upon some great martial design, the bottom whereof is not known to this day; and being rich, (for he had heaped up in the *Bastile* a mount of gold that was as high as a lance) he levied a huge army of 40,000 men; whence came the song, *The King of* France *with forty thousand men;* and upon a sudden he put this army in perfect equipage, and some say he invited our Prince *Henry* to come unto him to be a sharer in his exploits; but going one afternoon to the *Bastile*, to see his treasure and ammunition; his coach stopped suddenly, by reason of some colliers and other carts that were in that narrow street; *Ravillac* a lay-jesuit (who had a whole twelve month watched an opportunity to do

C 2   the

the act) put his foot boldly upon one of the wheels of the coach, and with a long knife stretched himself over their shoulders who were in the boot of the coach, and reached the King at the end, and stabed him right in the left-side to the heart ; and pulling out the fatal steel, he doubled his thrust : the King with a ruthful voice cried out, *Jesu suis blesse* (I am hurt) and suddenly the blood issued out at his mouth : the regicide villain was apprehended, and command given, that no violence should be offered him, that he might be reserved for the law, and some exquisite torture. The Queen grew half distracted hereupon, who had been crowned Queen of *France* the day before in great triumph ; but a few days after she had something to countervail, if not to overmatch her *sorrow*; for according to St. *Lewis's* law, she was made Queen Regent of *France* during the King's minority, who was then but about ten years of age. Many consultations were held how to punish *Ravillac*, and there were some *Italian* physicians that undertook to prescribe a torment, that should last a constant torment for three days, but he escaped only with this, his body was pulled between four horses, that one might hear his bones crack, and after the dislocation they were set again, and so he was carried in a cart standing half naked, with a torch in that hand which had committed the murder ; and in the place where the act was done, it was cut off, and a gauntlet of hot oil was clapt upon the stump, to stanch the blood, whereat he gave a doleful shriek, then was he brought upon a stage, where a new pair of *boots* was provided for him, half filled with boiling oil ; then his body was pincered, and hot oil poured into the holes. In all the extremity of this torture, he scarce shewed any sense of pain, but when the gauntlet was clapt upon his arm to stanch the flux of reaking blood, at that time, he gave a shriek only. He bore up against all these torments about three hours before he died : all the *confession* that could be drawn from him, was, *That he thought he had done God good service to take away that King, which would have embroiled all christendom in an endless war.*

A

A fatal thing it was, that *France* fhould have three of her kings come to fuch violent deaths, in fo fbort a *revolution* of time. *Henry* II. at tilt with Monfieur *Montgomery*, was killed by a fplinter of a lance that pierced his eye: *Henry* the III. not long after, was killed by a young friar, who in lieu of a *letter* which he pretended to have for him, pulled out of his long fleeve a knife, and thruft him into the *bottom* of the belly, as he was coming from his *clofe-ftool*, and fo difpatched him; but that regicide was hacked to pieces in the place by the nobles. The fame deftiny attended this King by *Ravillac*, which is become now a common name of reproach and infamy in *France*.

Never was King fo much lamented as this; there are a world not only of his pictures, but ftatues up and down *France*, and there's fcarce a market-town, but hath him erected in the market-place, or over fome gate, not upon fign-polls, as our *Henry* the VIII. and by a public act of parliament which was confirmed in the confiftory at *Rome*, he was entitled, *Henry the Great*, and fo placed in the temple of immortality. A notable Prince he was, and of an admirable temper of body and mind; he had a graceful facetious way to gain both love and awe: he would be never tranfported beyond himfelf with choller, but he would pafs by any thing with fome *repartee*, fome witty ftrain, wherein he was excellent. I will inftance in a few which were told me from a good hand: one day he was charged by the Duke of *Bouillon* to have changed his religion, he anfwered, *No coufin, I have changed no religion, but an opinion*: and the Cardinal of *Perron* being by, he enjoined him to write a treatife for his vindication; the Cardinal was long about the work, and when the King afked from time to time where his *book* was, he would ftill anfwer him, *That he expected fome manufcripts from* Rome, *before he could finifh it*. It happened, that one day the King took the Cardinal along with him to look on his workmen and new buildings at the *Louvre*; and paffing by one corner which had been a long time begun, but left unfinifhed, the King afked the chief *mafon* why

that corner was not all this while perfected ? Sir, it is
because I want some choice stones ; *No, no,* said the King,
looking upon the Cardinal, *It is because thou wantest
manuscripts from* Rome. Another time, the old Duke
of *Main,* who was used to play the droll with him, coming
softly into his bed-chamber and thrusting in his bald-head,
and long neck, in a posture to make the King merry, it
happened the King was coming from doing his case ; and
spying him, he took the round cover of the *close-stool,*
and clapt it on his bald sconce, saying, *Ah, cousin, you
thought once to have taken the crown off my head, and
wear it on your own ; but this of my tail shall now serve
your turn.* Another time, when at the siege of *Amiens,*
he having sent for the Count of *Soissons* (who had 100000
franks a year pension from the crown) to assist him in
those wars, and that the Count excused himself, by reason of his years and poverty, having exhausted himself in
the former wars, and all that he could do now, was to
pray for his Majesty, which he would do heartily : this
answer being brought to the King, he replied, *Will my
cousin, the Count of* Soissons, *do nothing else but pray for
me ? Tell him that prayer without fasting, is not avail-
able ; therefore I will make my cousin fast also from his
pension of* 100000 *per annum.*

He was once troubled with a fit of the gout ; and the
Spanish Ambassador coming then to visit him, and saying
he was sorry to see his Majesty so lame ; he answered,
*As lame as I am, if there were occasion, your master the
King of* Spain *should no sooner have his foot in the stirrup,
but he should find me on horseback.*

By these few you may guess at the *genius* of this spright-
ful Prince : I could make many more instances, but then I
should exceed the bounds of a letter. When I am in
Spain, you shall hear further from me ; and if you can
think on any thing wherein I may serve you, believe it,
Sir, that any employment from you shall be welcome to

Your much obliged servant,

Paris, *May,* 12. 1620.   J. H.

L E T-

L E T T E R .XV.

To my Brother Dr, HOWELL.

Brother,

BEING to-morrow to part with *Paris,* and begin my journey for *Spain,* I thought it not amiſs to ſend you this, in regard I know not when I ſhall have opportunity to write unto you again.

This kingdom ſince the young King hath taken., the ſcepter into his own hands, doth flouriſh very much with quietneſs and commerce ; nor is there any motion or the leaſt tintamar of trouble in any part of the country, which is rare in *France.* 'Tis true, the Queen-mother is diſcontented ſince ſhe left her regency, being confined; and I know not what it may come unto in time, for ſhe hath a ſtrong party, and the murdering of her Marquis of *Ancre* will yet bleed, as ſome fear.

I was lately in ſociety of a gentleman who was a ſpectator of that tragedy, and he was pleaſed to relate unto me the particulars of it, which was thus: when *Henry* IV. was ſlain, the Queen Dowager took the reins of the government into her hands during the young King's minority; and amongſt others whom ſhe advanced, Signior *Conchino* a *Florentine ;* and her foſter-brother was one : her countenance came to ſhine ſo ſtrongly upon him, that he became her only confident and favourite, inſomuch, that ſhe made him Marquis of *Ancre,* one of the twelve Marſhals of *France,* Governor of *Normandy,* and conferred other honours and offices of truſt upon him, and who but he. The princes of *France* could not endure this domineering of a ſtranger, therefore, they leagued together to ſuppreſs him by arms : the Queen Regent having intelligence hereof, ſurprized the Prince of *Conde,* and clapt him up in the *Baſtile :* the Duke of *Main* fled hereupon to *Peronne* in *Picardy,* and other great men put themſelves in an armed poſture to ſtand upon their guard. The young King being told that the Marquis of

Ancre

Ancre was the ground of this difcontentment, commanded Monfieur *de Vitry* Captain of his guard to arreft him,
and in cafe of refiftance to kill him.   This bufinefs was
carried very clofely till the next morning, that the faid
Marquis was coming to the *Louvre* with a ruffling train of
gallants after him, and paffing over the draw-bridge at
the court-gate, *Vitry* ftood there with the King's guard
about him ; and as the Marquis entered, he told him,
that he had a commiffion from the King to apprehend
him, therefore he demanded his fword :   the Marquis
hereupon put his hand upon his fword, fome thought to
yield it up, others to make oppofition ; in the mean
time, *Vitry* difcharged a piftol at him, and fo difpatched
him.   The King being above in his gallery, afked what
noife that was below, one fmilingly anfwered, nothing
Sir, but that the Marfhall of *Ancre* is flain : who flew
him ? The Captain of your guard : why ? Becaufe he
would have drawn his fword at your Majefty's royal commiffion : then the King replied, *Vitry hath done well, and
I will maintain the aƈt.*   Prefently, the Queen-mother
had all her guard taken from her, except fix men and fixteen women ; and fo fhe was banifhed *Paris*, and commanded to retire to *Blois.*   *Ancre*'s body was buried
that night in a church hard by the court ; but the next
morning; the lacqueys and pages (who are more unhappy here then the *apprentices* in *London*) broke up
his grave, tore his coffin to pieces, ript the winding-
fheet, and tied his body to an afs's tail, and fo dragged
him up and down the ftreets of *Paris*, which are none of
the fweeteft ; they then fliced off his ears and nailed
them upon the gates of the city ; they cut off his genitories, (and they fay he was hung like an afs) and fent
them for a prefent to the Duke of *Main ;* the reft of
his body they carried to the new-bridge, and hung him
his heels upwards and head downwards, upon a new gib-
bet that had been fet up a little before to punifh them
who fhould fpeak ill of the prefent government ; and it
was his chance to have the maidenhead of it himfelf.
His wife was hereupon apprehended, imprifoned, and
beheaded

beheaded for a witch some few days after, upon a surmise that she had enchanted the Queen to dote so upon her husband; and they say, the young King's picture was found in her closet in *virgin-wax* with one leg melted away. A little after a process was formed against the Marquis (her husband), and so he was *condemned after death*. This was a right act of a *French* popular fury, which like an angry torrent is irresistible, nor can any hanks, boundaries, or dikes stop the impetuous rage of it. How the young King will prosper after so high and an unexampled act of violence, by beginning his reign, and imbruing the walls of his own court with blood in that manner, there are divers censures.

When I am settled in *Spain* you shall hear from me; in the interim, I pray let your prayers accompany me in this long journey, and when you write to *Wales*, I pray acquaint our friends with my welfare: so, I pray God bless us both, and send us a happy interview,

Your loving brother,

Paris, Sept. 8. 1620.   J. H.

LETTER XVI.

To my Cousin W. VAUGHAN, *Esq; from* St. Malo.

COUSIN,

I Am now in *French Britany;* I went back from *Paris* to *Rouen*, and so through all *Normandy* to a little port called *Granville*, where I embarked for this town of *St. Malo*, but I did purge so violently at sea, that it put me into a burning fever for some few days, whereof (I thank God) I am newly recovered; and finding no opportunity of shipping here, I must be forced to turn my intended sea-voyage to a land-journey.

Since I came to this province, I was curious to converse with some of the lower *Britons*, who speak no other language but our *Welsh;* for their radical words are no
other;

other; but 'tis no wonder, for they were a colony of *Welsh* at first, as the *name* of this province doth imply, as also the Latin name *Armorica;* which though it pass for Latin, yet it is but pure *Welsh,* and signifies a country bordering upon the sea, as that arch-heretick was called *Pelagius, a Pelago,* his name being *Morgan.* I was a little curious to peruse the annals of this province; and, during the time that it was a kingdom, there were four kings of the name *Hoell,* whereof one was called *Hoell the Great.*

This town of *St. Malo* hath one rarity in it; for there is here a perpetual garrison of *English,* but they are of *English* dogs, which are let out in the night to guard the ships and eat the carrion up and down the streets, and so they are shut up again in the morning.

It will be now a good while before I shall have conveniency to send to you, or receive from you: howsoever, let me retain still some little room in your memory, and sometimes in your meditations, while I carry you about me perpetually, not only in my head, but in heart, and make you travel all along with me thus from town to country, from hill to dale, from sea to land up and down the world; and you must be contented to be subject to these uncertain removes and perambulations, until it shall please God to fix me again in *England:* nor need you, while you are thus my concomitant through new places every day, to fear any ill usage while I fare well.

Yours, Χρήσει ἢ κλήσει.

J. H.

LETTER XVII.
To Sir JOHN NORTH, *from* Rochel.

S I R,

I Am newly come to *Rochel;* nor am I sorry that I went somewhat out of my way to see this town, not (to tell you true) out of an extraordinary love I bear to
the

the people; for I do not find them so gentle and debonair to strangers, nor so hospitable as the rest of *France;* but I excuse them for it, in regard it is commonly so with all republick and banse-towns, whereof this smells very rank; nor indeed hath any *Englishman* much cause to love this town, in regard in ages past, lhe played the most treacherous part with *England* of any other part in *France :* for the story tells us, that this town having by a perfidious stratagem (by forging a counterfeit commission from *England*), induced the *English* Governor to make a general muster of all his forces out of the town : this being one day done, they shut their gates against him, and made him go shake his ears and shift for his lodging, and so rendered themselves to the *French* King, who sent them a blank to write their own conditions. I think they have the strongest ramparts by sea of any place of *christendom,* nor have I seen the like in any town of *Holland,* whose safety depends upon water. I am bound to-morrow for *Bordeaux,* then through *Gascogny* to *Tholouse,* so through *Languedoc* over the hills to *Spain :* I go in the best season of the year, for I make an *autumnal* journey of it. I pray let your prayers accompany me all along, they are the best offices of love, and fruits of friendship : so God prosper you at home, as me abroad, and send us in good time a joyful conjuncture.

Yours,

Rochel, Oct. 8. 1620.   J. H.

LETTER XVIII.

To Mr. Tho. Porter, *after Capt.* Porter, *from* Barcelona.

MY dear *Tom,* I had no sooner set foot upon this soil, and breathed *Spanish* air, but my thoughts presently reflected upon you. Of all my friends in *England,* you were the first I met here, you were the prime object of my speculation, methought the very winds in
gentle

gentle whifpers did breathe out your name, and blow it
on 'me : you feemed to reverberate upon me with the
beams of the fun, which you know hath fuch a powerful
influence, and indeed too great a ftroke in this country :
all this you muft afcribe to the operations of love, which
hath fuch a ftrong virtual force, that when it fafteneth upon a pleafant fubject, it fets the imagination in a ftrange
fit of working ; it employs all the faculties of the foul,
fo that not one cell in the brain is idle ; it bufieth the
whole inward man, it affects the heart, amufeth the underftanding ; it quickeneth the fancy, and leads the will
as it were by a filken thread to co-operate with them all,
I have felt thefe motions often in me, fpecially at this
time that my memory is fixed upon you ; but the reafon
that I fell firft upon you in *Spain*, was that I remembered
I had heard you often difcourfing how you have received
part of your education here, which brought you to fpeak
the lauguage fo exactly well : I think often of the relations I have heard you make of this country, and the
good inftructions you pleafed to give me.

I am now in *Barcelona*, but the next week I intend to
go on through *your* town of *Valentia* to *Alicant*, and
thence you fhall be fure to hear from me further, for I
make account to winter there. The Duke of *Offunu*
paffed by here lately ; and, having got leave of grace to
relcafe fome flaves, he went aboard the *Cape-Gallies*, and
palling through the *churma* of flaves, he afked divers of
them what their offences were ; every one excufed himfelf, one faying, that he was put in out of malice, another
by bribery of the judge, but all of them unjuftly ; a-
mongft the reft, there was one fturdy little black man,
and the Duke afking him what he was in for : Sir, faid
he, *I cannot deny but I am juftly put in here, for I
wanted money, and fo took a purfe hard by* Tarragona
to keep me from ftarving : the Duke with a little ftaff he
had in his hand, gave him two or three blows upon the
fhoulder, faying, *You rogue, what do you do amongft fo
many honeft innocent men ? Get you gone out of their*
company ;

company ; fo he was freed, and the reft remained ftill in *ftatu quo primus*, to tug at the oar.

I pray commend me to Signior *Camillo*, and *Mazalao*, with the reft of the *Venetians* with you ; and when you go aboard the fhip behind the *Exchange*, think upon

Yours,

Barcelona, Nov. 10. 1620. J. H.

L E T T E R XIX.

To Sir JAMES CROFTS.

S I R,

I Am now a good way within the body of *Spain*, at *Barcelona*, a proud wealthy city, fituated upon the *Mediterranean*, and is the *metropolis* of the kingdom of *Catalonia*, called of old *Hifpania Terraconenfis*. I had much ado to reach hither ; for befides the monftruous abruptnefs of the way, thefe parts of the *Pyreneys* that border upon the *Mediterranean* are never without thieves by the land (called *Bandeleros*) and pirates on the fea-fide, which lie fculking in the hollows of the rocks, and often furprize paffengers unawares, and carry them flaves to *Barbary* on the other fide. The fafeft way to pafs, is to take a *Bordon* in the habit of a pilgrim, whereof there are abundance that perform their vows this way to the Lady of *Monferrat*, one of the prime places of pilgrimage in *chriftendom :* it is a ftupenduous monaftery, built on the top of a huge land-rock, whether it is impoffible to go up or come down by a direct way, but a path is cut out full of windings and turning ; and on the crown of this craggy-hill there is a flat upon which the monaftery and pilgrimage place is founded, where there is a picture of the Virgin *Mary* fun-burnt and tanned, it feems when fhe went to *Egypt ;* and to this picture a marvellous confluence of people from all parts of *Europe* refort.

D As

As I paſſed between the *Pyreney-hills*, I obſerved the poor *Labradors*, ſome of the country people, live no better than brute animals in point of food; for their ordinary commons, is graſs and water, only they have always within their houſes a bottle of vinegar, and another of oil; and when dinner or ſupper time comes, they go abroad and gather their herbs, and ſo caſt vinegar or oil upon them, and will paſs thus two or three days without bread or wine; yet, they are ſtrong luſty men, and will ſtand ſtifly under a muſket.

There is a tradition, that there were divers mines of gold in ages paſt amongſt thoſe mountains: and the ſhepherds that kept goats then, having made a ſmall fire of roſemary-ſtubs, with other combuſtible ſtuff to warm themſelves, this fire grazed along, and grew ſo outrageous, that it conſumed the very entrails of the earth, and melted thoſe mines; which growing fluid by liquefaction, ran down into the ſmall rivulets that were in the valleys, and ſo carried all into the ſea, that monſtruous gulph which ſwalloweth all, but ſeldom diſgorgeth any thing; and in theſe brooks to this day ſome ſmall grains of gold are found.

The *Viceroy* of this country hath taken much pains to clear theſe hills of robbers, and there hath been a notable havock made of them this year; for in divers woods as I paſſed, I might ſpy ſome trees laden with dead carcaſſes, a better fruit far then *Diogenes*'s tree bore, whereon a woman had hanged herſelf; which the *Cynic* cried out to be the beſt bearing tree that ever he ſaw.

In this place there lives neither *Engliſh* merchant or factor; which I wonder at, conſidering it is a maritime town, and one of the greateſt in *Spain*, her chiefeſt arſenal for gallies, and the ſeale by which ſhe conveys her monies to *Italy*: but, I believe the reaſon is, that there is no commodious port here for ſhips of any burden, but a large bay. I will enlarge myſelf no further at this time, but leave you to the guard and guidance of God, whoſe ſweet hand of protection hath brought me through ſo many uncouth places and difficulties to this city. So hoping

ing to meet your letters in *Alicant*, where I fhall anchor a good while, I reft

Yours to difpofe of,

Barcelona, *Nov.* 24. 1620.　　　　　　J. H.

LETTER XX.

To Dr. Fr. Mansell, *from* Valentia.

S I R,

THOUGH it be the fame glorious fun that fhines upon you in *England*, which illuminates alfo this part of the hemifphere; though it be the fun that ripeneth your pippins, and pomegranates, your hops, and our vine-yards here, yet he difpenfeth his heat in different degrees of ftrength: thofe rays that do but warm you in *England*, do half roaft us here; thofe beams that irradiate only, and gild your honey-fuckled fields, do fcorch and parch this chinky gaping foil, and fo put too many wrink-les upon the face of our common mother the earth. O bleffed clime, O happy *England*, where there is fuch a rare temperature of the heat and cold, and all the reft of elementary qualities, that one may pafs (and fuffer little) all the year without either fhade in fummer, or fire in winter.

I am now in *Valentia*, one of the nobleft cities of all *Spain*, fituate in a large vega or valley, above fixty miles compafs: here are the ftrongeft filks, the fweeteft wines, the beft oils, and the beautifulleft females of all *Spain*; for the prime courtefans in *Madrid* and elfewhere are had hence. The very brute animals make themfelves beds of rofemary and other fragrant flowers hereabouts; and when one is at fea, if the wind blow from the fhore, he may fmell this foil before he come in fight of it many leagues off, by the ftrong odoriferous fcent it cafts. As it is the moft pleafant, fo it is alfo the temperateft cli-mate of all *Spain*, and fo they call it the fecond *Italy*; which made the *Moors*, whereof many thoufands were

D 2　　　　　　　　difterr'd

difterr'd and banifhed hence to *Barbary*, to think that paradife was in that part of the heavens which hung over this city. Some twelve miles off, is old *Sagunto*, now called *Morviedre*, through which I paffed, and faw'many monuments of *Roman* antiquities there ; amongft others, there is the temple dedicated to *Venus*, when the fnake came about her neck, a little before *Hannibal* came thi-ther. No more now, but that I heartily wifh you were here with me, and I believe you would not defire to be a good while in *England*. So, I am

Yours,

Valentia, March 1. 1620.   **J. H.**

LETTER XXI.

To CHRISTOPHER JONES, *Efq; at* Grays-Inn.

I Am now (thanks be to God) come to *Alicant*, the chief rendevouz I aimed at in *Spain ;* for I am to fend hence a commodity called *Barillia* to Sir *Robert Manfel*, for making of cryftal-glafs ; and I have treated with Signior *Andriotti* a *Genoa* merchant for a good round parcel of it, to the value of 2000 *l.* by letters of credit from Mr. *Richant ;* and upon his credit, I might have taken many thoufand pounds more, he is fo well known in the kingdom of *Valentia.* This *Barillia* is a ftrange kind of vegetable, and it grows nowhere upon the face of the earth, in that perfeétion as here : the *Vene-tians* have it hence ; and it is a commodity whereby this maritime town doth partly fubfift ; for, it is an ingredient that goes to the making of the beft caftile foap. It grows thus : 'tis a round thick earthy fhrub that bears berries like bar-berries, betwixt blue and green ; it lies clofe to the ground, and when it is ripe they dig it up by the roots, and put it together in cocks, where they leave it to dry many days like hay ; then they make a pit of a fa-thom deep in the earth, and with an inftrument like one

of

of our prongs, they take the tuffs and put fire to them, and when the flame comes to the berries, they melt and diffolve into an *azure* liquor, and fall down into the pit till it be full; then they dam it up, and fome days after they open it, and find this *Barillia* juice turned to a blue ftone, fo hard, that it is fcarce malleable: it is fold at one hundred crowns a tun, but I had it for lefs. There is alfo a fpurious flower called *Gazull*, that grows here, but the glafs that's made of that is not fo refplendent and clear. I have been here now thefe three months, and moft of my food hath been grapes and bread, with other roots, which have made me fo fat, that I think if you faw me, you would hardly know me, fuch nutriture this fanguine *Alicant* grape gives. I have not received a fyllable from you fince I was in *Antwerp*, which tranf-forms me to wonder, and engenders odd thoughts of jea-loufy in me, that as my body grows fatter, your love grows lanker towards me. I pray take off thefe fcruples, and let me hear from you, elfe it will make a fchifm in friendfhip, which I hold to be a very holy league, and no lefs than a piacle to infringe it; in which opinion, I reft

Your conftant friend,

Alicant, March 27. 1621.   J. H.

LETTER XXII.

To Sir JOHN NORTH, *Knight.*

SIR,

HAVING endured the brunt of a whole fummer in *Spain*, and tried the temper of all the other three feafons of the year, up and down the kingdoms of *Cata-lonia, Valentia* and *Marcia*, with fome parts of *Aragon,* I am now to direct my courfe for *Italy*. I hoped to have embarked at *Carthagena*, the beft port upon the *Mediterranean*; for what fhips and gallies get in thither, are fhut up as it were in a box from the violence and in-

jury

jury of all weathers ; which made *Andrea Doria*, being
asked by *Philip* II. which were his best harbours ? He
answered, *June, July*, and *Carthagena* ; meaning that
any port is good in these two months, but *Carthagena*
was good at any time of the year. There was a most
ruthful accident had happened there a little before I
came : for whereas five ships had gone thence laden with
soldiers for *Naples*, amongst whom there was the flower
of the gentry of the kingdom of *Mercia ;* those ships had
hardly sailed three leagues, but they met with sixteen
sail of *Algier* men of war, who had lien skulking in the
creeks thereabout ; and they had the winds and all things
else so favourable, that of those five ships, they took one,
sunk another, and burnt a third, and two fled back to
safe harbour. The report hereof being bruited up and
down the country, the gentlewomen came from the
country to have tidings, some of their children, others of
their brothers and kindred, and went tearing their hair,
and howling up and down the streets in a most piteous
manner. The Admiral of those five ships, as I heard
afterwards, was sent for to *Madrid*, and hanged at the
court-gate, because he did not fight. Had I come time
enough to have taken the opportunity, I might have been
made, either food for haddocks, or turned to cinders, or
have been by this time a slave in the bannier at *Algier*, or
tugging at an oar ; but I hope God hath reserved me for
a better destiny : so, I came back to *Alicant*, where I
lighted upon a lusty *Dutchman*, who hath carried me safe
hither, but we were near upon forty days in voyage.
We passed by *Majorca* and *Minorca*, the *Beleares In-
sulæ*, by some ports of *Barbary*, by *Sardinia, Corsica*,
and all the islands of the *Mediterranean* sea. We were
at the mouth of *Tyber*, and thence fetched our course for
Sicily ; we passed by those sulphureous fiery islands,
Mongibel and *Strombolo* ; and about the dawn of the
day we shot through *Scylla* and *Charybdis*, and so into
the phare of *Messina ;* thence we touched upon some of
the *Greek* islands, and so came to our first intended
course, into the *Venetian Gulph*, and are now here at
Malamocco,

Malamocco, where we remain yet aboard, and muſt be content to be ſo, to make up the month before we have *pratic*, that is, before any be permitted to go aſhore, and negotiate, in regard we touched at ſome infeƈted places : for there are no people upon earth ſo fearful of the plague as the *Italians*, eſpecially the *Venetians*, tho' their neighbours the *Greeks* hard by, and the *Turks*, have little or no apprehenſion at all of the danger of it ; for they will viſit and commerce with the ſick without any ſcruple, and will fix their longeſt finger in the midſt of their forehead, and ſay, their deſtiny and manner of death is pointed there. When we have gained yon maiden city, which lieth before us, you ſhall hear farther from me : ſo leaving you to his holy proteƈtion, who ✦ bath thus graciouſly vouchſafed to preſerve this ſhip, and me, in ſo long and dangerous a voyage, I reſt

Yours,

Malamocco, April 30. 1621.   J. H.

L E T T E R XXIII.

To my Brother Dr. HOWELL, *from on ſhipboard be‐ fore* Venice.

Brother,

IF this letter fail either in point of *orthography* or *ſtyle*, you muſt impute the firſt to the tumbling poſture my body was in at the writing hereof, being a ſhipboard ; the ſecond to the muddineſs of my brain, which like lees in a narrow veſſel, hath been ſhaken at ſea in divers tempeſts near upon forty days ; I mean natural days, which include the night alſo, and are compoſed of twenty four hours, by which number the *Italian* computes his clock : for at the writing hereof, I heard one from *Malamocco* ſtrike twenty-one hours. When I ſhall have ſaluted yonder virgin city that ſtands before me,

and

and hath tantalized me now this fe'n-night, I hope to cheer my spirits, and settle my *pericranium* again.

In this voyage we passed through, at least touched all those seas which *Horace* and other poets sing of so often, as the *Ionian*, the *Ægean*, the *Icarian*, the *Tyrrhene*, with others ; and now we are in the *Adrian* sea, in the mouth whereof *Venice* stands like a gold ring in a bear's muzzle. We passed also by *Ætna*, by the *Infames Scopulos*, *Acroceraunia*, and through *Scylla* and *Charybdis*, about which the antient poets, both *Greek* and *Latin*, keep such a coil; but, they are nothing so horrid or dangerous as they make them to be; they are two white keen-pointed rocks, that lie under water diametrically opposed; and like two dragons defying one another; and there are pilots, that in small shallops, are ready to steer all ships that pass. This amongst divers others, may serve for an instance, that the old poets used to heighten and hoise up things by their airy fancies above the reality of truth. *Ætna* was very furious when we past by, as she useth to be sometimes more than other, especially when the wind is Southward ; for, then she is more subject to belching out flakes of fire, (as stutterers use to stammer more when the wind is in that hole) some of the sparkles fell aboard us; but, they would make us believe in *Syracuse*, now *Messina*, that *Ætna* in times past hath cructated such huge gobbets of fire, that the sparks of them have burnt houses in *Malta* above fifty miles off, transported thither by a direct strong wind. We passed hard by *Corinth*, now *Ragusa*; but I was not so happy as to touch there, for you know

Non cuivis homini contingit adire Corinthum.

I conversed with many *Greeks*, but found none that could understand, much less practically speak any of the old dialects of the pristine *Greek*, it is so adulterated by the vulgar, as a bed of flowers by weeds : nor is there any people, either in the island, or on the continent, that speaks it conversably ; yet, there are in the *Morea* seven parishes called *Zacones*, where the original *Greek* is not

much

much degenerated, but they confound divers letters of the alphabet with one found; for in point of pronunciation, there is no difference betwixt *Epfilon*, *Iota*, and *Eta*.

The laft I received from you was in *Latin*, whereof I fent you an anfwer from *Spain* in the fame language, though in a coarfer dialeft. I fhall be a gueft to *Venice* a good while, therefore I defire a frequency of correfpondence between us by letters, for there will be conveniency every week of receiving and fending. When you write to *Wales*, I pray fend advice that I am come fafe to *Italy*, though not landed there yet: fo my dear brother, I pray God blefs us both, and all our friends, and referve me to fee you again with comfort, and you me, who am

Your loving Brother,

May 5. 1621. J. H.

L E T T E R XXIV.

To the honourable Sir ROBERT MANSELL, *Vice-Admiral of* England, *from* Venice.

S I R,

AS foon as I came to *Venice*, I applied myfelf to difpatch your bufinefs according to inftruftions, and Mr. *Seymor* was ready to contribute his beft furtherance. Thefe two *Italians*, who are the bearers hereof, by report here, are the beft gentlemen-workmen that ever blew cryftal; one is allied to *Antonio Miotti*, the other is coufin to *Mazalao;* for other things they fhall be fent in the fhip *Lion*, which rides here at *Malamocco*, as I fhall fend you account by conveyance of Mr. *Symns*. Herewith I have fent a letter to you from Sir *Henry Wotton*, the Lord Ambaffador here, of whom I have received fome favours: he wifhed me to write, that you have now a double intereft in him; for whereas, before he was only

your

your fervant, he is now your kinfman by your late mar‑
riage.

I was lately to fee the *arfenal* of *Venice*, one of the
wórthieſt things in chriſtendom ; they ſay there are as
many gallies and galeaſſes of all ſorts, belonging to *St*
Mark, either in courfe, at anchor, in dock, or upon the
careen, as there be days in the year : here they can build
a compleat galley in half a day, and put her afloat in per‑
fect equipage, having all the ingredients fitted before‑
hand ; as they did in three hours, when *Henry* III. paſ‑
fed this way to *France* from *Poland*, who wiſhed that
befides *Paris*, and his parliament towns, he had this *arfe‑*
nal in exchange for three of his chiefeſt cities. There are
300 people perpetually here at work ; and if one comes
young, and grows old in *St. Mark*'s ſervice, he hath a
penfion from the State during life. Being brought to fee
one of the *Clariſſimos* that govern this *arfenal*, this huge
fea ſtore-houfe ; among other matters reflecting upon
England, he was ſaying, that if *Cavaglier Don Roberto*
Manfell were here, he thought verily the republick would
make a proffer to him to be Admiral of the fleet of gal‑
lies and galeons, which are now going againſt the Duke
of *Oſſuna*, and the forces of *Naples*, you are ſo well known
here.

I was, fince I came hither, in *Murano*, a little iſland
about the diſtance of *Lambeth* from *London*, where cry‑
ſtal-glaſs is made ; and 'tis a rare fight to fee a whole
ſtreet, where on the one fide there are twenty furnaces
together at work. They ſay here, that altho' one ſhould
tranſplant a glaſs-furnace from *Murano* to *Venice* herſelf,
or to any of the little aſſembly of iſlands about her, or
to any other part of the earth befides, and ufe the fame
materials, the fame workmen, the fame fuel the felf‑
fame ingredients every way, yet they cannot make cry‑
ſtal-glaſs in that perfection, for beauty and luſtre, as in
Murano : fome impute it to the quality of the circum‑
ambient air that hangs over the place, which is purified
and attenuated by the concurrence of ſo many fires that
are in thoſe furnaces night and day perpetually; for they
are

are like the *veſtal-fire* which never goes out. And it is
well known, that ſome airs make more qualifying impreſſions than others ; as a *Greek* told me in *Sicily* of the
air of *Egypt*, where there be huge common furnaces to
hatch eggs by the thouſands in *camels* dung : for during
the time of hatching, if the air happen to come to be
overcaſt, and grow cloudy, it ſpoils all ; if the ſky continue ſtill, ſerene and clear, not one egg in an hundred
will miſcarry.

I met with *Camillo* your *Conſaorman* here lately ; and
could he be ſure of entertainment, he would return to
ſerve you again, and I believe for leſs ſalary.

I ſhall attend your commands herein by the next, and
touching other particulars, whereof I have written to
Capt. Bacon : ſo I reſt

Your moſt humble and ready ſervant,

Venice, May 30. 1621.   J. H.

L E T T E R XXV.

To my BROTHER, *from* Venice.

Brother,

I Found a letter of yours that had lain dormant here
a good while in Mr. *Symn*'s hands, to welcome me
to *Venice*, and I thank you for the variety of news
wherewith ſhe went freighted ; for ſhe was to me as a
ſhip richly laden from *London* uſeth to be to our merchants
here ; and I eſteem her *Cargazon* at no leſs a value, for
ſhe enriched me with the knowledge of my father's
health, and your own, with the reſt of my brothers and
ſiſters in the country, with divers other paſſages of contentment. Beſides, ſhe went alſo ballaſted with your
good inſtructions ; which as merchants uſe to do of their
commodities, I will turn to the beſt advantage ; and *Italy*
is no ill market to improve any thing. The only *procede*
(that I may uſe the mercantile term) you can expect is

thanks,

thanks, and this way fhall not be wanting to make you rich returns.

Since I came to this town, I difpatched fundry bufinef-fes of good value for Sir *Robert Manfell;* which I hope will give content. The art of glafs making here is very highly valued ; for whofoever be of that profeffion, are gentlemen *ipfo facto,* and it is not without reafon, it be-ing a rare kind of knowledge and *chymiftry* to tranfmute duft and fand (for they are the only main ingredients) to fuch a diaphanous pellucid dainty body as you fee a cry-ftal-glafs is, which hath this property above gold or filver, or any other mineral, to admit no poifon ; as alfo, that it never waftes or lofes a whit of its firft weight, though you ufe it never fo long. When I faw fo many forts of cu-rious glaffes made here, I thought upon the compliment which a gentleman put upon a Lady in *England,* who having five or fix comely daughters, faid, `He never faw in his life fuch a dainty cupboard of cryftal-glaffes.` The compliment proceeds, it feems, from a faying they have here, *That the firft handfome woman that ever was made, was made of* Venice *glafs* ; which implies *beauty,* but *brittlenefs* withal, (and *Venice* is not unfurnifhed with fome of that mould ; for no place abounds more with laffes and glaffes) but confidering the brittlenefs of the ftuff, it was an odd kind of melancholy in him, that could not be perfuaded but he was an *urinal;* furely he defer-ved to be piffed in the mouth. But, when I pryed into the materials, and obferved the furnaces and calcinations, the tranfubftantiations, the liquefactions that are incident to this art, my thoughts were raifed to a higher fpecula-tion ; that if this fmall furnace-fire hath virtue to con-vert fuch a fmall lump of dark duft and fand into fuch a precious clear body as cryftal, furely that grand univerfal fire at the day of judgment, may by its violent ardour *vitrify* and turn to one lump of cryftal the whole body of the earth; nor am I the firft that fell upon this conceit.

I will enlarge myfelf no further to you at this time, but conclude with this *tetaftric,* which my brain ran up-on in my bed this morning.

Vitrea.

Vitrea funt noſtræ commiſſa negotia curæ,
Hoc oculis ſpeculum mittimus ergo tuis :
Quod ſpeculum ? eſt inſtar ſpeculi mea litera, per quod
Vivida fraterni cordis imago nitet.

Adieu my dear brother, live happily, and love

Your brother,

Ven. June, 1. 1621.   J. H.

LETTER XXVI.

To Mr. RICHARD ALTHAM *at* Gray's-Inn, *from*
Venice.

Gentle Sir,

———*O dulcior illo*
Mille quod in ceris Attica ponit apis.

O thou that doſt in ſweetneſs far excel
That juice the Attic *bee ſtores in her cell.*

My dear DICK,

I Have now a good while ſince taken footing in *Venice,*
this admired maiden-city, ſo called, becauſe ſhe was
never defloured by any enemy ſince ſhe had a being, not
ſince her *rialto* was firſt erected, which is now above
twelve ages ago.

I proteſt to you, at my firſt landing I was for ſome days
raviſhed with the high beauty of this maid, with her lovely countenance. I admired her magnificent buildings,
her marvellous ſtuation, her dainty ſmooth neat ſtreets,
whereon you may walk moſt days in the year in a ſilk
ſtocking and ſattin ſlippers, without ſoiling them ; nor
can the ſtreets of *Paris* be ſo foul, as theſe are fair.
This beauteous maid hath been often attempted to be vi-
tiated ; ſome have *courted* her, ſome *bribed* her, ſome
would have *forced* her, yet ſhe hath ſtill preſerved her
chaſtity entire : and, though ſhe hath lived ſo many ages,

E   and

and paffed fo many fhrewd brunts; yet fhe continueth frefh to this very day without the leaft wrinkle of old age, or any fymptom of decay, whereunto political bodies, as well as natural, ufe to be liable. Befide, fhe hath wreftled with the greateft potentates upon earth; the Emperor, the King of *France*, and moft of the other princes of chriftendom, in that famous league of *Cambray*, would have funk her; but fhe bore up ftill within her lakes, and broke that league to pieces by her wit: the Grand *Turk* hath been often at her, and though he could not have his will of her, yet he took away the richeft jewel fhe wore in her *coronet*, and put it in his *turban*, I mean the kingdom of *Cyprus*, the only royal gem fhe had: he hath fet upon her fkirts often fince, and though fhe clofed with him fometimes, yet fhe came off ftill with her maidenhead; though fome that envy her happinefs would brand her to be of late times a kind of *concubine* to him, and that fhe gives him ready money once a year to lie with her, which fhe minceth by the name of *prefent*, though it be indeed rather a *tribute*.

I would I had you here with a wifh, and you would not defire in hafte to be at *Gray's-Inn*, though I hold your walks to be the pleafanteft place about *London*; and that you have there the choiceft fociety. I pray prefent my kind commendations to all there, and fervice at *Bifhopfgate-ftreet*, and let me hear from you by the next poft. So I am

Intirely yours,

Venice, June, 5. 1621.   J. H.

LETTER XXVII.

To Sir JAMES CROFTS *Knight, from* Venice.

SIR,

I Received one of yours the laft week, that came in my Lord Ambaffador *Wotton*'s packet; and being now upon point of parting with *Venice*, I could not do it without

out acquainting you (as far as the extent of a letter will permit) with her power, her policy, her wealth and pedigree. She was built out of the ruins of *Aquileia*, and *Padua*; for when those swarms of tough northern people over-ran *Italy*, under the conduct of that *scourge of heaven*, *Attila*, with others, and that this soft voluptuous nation after so long a defuetude from arms, could not repel their fury, many of the antient nobility and gentry fled into these lakes and little islands, amongst the fishermen, for their security; and finding the air good and commodious for habitation, they began to build upon those small islands, whereof there are in all sixty; and in tract of time, they conjoined and leagued them together by bridges, whereof there are now above 800; and this makes up the city of *Venice*, who is now above twelve ages old, and was contemporary with the *monarchy* of *France* : but the *Signory* glorieth in one thing above the *monarchy*, that she was born a *christian*, but the *monarchy* not. Though this city be thus hemed in with the *sea*, yet she spreads her wings far and wide upon the shote; she hath in *Lombardy* six considerable towns, *Padua*, *Verona*, *Vicenza*, *Brescia*, *Crema*, and *Bergamo*; she hath in the *marquisate*, *Bassan* and *Castlefranco* ; she hath all *Friuli* and *Istria* ; she commands the shores of *Dalmatia* and *Sclavonia* ; she keeps under the power of *St. Mark* the islands of *Corfu* (anciently *Cercyra*) *Cephalonia*, *Zant*, *Cerigo*, *Lucerigo*, and *Candy* (*Jove*'s cradle;) she had a long time the kingdom of *Cyprus*, but it was quite rent from her by the *Turk* ; which made that highspirited *Bassa*, being taken prisoner at the battle of *Lepanto*, where the Grand Signior lost above 200 gallies, to say, *That that defeat to his great master was but like to the shaving of his beard, or the pairing of his nails ; but the taking of* Cyprus *was like the cutting off of a limb, which will never grow again.* This mighty potentate being so near a neighbour to her, she is forced to comply with him, and give him an annual present in gold : she hath about 30 gallies most part of the year in course to scour

E 2 and

and fecure the *gulph;* fhe entertains by land in *Lom-bardy,* and other parts, 25000 foot, befides fome of the cantons of *Suiffes* whom fhe gives pay to ; fhe hath alfo in conftant pay 600 men of arms, and every of thefe muft keep two horfes a piece, for which they are allowed 120 ducats a year, and they are for the moft part gentlemen of *Lombardy.* When they have any great expedition to make, they have always a ftranger for their General, but he is fupervifed by two *proveditors,* without whom he cannot attempt any thing.

Her great council confifts of above 2000 gentlemen, and fome of them meet every Sunday and holiday to chufe officers and magiftrates ; and every gentleman be-ing paft 25 years of age, is capable to fit in this council. The *Doge,* or Duke (their *fovereign magiftrate*) is chofen by lots ; which would be too tedious here to de-monftrate ; and commonly he is an aged man, who is created like that courfe they hold in the popedom. When he is dead, there is *inquifitors* that examine his actions, and his mifdemeanours are punifhable in his heirs : there is a furintendent council of ten, and fix of them may dif-patch bufinefs without the *Doge :* but the *Doge* never without fome of them, not as much as open a letter from any foreign ftate, though addreffed to himfelf ; which makes him to be called by other princes, *tefta di legno, a head of wood.*

-The wealth of this *republick* hath been at a ftand, or rather declining fince the *Portugal* found a road to the *Eaft-Indies,* by the *Cape of Good-Hope ;* for this city was ufed to fetch all thofe fpices and other *Indian* commodi-ties from *Grand Cairo* down the *Nile,* being formerly carried to *Cairo* from the *Red-fea* upon camels and dro-medaries backs, fixty days Journey : and fo *Venice* ufed to difpenfe thofe commodities through all *chriftendom,* which not only the *Portugal,* but the *Englifh* and *Hol-lander* now tranfport, and are mafters of the trade. Yet there is no outward appearance at all of poverty, or any decay in this city ; but fhe is ftill gay, flourifhing and frefh, and flowing with all kinds of bravery and delight which

may

may be had at cheap rates. Much more might be written of this antient wife republick, which cannot be comprehended within the narrow inclofure of a letter. So with my due and daily prayers for a continuance of your health, and increafe of honour, I reft,

Your moft humble and ready fervant,

Venice, Auguft, 1. 1621.   J. H.

LETTER XXVIII.

To Sir WILLIAM St. JOHN *Knight, from* Rome.

SIR,

HAVING feen *Antenor*'s tomb in *Padua*, and the amphitheatre of *Flaminius* in *Verona*, with other brave towns in *Lombardy*, I am now come to *Rome* ; and *Rome*, they fay, is every man's country, fhe is called *Communis Patria ;* for every one that is within the compafs of the *Latin* church, finds himfelf here, as it were, at home, and in his mother's houfe, in regard of intereft in religion, which is the caufe that for one native, there be five ftrangers that fojourn in this city ; and without any diftinction or mark of ftrangenefs, they come to preferments and offices, both in church and ftate, according to merit, which is more valued and fought after here than anywhere.

But whereas I expected to have found *Rome* elevated upon feven hills, I met her rather fpreading upon a flat, having humbled herfelf fince fhe was made a *chriftian*, and defcended from thofe hills *Campus Martius*, with *Traftevere*, and the fuburbs of *St. Peter ;* fhe hath yet in compafs about fourteen miles, which is far fhort of that vaft circuit fhe had in *Claudius* his time : for *Vopifcus* writes, fhe was then of fifty miles circumference, and fhe had five hundred thoufand free citizens, in a famous cenfe that was made ; which, allowing but fix to every family, in women, children, and fervants, came to three

million

million of fouls : but fhe is now a wildernefs in comparifon of that number.   The *Pope* is grown to be a great
temporal Prince of late years, for the ftate of the church
extends above 300 miles in length, and 200 miles. in
breadth ; it contains *Ferrara, Bologna, Romagnia,* the
marquifate of *Ancona, Umbria, Sabina, Perugia,* with
a part of *Tufcany,* the *Patrimony, Rome* herfelf, and *Latium :* in thefe arc above fifty bifhopricks ; the *Pope*
hath alfo the dutchy of *Spoleto,* and the exarchate of *Ra-
venna ;* he hath the town of *Benevento* in the kingdom
of *Naples,* and the country of *Veniffe,* called *Avignon,*
in *France* ; he hath title alfo good enough to *Naples* itfelf, but rather than offend his champion the King of
Spain, he is contented with a white mule, and purfe of
piftoles about the neck, which he receives every year for
a herriot or homage, or what you will call it : he pretends alfo to be Lord Paramount of *Sicily, Urbin, Parma,* and *Maferan,* of *Norway, Ireland* and *England,*
fince King *John* did proftrate our crown at *Pandulfa* his
legate's feet.

   The ftate of the apoftolic See here in *Italy* lies betwixt two feas, the *Adriatic* and the *Tyrrhene ;* and it runs
through the midft of *Italy,* which makes the Pope powerful to do good or harm, and more capable than any other
to be an umpire or an enemy. His authority being mixt between temporal and fpiritual, difperfeth itfelf into fo many members, that a young man may grow old here, before he can well underftand the form of government.

   The confiftory of cardinals meet but once a week, and
once a week they folemnly wait all upon the Pope.   I am
told there are now in chriftendom but fixty eight cardinals, whereof there are fix cardinal-bifhops, fifty one
cardinal-priefts, and eleven cardinal-deacons : the cardinal-bifhops attend and fit near the Pope, when he ecle-
brates any feftival : the cardinal-priefts affift him at mafs,
and the cardinal-deacons attire him.   A cardinal is made
by a fhort *breve* or *writ* from the Pope, in thefe words,
*Creamus te focium regibus, fuperiorum ducibus, & fra-
trem noftrum : We create thee a companion to kings, fupe-
                                                              rior*

rior to dukes, and our brother. If a cardinal-bishop should be questioned for any offence, there must be twenty four witnesses produced against him.

The Bishop of *Ostia* hath most privilege of any other, for he consecrates and instals the Pope, and goes always next to him. All these cardinals have the repute of princes, and besides other incomes, they have the annats of benefices to support their greatness.

For point of power the Pope is able to put 50000 men in the field, in case of necessity, besides his naval strength in gallies. We read how *Paul* III. sent *Charles* III. 12000 foot, and 500 horse. *Pius* V. sent a great aid to *Charles* IX. and for riches, besides the temporal dominions, he hath in all the countries before-named, the datary or dispatching of *bulls.* The triennial subsidies, annats, and other ecclesiastic rights, amount to an unknown sum ; and it is a common saying here, *That as long as the Pope can finger a pen, he can want no pence. Pius* V. notwithstanding his expences in buildings, left four millions in the castle of *St. Angelo,* in less than five years ; more I believe than this *Gregory* XV. will, for he hath many nephews ; and better it is to be the Pope's nephew, than to be favourite to any Prince in christendom.

Touching the temporal government of *Rome*, and oppidan affairs, there is a pretor, and some choice citizens, who sit in the capitol. Among other pieces of policy, there is a synagogue of *Jews* permitted here (as in other parts of *Italy*) under the Pope's nose, but they go with a mark of distinction in their hats ; they are tolerated for advantage of commerce, wherein the *Jews* are very dexterous, though most of them be only brokers and lombardeers ; and they are held to be here, as the *Cynic* held women to be, *malum necessarium.* There be few of the *Romans* that use to pray heartily for the Pope's long life, in regard the oftner the change is, the more advantageous it is for the city, because commonly it brings Strangers, and a recruit of new people. The air of *Rome* is not so wholsome as of old ; and among other reasons, one is, because of the burning of stubble to fatten their fields. For her

antiquities,

antiquities, it would take up a whole volume to write them; thofe which I hold the chiefeft are, *Vefpafian's amphitheatre,* where eighty thoufand people might fit; the ftoves of *Anthony,* divers rare ftatues at *Belveder* and *St. Peters,* efpecially that of *Laocoon,* the *Obelifk*; for the genius of the *Roman* hath always been much taken with imagery, limning and fculptures, infomuch, that as in former times, fo now, I believe the ftatues and pictures in *Rome* exceed the number of living people. One antiquity, among others, is very remarkable, becaufe of the change of language; which is an ancient column erected as a trophy for *Duillius* the Conful, after a famous naval victory obtained againft the *Carthaginians* in the fecond *Punic* war, where thefe words are engraven, and remain legible to this day: *Exemet lecoines macif- trates caftreis exfocient pugnandod capet enque, navebos marid Conful, &c.* and half a dozen lines after, it is called *columna reftrata,* having the beaks and prows of fhips engraven up and down; whereby it appears, that the *Latin* then fpoken was much different from that which was ufed in *Cicero's* time 150 years after. Since the difmembering of the empire, *Rome* hath run through many viciffitudes and turns of fortune: and had it not been for the refidence of the Pope, I believe fhe had become a heap of ftones, a mount of rubbifh by this time; and howfoever that fhe bears up indifferent well, yet one may fay,

Qui miferanda videt veteris veftigia Romæ,
Ille poteft merito dicere Roma *fuit.*

They who the ruins of firft Rome *behold,*
May fay, Rome *is not now, but was of old.*

Prefent *Rome* may be faid to be but the monument of *Rome* paffed, when fhe was in that flourifh that *St. Auftin* defired to fee her in: fhe who tamed the world, tamed herfelf at laft, and falling under her own weight, fell to be a prey to time; yet, there is a providence feems to have a care of her ftill; for though her air be not fo good,

nor

nor her circumjacent foil fo kindly as it was, yet fhe hath wherewith to keep life and foul together ftill, by her ec-clefiaftical courts, which is the fole caufe of her peopling now. So it may be faid, when the Pope came to be her head, fhe was reduced to her firft principles : for as a fhepherd was founder, fo a fhepherd is ftill her Gover-nor and preferver ; but whereas the *French* have an odd faying, that

> *Jamais cheval ny homme,*
> *S'amenda pour aller à* Rome ;
>
> *Ne'er horfe, or man did mend,*
> *That unto* Rome *did wend :*

truly I muft confefs, that I find myfelf much bettered by it ; for the fight of fome of thefe ruins did fill me with fymptoms of mortification, and made me more fenfible of the frailty of all fublunary things, how all bodies, as well inanimate as animate, are fubject to diffolution and chan e, and every thing elfe under the moon, except the love gf

Your faithful fervitor,

Sept. 13. 1621.   J. H.

LETTER XXIX.

To Sir T. H. *Knight, from* Naples.

S I R,

I Am now in the gentle city of *Naples,* a city fwelling with all delight, gallantry and wealth ; and truly, in my opinion, the King of *Spain*'s greatnefs appears here more eminently than in *Spain* itfelf. This is a delicate luxurious city, fuller of true bred cavaliers than any place I faw yet. The clime is hot, and the conftitutions of the inhabitants more hot.

The

The *Neapolitan* is accounted the beft courtier of ladies, and the greateft embracer of pleafure of any other people: they fay there are no lefs here than twenty thoufand courtefans regiftered in the office of *Savelli*. This kingdom, with *Calabria*, may be faid to be the one moiety of *Italy*; it extends itfelf 450 miles, and fpreads in breadth 112; it contains 2700 towns; it hath 20 Archbifhops, 127 Bifhops, 13 Princes, 24 Dukes, 25 Marquiffes, and 800 Barons. There are three prefidial caftles in this city; and though the kingdom abound in rich ftaple commodities; as filks, cottons, and wine, and that there is a mighty revenue comes to the crown; yet the King of *Spain*, when he cafts up his account at the year's end, makes but little benefit thereof; for, it is eaten up betwixt governors, garrifons, and officers. He is forced to maintain 4000 *Spanifh* foot, called the *Tercia* of *Naples*; in the caftles he hath 1600 in perpetual garrifon; he hath a thoufand men of arms, 450 light-horfe; befides, there are five footmen enrolled for every hundred fire: and he had need to do all this, to keep this voluptuous people in awe: for, the ftory mufters up feven and twenty famous rebellions of the *Neapolitans* in lefs than 300 years; but now they pay foundly for it, for one fhall hear them groan up and down under the *Spanifh* yoke; and commonly the King of *Spain* fends fome of his *grandees* hither, to repair their decayed fortunes; whence the faying fprung, *That the Viceroy of* Sicily *gnaws, the* Governor *of* Millan *eats, but the Viceroy of* Naples *devours.* Our *Englifh* merchants here, bear a confiderable trade, and their factors live in better equipage, and in a more fplendid manner than in all *Italy* befides, than their mafters and principals in *London*; they ruffle in filks and fattins, and wear good *Spanifh* leather fhoes, while their mafters fhoes upon our *Exchange* in *London* fhine with blacking. At *Puzzoli* not far off, amongft the *Grottoes*, there are fo many ftrange ftupenduous things, that nature herfelf feemed to have ftudied of purpofe how to make herfelf there admired. I referve the difcourfing of them, with the nature of the

Taran-

Tarantula and *Manna*, which is gathered here and no-where else, with other things, till I fee you; for they are fitter for difcourfes than a letter. I will conclude with a proverb they have in *Italy* for this people:

> *Napolitano*
> *Largo di bocca, ſtretto dimano.*
>
> *The Neapolitans*
> *Have wide mouths, but narrow hands.*

They make ſtrong maſculine promifes, but female per-formances, (*for deeds are men, but words are women*) and if in a whole *flood* of compliments one find a *drop* of reality 'tis well. The firſt acceptance of a courtefy is accounted the greateſt incivility that can be amongſt them, and a ground for a quarrel; as I heard of a *German* gentleman that was baffled for accepting only one invita-tion to a dinner. So defiring to be preferved ſtill in your good opinion, and in the rank of your fervants, I reſt al-ways moſt ready

At your difpofing,

Oƈt. 1. 1621.   J. H.

LETTER XXX.

To CHRISTOPHER JONES, *Efq;* at Grays-Inn,
from Naples.

Honoured FATHER,

I Muſt ſtill ſtyle you fo, fince I was adopted your fon by fo good a mother as *Oxford:* my mind lately prompted me, that I ſhould commit a great folecifm, if among the reſt of my friends in *England*, I ſhould leave you unfaluted; whom I love fo dearly well, fpecially ha-ving fuch a fair and pregnant opportunity as the hand of this worthy gentleman your coufin *Morgan*, who is now poſting hence for *England*: he will tell you how it

fares

fares with me, how any time thefe thirty odd months I
have been toffed from fhore to fhore, and paffed under
various meridians, and am now in this voluptuous city of
Naples; and, though thefe frequent removes and tumblings under climes of differing temper were not without
fome danger, yet the delight which accompanied them
was far greater ; and it is impoffible for any man to conceive the true pleafure of perigrination, but he who actually enjoys and puts it in practice.   Believe it, Sir, that
one year well employed abroad by one of mature judgment, (which you know I want very much) advantageth
more in point of ufeful and folid knowledge than three in
any of our *Univerfities.*   You know *running waters are
the pureft,* fo they that traverfe the world up and down
have the cleareft underftanding ; being faithful eye-wit-
neffes of thofe things which others receive but in truft,
whereunto they muft yield an intuitive confent, and a
kind of implicit Faith.   When I paffed through fome
parts of *Lombardy*, among other things, I obferved the
phyfiognomies and complexions of the people, men and
women ; and, I thought I was in *Wales;* for divers of
them have a caft of countenance, and a nearer refemblance with our nation than any I ever faw yet : and the
reafon is obvious, for the *Romans* having been near upon
three hundred years among us, where they had four legions (before the *Englifh* nation or language had any being) by fo long a coalition and tract of time, the two nations muft needs copulate and mix, infomuch, that I believe there is yet remaining in *Wales* many of the *Roman*
race, and divers in *Italy* of the *Britifh.*   Among other
refemblances, one was in their profody, and vein of verfifying or rhyming ; which is like our *bards*, who hold
agnominations, and enforcing of confonant words or
fyllables one upon the other, to be the greateft elegance.
As for example, in *Welfh*, *tewgris, todyrris, ty'r derryn,
gwillt,* &c. fo have I feen divers old rhymes in *Italian*
running fo ; *Donne, O danno, che felo affronto affronta :
in felva falvo a me : piu caro cuore,* &c

Being

Being lately in *Rome*, among other pasquils, I met with one that was againſt the *Scots*; though it had ſome gall in it, yet it had a great deal of wit, eſpecially towards the concluſion: ſo that I think if King *James* ſaw it, he would but laugh at it.

As I remember, ſome years ſince, there was a very a-buſive ſatire in verſe brought to our King; and as the paſſages were a reading before him, he often ſaid, that if there were no more men in *England*, the rogue ſhould hang for it. At laſt being come to the concluſion, which was, after all his railing,

Now God preſerve the King, the Queen, the peers,
And grant the author long may wear his ears;

This pleaſed his majeſty ſo well, that he broke into a laughter, and ſaid, *By my ſoul ſo thou ſhalt for me*: thou art a bitter, but thou art a witty knave.

When you write to *Monmouthſhire*, I pray ſend my reſpects to my tutor, Mr. *Moor Fortune*, and my ſervice to Sir *Charles Williams*; and according to that relation which was betwixt us at *Oxford*, I reſt

Your conſtant ſon to ſerve you,

Naples, Octr. 8. 1621. J. H.

LETTER XXXI.

To Sir J. C. *from* Florence.

S I R,

THIS letter comes to kiſs your hands from fair *Florence*, a city ſo beautiful, that the great Emperor *Charles* V. ſaid, *That ſhe was fitting to be ſhewn, and ſeen only upon holidays*. She marvellouſly flouriſheth with buildings, with wealth and artiſans; for it is thought that in ſerges, which is but one commodity, there are made two millions every year. All degrees of people

live

live here, not only well, but fplendidly well, notwithftanding the manifold exactions of the Duke upon all
things : for none can buy here lands or houfes, but he
muft pay eight in the hundred to the Duke ; none can
hire or build a houfe, but he muft pay the tenth penny ;
none can marry or commence a fuit in law, but there is
a fee to the Duke : none can bring as much as an egg or
fallet to the market, but the Duke hath fhare therein.
Moreover *Leghorn*, which is the key of *Tufcany*, being
a maritime and a great mercantile town, hath mightily in-
riched this country, by being a frank port to all comers,
and a fafe rendezvous to pirates as well as to merchants.
Add hereunto, that the Duke himfelf in fome refpect
is a merchant ; for he fometimes engroffeth all the
corn of the country, and retails it at what rate he pleaf-
eth.   This enables the Duke to have perpetually 20000
men enrolled, trained up and paid, and none but they
can carry arms ; he hath 400 light-borfe in conftant pay,
and 100 men at arms befides ; and all thefe quartered
in fo narrow a compafs, that he can command them all
to *Florence* in twenty four hours.   He hath twelve
gallies, two galeons, and fix galeaffes befides ; and his
gallies are called, *The black fleet*, becaufe they annoy the
Turk more in the bottom of the *Straits* than any other.

This ftate is bound to keep good quarter with the
Pope more than others ; for all *Tufcany* is fenced by
nature herfelf, I mean with mountains, except towards
the territories of the apoftolic See, and the fea itfelf :
therefore it is called *a country of Iron*.

The Duke's palace is fo fpacious, that it occupieth
the room of fifty houfes at leaft ; yet though his court
furpaffeth the bounds of a Duke's, it reacheth not to the
magnificence of a King's.   The Pope was follicited to
make the grand Duke a King, and he anfwered, that he
was content he fhould be King in *Tufcany*, not of *Tufcany* ; whereupon one of his counfellors replied, that it
was a more glorious thing to be a grand Duke than a
petty King.

Among

Among other cities which I defired to fee in *Italy*, *Genoa* was one, where I lately was, and found her to be the proudeft for buildings of any I met withal ; yet the people go the plaineft of any other, and are alfo moft parfimonious in their diet : they are the fubtileft, I will not fay the moft fubdolous dealers : they are wonderful wealthy, efpecially in money. In the year 1600, the King of *Spain* owed them 18 millions, and they fay it is double as much now.

From the time they began to finger the *Indian* gold, and that this town hath been the fcale by which he hath conveyed his treafure to *Flanders*, fince the wars in the *Netherlands*, for the fupport of his armies, and that fhe hath got fome privileges for the exportation of wools and other commodities (prohibited to others) out of *Spain*, fhe hath improved extremely in riches, and made *St. George*'s mount fwell higher than *St. Mark's* in *Venice*.

She hath been often ill-favouredly fhaken by the *Venetians*, and hath had other enemies, which have put her to hard fhifts for her own defence, efpecially in the time of *Lewis* XI. of *France ;* at which time, when fhe would have given herfelf up to him for protection, King *Lewis* being told that *Genoa* was content to be his, he anfwered, *She fhould not be his long, for he would give her up to the devil, and rid his hands of her.*

Indeed the *Genoefe* have not the fortune to be fo well beloved, as other people in *Italy* ; which proceeds, I believe, from their cunningnefs and over-reachings in bargaining, wherein they have fomething of the *Jew*. The Duke is there but biennial, being changed every two years : he hath fifty *Germans* for his guard. There be four *Centurions* that have two men a piece, which upon occafions attend the *Signory* abroad in velvet coats ; there be eight chief governors, and 400 counfellors, among whom there be five fovereign *fyndics*, who have authority to cenfure the Duke himfelf, his time being expired, and punifh any Governor elfe, though after death, upon the heir.

Among

Among other cuſtoms they have in this town, one is, that none muſt carry a pointed knife about him ; which makes the *Hollander*, who is uſed to *ſnick* and *ſnee*, to leave his horn-ſheath and knife a ſhipboard when he comes a-ſhore. I met not with an *Engliſhman* in all the town; nor could I learn of any factor of ours that ever reſided here.

There is a notable little active republic towards the midſt of *Tuſcany*, called *Lucca ;* which in regard ſhe is under the Emperor's protection, he dares not meddle with-al, though ſhe lie as a partridge under a faulcon's wings, in relation to the Grand Duke : beſides, there is another reaſon of ſtate, why he meddles not with her, becauſe ſhe is more beneficial to him, now that ſhe is free, and more induſtrious to ſupport this freedom, than if ſhe were become his vaſſal ; for then it is probable ſhe would become more careleſs and idle, and ſo could not vent his commodities ſo ſoon, which ſhe buys for ready money, wherein moſt of her wealth conſiſts. There is no ſtate that wins the penny more nimbly, and makes quicker returns.

She hath a council called the *Diſcoli*, which pries in-to the profeſſion and life of every one, and once a year they rid the State of all vagabonds : ſo that this petty pretty republic may not be improperly paralleled to a hive of bees, which have been always the emblems of induſtry and order.

In this ſplendid city of *Florence*, there be many ra-rities, which if I ſhould inſert in this letter, it would make it ſwell too big ; and indeed they are fitter for parole communication. Here is the prime dialect of the *Italian* ſpoken, though the pronunciation be a little more guttural than that of *Siena*, and that of the court of *Rome*, which occaſions the proverb,

Lingua Toſcana *in bocca* Romana,

The Tuſcan *tongue ſounds beſt in a* Roman *mouth.*

The people here generally ſeem to be more generous,
and

and of a higher comportment than elsewhere, very cautious and circumspect in their negotiation; whence ariseth the proverb,

> *Chi ha da far con* Tosco,
> *Non bisogna che fia losco.*

> *Who dealeth with a* Florentine,
> *Must have the use of both his eyne.*

· I shall bid *Italy* farewel very shortly, and make my way over the *Alps* to *France*, and so home by God's grace, to take a review of my friends in *England;* among whom the, sight of yourself will be as gladsome to me as of any other: for I profess myself, and purpose to be ever

Your thrice affectionate servitor,

Nov. 1. 1621. J. H.

LETTER XXXII.

To Capt. FRANCIS BACON, *from* Turin.

SIR,

I Am now upon the point of shaking hands with *Ita'y;* for I am come to *Turin*, having already seen *Venice* the rich, *Padua* the learned, *Bologna* the fat, *Rome* the holy, *Naples* the gentle, *Genoa* the proud, *Florence* the fair, and *Milan* the great: from this last I came hither; and in that city also appears the grandeur of *Spain's* monarchy very much: the Governor of *Milan* is always Captain-General of the cavalry to the King of *Spain*, throughout *Italy*. The Duke of *Feria* is now Governor; and being brought to kiss his hand, he used me with extraordinary respect, as he doth all of our nation, being by maternal side a *Dormer*. The *Spaniard* entertains there also 3000 foot, 1000 light-horse, and 600 men at arms in perpetual pay; so that I believe the benefit of

F 3 that

that dutchy alſo, though ſeated in the richeſt ſoil of *Italy*, hardly countervails the charge.   Three things are admired in *Milan*; the *dome*, or great church, (built all of white marble within and without) the hoſpital, and the caſtle, by which the citadel of *Antwerp* was traced, and is the beſt conditioned fortreſs of chriſtendom; though *Nova Palma*, a late fortreſs of the *Venetian*, would go beyond it ; which is built according to the exact rules of the moſt modern enginery, being of a round form, with nine baſtions, and a ſtreet level to every baſtion.

The Duke of *Savoy*, though he paſs for one of the princes of *Italy*, yet the leaſt part of his territories lie there, being ſquandered up and down amongſt the *Alps ;* but as much as he hath in *Italy*, which is *Piedmont*, is a well peopled, and paſſing good country.

The Duke of *Savoy*, *Emanuel*, is accounted to be of the antienteſt and pureſt extraction of any Prince in *Europe ;* and his knights alſo of the *Annunciade*, to be one of the antienteſt orders : though this preſent Duke be little in ſtature, yet he is of a lofty ſpirit, and one of the helt ſoldiers now living; and though he be valiant enough, yet he knows how to patch the lion's ſkin with a fox's tail.   And, whoſoever is Duke of *Savoy* had need be cunning, and more than any other Prince, in regard, that ying between two potent neighbours‘ the *French* and the *Spaniard*, he muſt comply with both.

Before I wean myſelf from *italy*, a word or two touching the *genius* of the nation.   I find the *Italian* a degree higher in compliment than the *French :* he is longer and more grave in the delivery of it, and more prodigal of words, infomuch, that if one were to be worded to death, *Italian* is the ſitteſt language, in regard of the fluency and ſoftneſs of it: for throughout the whole body of it, you have not a word ends with a conſonant, except ſome few monoſyllable conjunctions and prepoſitions, and this renders the ſpeech more ſmooth ; which made one ſay, *That when the confuſion of tongues happened at the building of the tower of* Babel, *if the*
Italian

Italian *had been there,* Nimrod *had made him a plai-*
flerer. They are generally indulgent of themfelves, and
great embracers of pleafure; which may proceed from
the lufcious rich wines, and luxurious food, fruits and
roots, wherewith the country abounds; infomuch, that
in fome places, nature may be faid to be *Lena fui, A*
bawd to herfelf. The Cardinal *de Medicis*'s rule is of
much authority among them, *That there is no religion*
under the navel; and fome of them are of the opinion
of the *Afians,* who hold, that touching thofe natural paffions, defires and motions which run up and down in the
blood, God almighty and his handmaid Nature, did not
intend they fhould be a torment to us, but to be ufed
with comfort and delight. To conclude, in *Italy* there
be *Virtutes magnæ, nec minora vitia; Great virtues,*
and no lefs vices. So with a tender of my moft affectionate refpects unto you, I reft

Your humble fervitor,

Nov. 30. 1621.   J. H.

LETTER XXXIII.

To Sir J. H. *from* Lions.

S I R,

I Am now got over the *Alps,* and returned to *France :*
I had croffed and clambered up the *Pyreneans* to
Spain before; they are not fo high and hideous as the
Alps; but for our mountains in *Wales,* as *Eppint,* and
Penwinmaur, which are fo much cried up among us,
they are *molehills* in comparifon of thefe: they are but
pigmies compared to *giants,* but *blifters* compared to *im-*
pofthumes, or *pimples* to *warts.* Befides, our mountains
in *Wales* bear always fomething ufeful to man or beaft,
fome grafs at leaft; but thefe uncouth huge monftrous
excrefcences of nature bear nothing (moft of them) but
craggy ftones; the tops of fome of them are blanched
over

over all the year long with fnow ; and the people who dwell in the valleys drinking, for want of other, this fnow-water, are fubject to a ftrange fwelling in the throat, called *goytre*, which is common among them.

As I fealed the *Alps*, my thoughts reflected upon *Hannibal*, who with *vinegar* and *ftrong waters*, did eat out a paffage through thofe hills, but of late years they have found a fpeedier way to do it by *gunpowder*.

Being at *Turin*, I was by fome difafter brought to an extreme low ebb in money, fo that I was forced to foot it along with fome pilgrims, and with gentle pace and eafy journeys to climb up thofe hills, till I came to this town of *Lions*, where a countryman of ours, one Mr. *Lewis*, whom I knew in *Alicant*, lives factor ; fo that now I want not any thing for my accommodation.

This is a ftately rich town, and a renowned mart for the filks of *Italy*, and other *Levantine* commodities, and a great bank for money ; and indeed the greateft of *France :* before this bank was founded, which was by *Henry* I. *France* had but little gold and fiiver, infomuch, that we read how King *John* their captive King, could not in four years raife 60000 crowns to pay his ranfom to our King *Edward*, and *St. Lewis* was in the fame cafe when he was prifoner in *Egypt*, where he had left the facrament for a gage. But after this bank was erected, it filled *France* full of money : they of *Luca*, *Florence*, and *Genoa*, with the *Venetian*, got quickly over the hills, and brought their monies hither to get twelve in the hundred profit ; which was the intereft at firft, though it be now much lower.

In this great mercantile town, there be two deep navigable rivers, the *Rhone* and the *Soane :* the one hath a fwift rapid courfe, the other flow and fmooth ; and one day as I walked upon their banks, and obferved fo much difference in their courfe, I fell into a contemplation of the humours of the *French* and *Spaniard*, how they might be not improperly compared to thefe rivers ; the *French* to the fwift, the *Spaniard* to the flow river.

I ſhall write you no more letters until I preſent myſelf unto you for a ſpeaking letter, which I ſhall do as ſoon as I may tread *London* ſtones.

Your moſt affectionate ſervitor,

Lions, Nov. 6. 1621. J. H.

L E T T E R XXXIV.

To Mr. THO. BOWYER, *from* Lions.

BEING ſo near the lake of *Geneva*, curioſity would carry any one to ſee it: the inhabitants of that town methinks are made of another paſte differing from the affable nature of thoſe people I had converſed withal formerly: they have one policy, leſt that their pretty republic ſhould be peſter'd with fugitives, their law is, *That what ſtranger ſoever flies thither for ſanctuary, he is puniſhable there, in the ſame degree, as in the country where he committed the offence.*

Geneva is governed by four ſyndics, and four hundred ſenators: ſhe lies like a bone betwixt three maſtiffs; the Emperor, the *French* King, and the Duke of *Savoy*, they all three look upon the bone, but neither of them dare touch it ſingly, for fear the other two would fly upon him; but, they ſay the Savoyard hath the juſteſt title; for there are imperial records extant, *That although the* biſhops *of* Geneva *were* lords ſpiritual *and* temporal, *yet they ſhould acknowledge the* Duke *of* Savoy *for their ſuperior.* This man's anceſtors went frequently to the town, and the keys were preſently tendered to them; but ſince *Calvin*'s time, who had been once baniſhed and then called in again, which made him to apply that ſpeech unto himſelf, *The ſtone which the builders refuſed, is become the head-ſtone of the corner.* I ſay, ſince they were refined by *Calvin*, they ſeem to ſhun and ſcorn all the world beſides, being caſt as it were

into

into another mould, which hath quite altered their very natural difpofition in point of moral fociety.

Before I part with this famous city of *Lions*, I will relate unto you a wonderful accident that happened here not many years ago : there is an officer called *Le Cheva-lier du Guet* (which is a kind of night-guard) here as well as in *Paris;* and his Lieutenant called *Jaquette* having fupped one night in a rich merchant's houfe, as he was paffing the round afterwards, he faid, *I wonder what I have eaten and drunken in the merchant's houfe, for I find myfelf fo hot, that if I met with the* devil's *dam to-night, I fhould not forbear ufing of her.* Hereupon, a little after he overtook a young gentlewoman mafked, whom he would needs ufher to her lodging, but difcharged all his watch except two : fhe brought him, to his think-ing, to a little low lodging hard by the city wall, where there were only two rooms : after he had enjoyed her, he defired, that according to the cuftom of *French* gentle-men, his two comerades might partake alfo of the fame pleafure, fo fhe admitted them one after the other ; and when all this was done, as they fat together, fhe told them, if they knew well who fhe was, none of them would have ventured upon her ; thereupon, fhe whiftled three times, and all vanifhed. The next morning, the two foldiers that had gone with Lieutenant *Jaquette* were found dead under the city wall, amongft the ordure and excrements, and *Jaquette* himfelf a little way off half dead, who was taken up, and coming to himfelf again, confeffed all this, but died prefently after.

The next week I am to go down the *Loire* towards *Paris*, and thence as foon as I can for *England*, where, amongft the reft of my friends, whom I fo much long to fee after this triennial feparation, you are like to be one of my firft objects. In the mean time, I wifh the fame happinefs may attend you at *home*, as I defire to attend me *homeward :* for I am

Truly yours,

Lions, Dec. 5. 1621.   J. H.

L E T-

LETTER XXXV.

To my FATHER.

SIR,

IT hath pleafed God, after almoft three years peregrination by land and fea, to bring me back fafely to *London;* but although I am come fafely, I am come fickly: for when I landed in *Venice*, after fo long a voyage from *Spain*, I was afraid the fame defluxion of falt rheum which fell from my temples into my throat in *Oxford*, and diftilling upon the *uvula*, impeached my utterance a little to this day, had found the fame channel again; which caufed me to have an iffue made in my left arm for the diverfion of the humour. I was well ever after till I came to *Rouen*, and there I fell fick of a pain in the head, which, with the iffue, I have carried with me to *England*. Dr. *Harvey* who is my phyfician, tells me, that it may turn to a confumption, therefore he hath ftoped the iffue, telling me there is no danger at all in it, in regard I have not worn it a full twelvemonth. My brother, I thank him, hath been very careful of me in this my ficknefs, and hath come often to vifit me: I thank God I have paffed the brunt of it, and am recovering and picking up my crumbs apace. There is a flaunting *French* Ambaffador come over lately, and I believe his errand is nought elfe but compliment; for the King of *France* being lately at *Calais*, and fo in fight of *England*, he fent his Ambaffador M. *Cadenet*, exprefsly to vifit our King. He had audience two days fince, where he with his train of ruffling long-haired monfieurs, carried himfelf in fuch a light garb, that after the audience, the King afked my Lord Keeper *Bacon* what he thought of the *French* Ambaffador; he anfwered, that he was a tall proper man: ay, his majefty replied, but what think you of his head-piece? Is he a proper man for the office of an Ambaffador? *Sir,* faid *Bacon, Tall men are like high houfes of four or five ftories, wherein, commonly the uppermoft room is worft furnifhed.*

So

So defiring my brothers and fifters, with the reft of my coufins and friends in the country, may be acquainted with my fafe return to *England,* and that you would pleafe to let me hear from you by the next conveniency, I reft

Your dutiful fon,

Lond. Feb. 2. 1621.   J. H.

LETTER XXXVI.

To Sir JAMES CROFTS *at the Lord* DARCY'S *in*
St. Ofith.

SIR, I am got again fafely to this fide of the fea, and though I was in a very fickly cafe when I firft arrived, yet thanks be to God I am upon the point of perfect recovery, whereunto the fucking in of *Englifh* air, and the fight of fome friends, conduced not a little.

There is fearful news come from *Germany :* you know how the *Bohemians* fhook off the Emperor's yoke, and how the great council of *Prague* fell to fuch a hurly-burly, that fome of the imperial counfellors were hurled out at the windows: you heard alfo, I doubt not, how they offered the crown to the Duke of *Saxony,* and he waving it, they fent ambaffadors to the *Palfgrave,* whom they thought might prove *par negotio,* and to be able to go through-ftitch with the work, in regard of his powerful alliance, the King of *Britain* being his father-in-law, the King of *Denmark,* the Prince of *Orange,* the Marquis of *Brandenburg,* the Duke of *Bouillon* his uncles, the States of *Holland* his confederates, the *French* King his friend, and the Duke of *Brunfwick* his near ally: the Prince *Palfgrave* made fome difficulty at firft, and moft of his counfellors oppofed it ; others incited him to it, and among other hortatives they told him, *That if he had the courage to venture upon a King of* England's *fole daughter, he might very well venture upon a fovereign*

crown

crown when it was tendered him. Add hereunto, that
the States of *Holland* did mainly advance the work, and
there was a good reafon in policy for it; for their twelve
years truce being then upon point of expiring with *Spain*,
and finding our King fo wedded to peace, that nothing
could divorce him from it, they lighted upon this defign
to make him draw his fword, and engage him againft the
houfe of *Auftria* for the defence of his fole daughter, and
his grand-children. What his majefty will do hereafter.
I will not prefume to foretell, but hitherto he hath given
little countenance to the bufinefs; nay, he utterly mifliked it at firft: for whereas, Dr. *Hall* gave the Prince
Palfgrave the title of King of *Bohemia* in his pulpit-
prayer, he had a check for it; for I heard his majefty
fhould fay, that there is an implicite tie among kings.
which obligeth them, though there be no other intereft
or particular engagement, to ftick to, and right one another upon an infurrection of fubjects; therefore he had
more reafon to be againft the *Bohemians*, than to adhere
to them in the depofition of their fovereign Prince. The
King of *Denmark* fings the fame note, nor will he alfo allow him the appellation of King. But the fearful
news I told you of at the beginning of this letter is, that
there are frefh tidings brought how the Prince *Palfgrave*
had a well appointed army of about 25000 horfe and
foot near *Prague*; but the Duke of *Bavaria* came with
fcarce half the number; and, notwithftanding his long
march, gave them a fudden battle, and utterly routed
them, infomuch, that the new King of *Bohemia* having
not worn the crown a whole twelvemonth, was forced to
fly with his Queen and children; and after many difficulties, they write, that they are come to the caftle of *Ca-
ftrein*, the Duke of *Brandenburg*'s country, his uncle.
The news affects both court and city here with much
heavinefs.

I fend you my humble thanks for the noble correfpondence you were pleafed to hold with me abroad; and I
defire to know by the next, when you come to *London*,

G   that

that I may have the comfort of the fight of you, after fo
long an abfence.

Your true fervitor,

March 1. 1621.   J., H.

LETTER XXXVII.

To Sir EUBULE THEOLALL, *Knight, and Principal
of* Jefus College *in* Oxford.

SIR, I fend you moft due and humble thanks, that
notwithftanding I have played the truant, and been
abfent fo long from *Oxford*, you have been pleafed lately
to make choice of me to be fellow of your new foundation
in *Jefus College*, whereof I was once a member. As
the quality of my fortunes and courfe of life run now, I
cannot make prefent ufe of this your great favour, or
promotion rather ; yet, I do highly value it, and humbly
accept of it, and intend by your permiffion, to referve and
lay it by, as a good warm garment againft rough weather,
if any fall on me.   With this my expreffion of thankful-
nefs, I do congratulate the great honour you have pur-
chafed both by your beneficence, and by your painful endeavour befides, to perfect that national college, which
hereafter is like to be a monument of your fame, as well
as a feminary of learning, and will perpetuate your memory to all pofterity.

God almighty profper and perfect your undertakings,
and provide for you in heaven thofe rewards which fuch
publick works of piety ufe to be crowned withal ; it is
the apprecation of

Your truly devoted fervitor,

Lond. March 5. 1621.   J. H.

LET.

LETTER XXXVIII.

To my FATHER.

SIR, according to the advice you fent me in your laft, while I fought after a new courfe of employment, a new employment hath lately fought after me : my Lord *Savage* hath two young gentlemen to his fons, and I am to go travel with them. Sir *James Crofts* (who fo much refpects you) was the main agent in this bufinefs; and I am to go fhortly to *Long-Melford* in *Suffolk*, and thence to *St. Ofith* in *Effex* to the Lord *Darcy*. Queen *Anne* is lately dead of a dropfy in *Denmark-houfe* : which is held to be one of the fatal events that followed the laft fearful *comet* that rofe in the tail of the *conftellation* of *Virgo*; which fome ignorant. aftronomers that write of it, would fix in the heavens ; and that as far above the orb of the moon, as the moon is from the earth : but this is nothing in comparifon of thofe hideous fires that are kindled in *Germany*, blown firft by the *Bohemians*, which is like to be a war without end; for the whole houfe of *Auftria* is interefted in the quarrel ; and it is not the cuftom of that houfe to fet by any affront, or forget it quickly. Queen *Anne* left a world of brave jewels behind, but one *Piero* an outlandifh man, who had the keeping of them, embezzled many, and is run away : fhe left all fhe had to Prince *Charles*, whom fhe ever loved beft of all her children; nor do I hear of any legacy fhe left at all to her daughter in *Germany* : for that match, fome fay, leffened fomething of her affection towards her ever fince, fo that fhe would often call her goody *Palfgrave*; nor could fhe abide Secretary *Winwood* ever after, who was one of the chiefeft inftruments to bring that match about, as alfo for the rendition of the cautionary towns in the *Low-Countries*, *Flufhing* and *Brill*, with the *Rammakins*. I was lately with Sir *John Walter* and others of your counfel about law-bufinefs; and fome of them told me that Mr. *J. Lloyd*, your adverfary,

verfary, is one of the fhrewdeft follicitors in all the
thirteen fhires of *Wales*, being fo habituated to law-fuits
and wrangling, that he knows any of the leaft ftatting-
holes in every court : I could wifh you had made a fair
end with him; for befides the cumber and trouble, efpecially to thofe that dwell at fuch a huge diftance from
Weftminfter-hall as you do, law is a fhrewd pick-purfe,
and the lawyer, as I heard one fay wittily not long fince,
is like a *chriftmafs-box, which is fure to get whofoever
lofeth.*

So with the continuance of my due and daily prayers
for your health, with my love to my brothers and fifters,
I reft

Your dutiful fon,

March, 20. 1621   J. H.

L E T T E R   XXXIX.

To DANIEL CALDWALL *Efq; from the* Lord Savage's
Houfe in Long-Melford.

My dear DAN.

THOUGH confidering my former condition of life,
I may now be called a countryman, yet you cannot call me a ruftic (as you would imply in your letter)
as long as I live in fo civil and noble a family, as long
as I lodge in fo virtuous and regular a houfe as any I
believe in the land, both for *œconomical* government, and
the choice company ; for I never faw yet fuch a dainty
race of children in all my life together; I never faw yet
fuch an orderly and punctual attendance of fervants, nor
a great houfe fo neatly kept : here one fhall fee no dog,
nor a cat, nor cage to caufe any naftinefs within the body
of the houfe : the kitchen and gutters and other offices
of noife and drudgery are at the fag-end ; there is a back-
gate for the beggars and the meaner fort of fwains to
come in at ; the ftables butt upon the park, which for

a

a chearful rising ground, for groves and browsings for the
deer, for rivulets of water, may compare with any of
its bigness in the whole land ; it is opposite to the front
of the great house, whence from the gallery one may see
much of the game when they are a hunting.   Now for
the gardening and costly choice flowers, for ponds, for
stately large walks green and gravelly, for orchards and
choice fruits of all sorts, there are few the like in *England :* here you have your *bon chrestién pear* and *berga-
mot* in perfection, your *Muscadel* grapes in such plenty,
that there are some bottles of wine sent every year to the
King ; and one Mr. *Daniel*, a worthy gentleman hard
by, who hath been long abroad, makes good store in his
vintage.   Truly this house of *Long-Melford*, though it
be not so great, yet it is so well compacted and contrived
with such dainty conveniencies every way, that if you
saw the landskip of it, you would be mightily taken with
it, and it would serve for a choice pattern to build and
contrive a house by.   If you come this summer to your
manor of *Sheriff* in *Essex*, you will not be far off hence :
if your occasions will permit, it will be worth your coming hither, though it be only to see him, who would
think it a short journey to go from *St. David*'s head to
Dover cliffs to see and serve you, were there occasion :
if you would know who the same is, it is

Yours,

May, 20. 1621.   J. H.

LETTER XL.

To ROBERT BROWN *Esq;*

S. I R,

THANKS *for one courtesy, is a good usher to
bring on another ;* therefore it is my policy at this
time to thank you most heartily for your late copious
letter, to draw on a second : I say, I thank you a thou-

sand

fand times over for yours of the third of this prefent, which abounded with fuch variety of news, and ample well-couched relations, that I made many friends by it ; yet I.am forry for the quality of fome of your news, that Sir *Robert Manfel* being now in the *Mediterranean* with a confiderable naval ftrength of ours againft the *Moors,* to do the *Spaniards* a pleafure, Marquis *Spinola* fhould in a hogling way, change his mafter for the time, and taking commiffion from the Emperor, become his fervant for invading the *Palatinate* with the forces of the King of *Spain* in the *Netherlands*.   I am forry the princes of the *union* fhould be fo ftupid as to fuffer him to take *Oppenheim* by a *Parthian* kind of back ftratagem, in appearing before the town, and making femblance afterwards to go to *Worms;* and then perceiving the forces of the *united princes* to go for fuccouring of that, to turn back and take the town he intended firft, whereby I fear he will be quickly mafter of the reft.   Surely I believe there may be fome treachery in it, and that the Marquis of *Anfpach*, the General, was overcome by piftols made of *Indian* ingots, rather than of fteel ; elfe an army of 40000 which he had under his command, might have made its party good againft *Spinola*'s lefs than 20000, though never fuch choice veterans ; but what will not gold do ? It will make a pigmy too hard for a giant.   There is no fence or fortrefs *againft an afs laden with gold*.   It was the faying you know of *his* father, whom partial and ignorant antiquity cries up to have conquered the world, and that he fighed there were no more worlds to conquer, though he had never one of the three old parts of the then known world entirely to himfelf.   I defire to know what is become of that handful of men his majefty fent to *Germany* under Sir *Horace Vere*, which he was bound to do as he was one of the *proteftant* princes of the *union ;* and what is become of Sir *Arthur Chichefter,* who is gone Ambaffador to thofe parts ?

    Dear Sir, I pray make me happy ftill with your letters ; it is a mighty pleafure for us country-folks to hear how matters pafs in *London* and abroad : you know I have not the opportunity to correfpond with you in like kind, but may happily hereafter when the tables are turned, when I am in *London*, and you in the Weft. Whereas you are defirous to hear how it fares with me, I pray know that I live in one of the noblest houfes, and beft air in *England*. There is a dainty park adjoining ; where I often wander up and down, and I have my feveral walks. I make one to reprefent the *Royal Exchange*, the other the middle ifle of *Paul's*, another *Wefminfter-hall* ; and when I pafs through the herd of deer, methinks I am in *Cheapfide*. So with a full return of the fame mea-fure of love, as you pleafed to fend me, I reft

Yours,

May, 24. 1621.   J. H.

LETTER XLI.

To Captain THOMAS PORTER, *upon his return from an* Algier *Voyage.*

Noble Captain,

I Congratulate your fafe return from the *Straits*, but am forry you were fo ftraitened in your commiffi-on, that you could not attempt what fuch a brave naval power of twenty men of war, fuch a gallant General, and other choice knowing commanders might have performed, if they had had line enough. I know the lightnefs and nimblenefs of *Algier* fhips ; when I lived lately in *Alicant* and other places upon the *Mediterranean*, we fhould e-very week hear of fome of them chafed, but very feldom taken ; for a great fhip following one of them, may be faid to be as a maftiff dog running after a hare. I wonder the *Spaniards* came fhort of the promifed fupply for fur-therance of that noble adventurous defign you had to fire the fhips and gallies in *Algier* road : and according to the relation you pleafed to fend me, it was one of the braveft enterprizes, and had proved fuch a glorious exploit

that

that no story could have paralleled; but it seems their *hoggies, magicians* and *maribots* were tampering with the ill spirit of the air all the while, which brought down such a still cataract of rain-waters suddenly upon you, to hinder the working of your fire-works; such a disaster the story tells us befel *Charles* the Emperor, but far worse than yours, for he lost ships and multitudes of men, who were made slaves, but you came off with loss of eight men only, and *Algier* is another gess thing now than she was then, being I believe a hundred degrees stronger by land and sea; and for the latter strength, we may thank our countryman *Ward*, and *Danskey* the butter-bag *Hollander*, who may be said to have been two of the fatallest and most infamous men that ever christendom bred; for the one taking all *Englishmen*, and the other all *Dutchmen*, and bringing the ships and ordnance to *Algier*, they may be said to have been the chief raisers of those *Picaroons* to be pirates, who are now come to that height of strength, they daily endamage and affront all christendom. When I consider all the circumstances and success of this your voyage; when I consider the narrowness of your commission, which was as lame as the clerk that kept it; when I find that you secured the seas and traffick all the while, for I did not hear of one ship taken while you were abroad; when I hear how you brought back all the fleet, without the least disgrace or damage by foe or foul weather to any ship; I conclude, and so do far better judgments than mine, that you did what possibly could be done: let those that repine at the one in the hundred (which was imposed upon all the *Levant* merchants for the support of this fleet) mutter what they will, that you went first to *Gravesend, then to the Lands-end, and after to no end.*

I have sent you for your welcome home (in part) two barrels of *Colchester* oysters, which were provided for my Lord *Colchester* himself, therefore I presume they are good, and all green-fined: I shall shortly follow, but not to stay long in *England*, for I think I must over-

again

again speedily to push on my fortunes : so my dear *Tom,*
I am *de todas mis entranas* from the center of my heart,

Yours,

St. Osith, Dec. 1722. J. H.

LETTER XLII.

To my FATHER, *upon my second going to travel.*

S I R,

I Am lately returned to *London,* having been all this
while in a very noble family in the country, where I
found far greater respects than I deserved ; I was to go
with two of my Lord *Savage's* sons to travel, but finding
my self too young for such a charge, and our religion
differing, I have now made choice to go over comrade
to a very worthy gentleman, Baron *Altham's* son, whom
I knew in *Stanes* when my brother was there. Truly
I hold him to be one of the hopefullest young men of this
kingdom for parts and person ; he is full of excellent solid
knowledge, as the mathematics, the law, and other material studies : besides, I should have been tied to have
stayed three years abroad in the other employment at
least, but I hope to get back from this by God's grace
before a year be at an end ; at which time I hope the
hand of providence will settle me in some stable home-
fortune.

The news is, that the Prince *Palsgrave,* with his
lady and children, are come to the *Hague* in *Holland,*
having made a long progress or rather a pilgrimage about
Germany from *Prague.* The old Duke of *Bavaria* his
uncle, is chosen Elector and Arch-sewer of the *Roman*
empire in his place, (but as they say, in an imperfect
diet) and with this *proviso,* that the transferring of this
election upon the *Bavarian* shall not prejudice the next
heir. There is one Count *Mansfelt* that begins to get

a

a great name in *Germany*, and he with the Duke of *Brunſ-wick*, who is a temporal Biſhop of *Halverſtade*, have a conſiderable army on foot for the Lady *Elizabeth*, who in the *Low-Countries*, and ſome parts of *Germany* is called the Queen of *Boheme*, and for her winning princely comportment, the Queen of *Hearts*. Sir *Arthur Chicheſter* is come back from the *Palatinate*, much complaining of the ſmall army that was ſent thither under Sir *Horace Vere*, which ſhould have been greater, or none at all.

My Lord of *Buckingham* having been long ſince maſter of the horſe at court, is now made maſter alſo of all the *wooden-horſes* in the kingdom, which indeed are our beſt horſes, for he is to be High-Admiral of *England;* ſo he is become *Dominus equorum & aquarum.* The late Lord Treaſurer *Cranfield* grows alſo very powerful, but the city hates him for having betrayed their greateſt ſecrets, which he was capable to know more than another; having been formerly a merchant.

I think I ſhall have no opportunity to write to you again, until I be to the other ſide of the ſea ; therefore I humbly take my leave, and aſk your bleſſing, that I may the better proſper in my proceedings : ſo I am

Your dutiful ſon,

March, 19. 1622.   J. H.

LETTER XLIII.

To Sir JOHN SMITH, *Knight.*

S I R,

THE firſt ground I ſet foot upon after this my ſecond tranſmarine voyage, was *Trevere* (the *Scots* ſtapie) in *Zealand;* thence we ſailed to *Holland,* in which paſſage we might ſee divers ſteeples and turrets under water, of towns that we were told were ſwallowed up by a deluge within the memory of man : we went afterwards

to

to the *Hague*, where there are hard by, though in several places, two wonderful things to be seen, the one of *art*, the other of *nature* ; that of *art* is a waggon, or ship, or a monster mixt of both, like the *hippocentaur*, who was half man and half horse ; this engine hath wheels and sails that will hold above twenty people, and goes with the wind, being drawn or moved by nothing else, and will run, the wind being good, and the sails hoised up, above fifteen miles an hour upon the even hard sands : they say this invention was found out to entertain *Spinola* when he came hither to treat of the last truce. That wonder of *nature*, is a church-monument, where an Earl and a Lady are engraven with 365 Children about them, which were all delivered at one birth ; they were half male, half female : the two bafons in which they were christened hang still in the church, and the Bishop's name who did it ; and the story of this miracle, with the year and the day of the month mentioned, which is not yet 200 years ago ; and the story is this : that as the Countefs walked about the door after dinner, there came a beggar-woman, with two children upon her back, to beg alms ; the Countefs asked whether those children were her own, she answered she had them both at one birth, and by one father, who was her husband. The Countefs would not only not give her any alms, but reviled her bitterly, saying, it was impossible for one man to get two children at once : the beggar-woman being thus provocked with ill words, and without alms, fell to imprecations, that it should please God to shew his judgments upon her, and that she might bear at one birth as many children as there are days in the year, which she did before the years end, having never born child before. We are now in *North-Holland*, where I never saw so many, among so few, sick of leprofies ; and the reason is, becaufe they commonly eat abundance of fresh fish. A gentleman told me, that the women of this country, when they are delivered, there comes out of the womb a living creature befides the child, called *zucchie*, likeft a *bat* of any other creature, which the midwives throw into the fire, holding sheets before the chimney left it should fly away. Mr. *Altham* desires his service be presented to you and your lady, to Sir *John Franklin*, and all at the *Hill*; the like do I humbly crave at your hand : the *Italian* and *French* manuscripts you pleased to favour me withal, I left at Mr. *Seil*'s the stationer, whence if you have not them already, you may please to send for them. So in all affection I kiss your hands, and am

Your humble servant,

Trevere, April, 10. 1623.   J. H.

LETTER XLIV.

To the Right Honourable the Lord Viscount Colchester, *after Earl* Rivers,

Right Honourable,

THE commands your Lordship pleased to impose upon me when I left *England*, and those high favours wherein I stand bound to your Lordship, call upon me at this time to send your Lordship some small fruits of my foreign travel : Marquis *Spinola* is returned from the *Palatinate*, where he was so fortunate, that (like *Cæsar*) he came, saw, and overcame, notwithstanding the huge army of the princes of the *Union*, consisting of 40000 men; whereas his was under twenty, but made up of old tough blades, and veteran commanders. He hath now changed his coat, and taken up his old commission again from *Don Philippo*, whereas during that expedition he called himself *Cæsar*'s servant. I hear the Emperor hath transmitted the upper *Palatinate* to the Duke of *Bavaria*, as caution for those monies he hath expended in those wars. And the King of *Spain* is the Emperor's commissary for the lower *Palatinate* : they both pretend that they were bound to obey the imperial Summons, to assist *Cæsar* in these wars; the one as he was Duke of *Burgundy*, the other of *Bavaria*, both which countries

are

are feudatory to the empire ; elfe they had incured the imperial ban. It is feared this *German* war will be as the *Frenchman* faid, *de longue halaine*, long breathed ; for there are great powers on both fides, and they fay the King of *Denmark* is arming.

Having made a leifurely fojourn in this town, I had fpare hours to couch in writing a furvey of thefe countries, which I have now traverfed the fecond time ; but in regard it would be a great bulk for a letter, I fend it your Lordfhip apart, and when I return to *England* I fhall be bold to attend your Lordfhip for correcting of my faults : in the interim I reft, my Lord,

Your thrice humble fervant,

Antwerp, May, 1. 1623.　　　　　　　J. H.

L E T T E R XLV.

A Survey of the feventeen Provinces.

My Lora,

TO attempt a precife defcription of each of the feven-teen *provinces*, and of its progreffion, privileges, and primitive government, were a tafk of no lefs confufi-on than labour : let it fuffice to know, that fince *Flanders* and *Holland* were erected to earldoms, and fo left to be an appendix to the crown of *France*, fome of them have had abfolute and fupreme governors, fome fubaltern and fubject to a fuperior power. Among the reft, the earls of *Flanders* and *Holland* were moft confiderable ; but of them two, he of *Holland* being homageable to none, and having *Friefland* and *Zealand* added, was the more potent. In procefs of time all the feventeen met in one ; fome by conqueft, others by donation and legacy, but moft by alliance. In the houfe of *Burgundy* this union received moft growth, but in the houfe of *Auftria* it came to its full perfection ; for in *Charles* V. they all met as fo many lines drawn from the circumference to

H　　　　　　　　　　　　the

the centre ; who lording as fupreme head, not only over
the fifteen temporal, but the two fpiritual, *Liege* and
Utrecht, had a defign to reduce them to a kingdom,
which his fon *Philip* II. attempted after him ; but they
could not bring their intents home to their aim ; the caufe
is imputed to that multiplicity and difference of privileges
which they are fo eager to maintain, and whereof fome
cannot ftand with a monarchy without incongruity. *Philip* II. at his inauguration was fworn to obferve them, and
at his departure he obliged himfelf by an oath to fend ftill
one of his own blood to govern them. Moreover, at the
requeft of the knights of the golden fleece, he promifed
that all foreign foldiers fhould retire, and that he himfelf would come to vifit them once every feven years ;
but being once gone, and leaving in lieu of a *fword* a
diftaff, an unweildy woman to govern, he came not only
fhort of his promife, but procured a difpenfation from
the Pope to be abfolved of his oath ; and all this by the
counfel of Cardinal *Granvill*, who, as the States chroni-
cler writes, was the firft firebrand that kindled that la-
mentable and longfome war wherein the *Netherlands*
have traded above fifty years in blood : for intending to
increafe the number of *bifhops*, to eftablifh the decrees of
the council of *Trent*, and to chip the power of the council
of ftate compofed of the natives of the land, by making
it appealable to the council of *Spain*, and by adding to
the former oath of allegiance, (all which conduced
to fettle the inquifition, and to curb the confcience) the
broils began ; to appeafe which, ambaffadors were difpatched to *Spain*, whereof the two firft came to violent deaths, the one being beheaded, the other poifoned ;
but the two laft, *Egmond* and *Horn*, were nourifhed ftil
with hopes, until *Philip* II. had prepared an army under
the conduct of the Duke of *Alva*, to compofe the differ
ence by arms. For as foon as he came to the govern
ment, he eftablifhed the *Bloet-rad*, as the complainant
termed it, *a council of blood*, made up moft of *Spaniards*
Egmond and *Horn* were apprehended, and afterward
beheaded ; citadels were erected, and the oath of alle
giance

giance, with the political government of the country, in divers things altered. This poured oil on the fire formerly kindled, and put all in combustion : the Prince of *Orange* retires, thereupon his eldest son was surprized, and sent as hostage to *Spain*, and above 5000 families quit the country ; many towns revolted, but were afterwards reduced to obedience ; which made the Duke of *Alva* say, that the *Netherlands* appertained to the King of *Spain* not only by *descent*, but *conquest ;* and for a cumble of his victories, when he attempted to impose the tenthpenny for the maintenance of the garrisons in the citadels he had erected at *Grave, Utrecht* and *Antwerp* (where he caused his statue made of *cannon-brass* to be erected, trampling the *Belgians* under his feet) all the towns withstood this imposition ; so that at last matters succeeded ill with him, and having had his cousin *Paccecio* hanged at *Flushing* gate, after he had traced out the plat-form of a citadel in that town also, he received letters of revocation from *Spain*. To him succeeded *Don Luys de Requilius*, who came short of his predecessor in exploits ; and dying suddenly in the field, the government was vested for a time in the council of state : the *Spanish* soldiers being without a head, gathered together to the number of 1600, and committed such outrages up and down, that they were proclaimed enemies to the state. Hereupon the pacification of *Ghent* was transacted, whereof, among other articles one was, that all foreign soldiers should quite the country. This was ratified by the King, and observed by *Don John* of *Austria*, who succeeded in the government ; yet *Don John* retained the *Landskneghts* at his devotion still for some secret design, and as some conjectured for the invasion of *England ;* he kept the *Spaniards* also still hovering about the frontiers ready upon all occasions. Certain letters were intercepted that made a discovery of some projects, which made the war to bleed afresh : *Don John* was proclaimed enemy to the state ; so the Archduke *Matthias* was sent for, who being a man of small performance and improper for the times, was dismissed, but upon honourable terms.

Don John a little after dies, and as some gave out, of
the pox ; then comes in the Duke of *Parma*, a man as
of a different nation, being an *Italian*, so of a different
temper, and more moderate spirit, and of greater per-
formances than all the rest ; for whereas all the provinces except *Luxemburg*, and *Hainault* had revolted, he
reduced *Ghent*, *Tournay*, *Bruges*, *Malines*, *Bruffels*,
Antwerp, (which three last he beleaguered at one time)
and divers other great towns to the *Spanish* obedience
again : he had 60,000 men in pay, and the choicest which
Spain and *Italy* could afford. The *French* and *English*
ambassadors interceeding for a peace, had a short answer
of *Philip* II. who said, that he needed not the help of
any to reconcile himself to his own subjects, and reduce
them to conformity ; but the difference that was, he
would refer to his coufin the Emperor : hereupon the
business was agitated at *Colin*, where the *Spaniards* stood
as high a-tiptoe as ever, and notwithstanding the vast
expence of treasure and blood he had been at for so many
years, and that matters began to exasperate more and
more, which were like to prolong the wars *in infinitum*,
he would abate nothing in point of ecclesiastic government :
hereupon, the States perceived that King *Philip* could
not be wrought either by the follicitations of other princes,
or their own fupplications so often reiterated, that they
might enjoy the freedom of religion, with other infran-
chisements ; and finding him inexorable, being incited also
by the ban which was publifhed againft the Prince of
Orange, that whofoever killed him fhould have 5000
crowns ; they at laft abfolutely renounced and abjured
the King of *Spain* for their fovereign : they broke his
feals, changed the oath of allegiance, and fled to *France*
for fhelter ; they inaugurated the Duke of *Anjou* (recommended to them by the Queen of *England*, to whom
he was a fuitor) for their Prince, who attempted to render himfelf abfolute, and so thought to furprize *Antwerp*,
where he received an ill-favoured repulfe ; yet neverthe-
lefs the *United Provinces*, for so they termed themfelves
ever after, fearing to diftafte their next great neighbour
France,

France, made a fecond proffer of their protection and fovereignty to that King, who having too many irons in the fire at his own home, the *league* growing ftronger and ftronger, he anfwered them, that his *fhirt* was nearer to him than his *doublet*. Then had they recourfe to Queen *Elizabeth*, who partly for her own fecurity, partly for intereft in religion, reached them a fupporting hand, and fo fent them men, money, and a Governor, (the Earl of *Leicefter*,) who not fymbolizing with their humour, was quickly revoked, yet without any outward diflike on the Queen's fide, for fhe left her forces ftill with them, but upon their expence : fhe lent them afterwards fome confiderable fums of money, and fhe received *Flufhing* and the *Brill* for caution. Ever fince, the *Englifh* have been the beft finews of their war, and atchievers of the greateft exploits amongft them. Having thus made fure work with the *Englifh*, they made young Count *Maurice* their Governor, who for twenty-five years together held tack with the *Spaniard*; and during thofe traverfes of war was very fortunate : an overture of peace was then propounded, which the States would not hearken to *fingly* with the King of *Spain*, unlefs the provinces that yet remained under him would engage themfelves for the performance of what was articled; befides, they would not treat either of peace, or truce, unlefs they were declared *free States;* all which was granted : fo, by the intervention of the *Englifh* and *French* ambaffadors, a truce was concluded for twelve years.

Thefe wars did fo drain and difcommodate the King of *Spain*, by reafon of his diftance, (every foldier that he fent either from *Spain* or *Italy* cofting him near upon 100 crowns before he could be rendered in *Flanders*) that notwithftanding his mines of *Mexico* and *Peru*, it plunged him fo deeply in debt, that having taken up monies in all the chief banks of *chriftendom*, he was forced to publifh a *diploma*, wherein, he difpenfed with himfelf (as the *Holland* ftory hath it) from payment, alledging that he had employed thofe monies for the public peace of *chriftendom* : this broke many great bankers ; and, they

fay, his credit was not current in *Sevil* or *Lisbon*, his
own towns ; and which was worfe, while he ftood wreft-
ling thus with his own fubjects, the *Turk* took his opportunity to get from him *Tunis* and the *Goletta*, the
trophies of *Charles* V. his father.   So eager he was in
this quarrel, that he employed the utmoft of his ftrength
and induftry to reduce his people to his will, in regard
he had an intent to make thefe provinces his main rendezvous and magazine of men of war ; which his neighbours perceiving, and that he had a kind of aim to be
Weftern Monarch, being led not fo much for love as
reafons of ftate, they ftuck clofe to the revolted provinces : and, this was the *bone* that Secretary *Walfingham*
told Queen *Elizabeth,* he would caft the King of *Spain,*
that fhould laft him twenty years, and perhaps make his
teeth fhake in his head.

But to return to my firft difcourfe, whence this digref-
fion hath fnatched me : the *Netherlands,* who had been
formerly knit and concentred under one fovereign Prince,
were thus difmembered ; and as they fubfift now, they
are a ftate, and a province : the province having ten of the
feventeen at leaft, is far greater, more populous, better foiled and more ftored with gentry.   The ftate is
the richer and ftronger, the one proceeding from their
vaft navagation and commerce, the other from the quality of their country, being defenfible by rivers and
fluices, by means whereof they can fuddenly overwhelm
all the whole country ; witnefs that ftupendous fiege of
Leyden and *Haerlem ;* for moft of their towns, the marks
being taken away, are inacceffible, by reafon of fhelves
of fands.   Touching the tranfaction of thefe provinces,
which the King of *Spain* made as a dowry to the Archduke *Albertus,* upon marriage with the *Infanta,* (who
thereupon left his red hat, and *Toledo* miter, the chiefeft
fpiritual dignity in *chriftendom* for revenue, after the
papacy) it was fringed with fuch cautelous reftraints, that
he was fure to keep the better end of the ftaff ftill to himfelf ; for he was to have the tutelage and ward of his
children, that, they were to marry with one of the *Au-*
ftrian

ftrian family recommended by *Spain*, and in default of iffue, and in cafe *Albertus* fhould furvive the *Infanta*, he fhould be but Governor only. Add hereunto, that King *Philip* referved ftill to himfelf all the citadels and caftles, with the order of the golden fleece, whereof he is mafter, as he is Duke of *Burgundy*.

The Archduke for the time hath a very princely command, all coins bear his ftamp, all placarts or edicts are publifhed in his name; he hath the election of all civil officers and magiftrates; he nominates alfo bifhops and abbots, for the Pope hath only the confirmation of them here; nor can he adjourn any out of the country to anfwer any thing, neither are his bulls of any ftrength without the princes *placet*, which makes him have always fome commiffioners to execute his authority. The people here grow hotter and hotter in the *Roman* caufe, by reafon of the mixture with *Spaniards* and *Italians*; as alfo, by the example of the Archduke and the *Infanta*, who are devout in an intenfe degree. There are two fupreme councils, the Privy-council, and that of the State; this treats of confederations and intelligence with foreign princes, of peace and war, of entertaining or of difmiffing colonels and captains of fortifications; and they have the furintendency of the higheft affairs that concern the Prince and the polity of the provinces; the private hath the granting of all patents and requefts, the publifhing of all edicts and proclamations, the prizing of coin, the looking to the confines and extent of the provinces, and the enacting of all new ordinances. Of thefe two councils there is never a *Spaniard*, but in the actual council of war their voices are predominant. There is alfo a court of finances, or exchequer, whence all they that have the fingering of the King's money muft draw a difcharge. Touching matters of juftice, their law is mixt between civil and common, with fome claufes of canonical. The high-court of parliament is at *Maline*, whether all civil caufes may be brought by appeal from other towns, except fome that have municipal privileges, and are fovereign in their own jurifdictions, as *Mons* in *Hai-nalt*, and a few more.

The prime province for dignity is *Brabant*, which a-mongft many other privileges it enjoyeth, hath this for one, not to appear upon any fummons out of its own pre-cinct, which is one of the reafons why the Prince makes his refidence there: but the prime for extent and fame is *Flanders*, the chiefeft earldom in chriftendom, which is three days journey in length; *Ghent* its metropolis, is reputed the greateft town in *Europe*, whence arofe the proverb, *Les flamene tient un Gan, qui tiendra Paris dedans*. But the beautifulleft, richeft, ftrongeft, and moft privileged city is *Antwerp* in *Brabant*, being the *marquifate* of the holy empire, and drawing near to the nature of a hanfe-town, for lhe pays the Prince no other tax but the impoft. Before the diffociation of the feven-teen provinces, this town was one of the greateft marts of *Europe*, and greateft bank on this fide the *Alps*, moft princes having their factors here, to take up or let out monies; and here our *Grefham* got all his wealth, and built our royal-exchange by model of that here. The merchandize which was brought hither from *Germany*, *France*, and *Italy*, by land, and from *England*, *Spain*, and the hanfe-towns by fea was eftimated at above twenty millions of crowns every year; but as no violent thing is long lafting, and as 'tis fatal to all kingdoms, ftates, towns and languages to have their period, fo this re-nowned mart hath fuffered a fhrewd eclipfe, yet no ut-ter downfal, the exchange of the King of *Spain's* money and fome land-traffick keeping ftill life in her, though nothing fo full of vigour as it was; therefore, there is no town under the Archduke where the States have more concealed friends than in *Antwerp*, who would willingly make them her mafters in hope to recover her former commerce; which, after the laft twelve years truce began to revive a little, the States permitting to pafs by *Lillo's* fconce (which commands the river of *Scheld*, and lieth in the teeth of the town) fome fmall crofs-failed fhips to pafs hither. There is no place hath been more paffive

than.

than this, and more often pillaged; amongſt other times,
ſhe was once plundered moſt miſerably by the *Spaniards*
under the conduct of a prieſt, immediately upon *Don
John* of *Auſtria*'s death; ſhe had then her *ſtadt-houſe*

crowns the building; and the ſpoils that were carried a-
way thence amounted to forty tuns of gold: thus ſhe was

ing commanded by a citadel, which ſhe preferred before
a garriſon: this made the merchants retire and ſeek a
more free rendezvous, ſome in *Zealand*, ſome in *Holland*, ſpecially in *Amſterdam*, which roſe upon the fall
of this town, as *Lisbon* did from *Venice* upon the diſcovery of the *Cape of good Hope*, though *Venice* be not
near ſo much creſt-fallen.

I will now ſteer my diſcourſe to the *United Provinces*,
as they term themſelves, which are ſix in number, *viz.*
Holland, *Zealand*, *Frieſland*, *Overyſſell*, *Groninghen* and
Utrecht, three parts of *Gilderland*, and ſome frontier
towns and places of contribution in *Brabant* and *Flanders*. In all theſe there is no innovation at all introduced,
notwithſtanding this great change in point of government,
except that the college of States repreſents the Duke or
Earl in times paſt; which college conſiſts of the chiefeſt
gentry of the country, ſurintendants of towns, and the
principal magiſtrates. Every province and great town
chuſe yearly certain deputies, to whom they give plenary
power to deliberate with the other States of all affairs
touching the public welfare of the whole province, and
what they vote ſtands for law. Theſe being aſſembled,
conſult of all matters of ſtate, juſtice, and war: the Advocate, who is prime in the aſſembly propounds the buſineſs, and after, collects the ſuffrages, firſt of the provinces, then of the towns; which being put in form, he de-
livers in pregnant and moving ſpeeches; and in caſe there
be a diſſonance and reluctancy of opinions, he labours to
accord and reconcile them, concluding always with the
major voices.

Touching

Touching the adminiftration of juftice, the Prefident who is monthly changed, with the great council, have the fupreme judicature, from whofe decrees there is no appeal but a revifion; and then, fome of the choiceft lawyers amongft them are appointed.

For their *oppidan* government, they have variety of offices, a fcout, burgomafters, a balue, and *Vroetfchap-pens.* The fcout is chofen by the States, who with the halues have the judging of all criminal matters in laft refort, without appeal: they have alfo the determining of civil caufes, but thofe are appealable to the *Hague.* Touching their chiefeft Governor (or General rather now) having made proof of the *Spaniard, German, French* and *Englifh,* and agreeing with none of them, they lighted at laft upon a man of their own mould, Prince *Maurice,* now their General, in whom concurred divers parts fuitable to fuch a charge, having been trained up in the wars by his father, who with three of his uncles, and divers of his kindred, facrificed their lives in the States quarrel: he hath thriven well fince he came to the government; he cleared *Friefland, Overyffell* and *Gronighen,* in lefs than eighteen months. He hath now continued their Governor and General by fea and land above thirty-three years: he hath the election of magiftrates, the pardoning of malefactors, and divers other prerogatives, yet they are fhort of the reach of fovereignty, and of the authority of the antient counts of *Holland.* Though I cannot fay 'tis a mercenary employment, yet he hath a limited allowance; nor hath he any implicite command when he goes to the field: for either the council of war marcheth with him, or elfe he receives daily directions from them. Moreover, the States themfelves referve the power of nominating all commanders in the army, which being of fundry nations, deprive him of thofe advantages he might have to make himfelf abfolute. Martial difcipline is nowhere fo regular as amongft the States; nowhere are there leffer infolencies committed upon the burgher, nor robberies upon the country boors; nor are the officers permitted to infult over

the

the common foldiers. When the army marcheth, not one dares take fo much as an apple off a tree, or a root out of the earth in their paffage; and the reafon is, they are punctually paid their pay, elfe I believe they would be infolent enough; and were not the pay fo certain, I think few or none would ferve them. They fpeak of 60,000 they have in perpetual pay by land and fea, at home, and in the *Indies:* the King of *France* was ufed to maintain a regiment, but fince *Henry the Great's* death the payment hath been neglected. The means they have to maintain thefe forces, to pay their Governor, to difcharge all other expence; as the prefervation of their dikes, which comes to a vaft expence yearly, is the antient revenue of the counts of *Holland,* the impropriate church-livings, impofts upon all merchandize, which is greater upon exported than imported goods; excife upon all commodities, as well for neceffity as pleafure; taxes upon every acre of ground, which is fuch, that the whole country returns into their hands every three years. Add hereunto the art they ufe in their bank by the rife and fall of money, the fifhing upon our coafts, whither they fend every autumn above 700 holks or buffes; which in the voyages they make, return above a million in herrings. Moreover, their fifhing for greenfifh and falmond, amounts to fo much more; and for their cheefe and butter, 'tis thought they vent as much every year as *Lisbon* doth fpices. This keeps the common treafury always full, that upon any extraordinary fervice or defign there is feldom any new tax upon the people. Traffick is their general profeffion, being all either merchants or mariners; and having no land to manure, they furrow the fea for their living; and, this univerfallity of trade, and their banks of adventures, diftributes the wealth fo equally, that few amongft them are exceeding rich or exceeding poor. Gentry amongft them is very thin, and as in all democracies, little refpected; and coming to dwell in towns, they foon mingle with the merchants, and fo degenerate: their foil being all betwixt marfh and meadow is fo fat in pafturage, that one

cow

cow will give eight quarts of milk a-day, so that as a boor told me, in four little dorps near *Harlem*, 'tis thought there is as much milk milked in the year as there is *Rhenish* wine brought to *Dort*, which is the staple of it. Their towns are beautiful and neatly built, and with such uniformity, that who sees one sees all. In some places, as in *Amsterdam*, the foundation costs more than the superstructure; for the ground being soft, they are constrained to ram in huge stakes of timber (with wool about it to preserve it from putrifaction) till they come to a firm basis; so that as one said, whosoever could see *Amsterdam* under ground should see a huge winter-forrest.

Among all the confederate provinces, *Holland* is most predominant, which being but six hours journey in breadth, contains forty-nine walled towns, and all these within a day's journey one of another. *Amsterdam* for the present is one of the greatest mercantile towns in *Europe*. To her is appropriated the *East* and *West-India* trade, whither she sends yearly forty great ships, with another fleet to the *Baltick* sea; but they send not near so many to the *Mediterranean* as *England* : other towns are passably rich, and stored with shipping, but not one very poor; which proceeds from the wholesome policy they use, to assign every town some firm staple commodity; as to (their maiden-town) *Dort* the *German* wines and corn, to *Middleburgh* the *French* and *Spanish* wines, to *Trevere* (the Prince of *Orange*'s town (the *Scots* trade: *Leyden* in recompence of her long siege was erected to an university, which with *Franeker* in *Friesland* is all they have; *Harlem* for knitting and weaving hath some privilege; *Rotterdam* hath the *English* cloth : and this renders their towns so equally rich and populous. They allow free harbour to all nations, with liberty of religion, (the *Roman* only excepted) as far as the *Jew*, who hath two *synagogues* allowed him, but only in *Amsterdam*; which piece of policy they borrow of the *Venetians*, with whom they have very intimate intelligence : only the *Jews* in *Venice*, in *Rome*, and other places, go with some outward mark of distinction, but here they wear none; and these thefe two republics, that in the *Eaft*, and this in the *Weft*, are the two *remoras* that ftick to the great veſſel of *Spain*, that it cannot fail to the Weſtern monarchy.

I have been long in the ſurvey of theſe provinces, yet not long enough ; for much more might be ſaid, which is fitter for a ſtory than a ſurvey : I will conclude with a *mot* or two of the people, whereof ſome have been renowned in time paſt for feats of war. A mong the States, the *Hollander* or *Batavian* hath been moſt known, for ſome of the *Roman* emperors have had a ſelected guard of them about their perſons for their fidelity and valour, as now the King of *France* hath of the *Swiſſe*. The *Friſians* alſo have been famous for thoſe large privileges wherewith *Charlemain* endued them ; the *Flemins* alſo have been illuſtrious for the martial exploits they achieved in the Eaſt, where two of the earls of *Flanders* were crowned emperors. They have all a *genius* inclined to commerce, very inventive and witty in manufactures, witneſs the art of *printing*, *painting*, and *colouring* in glaſs ; thoſe curious quadrants, chimes and dials, thoſe kind of waggons which are uſed up and down *chriſtendom*, were firſt uſed by them ; and for the mariners compaſs, though the matter be diſputable betwixt the *Neapolitan*, the *Portugal* and them, yet there is a ſtrong argument on their ſide, in regard they were the firſt that ſubdivided the four cardinal winds to thirty two, others naming them in their language.

There is no part of *Europe* ſo haunted with all ſorts of foreigners as the *Netherlands*, which makes the inhabitants, as well women as men, ſo well verſed in all ſorts of languages, ſo that in exchange-time one may hear ſeven or eight ſorts of tongues ſpoken upon their burſes ; nor are the men only expert herein, but the women and maids alſo in their common hoſtries ; and in *Holland* the wives are ſo well verſed in bargaining, cyphering and writing, that in the abſence of their huſbands in long ſea-voyages, they beat the trade at home, and their words will paſs in equal credit. Theſe women are wonderfully ſober, though their huſbands make commonly their bar-

I   gains

:gains in drink, and then are they more cautelous.· This confluence of ſtrangers makes them very populous, which was the cauſe that *Charles* the Emperor ſaid, that all the *Netherlands* ſeemed to him but as one continued town. He and his grandfather *Maximilian*, notwithſtanding the choice of kingdoms they had, kept their courts moſt frequently in them, which ſhewed how highly they eſteemed them ; and, I believe if *Philip* II. had viſited them ſometimes, matters had not gone ſo ill.

There is no part of the earth, conſidering the ſmall circuit of the country, which is eſtimated to be but as big as the fifth part of *Italy*, where one may find more differing cuſtoms, tempers and humours of people, than in the *Netherlands :* the *Walloon* is quick and ſprightful; accoſtable and full of compliment, and gaudy in apparel, like his next neighbour the *French :* the *Fleming* and *Brabanter*, ſomewhat more flow and more ſparing of ſpeech : the *Hollander* flower than he, more ſurly and reſpectleſs of gentry and ſtrangers, homely in his clothing, of very few words, and heavy in action ; which may be well imputed to the quality of the ſoil, which works ſo ſtrongly upon the humours, that when people of a more vivacious and nimble temper come to mingle with them, their children are obſerved to partake rather of the ſoil than the ſire ; and ſo it is in all animals beſides.

Thus have I huddled up ſome obſervations of the *Low-Countries*, beſeeching your Lordſhip would be pleaſed to pardon the imperfections, and correct the errors of them ; for I know none ſo capable to do it as your Lordſhip, to whom I am

A moſt humble and ready ſervant,

Antwerp, May, 1. 1622.   J. H.

L E T-

LETTER XLVI.

To my Brother Dr. HOWELL *from* Bruffels.

SIR,

I Had yours in *Latin* at *Rotterdam*, whence I corre-
fponded with you in the fame language; I heard,
though not from you, fince I came from *Bruffels*, that
our fifter *Anne* is lately married to Mr. *Hugh Penry*, I
am heartily glad of it, and wifh the reft of our fifters were
fo well beftowed, for I know Mr. *Penry* to be a gentleman of a great deal of folid worth and integrity, and
one that will prove a good hufband, and a great *œcono-
mift*.

Here is news that *Mansfelt* hath received a foil in *Germany*, and that the Duke of *Brunfwick*, alias Bifhop of
Halverftadt, hath loft one of his arms : this makes them
vapour here extremely; and the laft week I heard of a
play the jefuits of *Antwerp* made in derogation, or rather derifion of the proceedings of the Prince *Palfgrave*,
where, amongft divers other paffages, they feigned a poft
to come puffing upon the ftage; and being afked what
news; he anfwered how the *Palfgrave* was like to have
fhortly a huge formidable army ; for the King of *Denmark* was to fend him 100,000, the *Hollanders* 100,000,
and the King of *Great Britain* 100,000 ; but being afked
thoufands of what? He replied, the firft would fend
100,000 *red herring*, the fecond 100,000 *cheefes*, and
the laft 100,000 ambaffadors, alluding to Sir *Richard
Wefton*, and Sir *Edward Conway*, my Lord *Carlifle*, Sir
Arthur Chichefter, and laftly, the Lord *Digby*, who have
been all employed in quality of ambaffadors in lefs than
two years, fince the beginning of thefe *German* broils.
Touching the *laft*, having been with the Emperor and
the Duke of *Bavaria*, and carried himfelf with fuch
high wifdom in his negotiations with the one, and ftout-
nefs with the other; and having preferved Count *Mansfelt's* troops from difbanding, by pawning his own argen-

try and jewels, he paſſed this way, where they ſay the Archduke did eſteem him more than any Ambaſſador that ever was in this Court; and the report is yet very freſh of his high abilities.

We are to remove hence in coach towards *Paris* the next week, where we intend to winter, or hard by ; when you have opportunity to write to *Wales*, I pray preſent my duty to my father, and my love to the reſt ; I pray remember me alſo to all at the *Hill* and the *Dale*, eſpecially to that moſt virtuous gentleman, Sir *John Frankling*. So my dear brother, I pray God continue and improve his bleſſings to us both, and bring us together again with comfort.

Your Brother,

June, 10. 1622.   J. H.

LETTER XLVII.

To Dr. THOMAS PRICHARD *at* Worceſter *Houſe.*

SIR,

FRIENDSHIP *is the great chain of human ſociety ; and intercourſe of letters is one of the chiefeſt links of that chain :* you know this as well as I ; therefore, I pray let our friendſhip, let our love, that nationality of *Britiſh* love, that virtuous tie of *academic* love be ſtill ſtrengthened (as heretofore) and receive daily more and more vigour. I am now in *Paris*, and there is weekly opportunity to receive and ſend ; and if you pleaſe to ſend, you ſhall be ſure to receive ; for I make it a kind of religion to be punctual in this kind of payment. I am heartily glad to hear that you are become a *domeſtic* member to that moſt noble family of the *Worceſters*, and I hold it to be a very good foundation for future preferment ; I wiſh you may be as happy in them, as I know they will be happy in you. *France* is now barren of news, only there was a ſhrewd bruſh lately betwixt the young

King

King and his mother, who having the Duke of *Efpernon*
and others for her champions, met him in open field
about *pont de ce,* but fhe went away with the worft ; fuch
was the rare dutifulnefs of the King, that he forgave
her upon his knees, and pardoned all her complices :
and now there is an univerfal peace in this country, which
it is thought will not laft long, for there is a war intended againft them of the reformed religion ; for this King,
though he be flow in fpeech, yet he is active in fpirit,
and loves motion.   I am here comrade to a gallant young
gentleman, my old acquaintance, who is full of excellent parts, which he hath acquired by a choice breeding,.
the Baron his father gave him both in the univerfity,.
and in the inns of court ; fo that for the time, I envy no
man's happinefs.   So with my hearty commends, and.
much endeared love unto you, I feft

Yours while,

Paris, Auguft 3. 1622.   J. H..

LETTER XLVIII.

To the Honourable Sir THOMAS SAVAGE (*after Lord*
SAVAGE) *at his Houfe upon* Tower-Hill..

Honourable S I R,

THOSE many undeferved favours for which I ftand.
obliged to yourfelf and my noble Lady, fince the
time I had the happinefs to come firft under your roof,
and the command you pleafed to lay upon me at my departure thence, called upon me at this time to give you
account how matters pafs in *France.*

That which for the prefent affords moft plenty of
news, is *Rochel,* which the King threateneth to block up
this fpring with an army by fea, under the command of
the Duke of *Nevers,* and by a land army under his own
conduct : both fides prepare, he to affault, the *Rochellers*
to defend.   The King declares that he proceeds not

I 3   againft

againſt them for their religion, which he is ſtill contented to tolerate, but for holding an aſſembly againſt his declarations: they anſwer, that their aſſembly is grounded upon his Majeſty's royal warrant, given at the diſſolution of the laſt aſſembly at *Lodun*, where he ſolemnly gave his word to permit them to reaſſemble when they would, ſix months after, if the breaches of their liberty and grievances which they then propounded were not redreſſed; and they ſay, this being unperformed, it ſtands not with the ſacred perſon of a King to violate his promiſe, being the firſt that ever he made them. The King is ſo incenſed againſt them, that their deputies can have neither acceſs to his perſon, nor audience of his counſel, as they ſtile themſelves the deputies of the aſſembly at *Rochel;* but if they ſay, they come from the whole body of them of the *pretended reformed religion,* he will hear them. The breach between them is grown ſo wide, that the King reſolves on a ſiege. This reſolution of the King is much fomented by the *Roman* clergy; eſpecially by the *Celeſtines,* who have 200,000 crowns of gold in the arſenal of *Paris,* which they would ſacrifice all to this ſervice; beſides, the Pope ſent him a bull to levy what ſums he would of the *Gallican* church, for the advancement of his deſign. This reſolution alſo is much puſhed on by the gentry, who beſides the particular employments and pay they ſhall receive hereby, are glad to have their young King trained up in arms, to make him a martial man; but for the merchant and poor peaſant, they tremble at the name of this war, fearing their teeth ſhould be ſet on edge with thoſe four grapes their fathers taſted in the time of the *league:* for, if the King begins with *Rochel,* 'tis feared all the four corners of the kingdom will be ſet on fire.

Of all the towns of ſurety which they of the religion hold, *Rochel* is the chiefeſt, a place ſtrong by nature, but ſtronger by art. It is a maritime town, and landward they can by ſluices drown a league's diſtance; 'tis fortified with mighty thick walls, baſtions, and counterſcarps; and thoſe according to the modern rules of enginery.

This,

This, among other cautionary towns, was granted by
Henry IV. to them of the religion for a certain term of
years; which being expired, the King faith, they are de-
volved again to the crown, and so demands them. They
of the religion pretend to have divers grievances; first,
they have not been paid these two years the 160,000
crowns which the last King gave them annually, to maintain their ministers and garrisons: they complain of the
King's carriage lately at *Bearn* (*Henry the Great's* country) which was merely protestant, where he hath introduced two years since the publick exercise of the *mass*,
which had not been sung there fifty years before; he altered also there the government of the country, and in
lieu of a *Viceroy*, left a *Governor* only: and whereas,
Navarrin was formerly a court of parliament for the
whole kingdom of *Navarre* (that is under *France*) he
hath put it down, and published an edict, that the *Na-*
varrois should come to *Toloufe*, the chief town of *Lan-*
guedoc; and lastly, he left behind him a garrison in the
said town of *Navarrin*. These and other grievances
they of the religion proposed to the King lately, desiring
his Majesty would let them enjoy still those privileges his
predecessor *Henry* III. and his father *Henry* IV. afforded
them by act of pacification; but, he made them a short
answer, that what the one did in this point, he did it out
of *fear;* what the other did, he did it out of *love;* but,
he would have them know, that he neither *loved* them
nor *feared* them; so the business is like to bleed sore on
both sides, nor is there yet any appearance of prevention.

There was a scuffle lately here betwixt the Duke of
Nevers and the Cardinal of *Guise*, who have had a long
suit in law about an abbey; and meeting the last week a-
bout the palace, from words they fell to blows, the Cardinal struck the Duke first, and so were parted; but in
the afternoon there appeared on both sides no less than
3000 horse in a field hard by, which shews the populouf-
ness and sudden strength of this huge city; but the matter was taken up by the King himself, and the Cardinal

clapt

clapt up in the *Baſtile*, where the King ſaith he ſhall abide to *ripen:* for he is but young, and they ſpeak of a *bull* that is to come from *Rome* to decardinalize him.   I fear to have treſpaſſed too much upon your patience, therefore I will conclude for the preſent, but will never ecaſe to profeſs myſelf

Your thrice humble and ready ſervitor,

Paris, Auguſt 18. 1622.   J. H.

LETTER XLIX.

To DAN. CALDWALL, *Eſq; from* Poiſſy.

My dear DAN.

TO be free from *Engliſh,* and to have the more conveniency to fall cloſe to our buſineſs, Mr. *Altham* and I are lately retired from *Paris* to this town of *Poiſſy,* a pretty genteel place, at the foot of the great foreſt of *St. Germain,* upon the river *Sequana,* and within a mile of one of the King's chiefeſt ſtanding houſes, and about fifteen miles from *Paris:* here is one of the prime nunneries of all *France.*   *Lewis* IX. who in the catalogue of the *French* kings is called St. *Lewis,* which title was confirmed by the *Pope,* was baptized in this little town; and after his return from *Egypt* and other places againſt the *Saracens,* being aſked by what title he would be diſtinguiſhed from the reſt of his predeceſſors after his death, he anſwered, that he deſired to be called *Lewis of Poiſſy.* Reply being made, that there were divers other places and cities of renown, where he had performed brave exploits and obtained famous victories, therefore, it was more fitting that ſome of thoſe places ſhould denominate him: no, ſaid he, I deſire to be called *Lewis of Poiſſy,* becauſe there I got the moſt glorious victory that ever I had, for *there I overcame the devil*; meaning, that he was chriſtened there.

I sent you from *Antwerp* a silver *Dutch* table-book;
I desire to hear of the receipt of it in your next. I must
desire you (as I did once at *Rouen*) to send me a dozen
pairs of the whitest kidskin gloves for women, and half a
dozen pairs of knives by the merchants post; and if you
want any thing that *France* can afford, I hope you know
what power you have to dispose of

Yours,

Poissy, Sept. 7. 1622. J. H.

L E T T E R L.

To my F A T H E R, *from* Paris.

S I R,

I Was afraid I should never have had ability to write to
you again, I had lately such a dangerous fit of sickness, but I have now past the brunt of it. God hath
been pleased to reprieve me, and reserve me for more
days, which I hope to have grace to number better,
Mr. *Altham* and I having retired to a small town from
Paris for more privacy, and sole conversation with the
nation: I tied myself to a talk for the reading of so many
books in such a compass of time; and thereupon, to make
good my word to myself, I used to watch many nights
together, though it was in the depth of winter; but returning to this town, I took cold in the head, and so
that mass of rheum which had gathered by my former
watching, turned to an imposthume in my head, whereof
I was sick above forty days; at the end they cauterized
and made an issue in my cheek to make vent for the imposthume, and that saved my life. At first they let me
blood, and I parted with above fifty ounces in less than
a fortnight: for *phlebotomy* is so much practised here,
that if one's little finger ache they presently open a vein,
and to ballance the blood on both sides, they usually let
blood in both arms; and, the commonness of the thing

seems

seems to take away all fear, insomuch, that the very women when they find themselves indisposed, will open a
vein themselves: for they hold, that the blood which
hath a circulation and fetcheth a round every twenty four
hours about the body is quickly repaired again. I was
eighteen days and nights that I had no sleep, but short
imperfect slumbers, and those too procured by potions :
the tumour at last came so about my throat, that I had
scarce vent left for respiration, and my body was brought
so low with all sorts of physick, that I appeared like a
mere *skeleton.* When I was indifferently well recovered,
some of the doctors and chirurgeons that tended me,
gave me a visit; and amongst other things, 'they fell in
discourse of wines, which was the best, and so by degrees they fell upon other beverages ; and one doctor in
the company who had been in *England,* told me, that we
have a drink in *England* called ale, which he thought
was the wholesomest liquor that could go into one's guts :
for, whereas the body of man is supported by two co-
lumns, *viz.* the natural heat, and radical moisture, he
said, there is no drink conduceth more to the preservation of the one and the increase of the other than ale ;
for, while the *Englishmen* drank only ale, they were
strong brawny able men, and could draw an arrow an ell
long, but since they fell to wine and beer, they are
found to be much impaired in their strength and age ;
so the ale bore away the bell among the doctors.

    The next week we advance our course further into
France, towards the river of *Loire* to *Orleans,* whence
I shall continue to convey my duty to you. In the mean
time, I humbly crave your blessing, and your acknowledgment to God almighty for my recovery: be pleased
further, to impart my love amongst my brothers and
sisters, with all my kinsmen and friends in the country :.
so I rest,

Your dutiful son,

Paris, Dec. 10. 1622.   J. H.

L E T.

LETTER LI.

To Sir THO. SAVAGE, *Knight and Baronet.*

Honourable Sir,

THAT of the fifth of this prefent which you pleafed to fend me was received, and I begin to think myfelf fomething more than I was, that you value fo much the flender endeavours of my pen to do you fervice, I fhall continue to improve your good opinion of me as opportunity fhall ferve.

Touching the great threats againft *Rochel,* whereof I gave you an ample relation in my laft, matters are become now more calm, and rather inclining to an accommodation ; for 'tis thought a fum of money will make up the breach; and to this end fome think all thefe bravadoes were made. The Duke of *Luynes* is at laft made Lord High Conftable of *France,* the prime officer of the crown: he hath a peculiar court to himfelf, a guard of 100 men in rich liveries, and 100,000 livres every year penfion: the old Duke of *Lefdiguieres,* one of the antienteft foldiers of *France,* and a proteftant, is made his Lieutenant.

But in regard all chriftendom rings of this favourite, being the greateft that ever was in *France,* fince the *Maires of the palace* who came to be kings afterwards, I will fend you herein his legend. He was born in *Provence,* and is a gentleman by defcent, though of a petty extraction; in the laft King's time he was preferred to be one of his *pages,* who finding him induftrious, and a good waiter, allowed him 300 crowns penfion *per annum;* which he hufbanded fo well, that he maintained himfelf and two brothers in paffable good fafhion therewith. The King obferving that, doubled his penfion, and taking notice that he was a ferviceable inftrument and apt to pleafe, he thought him fit to be about his fon, in whofe fervice he hath continued above fifteen years; and he hath *flown* fo high into his favour by a fingular dexterity and art he

hath

hath in *faulconry*, and by ſhooting at birds flying, wherein the King took great pleaſure, that he hath *ſoared* to
this pitch of honour. He is a man of a paſſable good
underſtanding and forecaſt, of a mild comportment,
humble and debonair to all, and of a winning converſation : he hath about him choice and ſolid heads, who pre-
ſcribe to him rules of policy, by whoſe compaſs he ſteers
his courſe ; which 'tis likely will make him ſubſiſt long :
he is now come to that tranſcendent altitude, that he
ſeems to have mounted above the reach of envy, and
made all hopes of ſupplanting him fruſtrate, both by the
politic guidance of his own actions, and the powerful
alliances he hath got for himſelf and his two brothers :
he is married to the Duke of *Montbazon*'s daughter, one
of the prime peers of *France :* his ſecond brother *Cadenet* (who is reputed the wiſeſt of the three) married the
heireſs of *Picardy*, with whom he had 9000*l.* lands a-
year ; his third brother *Brand*, to the great heireſs of
Luxemburgh, of which houſe there have been five emperors : ſo that theſe three brothers and their allies would
be able to counterbalance any one faction in *France*, the
eldeſt and youngeſt being made dukes and peers of
France, the other Marſhal. There are lately two ambaſſadors extraordinary come hither from *Venice* about
the *Valtolin*, but their negotiation is at a ſtand, until the
return of an ambaſſador extraordinary, who is gone to
Spain. Ambaſſadors alſo are come from the *Hague* for
payment of the *French* regiment there, which hath been
neglected theſe ten years, and to know whether his Majeſty will be pleaſed to continue their pay any longer ;
but their anſwer is yet ſuſpended. They have brought
news that the ſeven ſhips which were built for his Majeſty
in the *Teſſel* are ready : to this he anſwered, that he deſires to have ten more built ; for he intends to finiſh that
deſign which his father had a-foot a little before his
death, to eſtabliſh a royal company of merchants.

    This is all the news that *France* affords for the preſent,
the relation whereof if it proves as acceptable, as my endeavours to ſerve you herein are pleaſing unto me, I
                                             ſhall

ſhall eſteem myſelf happy: ſo, wiſhing you and my noble
Lady continuance of health, and increaſe of honour, I
reſt

Your moſt humble ſerviter,

Paris, Dec. 15. 1622.   J. H.

LETTER LII.

To Sir JOHN NORTH, *Knight.*

S I R,

I Confeſs you have made a perfect conqueſt of me by
your late favours, and I yield myſelf your captive;
a day may come that will enable me to pay my ranſom:
in the interim, let a moſt thankful acknowledgment be
my bail and enterprize.

I am now removed from off the *Seine* to the *Loire,* to
the fair town of *Orleans*: there was here lately a mixt
proceſſion betwixt military and eccleſiaſtic for the maid of
Orleans, which is performed every year very ſolemnly:
her ſtatue ſtands upon the bridge, and her cloaths are
preſerved to this day, which a young man wore in the
proceſſion; which makes me think that her ſtory (though
it ſound like a romance) is very true; and I read it thus,
in two or three chronicles: when the *Engliſh* had made
ſuch firm invaſions in *France,* that their armies had
marched into the heart of the country, beſieged *Orleans,*
and driven *Charles* VII. to *Bourges* in *Berry,* which
made him to be called (for the time) King of *Berry,*
there came to his army a ſhepherdeſs, one *Anne de Ar-*
que, who with a confident look and language told the
King, that ſhe was deſigned by heaven to beat the *Eng-*
liſh, and drive them out of *France:* therefore, ſhe deſired a command in the army; which by her extraordinary confidence and importunity ſhe obtained; and putting on man's apparel, ſhe proved ſo proſperous, that the
ſiege was raiſed from before *Orleans,* and the *Engliſh*

K   were

were purfued to *Paris*, and forced to quit that, and driven to *Normandy*. She ufed to go on with marvellous courage and refolution, and her word was *har à ha;* but in *Normandy* fhe was taken prifoner, and the *Englifh* had a fair revenge upon her; for, by an arreft of the parliament of *Rouen* fhe was burnt for a witch. There is a great bufinefs now a-foot in *Paris*, called the *Polette;* which if it take effect, will tend to correct, at leaftwife to cover a great error in the *French* government. The cuftom is, that all the chief places of juftice throughout all the eight courts of parliament in *France*, befides a great number of other offices, are fet to fale by the King, and they return to him unlefs the buyer liveth *forty* days after his refignation to another. It is now propounded that thefe cafual offices fhall be abfolutely hereditary, provided that every officer pay a yearly revenue unto the King, according to the valuation of, and perquifites of the office. This bufinefs is now in agitation, but the iffue is yet doubtful.

The laft you fent I received by *Vacandary* in *Paris:* fo, highly honouring your excellent parts and merit, I reft, now that I underftand *French* indifferent well, no more your (*fhe*) fervant, but

Your moft faithful fervitor,

Orleans, March 3. 1622.   J. H.

LETTER LIII.

To Sir JAMES CROFTS, *Knight.*

SIR,

WERE I to freight a Letter with compliments, this country would furnifh me with variety, but of news a fmall ftore at this prefent; and for compliments it is dangerous to ufe any to you who have fuch a piercing judgment to difcern femblances from realities.

The

The Queen-mother is at laſt come to *Paris*, where ſhe hath not been ſince *Ancre*'s death. The King is alſo returned poſt from *Bordeaux*, having traverſed moſt part of his kingdom, he ſettled peace everywhere he paſſed, and quaſhed divers inſurrections; and by his obedience to his mother, and his lenity towards all her partiſans at *pont de Ce*, where aboye 400 were ſlain; and notwithſtanding that he was victorious, yet he gave à general pardon, he hath gained much upon the affections of his people. His council of ſtate went ambulatory always with him; and as they ſay here, never did men manage things with more wiſdom. There is a war queſtionleſs a fermenting againſt the proteſtants: the Duke of *Eſpernon* in a kind of *rodomantado* way, deſired leave of the King to block up *Rochel*, and in ſix weeks he would undertake to deliver her to his hands, but I believe he reckons without his hoſt. I was told a merry paſſage of this little *Gaſcon* Duke, who is now the oldeſt ſoldier of *France;* having come lately to *Paris*, he treated with a pander to procure him a courteſan; and if ſhe was a *damoiſel* (a gentlewoman) he would give ſo much; and if a *citizen* he would give ſo much: the pander did his office, but brought him a citizen clad in *damoiſels* apparel; ſo ſhe and her maquerel were paid accordingly: the next day after, ſome of his familiars having underſtood hereof, began to be pleaſant with the Duke, and to jeer him, that he being a *vieil routier*, an old tried ſoldier ſhould ſuffer himſelf to be ſo cozened, as to pay for a citizen after the rate of a gentlewoman: the little Duke grew wild hereupon, and commenced an action of fraud againſt the pander, but what became of it I cannot tell you, but all *Paris* rung of it. I hope to return now very ſhortly to *England*, where, amongſt the reſt of my noble friends, I ſhall much rejoice to ſee and ſerve you whom I honour with no vulgar affection, ſo I am

Your true ſervitor,

Orleans, *March* 5, 1622.   J. H.

K 2   LET-

LETTER LIV.

To my Cousin Mr. WILLIAM MARTIN *at* Brussels,
from Paris.

Dear Cousin,

I Find you are very punctual in your performances, and a precise observer of the promise you made here to correspond with Mr. *Altham* and me by letters. I thank you for the variety of *German* news you imparted unto me, which was so neatly couched and curiously knit together, that your letter might serve for a pattern to the best intelligencer. I am sorry the affairs of the Prince *Palsgrave* go on so untowardly; the wheel of war may turn, and that spoke which is now up may down again. For *French* occurrences, there is a war certainly intended against them of the religion here; and there are visible preparations a-foot already: amongst others that shrink in the shoulders at it, the King's servants are not very well pleased with it, in regard besides *Scots* and *Swissers*, there are divers of the King's servants that are protestants. If a man go to *ragion' di stato*, to reason of state; the *French* King hath something to justify this design; for the protestants being so numerous, and having near upon fifty presidiary walled towns in their hands for caution, they have power to disturb *France* when they please, and being abetted by a foreign Prince to give the King law; and you know as well as I, how they have been made use of to kindle a fire in *France*: therefore, rather than they should be utterly suppressed, I believe the *Spaniard* himself would reach them his *ragged-staff* to defend them.

I send you here inclosed another from Mr. *Altham*, who respects you dearly; and we remembered you lately at *la pomme du pin* in the best liquor of the *French* grape. I shall be shortly for *London*, where I shall not rejoice a little to meet you: the *English* air may confirm what foreign begun, I mean our friendship and affecti-

ons:

ons; and in *me*, (that I may return you in *Englifh* the *Latin* verfes you fent me)

> *As foon a little ant*
> *Shall bibe the ocean dry,*
> *A fnail fhall creep about the world,*
> *E'er thefe affections die.*

So my dear coufin, may virtue be your guide, and fortune your companion.

Yours while,

Paris, *March* 18. 1622.   J. H.

LETTER LV.

To my FATHER.

S I R;

I Am fafely returned now the fecond time from beyond the feas, but I have yet no employment.   God and good friends I hope will fhortly provide one for me.

The *Spanifh* Ambaffador Count *Gondamar* doth ftrongly negotiate a match betwixt our Prince and the *Infanta* of *Spain*, but at his firft audience there happened an ill-favoured accident, (I pray God it prove no ill augury) for my Lord of *Arundell* being fent to accompany him to *Whitehall* upon a *Sunday* in the afternoon, as they were going over the terrafs, it broke under them, but only one was hurt in the arm.   *Gondamar* faid, that he had not cared to have died in fo good company: he faith, there is no other way to regain the *Palatinate*, but by this match, and to fettle an eternal peace in *chriftendom*.

The Marquis of *Buckingham* continueth ftill in fulnefs of grace and favour: the Countefs his mother fways alfo much at court; fhe brought Sir *Henry Montague* from delivering law on the *King's Bench* to look to his bags in the *Exchequer;* for, fhe made him Lord High Treafurer of *England,* but he parted with his white *ftaff* before the

K 3   year's year's end, though his purſe had bled deeply for it; (above 20,000 *l.*) which made a Lord of this land to aſk him at his return from court, *Whether he did not find that wood was extreme dear at* Newmarket, for there he received the white *ſtaff*. There is now a notable ſtirring man in the place, my Lord *Cranfield*, who from walking about the *Exchange*, is come to fit chief Judge in the *Chequer-Chamber*, and to have one of the higheſt places at the Council-table. He is married to one of the tribe of fortune, a kinſwoman of the Marquis of *Buckingham*. Thus there is riſing and falling at court; and as in our natural pace one foot cannot be up till the other be down, ſo it is in the affairs of the world commonly, one man riſeth at the fall of the other.

I have no more to write at this time, but that with tender of my duty to you, I deſire a continuance of your bleſſing and prayers.

Your dutiful ſon,

Lond. *March* 22. 1622.   J. H.

LETTER LVI.

To the Honourable M. JOHN SAVAGE (*now Earl* Rivers) *at* Florence.

SIR,

MY love is not ſo ſhort but it can reach to *Florence* to find you out, and further too if occaſion required; nor are theſe affections I have to ſerve you ſo dull but they can clamber over the *Alps* and *Apennine* to wait upon you, as they have adventured to do now in this paper. I am ſorry I was not in *London* to kiſs your hands before you ſet to ſea; and much more ſorry, that I had not the happineſs to meet you in *Holland* or *Brabant*, for we went the very ſame road, and lay in *Dort* and *Antwerp* in the ſame lodgings you had lain in a fortnight before. I preſume you have by this time taſted of the

ſweetneſs

fweetnefs of travel, and that you have weaned your affections from *England* for a good while, you muft now
think upon home, (as one faid) good men think upon
heaven, aiming ftill to go thither, but not till they finifh
their courfe; and yours I underftand will be three years:
in the mean time, you muft not fuffer any melting tendernefs of thoughts, or loving defires, to diftract or inter-
rupt you in that fair road you are in to virtue; and to
beautify within, that comely edifice which nature hath
built without you. I know your reputation is precious
to you, as it fhould be to every noble mind: you have
expofed it now to the hazard, therefore you muft be
careful it receive no taint at your return, by not anfwering
that expectation which your Prince and noble parents
have of you. You are now under the chiefeft clime of
wifdom, fair *Italy*, the darling of nature, the nurfe of
policy, the theatre of virtue; but, though *Italy* give
milk to *virtue* with one dug, fhe often fuffers *vice* to fuck
at the other, therefore you muft take heed you miftake
not the dug: for, there is an ill-favoured faying, that
Inglefe Italionato è diavolo incarnato; an *Englifhman*
Italianate, *is a devil incarnate.* I fear no fuch thing of
you, I have had fuch pregnant proofs of your ingenuity,
and noble inclinations to virtue and honour. I know you
have a mind to both, but I muft tell you, that you will
hardly get the good-will of the *latter,* unlefs the *firft* fpeak
a good word for you: when you go to *Rome,* you may
happily fee the ruins of two temples, one dedicated to
virtue, the other to *honour;* and there was no way to
enter into the laft, but through the firft. Noble Sir, I
wifh your good very ferioufly; and if you pleafe to call
to memory and examine the circumftance of things, and
my carriage towards you fince I had the happinefs to be
known firft to your honourable family, I know you will
conclude that I love and honour you in no vulgar way.

My Lord, your grandfather was complaining lately
that he had not heard from you a good while. By the
next fhipping to *Legborn,* amongft other things, he intends to fend you a whole brawn in collers. I pray be
pleafed

pleased to remember my affectionate service to Mr. *Thomas Savage*, and my kind respects to Mr. *Bold*: for *English* news, I know this pacquet comes freighted to you, therefore I forbear to send any. Farewel noble heir of honour, and command always

Your true servitor,

Lond. March 24. 1622. J. H.

LETTER LVII.

To Sir JAMES CROFTS, *Knight at St.* Osith *in* Essex.

SIR,

I Had yours upon *Tuesday* last; and whereas, you are desirous to know the proceedings of the parliament; I am sorry I must write to you that matters begin to grow boisterous: the King retired not long since to *Newmarket* not very well pleased, and this week there went thither twelve from the house of commons, to whom Sir *Richard Weston* was the mouth: the King not liking the message they brought, called them ambassadors; and in the large answer which he hath sent to the Speaker, he saith, that he must apply unto them a speech of Queen *Elizabeth*'s to an Ambassador of *Poland*; *Legatum expectavimus, Heraldum accepimus*; we expected an Ambassador, we have received a Herald. He takes it not well that they should meddle with the match betwixt his son and the *Infanta*, alleging an example of one of the kings of *France*, which would not marry his son without the advice of his parliament; but, afterwards that King grew so despicable abroad, that no foreign state would treat with him about any thing without his parliament. Sundry other high passages there was as a caveat he gave them, not to touch the honour of the King of *Spain*, with whom he was so far engaged in a matrimonial treaty that he could not go back. He gave them also a check

for

for taking cognizance of thofe things which had their motion in the ordinary courts of juftice; and that Sir *Edward Coke,* (though thefe words were not inferted in the anfwer) whom he thought to be *the fitteft inftrument for a tyrant that ever was in* England, fhould be fo bold as to call the *prerogative* of the crown a *great monfter.* The parliament after this was not long-lived, but broke up in difcontent, and upon the point of diffolution, they made a proteft againft divers particulars in the aforefaid anfwer of his Majefty. My Lord *Digby* is preparing for *Spain,* in quality of an Ambaffador extraordinary, to perfect the match betwixt our Prince and the Lady *Infanta;* in which bufinefs *Gondamar* hath waded already very deep, and been very active, and ingratiated himfelf with divers perfons of quality, ladies efpecially, yet he could do no good upon the Lady *Hatton* whom he defired lately, that in regard he was her next neighbour, (at *Ely* houfe) he might have the benefit of her back-gate to go abroad into the fields, but fhe put him off with a compliment, whereupon, in a private audience lately with the King, amongft other paffages of merriment, he told him, that my Lady *Hatton was a ftrange Lady, for fhe would not fuffer her husband Sir Edward* Coke *to come in at her fore-door, nor him to go out at her back-door,* and fo related the whole bufinefs. He was alfo difpatching a poft lately for *Spain;* and the poft having received his pacquet, and kiffed his hands, he called him back and told him he had forgot one thing, which was, that when he came to *Spain, he fhould commend him to the fun, for he had not feen him a good while, and in* Spain *he fhould be fure to find him.* So, with my moft humble fervice to my Lord of *Colchefter,* I reft

Your moft humble fervitor,

Lond. March 24. 1622.   J. H.

LET-

L E T T E R LVIII.

To my Brother, Mr. HUGH PENRY.

S I R,

THE *Welsh* nag you sent me, was delivered me
in a very good plight, and I give you a thousand
thanks for him ; I had occasion lately to try his mettle
and his lungs ; and every one tells me he is right, and of
no mungrel race, but a true mountaineer ; for besides his
toughness and strength of lungs up a hill, he is quickly
curried, and content with short commons. I believe he
hath not been long a highway traveller ; for whereas
other horses, when they pass by an inn or alehouse, use
to make towards them, to give them a friendly visit, this
nag roundly goes on, and scorns to cast as much as a
glance upon any of them ; which I know not whether I
shall impute it to his ignorance, or height of spirit ; but
conversing with the soft horses in *England*, I believe he
will quickly be brought to be more courteous.

The greatest news we have now, is the return of the
Lord Bishop of *Landaff, Davenant, Ward,* and *Belcan-
quell,* from the synod of *Dort,* where the Bishop had
precedence given him according to his episcopal dignity.
Arminius and *Vorstius* were sore baited there concerning
predestination, election, and reprobation ; as also touching *Christ*'s death, and man's redemption by it ; then
concerning man's corruption, and conversion ; lastly, concerning the perseverance of the saints. I shall have shortly the transactions of the synod. The *Jesuits* have put
out a jeering libel against it, and these two verses I remember in it :

Dordrecti synodus ? nodus ; chorus integer ?- æger ;
Conventus ? ventus ; sessio stramen ? amen.

But I will confront this *distich* with another I read in
France of the *Jesuits* in the town of *Dole,* towards *Lorain ;* they had a great house given them called *L'arc*
(arcum)

(*arcum*) and upon the river of *Loire*, *Henry* IV. gave them *la fleche*, *fagittam* in *Latin*, where they have two ſtately convents, that is, *bow* and *arrow;* whereupon one made theſe verſes :

Arcum Dola dedit, dedit illis alma fagittam
Francia ; quis chordam, quam meruere, dabit ?

Fair *France* the *arrow*, *Dole* gave them the *bow ;*
Who ſhall the *ſtring*, which they deſerve beſtow ?

No more now, but that with my dear love to my ſiſter, I .reſt

　　　　　　Your moſt affectionate brother,
London, *April* 16. 1622.　　　　J. H.

LETTER LIX.

To The Lord Viſcount Colcheſter.

ᶦ *My good Lord,*

I Received your Lordſhip's of the laſt week, and according to your commands, I ſend here incloſed the *Venetian* gazette : of foreign *avifo's*, they write that *Mansfelt* hath been beaten out of *Germany*, and is come to Sedan ; and it is thought that the Duke of *Bouillon* will ſet him up again with a new army.　Marquis *Spinola* hath newly ſat down before *Berghen op zoom* : your Lordſhip knows well what conſequence that town is of, therefore it is likely this will be a hot ſummer in the *Netherlands*.　The *French* King is in open war againſt them of the religion ; he hath already cleared the *Loire*, by taking *Jerſeau* and *Saumur*, where Monſieur *du Pleſſis* ſent him the keys, which are promiſed to be delivered him again, but I think *ad Græcas Calendas*.　He hath been alſo before *St. John d'Angeli*, where the young Cardinal .of *Guiſe* died, being ſtruck down by the puff of a cannon-bullet, which put him in a burning fever, and
　　　　　　　　　　　　　　　　made

made an end of him. The laſt town that is taken was *Clerac*, which was put to 50,000 Crowns ranſom ; many were put to the ſword, and divers gentlemen drowned as they thought to eſcape. This is the fifteenth cautionary town the King hath taken : and now they ſay he marcheth towards *Montauban*, and ſo to *Montpellier* and *Niſmes*, and then have at *Rochel*. My Lord *Hays* is by this time, it is thought, with the army ; for Sir *Edward Herbert* is returned, having had ſome claſhings and counterbuffs with the favourite *Luynes*, wherein he comported himſelf gallantly. There is a freſh report blown over, that *Luynes* is lately dead in the army of the plague, ſome ſay of the purples, the next couſin-german to it ; which the proteſtants give out to be the juſt judgment of heaven fallen upon him, becauſe he incited his maſter to theſe wars againſt them. If he be not dead, let him die when he will, he will leave a fame behind him, to have been the greateſt favourite for the time that ever was in *France*, having from a ſimple *falconer* come to be high Conſtable, and made himſelf and his younger brother grand dukes and peers ; and his ſecond brother *Cadenat*, Marſhal ; and all three married into princely families.

No more now, but that I moſt humbly kiſs your Lordſhip's hands, and ſhall be always moſt ready and chearful to receive your commandments, becauſe I am

Your Lordſhip's obliged ſervitor, ,

London, Aug. 12. 1622.   J. H.

LETTER LX.

To my FATHER, *from* London.

S I R,

I Was at a dead ſtand in the courſe of my fortunes, when it pleaſed God to provide me lately an employment to *Spain*, whence I hope there may ariſe both repute and profit. Some of the cape merchants of the
Turky

Turky company; among whom the chiefeft were Sir *Robert Napper*, and Captain *Leat*, propofed to me, that they had a great bufinefs in the court of *Spain* in agitation many years, nor was it now their bufinefs but the King's, in whofe name it is followed : they could have gentlemen of good quality, that would undertake it, yet if I would take it upon me, they would employ no other ; and affured me, that the employment fhould tend both to my benefit and credit. Now the bufinefs is this : there was a great *Turky* fhip called the *Vineyard*, failing through the *Straits* towards *Conftantinople*, but by diftrefs of weather lhe was forced to put into a little port called *Milo*, in *Sardinia ;* the fearchers came aboard of her, and finding her richly laden, for her cargazon of broadcloth was worth the firft penny, near upon 30,000 *l.* they cavilled at fome fmall proportion of lead and tin which they had only for the ufe of the fhip ; which the fearchers alledged to be *ropa de contrabando*, prohibited goods ; for by article of peace, nothing is to be carried to *Turky* that may arm or *vittle*. The Viceroy of *Sardinia* hereupon feized upon the whole fhip, and all their goods, landed the mafter and men in *Spain*, who coming to Sir *Charles Cornwalles* then Ambaffador at that court, Sir *Charles* could do them little good at prefent, therefore they came to *England*, and complained to the King and council : his Majefty was fo fenfible hereof, that he fent a particular commiffion in his own royal name, to demand a reftitution of the fhip and goods, and juftice upon the Viceroy of *Sardinia*, who had fo apparently broke the peace, and wronged his fubjects. Sir *Charles* (with Sir *Paul Pindar* a while) laboured in the bufinefs, and commenced a fuit in law, but he was called home before he could do any thing to purpofe. After him Sir *John Digby* (now Lord *Digby*) went Ambaffador to *Spain;* and among other things he had that particular commiffion from his Majefty invefted in him, to profecute the fuit in his own royal name : thereupon he fent a well qualified gentleman, Mr. *Walfingham Grefv*, to *Sardinia*,

L   who

who unfortunately meeting with fome men of war in the paffage, was carried prifoner to *Algier.* My Lord *Digby* being remanded home, left the bufinefs in Mr. *Cottington's* hands, the Agent, but refumed it at his return ; yet it proved fuch a tedious intricate fuit, that he returned again without finifhing the work, in regard of the remotenefs of the ifland of *Sardinia,* whence the witneffes and other difpatches were to be fetcht. The Lord *Digby* is going now Ambaffador extraordinary to the court of *Spain,* upon the bufinefs of the match, the reftitution of the *Palatinate,* and other high affairs of ftate ; therefore, he is defirous to tranfmit the King's commiffion touching this particular bufinefs to any gentleman that is capable to follow it, and promifeth to affift him with the utmoft of his power ; and in faith he hath good reafon to do fo, in regard he hath now a good round fhare himfelf in it. About this bufinefs I am now preparing to go to *Spain,* in company of the Ambaffador ; and I fhall kifs the King's hands as his Agent touching this particular commiffion. I humbly intreat that your bleffing and prayers may accompany me in this my new employment, which I have undertaken upon very good terms, touching expences and reward : fo, with my dear love to my brothers and fifters, with other kindred and friends in the country, I am

Your dutiful fon,

London, *Sept.* 8. 1622.   J. H.

LETTER LXI.

To Sir THOMAS SAVAGE, *Knight and Baronet, at his Houfe in* Long-Melford.

Honourable Sir,

I Received your commands in a letter which you fent me by Sir *John North,* and I fhall not fail to anfwer you in thofe particulars. It hath pleafed God to difpofe

of

of me once more for *Spain*, upon a bufinefs which I hope
will make me good returns : there have two ambaffadors
and a toyal Agent followed it hitherto, and I am the
fourth that is employed in it. I defer to trouble you
with the particulars of it, in regard I hope to have the
happinefs to kifs your hand at *Tower-hill* before my departure, which will not be till my Lord *Digby* fets forward. He goes in a gallant fplendid equipage, and one
of the King's fhips is to take him in at *Plymoath*, and
tranfport him to the *Corunna*, or *St. Anderas.*

Since that fad difafter which befel Archbifhop *Abbot*,
to kill the man by the glancing of an arrow as he was
fhooting at a deer, (which kind of death befel one of
our kings once in *New-Foreft*) there hath been a commiffion awarded to debate whether upon this fact, whereby he hath fhed human blood, he be not to be deprived
of his Archbifhoprick, and pronounced irregular : fome
were againft him ; but Bifhop *Andrews*, and Sir *Henry*
Martin ftood ftifly for him, that in regard it was no fpon-
taneous act, but a mere contingency, and that there is
no degree of men but is fubject to misfortunes, and ca-
fualties, they declared pofitively that he was not to fall
from his dignity or function, but fhould ftill remain regular, and in *ftatu quo prius*. During this debate, he pe-
titioned the King that he might be permitted to retire to
his alms-houfe at *Guilford* where he was born, to pafs
the remainder of his life ; but he is now come to be
again *rectus in curia*, abfolutely quitted, and reftored to
all things : but for the wife of him who was killed, it
was no misfortune to her, for he hath endued herfelf,
and her children with fuch an eftate, that they fay her
hufband could never have got. So I humbly kifs your
hands, and reft

Your moft obliged fervant,

London, *Nov.* 9. 1622.   J. H.

LETTER LXII.

To Capt. NICH. LEAT *at his House in* London.

SIR,

I Am fafely come to the court of *Spain* ; and although by reafon of that misfortune which befel Mr. *Altham* and me, of wounding the ferjeants in *Lombard-ftreet,* we ftaid three weeks behind my Lord Ambaffador, yet we came hither time enough to attend him to court at his firft audience.

'The *Englifh* nation is better looked on now in *Spain* than ordinary, becaufe of the hopes there are of a match, which the merchants and commonalty much defire, though the nobility and gentry be not fo forward for it : fo that in this point the pulfe of *Spain* beats quite contrary to that of *England,* where the people are averfe to this match, and the nobility with moft part of the gentry in-clinable.

I have perufed all the papers I could get into my hands, touching the bufinefs of the fhip *Vineyard,* and I find that they are higher than I in bulk, though clofely preft together : I have caft up what is awarded by all the fentences of view and review, by the council of ftate and war; and I find the whole fum, as well principal, as intereft upon intereft, all forts of damages, and proceffal charges, come to about 250,000 crowns. The *Conde del Real, quondam* Viceory of *Sardinia,* who is adjudged to pay moft part of this money, is here; and he is *Majordomo,* Lord Steward to the *Infant* Cardinal : if he hath wherewith, I doubt not but to recover the money ; for, I hope to have come in a favourable conjuncture of time, and my Lord Ambaffador who is fo highly efteemed here, doth affure me of his beft furtherance. So praying I may prove as fuccefsful, as I fhall be faithful in this great bufinefs, I reft

Yours to difpofe of,

Madrid, Dec 28. 1622. J. H.

L E T-

LETTER LXIII.

To Mr. ARTHUR HOPTON, *from* Madrid.

S I R,

SINCE I was made happy with your acquaintance, I have received fundry ſtrong evidences of your love and good wiſhes unto me, which have tied me to you in no common obligation of thanks : I am in deſpair ever to cancel this bond, nor would I do it, but rather endear the engagements more and more.

The treaty of the match betwixt our Prince and the Lady *Infanta* is now ſtrongly afoot : ſhe is a very comely Lady, rather of a *Flemiſh* complexion than *Spaniſh*, fair haired, and carrieth a moſt pure mixture of red and white in her face ; ſhe is full and big liped ; which is held a beauty rather than a blemiſh, or any exceſs, in the *Auſtrian* family, it being a thing incident to moſt of that race ; ſhe goes now upon ſixteen, and is of a tallneſs agreeable to thoſe years. The King is alſo of ſuch a complexion, and is under twenty ; he hath two brothers, *Don Carlos*, and *Don Hernando*, who, though a youth of twelve, yet is the Cardinal and Aichbiſhop of *Toledo* ; which, in regard it hath the chancellorſhip of *Caſtile* annexed to it, is the greateſt ſpiritual dignity in chriſtendom after the papacy, for it is valued at 300,000 crowns *per annum.* *Don Carlos* is of a different complexion from all the reſt, for he is black haired, and of a *Spaniſh* hue ; he hath neither office, command, dignity, or title, but is an individual companion to the King ; and what cloaths ſoever are provided for the King, he hath the very ſame, and as often, from top to toe : he is the better beloved of the people for his complexion ; for one ſhall hear the *Spaniards* ſigh and lament, ſaying, O when ſhall we have a King again of our own colour !

I pray recommend me kindly to all at your houſe, and ſend me word when the young gentleman returns.

L 3. from

from *Italy.* So with my moſt affectionate reſpects to yourſelf, I reſt.

Your true friend to ſerve you,

Madrid, Jan. 5. 1622.　　　　　　　　J. H.

LETTER LXIV.

To the Lord Viſcount Colcheſter, *from* Madrid.

Right Honourable,

THE grand buſineſs of the match goes ſo fairly on, that a ſpecial *junta* is appointed to treat of it, the names whereof I ſend you here incloſed : they have proceeded ſo far, that moſt of the articles are agreed upon. Mr. *George Gage* is lately come hither from *Rome,* a polite and prudent gentleman, who hath negotiated ſome things in that court for the advancement of the buſineſs, with the cardinals *Bandino, Ludoviſio,* and *la Suſanna,* who are the main men there, to whom the drawing of the diſpenſation, is referred.

The late taking of *Ormus* by the *Perſian* from the crown of *Portugal* keeps a great noiſe here, and the rather becauſe the exploit was done by the aſſiſtance of the *Engliſh* ſhips that were then thereabout. My Lord *Digby* went to court, and gave a round ſatisfaction in this point ; for it was no voluntary, but a conſtrained act in the *Engliſh,* who being in the *Perſian*'s port, were ſuddenly embargoed for the ſervice ; and the *Perſian* herein did no more than what is uſual among *chriſtian* princes themſelves, and which is oftner put in practice by the King of *Spain* and his *Viceroys,* than by any other, *viz.* to make an embargo of any ſtranger ſhips that rides within his port upon all occaſions. It was feared this ſurpriſal of *Ormus,* which was the greateſt mart in all the *Orient* for all ſorts of jewels, would have bred ill blood, and prejudiced the proceedings of the match ; but the

Spaniard

Spaniard is a rational man, and will be fatisfied with reafon. Count *Olivares* is the main man who fways all,
and it is thought he is not fo much affected to an alliance
with *England* as his predeceffor the Duke of *Lerma* was,
who fet it firft afoot betwixt Prince *Henry* and this Queen
of *France :* the Duke of *Lerma* was the greateft *priva-
do*, the greateft favourite that ever was in *Spain*, fince
Don Alvaro de Luna ; he brought himfelf, the Duke of
Uzeda his fon, and the Duke of *Cea* his grandchild, to
be all grandees of *Spain ;* which is the greateft title that
a *Spanifh* fubject is capable of : they have a privilege to
ftand covered before the King, and at their election there
is no other ceremony but only thefe three words by the
King, *cobbrefe por grande*, cover yourfelf for a grandee ;
and that is all. The Cardinal Duke of *Lerma* lives at
Volladolid, he officiates and fings mafs, and paffes his
old age in devotion and exercifes of piety. It is a common, and indeed a commendable cuftom of the *Spaniard*, when he hath paffed his *grand climacteric*, and
is grown decripit, to make a voluntary refignation of offices, be they never fo great and profitable (though I cannot fay *Lerma* did fo) and fequeftring and weaning themfelves, as it were, from all mundane negotiations and in-
cumbrances, to return to fome place of devotion, and
fpend the refidue of their days in meditation, and in preparing themfelves for another world. *Charles* the Em-
perot fhewed them the way, who left the empire to
his brother, and all the reft of his dominions to his fon
Philip II. and fo taking with him his two fifters, he retired into a monaftery, they into a nunnery. This does
not fuit with the genius of an *Englifhman*, who loves
not to pull off his cloaths till he goes to bed. I will con-
clnde with fome verfes I faw under a huge *rodomontado*
picture of the Duke of *Lerma*, wherein he is painted like
a giant, bearing up the monarchy of *Spain*, that of *France*,
and the *popedom* upon his fhoulders, with this ftanza :

Sobre

Sobre les ombres d'efte Atlante
Tazen eu aqueftos dias
Eftas tres monarquias.

Upon the ſhoulders of this *Atlas* lies -
The *popedom*, and two mighty *monarchies.*

So I moſt humbly kiſs your Lordſhip's hands, and reſt
ever moſt ready

At your Lordſhip's command,

Madrid, Feb. 3. 1622.   J. H.

L E T T E R LXV.

To my FATHER.

S I R,

ALL affairs went on fairly here, eſpecially that of
the match, when Mr. *Endymion Porter* brought
lately my Lord of *Briſtol* a diſpatch from *England* of a
high nature, wherein the Earl is commanded to repreſent
to this King, how much his Majeſty of *Great Britain*
ſince the beginning of theſe *German* wars hath laboured
to merit well of this crown, and of the whole houſe of
Auſtria, by a long and lingering patience, grounded ſtill
upon aſſurances hence, that care ſhould be had of his
honour, his daughter's jointure, and grandchildren's patrimony; yet how groſly all things had proceeded in
the treaty at *Bruſſels*, managed by Sir *Richard Weſton,*
as alſo that in the *Palatinate* by the Lord *Chicheſter ;*
how in treating-time the town and caſtle of *Heidelberg*
were taken, *Manheim* beſieged, and all acts of hoſtility
uſed, notwithſtanding the fair profeſſions made by this
King, the *Infanta* at *Bruſſels*, and other his miniſters ;
how merely out of reſpect to this King he had neglected
all martial means, which probably might have preſerved
the *Palatinate ;* thoſe thin garriſons which he had ſent
thither,

thither, being rather for honour's fake to keep a footing until a general accommodation, than that he relied any way upon their ftrength : and fince that there are no other fruits of all this but reproach and fcorn, and that thofe good offices which he ufed towards the Emperor on the behalf of his fon-in-law, which he was fo much encouraged by letters from hence fhould take effect, have not forted to any other iffue than to a plain affront, and a high injuring of both their majefties, though in a differing degree. The Earl is to tell him, that his Majefty of *Great Britain* hopes and defires, that out of a true apprehenfion of thefe wrongs offered unto them both, he will, as his dear and loving brother, faithfully promife and undertake upon his honour, confirming the fame under his hand and feal, either that *Heidelberg* fhall be within feventy days rendered into his hands; as alfo, that there fhall be within the faid term of feventy days a fufpenfion of arms in the *Palatinate;* and, that a treaty fhall recommence upon fuch terms as he propounded in *November* laft; which this King held then to be reafonable : and, in cafe that this be not yielded to by the Emperor, that then this King join forces with his Majefty of *England* for the recovery of the *Palatinate*, which upon this truft hath been loft; or in cafe his forces at this time be otherwife employed, that they cannot give his Majefty that affiftance he defires and deferves, that at leaft he will permit a free and friendly paffage through his territories, fuch forces as his Majefty of *Great Britain* fhall employ into *Germany:* of all which, if the Earl of *Briftol* hath not from the King of *Spain* a direct affurance under his hand and feal ten days after his audience, that then he take his leave and return to *England* to his Majefty's prefence, alfo to proceed in the negotiation of the match according to former inftructions.

This was the main fubftance of his Majefty's late letter; yet, there was a poftil added, that in cafe a rupture happen betwixt the two crowns, the Earl fhould not come inftantly and abruptly away, but that he fhould fend

advice

advice firft to *England*, and carry the bufinefs fo, that the world fhould not prefently know of it.

Notwithftanding all thefe traverfes, we are confident here that the match will take, otherwife my cake is dough.   There was a great difference in one of the capitulations betwixt the two kings, how long the children which fhould iffue of this marriage were to continue *fub regimine matris*, under the tutelage of the mother. This King demanded fourteen years at firft, then twelve, but now he is come to nine, which is newly condefcended unto.   I received yours of the firft of *September*, in another from Sir *James Crofts*, wherein it was no fmall comfort to me to hear of your health.   I am to go hence fhortly for *Sardinia*, a dangerous voyage, by reafon of *Algier* pirates.   I humbly defire your prayers may accompany

Your dutiful fon,

Madrid, Feb. 23. 1622.   J. H.

L E T T E R LXVI.

To Sir JAMES CROFTS, *Knight.*

S I R,

YOURS of the fecond of *October* came fafe to hand with the inclofed : you write that there came difpatches lately from *Rome*, wherein the Pope feems to endeavour to infinuate himfelf into a direct treaty with *England*, and to negotiate immediately with our King touching the difpenfation, which he not only labours to evade, but utterly difclaims, it being by article the tafk of this King to procure all difpatches thence.   I thank you for fending me this news.   You fhall underftand there came lately an exprefs from *Rome* alfo to this court, touching the bufinefs of the match, which gave very good content; but, the difpatch and new inftructions which Mr. *Endymion Porter* brought my Lord of *Briftol* lately from *England* touching the Prince *Palatinate,*

nate, fills us with apprehenfions of fear. Our ambaffadors here have had an audience of this King already a-
bout thofe propofitions; and we hope, that Mr. *Porter*
will carry back fuch things as will fatisfy, touching the
two points in the treaty wherein the two kings differed
moft, *viz.* about the education of the children, and the
exemption of the *Infanta*'s ecclefiaftic fervants from fecular jurifdiction. Both thefe points are cleared, for the
Spaniard is come from fourteen years to ten, and for fo
long time the *Infant* princes fhall remain under the mothers government: and for the other point, the ecclefiaftical fuperior fhall firft take notice of the offence that fhall
be committed by any fpiritual perfon belonging to the *Infanta*'s family; and according to the merit thereof, either
deliver him by degradation to the fecular juftice, or ba-
nifh him the kingdom, according to the quality of the de-
lict; and it is the fame that is practifed in this kingdom,
and other parts that adhere to *Rome*.

The *Conde de Monterry* goes *Viceroy* to *Naples*, the
Marquis *de Montefclaros* being put by, the gallanter man
of the two. I was told of a witty faying of his, when
the Duke of *Lerma* had the vogue in this court: for, going one morning to fpeak with the Duke, and having
danced attendance a long time, he peeped through a flit
in the hanging, and fpied *Don Rodrigo Calderon*, a great
man, (who was lately beheaded here for poifoning the
late Queen Dowager) delivering the Duke a paper upon
his knees, whereat the Marquis fmiled, and faid, *Voto
tal; aquel hombre fube mas a las rodillas, que yo no hago
a los pies; I fwear, that man climbs higher upon his
knees, than I can upon my feet.* Indeed, I have read
it to be a true court rule, that *defcendendo afcendendum
eft in aula,* defcending is the way to afcend at court.
There is a kind of humility and compliance that is far
from any fervile bafenefs, or fordid flattery, and may be
termed difcretion rather than adulation. I intend, God
willing, to go for *Sardinia* this fpring. I hope to have
better luck than Mr. *Walfingham Greffey* had, who fome
few years fince in his paffage thither upon the fame bufinefs

nefs that I have in agitation, met with fome *Turky* men of war, and fo was carried flave to *Algier:* fo, with my true refpects to you, I reft

Your faithful fervant,

Madrid, March 12. 1622. **J. H.**

LETTER LXVII.

To the Honourable Sir THOMAS SAVAGE, *Knight and Baronet.*

Honourable Sir,

THE great bufinefs of the match was tending to a period, the articles reflecting both upon church and ftate, being capitulated, and interchangeably accorded on both fides; and there wanted nothing to confummate all things, when to the wonderment of the world the Prince and the Marquis of *Buckingham* arrived at this court on *Friday* laft, upon the clofe of the evening: they lighted at my Lord of *Briftol's* houfe, and the Marquis (Mr. *Thomas Smith*) came in firft with a portmantle under his arm, then (Mr. *John Smith*) the Prince was fent for, who ftaid a while at the other fide of the ftreet in the dark, my Lord of *Briftol* in a kind of aftonifhment brought him up to his bed-chamber, where he prefently called for pen and ink, and difpatched a poft that night to *England,* to acquaint his Majefty how in lefs than fixteen days he was come fafely to the court of *Spain;* that poft went lightly laden, for he carried but three letters. The next day came Sir *Francis Cottington* and Mr. *Porter,* and dark rumours ran in every corner, how fome great man was come from *England;* and fome would not ftick to fay amongft the vulgar, it was the King, but towards the evening on *Saturday,* the Marquis went in a clofe coach to court, where he had private audience of this King, who fent *Olivares* to accompany him back to the Prince, where he kneeled, and kiffed his hands, and hugged his thighs,

thighs, and delivered how unmeafurably glad his Catholick Majefty was of his coming, with other high compliments, which Mr. *Porter* did interpret. About ten o' clock that night, the King himfelf came in a clofe coach with intent to vifit the Prince; who hearing of it, met him half way, and after falutations and divers embraces which paffed in the firft interview, they parted late. I forgot to tell you, that Count *Gondamar* being fworn counfellor of ftate that morning, having been before but one of the council of war, he came in great hafte to vifit the Prince, faying, he had ftrange news to tell him, which was, that an *Englifhman* was fworn Privy-counfellor of *Spain*, meaning himfelf, who he faid was an *Englifhman* in his heart. On *Sunday* following, the King in the afternoon came abroad to take the air with the Queen, his two brothers and the *Infanta*, who were all in one coach; but the *Infanta* fat in the boot with a blue ribband about her arm, of purpofe that the Prince might diftinguifh her: there were above twenty coaches befides, of grandees, noblemen, and ladies that attended them. And now, it was publickly known amongft the vulgar, that it was the Prince of *Wales* who was come; and the confluence of people before my Lord of *Briftol*'s houfe was fo great and greedy to fee the Prince, that to clear the way, Sir *Lewis Dives* went out and took coach, and all the crowd of people went after him; fo, the Prince himfelf took a coach, wherein were the Earl of *Briftol*, Sir *Walter Afhton*, and Count *Gondamar*, and fo went to the *Prado*, a place hard by, of purpofe to take the air, where they ftaid till the King paffed by. As foon as the *Infanta* faw the Prince her colour rofe very high; which, we hold to be an impreffion of love and affection, for the face is often-times a true index of the heart. Upon *Monday* morning after, the King fent fome of his prime nobles, and other gentlemen, to attend the Prince in quality of officers; as one to be his mayordom, (his fteward) another to be mafter of the horfe, and fo to inferior officers, fo that there is a compleat court now at my Lord of *Briftol*'s houfe;

M but

but upon *Sunday* next the Prince is to remove to the King's palace, where there is one of the chief quarters of the houfe providing for him. By the next opportunity you fhall hear more: in the interim, I take my leave and reft

Your moft humble and ready fervitor,

March 26. 1623. J. H.

LETTER LXVIII.

To Sir FRANCIS COTTINGTON, *Secretary to his Highnefs the Prince of* Wales, *at St.* james's.

SIR,

I Believe it will not be unpleafing unto you to hear of the procedure and fuccefs of that bufinefs wherein you have been fo long verfant; I mean, the great fuit againft the *quondam Viceroy* of *Sardinia*, the *Conde del Real.* Count *Gondamar's* coming was a great advantage unto me; who hath done me many favours: befides a confirmation of the two fentences of view and review, and of the execution againft the *Viceroy*, I have procured a royal *cedule*, which I caufed to be printed, and whereof I fend you here inclofed a copy; by which *cedule*, I have power to arreft his very perfon; and my lawyers tell me, there never was fuch a *cedule* granted before. I have alfo by virtue of it priority of all other his creditors. He hath made an imperfect overture of a compofition, and fhewed me fome trivial old fafhioned jewels, but nothing equivalent to the debt; and, now that I fpeak of jewels, the late furprifal of *Ormus* hy the affiftance of our fhips fink deep in their ftomachs here, and we were afraid it would have fpoiled all proceedings, but my Lord *Digby*, now Earl of *Briftol* ('for Count *Gondamar* brought him over his patent) hath calmed all things at his laft audience.

There

There were luminaries of joy lately here for the victory that *Don Gonzalez de Cordova* got over Count *Mansfelt* in the *Netherlands*, with that army which the Duke of *Bovillon* had levied for him; but some say, they have not much reason to rejoice, for though the infantry suffered, yet *Mansfelt* got clear with all his horse by a notable retreat; and they say here, it was the greatest piece of service and art that ever he did, it being a maxim, that there is nothing so difficult in the art of war as an honourable retreat. Besides, the report of his coming to *Breda* caused Marquis *Spinola* to raise the siege before *Berghen*, to burn his tents, and to pack away suddenly, for which he is much censured here.

Captain *Leat* and others have written to me of the favourable report you pleased to make of my endeavours here: for which, I return you humble thanks; and though you have left behind you a multitude of servants in this court, yet if occasion were offered, none should be more forward to go on your errand than

Your humble and faithful servitor,

Madrid, March 15. 1623.   J. H.

LETTER LXIX.

To Sir EUBULE THELOALL, *Knight*, *at* Grays-Inn.

SIR,

I Know the eyes of all *England* are earnestly fixed now upon *Spain*, her best jewel being here; but his journey was like to be spoiled in *France*, for if he had staid but a little longer, at *Bayonne*, the last town of that kingdom hitherwards, he had been discovered; for Monsieur *Gramond* the Governor had notice of him not long after he had taken post. The people here do mightily magnify the gallantry of the journey, and cry out, that he deserved to have the *Infanta* thrown into his arms the first night he came. He hath been entertained with all the magnificence that poffibly could be devifed. On *Sunday* laſt in the morning betimes he went to St. *Hierome*'s monaſtery, whence the kings of *Spain* uſe to be fetched the day they are crowned; and thither the King came in perſon with his two brothers, his eight counſels, and the flower of the nobility: he rode upon the King's right-hand through the heart of the town, under a great canopy, and was brought ſo into his lodgings to the King's palace; and the King himſelf accompanied him to his very bed-chamber. It was a very glorious ſight to behold; for the cuſtom of the *Spaniard* is, though he go plain in his ordinary habit, yet upon ſome feſtival or cauſe of triumph, there is none goes beyond him in gaudineſs.

We daily hope for the Pope's *breve*, or *diſpenſation*, to perfect the buſineſs, though there be dark whiſpers abroad that it is come already, but that upon this unexpected coming of the Prince, it was ſent back to *Rome*, and ſome new clauſes thruſt in for their further advantage. Until this diſpatch comes, matters are at a kind of a ſtand, yet, his Highneſs makes account to be back in *England* about the latter end of *May*. God almighty turn all to the beſt, and to what ſhall be moſt conducible to his glory: ſo, with my due reſpects unto you, I reſt

Your much obliged ſervitor,

April 1. 1623.   J. H.

L E T T E R LXX.

To Captain L E A T.

S I R,

HAVING brought up the law to the higheſt point againſt the Viceroy of *Sardinia*, and that in an extraordinary manner, as may appear unto you by that printed *cedule* I ſent you in my laſt; and finding an apparent diſability in him to ſatisfy the debt, I thought

upon

upon a new defign, and framed a memorial to the King, and wrought good ftrong means to have it feconded, that, in regard that predatory act of feizing upon the fhip *Vineyard* in *Sardinia* with all her goods, was done by his Majefty's Viceroy, his fovereign Minifter of State; one that immediately reprefented his own royal perfon, and that the faid Viceroy was infolvent, I defired his Majefty would be pleafed to grant a warrant for the relief of both parties to lade fo many thoufand *fterils*, or meafures of corn, out of *Sardinia* and *Sicily* cuftom free. I had gone far in the bufinefs when Sir *Francis Cottington* fent for me, and required me in the Prince's name to proceed no further herein till he was departed: fo, his Highnefs's prefence here hath turned rather to my difadvantage than otherwife. Amongft other *grandezas* which the King of *Spain* conferred upon our Prince, one was the releafement of prifoners, and that all petitions of grace fhould come to him for the firft month; but he hath been wonderful fparing in receiving any, efpecially from any *Englifh*, *Irifh*, or *Scot*. Your fon *Nicolas* is come hither from *Alicant*, about the fhip *Amity*, and I fhall be ready to fecond him in getting fatisfaction: fo I reft

Yours ready to ferve you,

Madrid, June 3. 1623.   J. H.

LETTER LXXI.

To Captain THOMAS PORTER.

Noble Captain,

MY laft unto you was in *Spanifh*, in anfwer to one of yours in the fame language; and amongft that confluence of *Englifh* gallants, which upon the occafion of his Highnefs being here, are come to this court, I fed myfelf with hopes a long while to have feen you; but, I find now that thofe hopes were imped with falfe

feathers.

feathers. I know your heart is here, and your beſt affections, therefore I wonder what keeps back your perſon ; but I conceive the reaſon to be, that you intend to
come like yourſelf, to come commander in chief of one
of the caſtles of the crown, one of the ſhips royal. If
you come to this lhote fide, I hope you will have time
to come to the court: I have at any time a good lodging for you, and my landlady is none of the meaneſt, and
her huſband hath many good parts. I heard her ſetting
him forth one day, and giving this character of him, *Mi
marido ei buen muſico, buen eſgrimido, buen eſcrivano,
excellente arithmetico, ſalvo que no multiplica;* my huſband is a good muſician, a good fencer, a good horſe-
man, a good penman, and an excellent *arithmetician,*
only he cannot *multiply.* For outward uſage, there is
all induſtry uſed to give the Prince and his ſervants all
poſſible contentment; and ſome of the King's own ſervants wait upon them at table in the palace, where, I
am ſorry to hear ſome of them jeer at the *Spaniſh* fare,
and uſe other ſlighting ſpeeches and demeanour. There
are many excellent poems made here ſince the Prince's
arrival, which are too long to couch in a letter, yet I
will venture to ſend you this one *ſtanza* of *Lope de Vegas.*

> *Carlos Eſtuardo ſoy*
> *Que ſiendo* Amor *mi guia,*
> *Al cielo d'Eſpana voy*
> *Par ver mi eſtrella* Maria.

There are comedians once a week come to the palace,
where under a great canopy, the Queen and the *Infanta*
ſit in the middle, our Prince and *Don Carlos* on the
Queen's right hand, the King and the little Cardinal on
the *Infanta's* left hand. I have ſeen the Prince have
his eyes immoveably fixed upon the *Infanta* half an hour
together in a thoughtful ſpeculative poſture, which ſure
would needs be tedious, unleſs affection did ſweeten it:
it was no handſome compariſon of *Olivares,* that he
watched her as a cat doth a mouſe. Not long ſince, the
Prince underſtanding that the *Infanta* was uſed to go
ſome

some mornings to the *casa de campo,* a summer-house the King hath the other side the river, to gather *May* dew, he did rise betimes and went thither, taking your brother with him, they were let into the house, and into the garden, but the *Infanta* was in the orchard; and there being a high partition-wall between, and the door doubly bolted, the Prince got on the top of the wall, and sprung down a great height, and so made towards her, but she spying him first of all the rest, gave a shriek and ran back: the old Marquis that was then her guardian, came towards the Prince, and fell on his knees, conjuring his Highness to retire, in regard he hazarded his head if he admitted any to her company; so the door was opened, and he came out under that wall over which he had got in. I have seen him watch a long hour together in a close coach in the open street to see her as she went abroad. I cannot say that the Prince did ever talk with her privately, yet publickly often, my Lord of *Bristol* being interpreter, but the King always sat hard by to over-hear all. Our cousin *Archy* hath more privilege than any, for he often goes with his fool's coat, where the *Infanta* is with her *meninas* and ladies of honour, and keeps a blowing and blustering amongst them, and flurts out what he lists.

One day they were discoursing what a marvellous thing it was, that the Duke of *Bavaria* with less than 15000 men, after a toilsome march, should dare to encounter the *Palsgrave*'s army, consisting of above 25000, and to give them utter discomfiture, and take *Prague* presently: whereunto *Archy* answered, that he would tell them a stranger thing than that. Was it not a strange thing, quoth he, that in the year 1588, there should come a fleet of 140 sails from *Spain* to invade *England,* and that ten of these could not go back to tell what became of the rest? By the next opportunity I will send you the *Cordouan* pockets and gloves you wrote for of *Francisco Marino*'s perfuming. So my dear Captain live long, and love his

Madrid, July 10. 1623.   J. H.
                                               L E T-

LETTER LXXII.

To my Coufin Tho. Guin, *Efq; at his Houfe* Trecaftle.

Cousin,

I Received lately one of yours, which I cannot compare more properly than to a pofie of curious flowers, there was therein fuch a variety of fweet ftrains
and dainty expreffions of love; and though it bore an
old date, for it was forty days before it came fafe to
hand, yet the flowers were ftill frefh, and not a whit
faded, but did caft as ftrong and as fragrant a fcent as
when your hands bound them up firft together, only
there was one flower that did not favour fo well, which
was the undeferved character you pleafe to give of my
fmall abilities; which in regard you look upon me
through the profpective of affection, appear greater unto
you than they are of themfelves; yet as fmall as they
are, I would be glad to ferve you upon any occafion.

Whereas you defire to know how matters pafs here,
you fhall underftand, that we are rather in affurance than
hopes that the match will take effect, when one difpatch
more is brought from *Rome*, which we greedily expect.
The *Spaniards* generally defire it; they are much taken
with our Prince, with the bravery of his journey, and his
difcreet comportment fince; and, they confefs there was
never Princefs courted with more gallantry. The wits
of the court here have made divers encomiums of him,
and of his affection to the Lady *Infanta*. Amongft o-
thers, I fend you a *Latin* poem of one *Marniorius* a
Valencian, to which, I add this enfuing *hexaftic;* which
in regard of the difficulty of the verfe, confifting of all
ternaries, (which is the hardeft way of verfifying) and of
the exactnefs of the tranflation, I believe will give you
content:

Fax grata eft, gratum eft vulnus, mihi grata catena eft;
Me quibus aftringit, ledit & urit amor;

Sed.

Sed flammam extingui, fanavi vulnera, folvi
Vincla, etiam ut poffem non ego poffe velim :
Mirum equidem genus hoc morbi eft, incendia & ictus
Vinclaque, vinctus adhuc, læfus & uftus, amo.

Grateful's to me the fire, the wound, the chain,
By which *love* burns, *love* binds and giveth pain ;
But for to quench this fire, thefe bonds to loofe,
Thefe wounds to heal, I would not could I chufe :
Strange ficknefs, where the wounds, the bonds, the fire
That burns, that bind, that hurt, I muft defire.

In your next, I pray fend me your opinion of thefe
verfes, for I know you are a *critic* in poetry. Mr.
Vaughan of the *Golden-grove* and I were comrades and
bedfellows here many months together : his father, Sir
John Vaughan the Prince's Controller, is lately come to
attend his mafter. My Lord of *Carlifle*, my Lord of
Holland, my Lord *Rochfort*, my Lord of *Denbigh*, and
divers others are here, fo that we have a very flourifhing
court ; and I could wifh you were here to make one of
the number. So my dear coufin, I wifh you all happinefs, and our noble Prince a fafe and fuccefsful return to
England.

Your moft affectionate coufin,

Madrid, Auguft 13. 1623.   J. H.

LETTER LXXIII.

To my noble Friend Sir JOHN NORTH.

S I R,

THE long looked for difpenfation is come from
Rome, but I hear it is clogged with new claufes ;
and one is, that the Pope, who alledgeth that the only
aim of the apoftolical See in granting this difpenfation, was
the advantage and eafe of the catholics in the King of
Great

Great Britain's dominions, therefore he defired a valueable caution for the performance of thofe articles which were ftipulated in their favour : this hath much puzzled the bufinefs; and Sir *Francis Cottington* comes now over about it: befides, there is fome diftafte taken at the Duke of *Buckingham* here; and I heard this King fhould fay he will treat no more with him, but with the ambaffadors, who, he faith, have a more plenary commiffion, and underftand the bufinefs better. As there is fome darknefs happened betwixt the two favourites, fo matters ftand not right betwixt the Duke and the Earl of *Briftol;* but, God forbid that a bufinefs of fo high a confequence as this, which is likely to tend fo much to the univerfal good of *chriftendom*, to the reftitution of the *Palatinate*, and the compofing thofe broils in *Germany*, fhould be ranverfed by differences betwixt a few private fubjects, though now public minifters.

Mr. *Wafhington* the Prince's page is lately dead of a calenture, and I was at his burial, under a fig-tree behind my Lord of *Briftol*'s houfe. A little before his death one *Ballard* an *Englifh* Prieft went to tamper with him; and Sir *Edward Varney* meeting him coming down the ftairs of *Wafhington*'s chamber, they fell from words to blows, but they were parted. The bufinefs was like to gather very ill blood, and come to a great height, had not Count *Gondamar* quafht it; which I believe he could not have done, unlefs the times had been favourable, for fuch is the reverence they bear to the church here, and fo holy a conceit they have of all ecclefiaftics, that the greateft *Don* in *Spain* will tremble to offer the meaneft of them any outrage or affront. Count *Gondamar* hath alfo helped to free fome *Englifh* that were in the Inquifition in *Toledo* and *Sevile;* and I could alledge many inftances how ready and chearful he is to affift any *Englifhman* whatfoever, notwithftanding the bafe affronts he hath often received of the *London* boys as he calls them. At his laft return hither, I heard of a merry faying of his to the Queen, who difcourfing with him about the greatnefs of *London*, and whether it was as populous

pulous as *Madrid;* yes *Madam,* and more populous when I came away, though I believe there is scarce a man left there now, but all women and children; for all the men both in court and city were ready booted and spured to go away: and I am sorry to hear how other nations do much tax the *English* of their incivility to public ministers of state; and what ballads, and pasquils, and fopperies and plays were made against *Gondamar* for doing his master's business. My Lord of *Bristol* coming from *Germany* to *Bruffels,* notwithstanding that at his arrival thither, the news was fresh that he had relieved *Frankindale* as he passed, yet was he not a whit the less welcome, but valued the more both by the Archdutchess herself and *Spinola* with all the rest; as also, that they knew well that the said Earl had been the sole adviser of keeping Sir *Robert Manfel* abroad with that fleet upon the coast of *Spain* till the *Palfgrave* should be restored. I pray Sir when you go to *London-wall* and *Towerhill,* be pleased to remember my humble service where you know it is due: so, I am

Your most faithful servitor,

Madrid, August 15. 1623.   J. H.

LETTER LXXIV.

To the Right Honourable the Lord Viscount Colchester.

My very good Lord,

I Received the letter and commands your Lordship pleased to send me by Mr. *Walfingham Grefley;* and touching the constitutions and orders of the *contratation* house of the *West-Indies* in *Sevile,* I cannot procure it for love or money, upon any terms, though I have done all possible diligence therein; and some tell me it is dangerous, and no less than treason in him that gives the copy of them to any, in regard it is counted the greatest mystery of all the *Spanish* government.

That

That difficulty which happened in the bufinefs of the match of giving caution to the Pope, is now overcome: for whereas our King anfwered, that he could give no other caution than his royal word and his fon's, exemplified under the great feal of *England*, and confirmed by his council of State, it being impoffible to have it done by parliament, in regard of the averfenefs the common people have to the alliance; and whereas this gave no fatisfaction to *Rome*, the King of *Spain* now offereth himfelf for caution, for putting in execution what is ftipulated in behalf of the *roman catholicks* throughout his Majefty of *Great Britain*'s dominions. But he defires to confult his ghoftly fathers to know, whether he may do it without wronging his confcience: hereupon there hath been a *junta* formed of bifhops and jefuits, who have been already a good while about it; and the Bifhop of *Segovia*, who is as it were Lord Treafurer, having written a treaty lately againft the match, was outted of his office, banifhed the court, and confined to his diocefs. The Duke of *Buckingham* hath been indifpofed a good while, and lies fick at court, where the Prince hath no public exercife of devotion, but only bed-chamber prayers: and fome think that his lodging in the King's houfe is like to prove a difadvantage to the main bufinefs: for whereas, moft forts of people here hardly holde us to be *chriftians.* If the Prince had a palace of his own, and been permitted to have ufed a room for an open chapel to exercife the liturgy of the church of *England*, it would have brought them to have a better opinion of us; and to this end there were fome of our church-plate and veftments brought hither, but never ufed. The flow pace of this *junta* troubles us a little, and to the *divines* there are fome civilians admitted lately; and the *quære* is this, whether the King of *Spain* may bind himfelf by oath in the behalf of the King of *England*, to perform fuch and fuch articles that are agreed on in favour of the *roman catholics* by virtue of this match; whether the King may do this *falva confcientia?*

There

There was a great show lately here of baiting of bulls with men, for the entertainment of the Prince; it is the chiefest of all *Spanish* sports; commonly there are men killed at it, therefore there are priests appointed to be there ready to confess them. It hath happened often-times, that a bull hath taken up two men upon his horns with their guts dangling about them; the horsemen run with lances and swords, the foot with goads. As I am told, the Pope hath sent divers bulls against this sport of bulling, yet it will not be left, the nation hath taken such an habitual delight in it. There was an ill-favoured accident like to have happened lately at the King's house, in that part where my Lord of *Carlisle* and my Lord *Denbigh* were lodged; for my Lord *Denbigh* late at night taking a pipe of tobacco in a *balcony*, which hung over the King's garden, he blew down the ashes, which falling upon some parched combustible matter, began to flame and spread; but Mr. *Davis*, my Lord of *Carlisle*'s barber, leapt down a great height, and quenched it. So with my continuance of my most humble service, I rest ever ready

At your Lordship's command,

Madrid, August 16. 1623.   J. H.

LETTER LXXV.

To Sir JAMES CROFTS, *from* Madrid.

S I R,

THE court of *Spain* affords now little news; for there is a *remora* sticks to the business of the match, till the *junta* of the *divines* give up their opinion; but from *Turky* there came a letter this week, wherein there is the strangest and most tragical news, that in my small reading no story can parallel, or shew with more pregnancy the instability and tottering estate of human greatness, and the sandy foundation whereon the vast

    Ottoman

Ottoman empire is reared: for *Sultan Ofman*, the *Grand Turk*, a man according to the humour of that nation warlike and flefhed in blood, and a violent hater of *chri-ftians*, was in the flower of his years, in the heat and height of his courage knocked in the head by one of his own flaves, and one of the meaneft of them, with a battle-axe, and the murderer never after proceeded againft or queftioned.

The ground of this tragedy was the late ill fuccefs he had againft the *Pole*, wherein he loft about 100,000 horfe for want of forage, and 80,000 men for want of fighting; which he imputed to the cowardice of his *Ja-nizaries*, who rather than bear the brunt of the battle, were more willing to return home to their wives and merchandizing; which they are now permitted to do, contrary to their firft inftitution, which makes them more worldly and lefs venturous. This difgraceful return from *Polland*, ftuck in *Ofman*'s ftomach, and fo he ftudi-ed a way to be revenged of the *Janizaries*; therefore, by the advice of his *Grand Vifier* (a ftout gallant man, who had been one of the chief *Beglerbegs* in the Eaft) he in-tended to erect a new foldiery in *Afia* about *Damafco*, of the *Coords*, a frontier people, and confequently hardy and inured to arms. Of thefe he purpofed to entertain 40,000 as a life-guard for his perfon, though the main defign was to fupprefs his lazy and luftful *Janizaries*, with men of frefh new fpirits.

To difguife this plot, he pretended a pilgrimage to *Mecca*, to vifit *Mahomet*'s tomb, and reconcile himfelf to the Prophet, who he thought was angry with him, becaufe of his late ill fuccefs in *Poland*: but this colour was not fpecious enough, in regard he might have performed this pilgrimage with a fmaller train and charge; therefore it was propounded that the *empire* of *Sidon* fhould be made to rife up in arms, that fo he might go with a great power and treafure; but this plot was held difadvantageous to him, in regard his *Janizaries* muft then have attended him: fo he pretends and prepares only for the pilgrimage, yet he makes ready as much treafure

treafure as he could make, and to that end he melts his plate, and furniture of horfes, with divers church-lamps: this fomented fome jealoufy in the *Janizaries*, with certain words which fhould drop from him, that he would find foldiers fhortly fhould whip them. Hereupon he had fent over to *Afia*'s fide his pavilions, many of his fervants, with his jewels and treafure, refolving upon the voyage, notwithftanding that divers petitions were delivered him by the clergy, the civil magiftrates, and the foldiery, that he fhould defift from the voyage, but all would not do: thereupon, on the point of his departure, the *Janizaries* and *Spahies* came in a tumultuary manner to the feraglio, and in a high infolent language diffuaded him from the pilgrimage, and demanded of him his ill counfellors. The firft he granted, but for the fecond, he faid that it ftood not with his honour, to have his neareft fervants torn from him fo, without any legal proceeding; but he affured them that they fhould appear in the *divan* the next day, to anfwer for themfelves: but this not fatisfying, they went away in a fury, and plundered the *Grand Vifier*'s palace, with divers others. *Ofman* hereupon was advifed to go from his private gardens that night to the *Afian* fhore, but his deftiny kept him from it: fo the next morning they came armed to the court, (but having made a covenant not to violate the imperial throne) and cut in pieces the *Grand Vifier* with divers other great officers; and not finding *Ofman*, who had hid himfelf in a fmall lodge in one of his gardens, they cried out, they muft have a *Mufulman* Emperor; therefore they broke into a dungeon, and brought out *Muftapha*, *Ofman*'s uncle, whom he had clapt there at the beginning of the tumult, and who had been King before, but was depofed for his fimplicity, being a kind of *Santon*, or holy man, that is, betwixt an *innocent* and an *idiot*: this *Muftapha* they did re-enthronize, and place in the *Ottoman* empire

The next day they found *Ofman*, and brought him before *Muftapha*, who excufed himfelf with tears in his eyes for his rafh attempts, which wrought tendernefs in

fome,

fome, but more fcorn and fury in others; who fell upon
the *Capi Aga*, with the other officers, and cut them in
pieces before his eyes.   *Ofman* then was carried to prifon,
and as he was getting on horfeback, a common foldier
took off his turban, and clapt his upon *Ofman's* head,
who in his paffage begged a draught of water at a fountain.   The next day, the new *Vifier* went with an executioner to ftrangle him, in regard there were two younger
brothers more of his to preferve the *Ottoman* race;
where, after they had rufhed in, he being newly awaked,
and ftaring upon them, and thinking to defend himfelf,
a robuft boifterous rogue knocked him down, and fo the
reft fell upon him, and ftrangled him with much ado.

Thus fell one of the greateft potentates upon earth,
hy the hands of a contemptible flave, for there is not a
free-born fubject in all that vaft empire.   Thus fell he
that intitles himfelf moft puiffant and higheft monarch of
the *Turks*, King above all kings, a King that dwelleth
upon the earthly paradife, fon of *Mahomet*, keeper of
the grave of the chriftian God, Lord of the tree of life,
and of the river *Flisky*, Prior of the earthly paradife,
Conqueror of the *Macedonians*, the feed of great *Alex-*
ander, Prince of the kingdoms of *Tartary*, *Mefopotamia*,
Media, and of the martial *Mammalucks*, *Anatolia*,
Bithynia, *Afia*, *Armenia*, *Servia*, *Thracia*, *Morea*,
Valachia, *Moldavia*, and of all warlike *Hungary*, fovereign Lord and commander of all *Greece*, *Perfia*, both
the *Arabias*, the moft noble kingdom of *Egypt Tremifen*,
and *African*, empire of *Trabefond*, and the moft glorious *Conftantinople*, Lord of all the white and black feas,
of the holy city *Mecca*, and *Medina*, fhining with divine
glory, commander of all thing that are to be commanded,
and the ftrongeft and mightieft Champion of the wide
world, a warriour appointed by heaven in the edge of the
fword, a perfecutor of his enemies, a moft perfect jewel
of the bleffed tree, the chiefeft keeper of the crucified
God, *&c.* with other fuch bombaftical titles.

This *Ofman* was a man of a goodly conftitution, an
amiable afpect, and of excefs of courage, but fordidly
covetous;

covetous ; which drove him to violate the church, and to melt the lamps therof, which made the *Mufti* fay, that this was a due judgment fallen upon him from heaven for his facrilege. He ufed alfo to make his perfon too cheap, for he would go ordinarily in the night time with two men after him, like a petty conftable, and peep into the *cauph-houfes* and *carabets*, and apprehend foldiers there : and thefe two things it feems was the caufe that when he was fo affaulted in the feraglio, not one of his domeftick fervants, whereof he had 3000, would lift up an arm to help him.

Some few days before his death he had a ftrange dream, for, he dreamed that he was mounted upon a great *camel*, who would not go, neither by fair nor foul means ; and lighting off him, and thinking to ftrike him with his fcimiter, the body of the beaft vanifhed, leaving the head and the bridle only in his hand. When the *Mufti* and the *hoggies* could not interpret this dream, *Muftapha* his uncle did it ; for he faid, the *camel* fignified his empire, his mounting of him, his excefs in goverment, his lighting down, his depofing. Another kind of prophetic fpeech dropt from the *Grand Vifier* to Sir *Thomas Roe*, our Ambaffador there, who having gone a little before this tragedy to vifit the faid *Vifier*, told him what whifperings and mutterings there were in every corner, for this *Afiatic* voyage, and what ill confequences might enfue from it ; but if it held, he defired him to leave a charge with the *Chimacham*, his deputy, that the *Englifh* nation in the port fhould be free from outrages : whereunto the *Grand Vifier* anfwered, trouble not yourfelf about that, for I will not remove fo far from *Conftantinople*, but I will leave one of my legs behind to ferve you ; which proved too true, for he was murdered afterwards, and one of his legs was hung up in the hippodrome.

This frefh tragedy makes me to give over wondering at any thing that ever I heard or read, to fhew the lubricity of *mundan* greatnefs, as alfo the fury of the vulgar, which like an impetuous torrent gathereth ftrength by degrees as it meets with divers dams, and being come to

the

the height, cannot ftop itfelf: for when this rage of the foldiers began firft, there was no defign at all to violate or hurt the Emperor, but to take from him his ill counfellors; but it being once a-foot, it grew by infenfible degrees to the utmoft of outrages.

The bringing out of *Muftapha*, from the dungeon, where he was prifoner, to be Emperor of the *Mufulmans*, put me in mind of what I read in Mr. *Cambden* of our late Queen *Elizabeth*, how fhe was brought from the fcaffold to the *Englifh* throne.

They who profefs to be critics in policy here, hope that this murdering of *Ofman* may in time bring good blood, and prove advantageous to chriftendom: for though this be the firft Emperor of the *Turks* that was difpatched fo, he is not like to be the laft, now that'the foldiers have this precedent. Others think, that if that defign in *Afia* had taken, it had been very probable 'the *Conftantinopolitans* had hoifed up another King, and fo the empire had been difmembered, and by this divifion had loft ftrength, as the *Roman* empire did, when it was broken into Eaft and Weft.

Excufe me that this my letter is become fuch a monfter, I mean that it hath paft the fize and ordinary proportion of a letter; for the matter it treats of is monftrous; befides, it is a rule, that hiftorical letters have more liberty to be long than others. In my next you fhall hear how matters pafs here: in the mean time, and always, I reft

Your honour's moft devoted fervant,

Madrid, Auguft 17. 1623.　　　　J. H.

L E T.

LETTER LXXVI.

To the Right Honourable Sir THOMAR SAVAGE, *Knight and Baronet.*

Honourable Sir,

THE procedure of things in relation to the grand bufinefs the match, was at a kind of ftand, when the long winded *junta* delivered their opinions, and fell at laft upon this refult, that his catholick Majefty, for the fatisfaction of *St. Peter*, might oblige himfelf in the behalf of *England*, for the performance of thofe capitulations which related to the *roman catholics* in that kingdom ; and in cafe of non-performance, then to right himfelf by war, fince that the matrimonial articles were folemnly fworn to by the King of *Spain*, and his Highnefs, the two favourites, our two ambaffadors, the Duke of *Infantado*, and other counfellors of ftate being prefent : hereupon, the eighth of *September* next is appointed to be the day of *defpoforios*, the day of *affiance*, or the betrothing-day. There was much gladnefs expreft here, and luminaries of joy were in every great ftreet throughout the city ; but there is an unlucky accident hath intervened, for the King gave the Prince a folemn vifit fince, and told him Pope *Gregory* was dead, who was fo great a friend to the match, but in regard the bufinefs was not yet come to perfection, he could not proceed further in it till the former difpenfation was ratified by the new Pope *Urban*, which to procure, he would make it his own tafk, and that all poffible expedition fhould be ufed in it, and therefore defired his patience in the interim. The Prince anfwered, and preft the neceffity of his fpeedy return with divers reafons ; he faid, there was a general kind of murmuring in *England* for his fo long abfence ; that the King his father was old and fickly, that the fleet of his fhips were already, he thought, at fea to fetch him, the winter drew on ; and withal, that the articles of the match were figned in *England* with this
provifo,

provifo, that if he be not come back by fuch a month, they fhould be of no validity. The King replied, that fince his Highnefs was refolved upon fo fudden a departure, he would pleafe to leave a proxy behind to finifh the marriage, and he would take it for a favour if he would depute *him* to perfonate him ; and ten days after the ratification fhall come from *Rome* the bufinefs fhall be done, and afterwards he might fend for his wife when he pleafed. The Prince rejoined, that among thofe multitudes of royal favours which he had received from his Majefty, this tranfcended all the reft, therefore he would moft willingly leave a proxy for his Majefty, and another for *Don Carlos* to this effect : fo they parted for that time without the leaft umbrage of difcontent ; nor do I hear of any ingendered fince. The laft month, it is true, the *junta* of divines dwelt fo long upon the bufinefs, that there were whifperings that the Prince intended to go away difguifed as he came ; and the queftion being afked by a perfon of quality, there was a brave anfwer made, that if love brought him thither, it is not fear fhall drive him away.

There are preparations already a-foot for his return, and the two proxies are drawn and left in my Lord of *Briftol*'s hands. Notwithftanding this ill-favoured ftop, yet we are all here confident the bufinefs will take effect: in which hopes I reft

Your moft humble and ready fervant,

Madrid, Auguft 18. 1623.   J. H.

L E T T E R LXXVII.

To Captain NICH. LEAT *at his Houfe in* London.

S I R,

THIS letter comes to you by Mr. *Richard Altham,* of whofe fudden departure hence I am very forry, it being occafioned by the late death of his brother Sir *James Altham.*

Altham. I have been at a ftand in the bufinefs a good while, for his Highnefs's coming hither was no advantage to me in the earth. He hath done the *Spaniards* divers courtefies, but he hath been very fparing in doing the *Englifh* any: it may be perhaps, becaufe it may be a dimunition of honour to be beholding to any foreign Prince to do his own fubjects favours, but my bufinefs requires no favour; all I defire is juftice, which I have not obtained yet in reality.

The Prince is preparing for his journey: I fhall to it again clofely when he is gone, and make a fhaft or a bolt of it. The Pope's death hath retarded the proceedings of the match, but we are fo far from defpairing of it, that one may have wagers thirty to one it will take effect ftill. He that deals with this nation muft have a great deal of phlegm; and if this *grand* bufinefs of ftate, (the match) fuffer fuch protractions and puttings off, you need not wonder that private negotiations as mine is, fhould be fubject to the fame inconveniencies. There fhall be no means left unattempted that my beft induftry can find out to put a period to it; and when his Highnefs is gone, I hope to find my Lord of *Briftol* more at leifure to continue his favour and furtherance, which hath been much already: fo, I reft

Yours ready to ferve you,

Madrid, Auguft 19. 1623. J. H.

L*E T T E R LXXVIII.

To Sir JAMES CROFTS, *Knight.*

S I R,

THE Prince is now upon his journey to the feafide, where my Lord of *Rutland* attends for him with a royal fleet. There are many here fhrink in their fhoulders, and are very fenfible of his departure, and the Lady *Infanta* refents it more than any: fhe hath caufed

a

a mafs to be fung every day ever fince for his good voy-age. The *Spaniards* themfelves confefs there was ne-ver *princefs* fo bravely wooed. The King and his two brothers accompanied his Highnefs to the *Efcurial,* fome twenty miles off, and would have brought him to the fea-fide, but that the Queen is big, and hath not many days to go. When the King and he parted, there paf-fed wonderful great endearments and embraces in divers poftures between them a long time; and in that place, there is a pillar to be erected as a monument to pofte-rity. There are fome *grandees* and Count *Gondamar,* with a great train befides gone with him to the *Marine,* to the fea-fide, which will be many days journey, and muft needs put the King of *Spain* to a mighty expence, befides his feven months entertainment here. We hear that when he paffed through *Valladolid,* the Duke of *Lerma* was retired thence for the time by fpecial com-mand from the King, left he might have difcourfe with the Prince, whom he extremely defired to fee: this funk deep into the old Duke, infomuch that he faid, that of all the acts of malice which *Olivares* had ever done him, he refented this more than any. He bears up yet very well under his cardinal's habit; which hath kept him from many a foul ftorm that might have fallen upon him elfe from the temporal power. The Duke of *Uzeda* his fon, finding himfelf decline in favour at court, had re-tired to the country, and died foon after of difcontent-ment. During his ficknefs, the Cardinal wrote this fhort weighty letter unto him: *Dizen me, que Mareys de ne-cio; por mi, mas temo mis a nos que mis Enmigos.* Lerma. I fhall not need to *Englifh* it to you, who are fo great a mafter of the language. Since I began this let-ter, we underftand the Prince is fafely embarked, but not without fome danger of being caft away, had not Sir *Sackvile Trevor* taken him up. I pray God fend him a good voyage, and us no ill news from *England.* My moft humble fervice at *Towerhill,* fo I am

Your humble fervitor,

Madrid, Auguft 21. 1623. J. H.

LETTER LXXIX.

To my Brother Dr. HOWELL.

My Brother,

SINCE our Prince's departure hence, the Lady *Infanta* ftudieth *Englifh* apace; and one Mr. *Wadfworth* and father *Boniface*, two *Englifhmen*, are appointed her teachers, and have accefs to her every day: we count her as it were our *Princefs* now, and as we give, fo fhe takes that title. Our ambaffadors, my Lord of *Briftol*, and Sir *Walter Afton*, will not ftand now covered before her, when they have audience, becaufe they hold her to be their Princefs. She is preparing divers fuits of rich cloaths for his Highnefs, of perfumed amber leather, fome embroidered with pearl, fome with gold, fome with filver: her family is fettling apace, and moft of her officers are known already. We want nothing now but one difpatch more from *Rome*, and then the marriage will be folemnized, and all things confummated; yet there is one Mr. *Clerk* (with the lame arm) that came hither from the fea-fide, as foon as the Prince was gone: he is one of the Duke of *Buckingham*'s creatures, yet he lies at the Earl of *Briftol*'s houfe; which we wonder at, confidering the darknefs that happened betwixt the Duke and the Earl: we fear that this *Clerk* hath brought fomething that may puzzle the bufinefs. Befides, having occafion to make my addrefs lately to the *Venetian* Ambaffador, who is interefted in fome part of that great bufinefs for which I am here, he told me confidently it would be no match, nor did he think it was ever intended; but, I want faith to believe him yet, for I know St. *Mark* is no friend to it, nor *France*, or any other Prince or ftate befides the King of *Denmark*, whofe grandmother was of the houfe of *Auftria*, being fifter to *Charles* the Emperor. Touching the bufinefs of the *Palatinate*, our ambaffadors were lately affured by *Olivares*, and all the counfellors here, and that in this

King's

King's name, that he would procure his Majesty of *Great
Britain* entire satisfaction herein; and *Olivares*, giving
them the joy, intreated them to assure their King upon
their honour, and upon their lives, of the reality hereof; for the *Infanta* herself (saith he) hath stirred in it,
and makes it her own business: for, it was a firm *peace*
and amity (which he confessed could never be without
the accommodation of things in *Germany*) as much as
an *alliance*, which his Catholic Majesty aimed at. But
we shall know shortly now what to trust to: we shall
walk no more in mists, though some give out yet that
our Prince shall embrace a cloud for *Juno* at last.

I pray present my service to Sir *John Franklin*, and
Sir *John Smith*, with all at the *Hill* and *Dale*; and
when you send to *Wales*, I pray convey the inclosed to
my father. So my dear brother, I pray God bless us
both, and bring us again joyfully together.

Your very loving brother,

Madrid, August 12. 1623. **J. H.**

L E T T E R LXXX.

To my noble Friend Sir JOHN NORTH, *Knight.*

S I R,

I Received lately one of yours, but it was of a very
old date. We have our eyes here now all fixed upon *Rome*, greedily expecting the ratification, and lately a
strong rumour ran it was come, insomuch that Mr. *Clerk*,
who was sent hither from the Prince, being a shipboard,
(and now lies sick at my Lord of *Bristol's* house of a calenture) hearing of it, he desired to speak with him, for
he had something to deliver him from the Prince, my
Lord Ambassador being come to him, Mr. *Clerk* delivered a letter from the Prince: the contents whereof were,
' that, whereas he had left certain *proxies* in his hand to
' be delivered to the King of *Spain* after the ratification

' was

' was come, he defired and required him not to do it
' till he fhould receive further orders from *England*.'
My Lord of *Briftol* hereupon went to Sir *Walter Afton,*
who was in joint commiffion with him for concluding the
match. and fhewing him the letter, what my Lord *Afton*
faid I know not, but my Lord of *Briftol* told him, that
they had a commiffion royal under the broad feal of
England, to conclude the match : he knew as well as
he how earneft the King their mafter had been any time
this ten years to have it done, how there could not be
a better pawn for the furrendry of the *Palatinate,* than
the *Infanta* in the Prince's arms, who could never reft
till fhe did the work to merit love of our nation. He
told him alfo, how their own particular fortunes de-
pended upon it ; befides, if he fhould delay one moment
to deliver the *proxy* after the ratification was come, according to agreement, the *Infanta* would hold herfelf fo
blemifhed in her honour, that it might overthrow all
things. Laftly, he told him, that they incurred the hazard of their heads, if they fhould fufpend the executing
his Majefty's commiffion upon any order, but from that
power who gave it, who was the King himfelf. Hereupon, both the ambaffadors proceeded ftill in their preparing matters for the folemnizing of the marriage : the
Earl of *Briftol* had caufed above thirty rich liveries to be
made of watched velvet, with filver-lace up to the very
eapes of the cloaks ; the beft forts whereof, were valued
at 80 *l.* a livery. My Lord *Afton* had alfo provided new
liveries ; and a fortnight after the faid politic report was
blown up, the ratification came indeed compleat and full ;
fo the marriage-day was appointed, a *terras* covered all
over with tapeftry was raifed from the King's palace to the
next church ; which might be about the fame extent as
from *Whitehall* to *Weftminfter-Abbey ;* and the King intended to make his fifter a *wife,* and his daughter
(whereof the Queen was delivered a little before) a
chriftian upon the fame day : the *grandees* and great ladies had been invited to the marriage, and orders was
fent to all the port-towns to difcharge their great ord-

O   nance,

nance, and fundry other things were prepared to honour
the folemnity: but, when we were thus at the height of
our hopes, a day or two before, there came Mr. *Keller-
gree*, *Grefly*, *Wood* and *Davies*, one upon the neck of
another, with a new commiffion to my Lord of *Briftol*
immediately from his Majefty, countermanding him to
deliver the *proxy* aforefaid, until a full and abfolute fatisfaction were had for the furrendry of the *Palatinate*
under this King's hand and feal, in regard he defired his
fon fhould be married to *Spain*, and his fon-in-law re-
married to the *Palatinate* at one time: hereupon, all
was dafhed in pieces, and that frame which was rearing
fo many years, was ruined in a moment. This news
ftruck a damp in the hearts of all people here, and they
wifhed that the poftillions that brought it had all broke
their necks in the way.

My Lord of *Briftol* hereupon went to court to acquaint
the King with his new commiffion, and fo propofed the
reftitution of the *Palatinate*. The King anfwered, it
was none of his to give: 'tis true, he had a few towns
there, but he held them as commiffioner only from the
Emperor, and he could not command an Emperor, yet if
his Majefty of *Great Britain* would put a treaty a-foot,
he would fend his own ambaffadors to join. In the interim, the Earl was commanded not to deliver the aforefaid *proxy* of the Prince, for the difponfories or efpoufal,
until *Chriftmas*: (and herein it feems his Majefty with
you was not well informed, for thofe powers of *proxies*
expired before). The King here faid further, that if
his uncle the Emperor, or the Duke of *Bavaria* would
not be conformable to reafon, he would raife as great an
army for the Prince *Palfgrave* as he did under *Spinola*
when he firft invaded the *Palatinate*; and to fecure this,
he would engage his contratation-houfe of the *Weft-Indies*, with his plate-fleet, and give the moft binding inftrument that could be under his hand and feal. But
this gave no fatisfaction, therefore my Lord of *Briftol* I
believe hath not long to ftay here, for, he is commanded
to deliver no more letters to the *Infanta*, nor demand

any

any more audience; and that fhe fhould be no more ftyled Princefs of *England* or *Wales*. The forefaid caution
which this King offered to my Lord of *Briftol*, made me
think of what I read of his grandfather *Philip* II. who
having been married to our Queen *Mary*, and it being
thought fhe was with child of him, and was accordingly
prayed for at *Paul's-crofs*, though it proved afterwards
but a tympany, King *Philip* propofed to our parliament,
that they would pafs an act that he might be Regent during his or her minority that fhould be born, and he would
give good caution to furrender the crown, when *he* or
fhe fhould come to age. The motion was hotly can-
vafed in the houfe of peers, and like to pafs, when the
Lord *Paget* rofe up and faid, *I, but who fhall fue for
the King's bond?* So the bufinefs was dafhed. I have
no more news to fend you now, and I am forry I have
fo much, unlefs it were better; for we that have bufinefs
to negotiate here are like to fuffer much by this rupture.
Welcome be the will of God, to whofe benediction I
commend you, and reft

Your moft humble fervitor,

Madrid, Auguft 25. 1623. J. H.

LETTER LXXXI.

To the Right Honourable Lord CLIFFORD.

My good Lord,

THOUGH this court cannot afford now fuch comfortable news in relation to *England* as I could
wifh, yet fuch as it is you fhall receive. My Lord of
Briftol is preparing for *England*: I waited upon him
lately when he went to take his leave at court, and the
King wafhing his hands, took a ring from off his own
finger, and put it upon his; which was the greateft honour that ever he did any Ambaffador as they fay here:
he gave him alfo a cupboard of plate, valued at 20,000.

crowns.

crowns. There were also large'and high promises made
him, that in case he feared to fail upon any rock in *England*, by reason of the power of those who maligned
him, if he would stay in any of his dominions, he would
give him means and honour equal to the highest of his
enemies. The Earl did not only wave, but disdained
these propositions made unto him by *Olivares*; and said,
he was so confident of the King his master's justice and
high judgment, and of his own innocency, that he conceived no power could be able to do him hurt. There
hath occurred nothing lately in this court worth the ad-
vertisement. They speak much of the strange carriage
of that boisterous Bishop of *Halverstadt*, (for so they
term him here) that having taken a place where there
were two monasteries of nuns and friers, he caused divers feather-beds to be riped, and all the feathers to be
thrown in a great hall, whither the nuns and friers were
thrust naked with their bodies oiled and pitched, and to
tumble among these feathers; which makes them here
presage him an ill death. So, I most affectionately kiss
your hands, and rest

Your very humble servitor,

Madrid, August 26. 1623.   J. H.

LETTER LXXXII.

To Sir JOHN NORTH.

S I R,

I Have many thanks to render you for the favour you
lately did to a kinsman of mine, Mr. *Vaughan*, and
for divers others, which I defer till I return to that
court, and that I hope will not be long. Touching the
procedure of matters here, you shall understand, that my
Lord *Aston* had special audience lately of the King of
Spain, and afterwards presented a memorial, wherein
there was a high complaint against the miscarriage of the

two

two *Spanish* ambaſſadors now in *England,* the Marquis
of *Inopiſa,* and *Don Carlos Coloma:* the ſubſtance of it
was, that the ſaid ambaſſadors in a private audience his
Majeſty of *Great Britain* had given them, informed him
of a pernicious plot againſt his perſon and royal authority;
which was, that at the beginning of your now parliament, the Duke of *Buckingham* with other his complices, often met and conſulted in a clandeſtine way, how
to break the treaty both of *match* and *Palatinate;* and
in caſe his Majeſty was unwilling thereunto, he ſhould
have a country-houſe or two to retire unto for his recrea-
tion and health, in regard the Prince is now of years and
judgment fit to govern. His Majeſty ſo reſented this,.

* that the next day he ſent them many thanks for the care
they had of him, and deſired them to perfect the work;
and now that they had detected the treaſon, to diſcover
alſo the traitors; but they were ſhy in that point. The
King ſent again, deſiring them to ſend him the names of
the conſpirators in a paper ſealed up by one of their own
confidents, which he would receive with his own hands,
and no ſoul ſhould ſee it elſe; adviſing them withal, that
they ſhould not prefer this diſcovery before their own
honours, to be accounted falſe accuſers: they replied,
that they had done enough already by inſtancing in the
Duke of *Buckingham,* and it might eaſily be gueſſed who
were his confidents and creatures. Hereupon his Majeſty put thoſe whom he had any grounds to ſuſpect to
their oaths; and afterward ſent my Lord *Conway,* and
Sir *Francis Cottington,* to tell the ambaſſadors that he
had left no means uneſſayed to diſcover the conſpiration;
that he had found upon oath ſuch a clearneſs of ingenuity
in the Duke of *Buckingham,* that ſatisfied him of his innocency; therefore, he had juſt cauſe to conceive that
this information of theirs, proceeded rather from malice
and ſome political ends than from truth; and in regard
they would not produce the authors of ſo dangerous a
treaſon, they made themſelves to be juſtly thought the
authors of it: and therefore, though he might by his
own royal juſtice and the law of nations puniſh this ex-

ceſs

cefs and infolence of theirs, and high wrong they had done to his beft fervánts, yea, to the Prince his fon: for through the fides of the Duke they wounded him, in regard it was impoffible that fuch a defign fhould be attempted without his privity, yet he would not be his own Judge herein, but would refer them to the King their mafter, whom he conceived to be fo juft, that he doubted not but he would fee him fatisfied, and therefore he would fend an exprefs unto him hereabouts, to demand juftice and reparation: this bufinefs is now in agitation, but we know not what will become of it. We are all here in a fad difconfolate condition, and the merchants fhake their heads up and down, out of an apprehenfion of fome fearful war to follow: fo I moft affectionately kifs your hands, and reft

Your very humble and ready fervitor,
Madrid, Auguft 26. 1623. J. H.

` L E T T E R   LXXXIII.

To Sir KENELME DIGBY, *Knight.*

S I R,

YOU have had knowledge (none better) of the progieffion and growings of the *Spanifh* match from time to time. I muft acquaint you now with the rupture and utter diffolution of it, which was not long a doing: for, it was done in one audience that my Lord of *Briftol* had lately at court; whence it may be inferred, that 'tis far more eafy to pull down than rear up; for that ftructure which was fo many years a rearing was dafhed as it were in a trice: diffolution goeth a fafter pace then compofition. And it may be faid, that the civil actions of men, efpecially great affairs of monarchs (as this was) have much analogy in degrees of progreffion with the natural production of man. To make man there are many acts muft precede, firft, a meeting and copulation of the
fexes,

fexes, then conception; which requires a well difpofed womb to retain the prolifical feed, by the conftriction and occlufion of the orifice of the matrix; which feed being firft, and afterwards cream, is by a gentle ebullition coagulated and turned to a cruded lump; which the womb by virtue of its natural heat prepares to be capable to receive form, and to be organized, whereupon nature falls a working to delineate all the members, beginning with thofe that are moft noble; as the heart, the brain, the liver, whereof, *Galen* would have the liver which is the fhop and fource of the blood, and *Ariftotle* the heart, to be firft framed, in regard 'tis *primum vivens, & ultimum moriens:* nature continues in this labour until a perfect fhape be introduced; and this is called
• *formation,* which is the third act, and is a production of an organical body out of the fpermatic fubftance, caufed by the plaftic virtue of the vital fpirits; and fometimes this act is finifhed thirty days after the conception, fometimes fifty, but moft commonly in forty two or forty five, and is fooner done in the male: this being done, the *embryo* is animated with three fouls; the firft with that of plants, called a vegetable foul, then with a fenfitive, which all brute animals have, and laftly, the rational foul is infufed; and thefe three in man are like *trigonus* in *tetragono,* the two firft are generated *ex traduce,* from the feed of the parents, but the laft is by immediate infufion from God; and, 'tis controverted betwixt philofophers and divines, when this infufion is made.

This is the fourth act that goeth to make a man, and is called *animation:* and as the naturalifts allow *animation* double the time that formation had from the conception, fo they allow to the ripening of the *embryo* in the womb, and to the birth thereof treble the time that *animation* had; which happeneth fometimes in nine, fometimes in ten months. This *grand* bufinefs of the *Spanifh* match may be faid to have had fuch degrees of progreffion; firft, there was a meeting and coupling on both fides, for, a *junta* in *Spain,* and fome felect counfellors of ftate were appointed in *England.* After this conjunction

junction the bufinefs was conceived, then it received form, then life, (though the quickening was flow) but having had near upon ten years in lieu of ten months to be perfected, it was unfortunately ftrangled when it was ripe ready for birth; and I would they had never been born that did it, for it is like to be out of my way 3000 *l.* And as the *embryo* in the womb is wrapt in three membranes, or tunicles; fo this great bufinefs you know better than I, was involved in many difficulties, and died fo intangled before it could break through them.

There is a buz here of a match betwixt *England* and *France:* I pray, God fend it a fpeedier formation and *animation* than this had, and that it may not prove an abortive.

I fend you herewith a letter from the paragon of the *Spánifh* court, *Donna Anna Maria Manrique,* the Duke of *Marquedas*'s fifter, who refpects you in a high degree. She told me this was the firft letter fhe ever writ to man in her life, except the Duke her brother: fhe was much folicited to write to Mr. *Thomas Cary,* but fhe would not. I did alfo your meffage to the *Marquefa d'Inojofa,* who put me to fit a good while with her upon her *eftrado;* which was no fimple favour: you are much in both thefe ladies books, and much fpoken of by divers others in this court. I could not recover your diamond hat-band which the *Picaroon* fnatched from you in the coach, though I ufed all means poffible, as far as book, bell, and candle, in point of excommunication againft the party in all the *churches* of *Madrid;* by which means you know things are recovered. So, I moft affectionately kifs your hands, and reft

Your moft faithful fervitor, J. H.

P. S. Yours of the 2d of *March* came fafe to hand. *Madrid.*

L E T T E R LXXXIV.

To the Lord Viscount Colchefter, *from* Madrid.

Right Honourable,

YOUR Lordfhips of the 3d current came fafe to hand; and, being now upon the point of parting with this court, I thought it worth the labour to fend your Lordfhip a fhort furvey of the monarchy of *Spain;* a bold undertaking your Lordfhip will fay, to comprehend within the narrow bounds of a letter fuch a huge bulk; but as in the bofs of a fmall diamond ring one may difcern the image of a mighty mountain, fo I will endeavour that your Lordfhip may behold the power of this great King in this paper :

Spain hath been always efteemed a country of antient renown ; and as it is incident to all others, fhe hath had her viciffitudes and turns of fortune : fhe hath been thrice overcome; by the *Romans,* by the *Goths,* and by the *Moors.* The middle conqueft continueth to this day; for this King and moft of the nobility profefs themfelves to have defcended of the *Goths.* The *Moors* kept here about 700 years; and it is a remarkable ftory how they got in firft, which was thus upon good record : there reigned in *Spain, Don Rodrigo,* who kept his court then at *Malaga,* he employed the Conde *Don Julian* Ambaffador to *Barbary,* who had a daughter, (a young beautiful lady) that was maid of honour to the Queen: the King fpying her one day refrefhing herfelf under an arbor, fell enamoured with her, and never left till he had deflowered her: fhe refenting much the difhonour, writ a letter to her father in *Barbary* under this allegory, *That there was a fair green apple upon the table, and the King's poignard fell upon it, and cleft it in two.* *Don Julian* apprehending the meaning, got letters of revocation, and came back to *Spain,* where he fo complied with the King, that he became his favourite. Amongft other things he advifed the King, that in regard he was

now

now in peace with all the world, he would difmifs his *gallies* and garrifons that were up and down the *fea-coafts*, becaufe it was a fuperfluous charge. This being done, and the country left open to any invader, he prevailed with the King to have leave to go with his Lady to fee her friends in *Tarragona*, which was 300 miles off. Having been there a while, his Lady made femblance to be fick, and fo fent to petition the King, that her daughter *Donna Cava* (whom they had left at court to fatiate the King's luft) might come to comfort her a while; *Cava* came, and the gate through which fhe went forth is called after her name to this day in *Malaga*. *Don Julian* having all his chief kindred there, he failed over to *Barbary*, and afterwards brought over the King of *Morocco*, and others with an army, who fuddenly invaded *Spain*, lying armlefs and open, and fo conquered it. *Don Rodrigo* died gallantly in the field, but what became of *Don Julian*, who for a particular revenge betrayed his own country, no ftory makes mention. A few years before this happened, *Rodrigo* came to *Toledo*, where, under the great church there was a vault with huge iron doors, and none of his predeceffors durft open it, becaufe there was an old prophecy, *That when that vault was opened* Spain *fhould be conquered*. *Rodrigo* flighting the prophecy, caufed the doors to be broke open, hoping to find there fome treafure; but when he entered, there was nothing found but the pictures of *Moors*, of fuch men that a little after fulfilled the prophecy.

Yet this laft conqueft of *Spain* was not perfect, for divers parts Northweft kept ftill under chriftian kings, efpecially *Bifcay*; which was never conquered, as *Wales* in *Britanny*; and the *Bifcayners* have much analogy with the *Welfh* in divers things. They retain to this day the original language of *Spain*; they are the moft mountaineous people, and they are reputed the antienteft gentry, fo that when any is to take the order of knighthood, there are no inquifitors appointed to find whether he be clear of the blood of the *Moors*, as in other places. The King when he comes upon the confines, pulls off one

one fhoe before he can tread upon any *Bifcay* ground; and he hath good reafon to efteem that province, in regard of divers advantages he hath by it, for, he hath his beft timber to build fhips, his beft marines, and all his iron thence.

There were divers bloody battles betwixt the remnant of chriftians and the *Moors* for 700 years together; and the *Spaniards* getting ground more and more, drove them at laft to *Granada*, and thence alfo in the time of *Ferdinand* and *Ifabella*, quite over to *Barbary*. Their laft King was *Chico*, who, when he fled from *Granada* crying and weeping, the people upbraided him, *that he might well weep like a woman, who could not defend himfelf, and them like a man.* This was that *Ferdinand* who obtained from *Rome* the title of *Catholic*, though fome ftories fay, that many ages before *Ricaredus*, the firft orthodox King of the *Goths*, was ftyled *Catholicus* in a provincial fynod held at *Toledo;* which was continued by *Alphonfus* I. and then made hereditary by this *Ferdinand*. This abfolute conqueft of the *Moors* happened about *Henry* VII's time, when the forefaid *Ferdinand* and *Ifabella* had by alliance joined *Caftile* and *Aragon;* which with the difcovery of the *Weft-Indies*, which happened a little after, was the firft foundation of that greatnefs whereunto *Spain* is now mounted. Afterwards there was an alliance with *Burgundy* and *Auftria :* by the firft houfe, the feventeen provinces fell to *Spain;* by the fecond *Charles* V. came to be Emperor: and remarkable it is how the houfe of *Auftria* came to that height from a mean Earl ; the Earl of *Hasburg* in *Germany*, who having been one day a hunting, he overtook a prieft who had been with the facrament to vifit a poor fick Lady, the Prieft being tired, the Earl lighted off his horfe, helped up the Prieft, and fo waited upon him a-foot all the while till he brought him to the church: the Prieft giving him his benediction at his going away, told him, that for this great act of humility and piety, *his race fhould be one of the greateft that ever the world had;* and ever fince, which is fome 240 years ago, the

empire

empire hath continued in that houfe; which afterwards was called the houfe of *Auftria*.

In *Philip* II's time the *Spanifh* monarchy came to its higheft cumble, by the conqueft of *Portugal*, whereby the *Eaft-Indies*, fundry iflands in the *Atlantic·* fea, and divers places in *Barbary* were added to the crown of *Spain*. By thefe fteps this crown came to this grandeur; and truly give the *Spaniard* his due, he is a mighty Monarch, he hath dominions in all parts of the world, (which none of the four monarchies had) both in *Europe*, *Afia*, *Africa*, and *America*, (which he hath folely to himfelf) though our *Henry* VII. had the fame proffer made him: fo, the fun fhines all the twenty four hours of the natural day upon fome part or other of his countries; for part of the *Antipodes* are fubject to him. He hath eight viceroys in *Europe*, two in the *Eaft-Indies*, two in the *Weft*, two in *Afric*, and about thirty provincial fovereign commanders more; yet, as I was told lately, in a difcourfe betwixt him and our Prince at his being here, when the Prince fell to magnify his fpacious dominions, the King anfwered, *Sir, 'tis true, it hath pleafed God to truft me with divers nations and countries; but of all thefe there are but two which yield me any clear revenues, viz.* Spain, *and my* Weft-Indies, *nor all* Spain *neither, but* Caftile *only: the reft do fcarce quit coft, for all is drunk up betwixt governors and garrifons; yet my advantage is, to have the opportunity to propagate the Chriftian religion, and to employ my fubjects.* For the laft, it muft be granted that no Prince hath better means to breed brave men, and more variety of commands to heighten their fpirits with no petty but princely employments.

This King befides, hath other means to oblige the gentry unto him by fuch a huge number of *commendams* which he hath in his gift to beftow on whom he pleafes of any of the three orders of knighthood; which *England* and *France* want. Some noblemen in *Spain* can fpend 50,000*l*. fome forty, fome thirty, and divers 20,000*l*. *per annum.* The church here is exceeding rich

rich both in revenues, plate and buildings ; one cannot go
to the meaneft country chapel, but he will find chalices,
lamps and candlefticks of filver.   There are fome bifhopricks of 30,000 *l. per annum* and divers of 10,000 *l.* and
Toledo is 100,000 *l.* yearly revenue.   As the church is
rich, fo it is mightily reverenced here, and very powerful ; which made *Philip* II. rather depend upon the
clergy than the fecular power.   Therefore I do not fee
how *Spain* can be called a poor country, confidering the
revenues aforefaid of princes and prelates ; nor is it fo
thin of people as the world makes it, and one reafon may
be that there are fixteen univerfities in *Spain*, and in one
of thefe there were 15,000 ftudents at one time when I
was there, I mean *Salamanca ;* and in the village of
Madrid (for the King of *Spain* cannot keep his conftant
court in any city) there are ordinarily 600,000 fouls.
It is true, that the colonizing of the *Indies*, and the
wars of *Flanders*, have much drained this country of
people. Since the expulfion of the *Moors* it is alfo grown
thinner, and not fo full of corn ; for thofe *Moors* would
grub up wheat out of the very tops of the craggy hills,
yet they ufed another grain for their bread ; fo, that the
Spaniard had nought elfe to do but to go with his afs to
the market, and buy corn of the *Moors.*   There lived
here alfo in times paft a great number of the *Jews*, till
they were expelled by *Ferdinand ;* and as I have read
in an old *Spanifh* legend, the caufe was this : the King
had a young Prince to his fon, who was ufed to play
with a *Jewifh* Doctor that was about the court, who
had a ball of gold in a ftring hanging down his breaft, the
little Prince one day fnatched away the faid golden ball,
and carried it to the next room ; the ball being hollow,
opened, and within there was painted our *Saviour* killing
a *Jew's* tail.   Hereupon they were all fuddenly difter-
red and exterminated, yet, I believe in *Portugal* there
lurks yet good ftore of them.

For the foil of *Spain*, the fruitfulnefs of their vallies
recompences the fterility of their hills ; corn is their greateft want, and want of rain is the caufe of that, which

P   makes

makes them have need of their neighbours ; yet as much
as *Spain* bears is passing good, and so is every thing else
for the quality ; nor hath any one a better horse under
him, a better cloak on his back, a better sword by his
side, better shoes on his feet than the *Spaniard ;* nor
doth any drink better wine, or eat better fruit than he,
nor flesh for the quantity.

Touching the people, the *Spaniard* looks as high,
though not so big as a *German ;* his excess is in too much
gravity, which some who know him not well, hold to
be a pride ; he cares not how little he labours, for poor
Gascons and *Morisco* slaves do most of his work in field
and vineyard : he can endure much in the war, yet he
loves not to fight in the dark, but in open day, or upon a
stage that all the world might be witnesses of his valour ;
so that you shall seldom hear of *Spaniards* employed in
night-service, nor shall one hear of a duel here in an age.
He hath one good quality, that he is wonderfully obedient to government ; for the proudest Don of *Spain*, when
he is prancing upon his ginet in the street, if an *algu-
azil* (a serjeant) shew him his *vare*, that is a little white
staff he carrieth as a badge of his office, my Don will
down presently off his horse and yield himself his prisoner. He hath another commendable quality, that when
he giveth alms, he pulls off his hat, and puts it in the
beggar's hand with a great deal of humility. His gravity is much lessened since the late proclamation came out
against ruffs, and the King himself shewed the first example : they were come to that height of excess herein,
that twenty shillings were used to be paid for starching of
a ruff ; and some, though perhaps he had never a shirt to
his back, yet he would have a toting huge swelling ruff
about his neck. He is sparing in his ordinary diet, but
when he makes a feast he is free and bountiful. As to
temporal authority, especially martial, so is he very obedient to the church, and believes all with an implicit
faith : he is a great servant of ladies, nor can he be blam-
ed, for, as I said before, he comes of a *Gotish* race ;
yet he never brags of, nor blazes abroad his doings that
                                                        way,

way, but is exceedingly careful of the repute of any woman, (a civility that we much want in *England*). He
will speak high words of Don *Philippo* his King, but
will not endure a stranger should do so. I have heard a
Biscayner make a *rodomantado*, that he was as good a
gentleman as *Don Philippo* himself, for, *Don Philippo*
was half a *Spaniard*, half a *German*, half an *Italian*,
half a *Frenchman*, half I know not what, but he was a
pure *Biscayner* without mixture. The *Spaniard* is not
so smooth and oily in his compliment as the *Italian* ;
and though he will make strong protestations, yet he will
not swear out compliments like the *French* and *English* :
as I heard when my Lord of *Carlisle* was Ambassador in
France, there came a great Monsieur to see him, and
having a long time banded, and swore compliments one
to another who should go first out at a door; at last my
Lord of *Carlisle* said, *ô Monseigneur ayez pitie. de mon
ame,* O my Lord have pity upon my soul.

The *Spaniard* is generally given to gaming, and that
in excess ; he will say his prayers before, and if he win
he will thank God for his good fortune after : their
common game at cards (for they very seldom play at
dice) is *primera,* at which the King never shews his game,
but throws his cards with their faces down on the table :
he is merchant of all the cards and dice through all the
kingdom, he hath them made for a penny a pair, and he
retails them for twelve-pence ; so that it is thought he
hath 30,000*l.* a year by this trick at cards. The *Spaniard* is very devout in his way, for I have seen him kneel
in the very dirt when the *Ave Mary* bell rings ; and some,
if they spy two straws or sticks ly cross-ways in the street,
they will take them up and kiss them, and lay them
down again. He walks as if he marched, and seldom
looks on the ground, as if he contemned it. I was told
of a *Spaniard,* who having got a fall by a stumble and
broke his nose, rose up, and in a disdainful manner said,
Voto a tal estoes caminar por la tierra, this it is to walk
upon earth. The *labradors* and country swains here are
sturdy and rational men, nothing so simple or servile as

P. 2.   the

the *French* peafant who is born in chains.   It is true,
the *Spaniard* is not fo converfable as other nations,
(unlefs he hath travelled) elfe he is like *Mars* among the
planets, impatient of conjunction; nor is he fo free in
his gifts and rewards ; as the laft fummer it hapened that
Count *Gondomar* with Sir *Francis Cottington*, went to
fee a curious houfe of the Conftable of *Caftile's*. which
had been newly built here, the keeper of the houfe was
very officious to fhew him every room, with the garden,
grottos and aqueducts, and prefented him with fome
fruit : *Gondomar* having been a long time in the houfe,
coming out, put many compliments of thanks upon the
man, and fo was going away, Sir *Francis* whifpered
him in the ear, and afked whether he would give the
man any thing that took fuch pains ?   Oh, quoth *Gondo-*
mar, well remembered, *Don Francifco*, have you ever a
double piftole about you ? If you have, you may give it
him, *and then you pay him after the* Englifh *manner, I*
have paid him already after the Spanifh.   The *Spaniard*
is much improved in policy fince he took footing in *Italy*,
and there is no nation agrees with him better.   I will
conclude this character with a faying that he hath, .

> *No ay hombre debaxo d'el fol,*
> *Como el* Italiano *y el* Efpanol.

Whereunto a *Frenchman* anfwered,

> *Dizes la verdad, y tienes razon,*
> *El uno es* puto, *el otro* ladron.

Englifhed thus :

> Beneath the fun there's no fuch man,
> As is the *Spaniard* and *Italian*.

The Frenchman *anfwers*,

> Thou tell'ft the truth, and reafon haft,
> The firft a *thief*, a *buggerer* the laft.

Touching

Touching their women, nature hath made a more viſible diſtinction betwixt the two Sexes here than elſewhere ; for the men for the moſt part are ſwarthy and rough, but the women are of a far finer mould, they are commonly little ; and whereas, there is a ſaying that makes a compleat woman, let her be *Engliſh* to the neck, *French* to the waiſt, and *Dutch* below : I may add, for hands and feet let her be *Spaniſh*, for they have the leaſt of any. They have another ſaying, a *French-woman* in a dance, a *Dutch-woman* in the kitchen, an *Italian* in a window, an *Engliſh-woman* at board, and the *Spaniſh* a bed. When they are married, they have a privilege to wear high ſhoes, and to paint ; which is generally practiſed here, and the Queen uſeth it herſelf. They are coy enough, but not ſo froward as our *Engliſh ;* for if a Lady go along the ſtreet (and all women going here vailed, and their habit ſo generally alike, one can hardly diſtinguiſh a Counteſs from a cobler's wife) if one ſhould caſt out an odd ill-ſounding word, and aſk her a favour, ſhe will not take it ill, but put it off, and anſwer you with ſome witty retort. After thirty they are commonly paſt childbearing ; and I have ſeen a woman in *England* look as youthful at fifty, as ſome here at twenty-five. Money will do miracles here in purchaſing the favour of ladies, or any thing elſe, though this be the country of money, for it furniſheth well near all the world beſides, yea their very enemies, as the *Turk* and *Hollander ;* inſomuch, that one may ſay, the *coin* of *Spain* is as *catholic* as her *King.* Yet though he be the greateſt King of gold and ſilver mines in the world, (I think) yet the common current coin here is copper ; and herein I believe the *Hollander* hath done him more miſchief by counterfeiting his copper coins, than by their arms, bringing it in by ſtrange ſurreptitious ways, as in hollow ſows of tin and lead, hollow maſts, in pitch buckets under water, and otherways. But I fear to be injurious to this great King, to ſpeak of him in ſo narrow a compaſs ; a great King indeed, though the *French* in a ſlighting way compare his monarchy to a *beggar's cloak made up of patches :* they

arc

are *patches* indeed, but such as he hath not the like. The *Eaft-Indies* is a patch embroidered with pearls, rubies, and diamonds : *Peru* is a patch embroidered with maffy gold, *Mexico* with filver, *Naples* and *Milan* are pathes of cloth of tiffue ; and if thefe patches were in one piece, what would become of his cloak embroidered with *flower-de-luces* ?

So, *defiring your Lordfhip to pardon this poor im-perfect paper, confidering the high quality of the fubject,. I reft*

Your Lordfhip's moft humble fervant,

Madrid, Feb. 1. 1623.   J. H.

L E T T E R   LXXXV.

To Mr. WALSINGHAM GRESLEY, *from* Madrid.

Don BALTHASAR,

I Thank you for my letter in my Lord's laft pacquet, wherein among other paffages, you write to me the circumftances of Marquis *Spinola*'s raifing his leaguer, by flatting and firing his works before *Berghen*. He is much taxed here, to have attempted it, and to have buried fo much of the King's treafure before that town, in fuch coftly trenches. A gentleman came hither late-ly, who was at the fiege all the while, and he told me one ftrange paffage ; how Sir *Ferdinando Cary*, a huge corpulent Knight, was fhot through his body ; the bullet entring at the navel, and coming out at his back, killed his man behind him, yet he lives ftill, and is like to recover. With this miraculous accident, he told me alfo a merry one ; how a Captain that had a wooden leg booted over, had it fhattered to pieces by a cannon-bul-let, his foldiers crying *a Surgeon, a Surgeon*, for the Captain ; no, no, faid he, *a carpenter, a carpenter will ferve the turn.* To this pleafant tale I will add another that happened lately in *Alcala*, hard by, of a *Dominican*

frier,

frier, who in a solemn proceffion which was held there upon *Afcenfion* day laft, had his ftones dangling under his habit cut off inftead of his pocket by a cut-purfe.

Before you return hither, which I underftand will be fpeedily, I pray beftow a vifit on our friends in *Bifhopf-gate-ftreet :* fo I am

Your faithful fervant,

Madrid, Feb. 3. 1623.   J. H.

L E T T E R LXXXVI.

To Sir ROBERT NAPIER *Knight, at his Houfe in* Bifh-opfgate-ftreet.

S I R,

THE late breach of the *match*, hath broke the neck of all bufinefs here, and mine fuffers as much as any : I had accefs lately to *Olivares*, once or twice ; I had audience alfo of the King, to whom I prefented a memorial that intimated *letters of mart*, unlefs fatisfa-ction were had from his *Viceroy* the *Conde del Real.* The King gave me a gracious anfwer, but *Olivares* a churlifh one, *viz. That when the* Spaniards *had juftice in* England, *we fhould have juftice here :* fo, that not-withftanding I have brought it to the higheft point and pitch of perfection in law that could be, and procured fome difpatches, the like whereof were never granted in this court before, yet I am in defpair now to do good. I hope to be fhortly in *England*, by God's grace, to give you and the reft of the proprietaries, a punctual account of all things ; and you may cafily conceive how forry I am that matters fucceeded not according to your expe-ctation, and my endeavours ; but I hope you are none of thofe that meafure things by the event. The Earl of *Briftol*, Count *Gondomar*, and my Lord Ambaffador *Afton*, did not only do courtefies, but they did co-operate

with

with me in it, and contribute their utmost endeavours.
So I rest

Yours to serve you,

Madrid, Feb. 19. 1623.   J. H.

L E T T E R   LXXXVII.

To the Honourable Sir T. S. *at* Towerhill.

·S I R,

I Was yesterday at the *Escurial* to see the monastery
of *St. Laurence*, the eight wonder of the world;
and truly considering the site of the place, the state of
the thing, and the symmetry of the structure, with divers
other rarities, it may be called so ; for what I have seen
in *Italy*, and other places, are but babbles to it. It is built
amongst a company of craggy barren hills, which makes
the air the hungrier, and wholesomer ; it is all built of
free-stone and marble, and that with such solidity and moderate height, that surely *Philip* II's chief design was
to make a sacrifice of it to eternity, and to contest with
the meteors, and *time* itself. It cost 8,000000, it was
twenty-four years a building, and the founder himself saw
it finished, and enjoyed it twelve years after, and carried his bones himself thither to be buried.

The reason that moved King *Philip* to waste so much
treasure, was a vow he had made at the battle of *St.
Quintin*, when he was forced to batter a monastery of
St. Laurence friers, that if he had the victory, he would
erect such a monastery to *St. Laurence*, that the world
had not the like ; therefore the form of it is like a grid-
iron, the handle is a huge royal palace, and the body a
vast monastery or assembly of quadrangular cloisters ; for
there are as many as there be months in the year. There
be a 100 monks, and every one hath his man and his
mule ; and a multitude of officers : besides, there are three
libraries there, full of the choicest books for all sciences.

It

It is beyond expreſſion what grotos, gardens, walks, and aqueduĉts there are there, and what curious fountains in the upper cloiſters, for there be two ſtages of cloiſters: in fine, there is nothing that is vulgar there. To take a view of every room in the houſe, one muſt make account to go ten miles; there is a vault called the *Pantheon* under the higheſt altar, which is all paved, walled, and arched with marble; there be a number of huge ſilver candleſticks, taller than I am; lamps three yards compaſs, and divers chalices and croſſes of maſſy gold: there is one quire made all of burniſhed braſs, piĉtures and ſtatues like giants, and a world of glorious things, that purely raviſhed me. By this mighty monument, it may be inferred, that *Philip* II. though he was a little man, yet had vaſt gigantick thoughts in him, to leave ſuch a huge pile for poſterity to gaze upon, and admire his memory. No more now, but that I reſt

Your humble ſervant,

Madrid, March 9. 1623. J. H.

LETTER LXXXVIII.

To the Lord Viſcount Colcheſteſter, *from* Madrid.

My Lord,

YOU writ to me not long ſince, to ſend you an account of the Duke of *Oſſuna*'s death, a little man, but of great fame and fortunes, and much cried up, and known up and down the world. He was revoked from being Viceroy of *Naples* (the beſt employment the King of *Spain* hath for a ſubjeĉt) upon ſome diſguſt; and being come to this court, when he was brought to give an account of his government, being troubled with the gout, he carried his ſword in his hand inſtead of a ſtaff: the King miſliking the manner of his poſture, turned his back to him, and ſo went away: thereupon he was overheard mutter, *Eſto es para ſervir muchachos: This it is to ſerve*

ferve boys. This coming to the King's ear, he was apprehended, and committed prifoner to a monaftery not
far off, where he continued fome years, until his beard
came to his girdle; then growing very ill, he was permitted to come to his houfe in this town, being carried in
a bed upon mens fhoulders, and fo died fome years ago.
There were divers accufations againft him; among the
reft, I remember thefe, that he had kept the Marquis
de Campolatoro's wife, fending her bufband out of the
way upon employment; that he had got a baftard of a
Turkifh woman, and fuffered the child to be brought up
in the *Mahometan* religion; that being one day at high
mafs, when the hoft was elevated, he drew out of his
pocket a piece of gold, and held it up, intimating that
that was his god; that he had invited fome of the prime
courtefans of *Naples* to a feaft, and after dinner made a
banquet for them in his garden; where he commanded
them to ftrip themfelves ftark naked, and go up and
down while he lhot fugar-plums at them out of a trunk,
which they were to take up from off their high chapins,
and fuch like extravagancies. One (amongft divers o-
ther) witty paffages was told me of him; which was, that
when he was Viceroy of *Sicily*, there died a great rich
Duke who left but one fon, whom with his whole eftate,
he bequeathed to the tutéle of the jefuits; and the words
of the will were, *When he is paft his minority*, (Darete
al mio figlivolo quelque voi volete) *you fhall give my
fon what you will*. It feems the jefuits took to themfelves two parts of three of the eftate, and gave the reft
to the heir: the young Duke complaining hereof to the
Duke of *Offuna*, (then Viceroy) he commanded the jefuits to appear before him: he afked them how much of
the eftate they would have, they anfwered, two parts of
three; which they had almoft employed already to build
monafteries and an hofpital, to erect particular altars, and
maffes, to fing dirges and refrigeriums for the foul of
the deceafed Duke. Hereupon, the Duke of *Offuna*
caufed the will to be produced, and found therein the
words afore-recited, *When he is paft his minority, you
fhall*.

shall give my son of my estate what you will. Then he told the jesuits, you must by virtue and tenor of these words, give *what you will* to the son, which by your own confession is two parts of three; and so he determined the business.

Thus have I in part satisfied your Lordship's desire; which I shall do more amply when I shall be made happy to attend you in person; which I hope will be before it be long. In the interim, I take my leave of you from *Spain,* and rest

Your Lordship's most ready and humble servitor,

Madrid, March 13. 1623. J. H.

LETTER LXXXIX.

To Sir James Crofts, *from* Bilboa.

S I R,

BEING safely come to the *Marine,* in convoy of his Majesty's jewels, and being to sojourn here some days, the conveniency of this gentleman, (who knows, and much honoureth you) he being to ride post through *France,* invited me to send you this.

We were but five horsemen in all our seven days journey from *Madrid* hither, and the charge Mr. *Wiches* had is valued at 400,000 crowns; but 'tis such safe travelling in *Spain,* that one may carry gold in the palm of his hand, the government is so good. When we had gained *Biscay* ground, we past one day through a forest, and lighting off our mules to take a little repast under a tree, we took down our *alforjas* and some bottles of wine, (and you know 'tis ordinary here to ride with one's victuals about him) but as we were eating we spied two huge wolves, who stared upon us a while, but had the good manners to go away. It put me in mind of a pleasant tale I heard Sir *Thomas Fairfax* relate of a soldier in *Ireland,* who having got his passport to go for *England,*

as

as he paſt through a wood with a knapſack upon his back, being weary, he ſat down under a tree, where he opened his knapſack and fell to ſome victuals he had, but upon a ſudden he was ſurprized with two or three wolves, who coming towards him, he threw them ſcraps of bread and cheeſe till all was done; then the wolves making a nearer approach unto him, he knew not what ſhift to make, but by taking a pair of bagpipes which he had; and as ſoon as he began to play upon them, the wolves ran all away as if they had been ſeared out of their wits; whereupon the ſoldier ſaid, *A pox take you all, if I had known you had loved muſic ſo well you ſhould have had it before dinner.*

If there be a lodging void at the three *Halbertsheads*, I pray be pleaſed to cauſe it be reſerved to me: ſo, I reſt

Your humble ſervitor,

Bilboa, Sept. 6. 1624.   J. H.

LETTER XC.

To my FATHER, *from* London.

S I R,

I Am newly returned from *Spain;* I came over in convoy of the Prince's jewels, for which, one of the ſhips royal with the *Catch* were ſent under the command of Captain *Love*. We landed at *Plymouth*, whence I came by poſt to *Theobald's* in leſs than two nights and a day, to bring his Majeſty news of their ſafe arrival. The Prince had newly got a fall off a horſe, and kept his chamber: the jewels were valued at above 100,000 pounds; ſome of them a little before the Prince's departure had been preſented to the *Infanta*, but ſhe waving to receive them, yet with a civil compliment they were left in the hands of one of the Secretaries of ſtate for her uſe upon the wedding-day; and, it was no unworthy thing in the *Spaniard* to deliver them back, notwithſtand-

ing

ing that the *treaties* both of *match* and *Palatinate* had been diffolved a pretty while by act of parliament, that a war was threatened and ambaffadors revoked. There were jewels alfo amongft them to be prefented to the King and Queen of *Spain*, to moft of the ladies of honour and the grandees. There was a great table diamond for *Olivares* of eighteen carrats weight; but the richeft of all was to the *Infanta* herfelf; which was a chain of great orient pearl, to the number of 276, weighing nine ounces. The *Spaniards* notwithftanding they are mafters of the ftaple of jewels, ftood aftonifhed at the beauty of thefe, and confeffed themfelves to be put down.

Touching the employment upon which I went to *Spain*, I had my charges born all the while, and that was all: had it taken effect, I had made good bufinefs of it; but 'tis no wonder (nor can it be I hope any difrepute unto me) that I could not bring to pafs what three ambaffadors could not do before me.

I am now cafting about for another fortune, and fome hopes I have of employment about the Duke of *Buckingham*: he fways more than ever, for whereas, he was before a favourite to the King, he is now a favourite to parliament, people, and city, for breaking the match with *Spain*. Touching his own intereft, he had reafon to do it, for the *Spaniards* love him not; but, whether the public intereft of the State will fuffer in it or no, I dare not determine: for my part, I hold the *Spanifh match* to be better than their *powder*, and their *wares* better than their *wars;* and I fhall be ever of that mind, that *no country is able to do* England *lefs hurt, and more good than* Spain, confidering the large traffick and treafure that is to be got thereby.

I fhall continue to give you an account of my courfes when opportunity ferves, and to difpofe of matters fo that I may attend you this fummer in the country: fo, defiring ftill your bleffing and prayers, I reft

Your dutiful fon,

London, Dec. 10. 1624.

J. H.

LET-

LETTER XCI.

To the Lord Viscount Colcheſter.

Right Honourable,

MY laſt to your Lordſhip was in *Italian*, with the *Venetian gazetta* incloſed. Count *Mansfelt* is upon point of parting, having obtained it ſeems the ſum of his deſires: he was lodged all the while in the ſame quarter of St. *James*'s which was appointed for the *Infanta*: he ſupped yeſternight with the council of war, and he hath a grant of 12000 men, *Engliſh* and *Scots*, whom he will have ready in the body of an army againſt the next ſpring; and they ſay, that *England, France, Venice,* and *Savoy,* do contribute for the maintenance thereof 60,000 *l.* a month. There can be no conjeſture, much leſs any judgment made of his deſign: moſt think it will be for relieving *Breda*, which is ſtraitly begirt by *Spinola*, who gives out, that he hath her already as a bird in a cage, and will have her maugre all the oppoſition of chriſtendom; yet, there is freſh news come over, that Prince *Maurice* hath got on the back of him, and hath belaggered him as he hath done the *town;* which I want faith to believe yet, in regard of the huge circuit of *Spinola*'s works; for his circumvallations are cried up to be near upon twenty miles. But while the *Spaniard* is ſpending millions here for getting ſmall towns, the *Hollander* gets kingdoms of him elſewhere. He hath invaded and taken lately from the *Portugal* part of *Brazil*, a rich country for ſugars, cottons, balſams, dyeing-wood, and divers commodities beſides.

The treaty of marriage betwixt our Prince and the youngeſt daughter of *France* goes on apace, and my Lords of *Carliſle*, and *Holland* are in *Paris* about it: we ſhall ſee now what difference there is betwixt the *French* and *Spaniſh* pace. The two *Spaniſh* ambaſſadors have been gone hence long ſince: they ſay, that they are both in priſon,

prifon, one in *Burgois* in *Spain*, the other in *Flanders*,
for the fcandalous information they made here againſt the
Duke of *Buchingham*; about which, the day before their
departure hence, they deſired to have one private audience more, but his Majeſty denied them. I believe
they will not continue long in difgrace, for matters grow
daily worſe and worſe betwixt us and *Spain:* for, diveis,
letters of mart are granted our merchants, and letters of
mart are commonly the fore-runners of a war; yet, they
fay *Gondomar* will be on his way hither again about the
Palatinate, for the King of *Denmark* appears now in his
niece's quarrel, and arms apace. No more now, but
that I kiſs your Lordſhip's hand, and'reſt

Your moſt humble and ready ſervitor,

Lond. Feb. 5. 1624.   J. H.

L E T T E R XCII.

To my FATHER, *from* London.

S I R,

I Received yours of the 3d of *February* by the hands
of my couſin *Thomas Guin* of *Trecaſtle.*

It was my fortune to be on *Sunday* was fortnight at
Theobald's, where his late Majeſty King *James* departed
this life, and went to his laſt reſt upon the *day of reſt,*
preſently after ſermon was done. A little before the
break of day he ſent for the Prince, who roſe out of his
bed and came in his night-gown; the King ſeemed to
have ſome carneſt thing to ſay unto him, and ſo endeavoured to rouſe himſelf upon his pillow, but his ſpirits
were ſo ſpent that he had not ſtrength to make his words
audible. He died of a fever which began with an ague;
and ſome *Scots* doctors mutter at a plaiſter the Counteſs
of *Buckingham* applied to the outſide of his ſtomach.
'Tis thought the late breach of the match with *Spain,*
which for many years he had ſo vehemently deſired,

took too deep an impreſſion in him, and that he was for-
eed to ruſh into a war now in his declining age, having lived in a continual uninterrupted peace his whole life,
except ſome collateral aids he had ſent his ſon-in-law.
As ſoon as he expired, the privy-council ſat, and in leſs
then a quarter of an hour, King *Charles* was proclaimed
at *Theobald*'s court-gate, by Sir *Edward Zouch* Knight-
marſhal, Maſter Secretary *Conway* dictating unto him,
*That whereas, it hath pleaſed God to take to his mercy
our moſt gracious Sovereign, King* James *of famous memory, We proclaim Prince* Charles *his rightful and in-
dubitable heir to be King of* England, Scotland, France
and Ireland, *&c.* The Knight-marſhal miſtook, ſaying,
his rightful and dubitable heir, but he was rectified by
the Secretary. This being done, I took my horſe inſtantly, and came to *London* firſt, except one, who was
come a little befoıe me, infomuch, that I found the
gates ſhut. His now Majeſty took coach, and the Duke
of *Buckingham* with him, and came to St. *James*'s. In
the evening he was proclaimed at *Whitehall* gate, in
Cheapſide and other places in a ſad ſhower of rain; and
the weather was ſuitable to the condition wherein he
finds the kingdom, which is cloudy: for, he is left engaged in a war with a potent Prince, the people by long
diſuetude unapt for arms, the fleet royal in quarter repair, himſelf without a Queen, his ſiſter without a country, the crown pitifully laden with debts, and the purſe
of the ſtate lightly hallaſted, though it never had better
opportınity to be rich than it had theſe laſt twenty
years; but God almighty, I hope will make him emerge,
and pull this iſland out of all theſe plagues, and preſerve
us from worſer times.

The plague is begun in *White-chapel;* and as they
ſay, in the ſame houſe, at the ſame day of the month,
with the ſame number that died twenty two years ſince
when Queen *Elizabeth* departed.

There are great preparations for the funeral; and
there is a deſign to buy all the cloth for mourning white,
and then to put it to the dyers in groſs; which is like to
ſave

fave the crown a good deal of money: the drapers murmur extremely at the Lord *Cranfield* for it.

I am not fettled yet in any ftable condition, but I ly
windbound at the *Cape of Good Hope*, expecting fome
gentle gale to launch out into an employment.

So, with my love to all my brothers and fifters at the
Bryn, and near *Brecknock*, I humbly crave a continuance
of your prayers and blefling to

Your dutiful fon,

London, Dec. 11: 1625.   J. H.

LETTER XCIII.

To Dr. PRICHARD.

S I R,

SINCE I was beholden to you for your many favours
in *Oxford*, I have not heard from you (*ne gry qui-
dem*), I pray let the wonted correfpondence be now te-
vived and receive new vigour between us.

My Lord Chancellor *Bacon* is lately dead of a languifh-
ing weaknefs: he died fo poor, that he fcarce left money
to bury him; which though he had a great wit, did argue
no great wifdom, it being one of the effential properties
of a wife man to provide for the main chance. I have
read, that it hath been the fortune of all poets commor-
ly to die beggars, but for an Orator, a Lawyer, and Philofopher as he was to die fo, is rare. It feems the fame
fate befel him that attended *Demofthenes*, *Seneca*, and
Cicero, (all great men); of whom, the two firft fell by
corruption. The faireft diamond may have a flaw in it,
but I believe he died poor out of a contempt of the pelf
of fortune; as alfo out of an excefs of generofity, which
appeared as in divers other paffages, fo once when the
King had fent him a ftag, he fent up for the under-
keeper, and having drunk the King's health unto him in
a great filver gilt-bowl, he gave it him for his fee.

Q 3

He

He writ a pitiful letter to King *James* not long before his death, and concludes, ' Help me dear Sovereign ' Lord and Master, and pity me so far, that I who have ' been born to a bag, be not now in my age forced in ' effect to bear a wallet; nor that I who desire to live to ' study, may be driven to study to live:' which words, in my opinion, argueth a little abjection of spirit, as his former letter to the Prince did of profaneness; wherein he hoped, that as the Father was his Creator, the Son will be his Redeemer. I write not this to derogate from the noble worth of the Lord Viscount *Verulam*, who was a rare man, a man *reconditæ scientiæ, & ad salutem literarum natus;* and I think the eloquentest that was born in this isle. They say he shall be the last Lord Chancellor, as Sir *Edward Coke* was the last Lord Chief Justice of *England;* for ever since, they have been termed Lord Chief Justices of the King's-bench, so hereafter they shall be only Keepers of the Great Seal, which for title and office are deposable; but they say the Lord Chancellor's title is indelible.

I was lately at *Grays-Inn* with Sir *Eubule,* and he desired me to remember him unto you, as I do also salute *meum* Prichardum *ex imis* præcordiis, *vale* κεφαλή μοι' προσφιλεσάτη.

Yours most affectionately while,

Lond. Jan. 6. 1625. J. H.

LETTER CIV.

To my Well-beloved Cousin Mr. T. V.

COUSIN,

YOU have a great work in hand; for you write unto me, that you are upon a treaty of marriage; a great work indeed, and a work of such consequence, that it may *make* you or *mar* you: it may make the whole remainder of your life uncouth or comfortable to **you;**

you; for of all civil actions that are incident to man, there is not any that tends more to his infelicity or happiness, therefore, it concerns you not to be over-hasty herein, nor to take the *ball before the bound:* you must be cautious how you thrust your neck into such a yoke, whence you will never have power to withdraw it again, for the *tongue* useth to tie so hard a knot that the *teeth* can never untie; no, not *Alexander*'s sword can cut asunder among us christians. If you are resolved to marry, *chuse where you love, and resolve to love your choice:* let love rather than *lucre,* be your guide in this election, though a concurrence of both be good, yet for my part, I had rather the latter should be wanting than the first; the one is the pilot, but the other the ballast of the ship which should carry us to the *harbour* of a happy life. If you are bent to wed, I wish you anothergets wife than *Socrates* had, who when she had scolded him out of doors, as he was going through the portal threw a chamber-pot of stale urine upon his head; whereat the Philosopher having been silent all the while, smilingly said, *I thought after so much thunder we should have rain;* and as I wish you may not light upon such an *Zantippe* (as the wisest men have had ill luck in this kind, as I could instance in two of our most eminent lawyers, *C. B.*) so, I pray that God may deliver you from a wife of such a generation, that *Strowd* our cook here at *Westminster* said his wife was of, who, when (out of a mislike of a preacher) he had on *Sunday* in the afternoon gone out of the church to a tavern, and returning towards the evening pretty well heated, to look to his roast, and his wife falling to read him a loud lesson in so furious a manner, as if she would have basted him instead of the mutton, and amongst other revilings, telling him often, that the *devil,* the *devil* would fetch him, at last he broke out of a long silence, and told her, I prithee good-wife hold thyself content, for I know the devil will do me no hurt, for I have married his kinswoman. If you light upon such a wife, (a wife that hath more bone than flesh) I wish you may have the same measure of pa-

tience

tience that *Socrates* and *Strowd* had, to suffer the *grey--mare* sometimes to be the *better horse*. I remember a *French* proverb:

> *La maison est miserable & meschante*
> *On la poule plus haut que le coc chante.*

That house doth every day more wretched grow,
Where the hen louder than the cock doth crow,

yet we have another *English* proverb almost counter to this, *That it is better to marry a shrew than a sheep:* for, though silence be the dumb orator of beauty, and the best ornament of a woman, yet a phlegmatic dull wife is fulsome and fastidious.

Excuse me cousin, that I jest with you in so serious a business. I know you need no counsel of mine herein, you are discreet enough of yourself; nor do I presume, do you want advice of parents, which by all means must go along with you: so, wishing you all conjugal joy, and a happy *confarreation*, I rest

Your affectionate cousin,

London, Feb. 5. 1625.   J. H.

L E T T E R XCV.

To my noble Lord, the Lord Clifford, *from* London.

My Lord,

THE Duke of *Buckingham* is lately returned from *Holland*, having renewed the peace with the states, and articled with them for a continuation of some naval forces for an expedition against *Spain*; as also, having taken up some monies upon private jewels, (not any of the crown's); and lastly, having comforted the Lady *Elizabeth* for the decease of his late Majesty her father, and of Prince *Frederick* her eldest son, whose disaster-ous manner of death, amongst the rest of her sad afflicti-
ons

ons is not the leaſt: for paſſing over *Harlem Mere*, an huge inland loch, in company of his father who had been in *Amſterdam*, to look how his bank of money did thrive, and coming (for more frugality) in the common boat, which was overſet with merchandize and other paſſengers in a thick fog, the veſſel turned over, and ſo many periſhed; the Prince *Palſgrave* ſaved himſelf by ſwimming, but the young Prince clinging to the maſt and being intangled among the tackling, was half drowned, and half frozen to death: a ſad deſtiny!

There is an open rupture betwixt us and the *Spaniard*, though he gives out, that he never broke with us to this day. Count *Gondomar* was on his way to *Flanders*, and thence to *England* (as they ſay), with a large commiſſion to treat for a ſurrender of the *Palatinate*, and ſo to piece matters together again, but he died in the journey at a place called *Bannol*, of pure apprehenſions of grief, it is given out.

The match betwixt his Majeſty and the Lady *Henrietta Maria*, youngeſt daughter to *Henry the Great*, (the eldeſt being married to the King of *Spain*, and the ſecond to the Duke of *Savoy*) goes roundly on, and is in a manner concluded; whereat the Count of *Soiſſons* is much diſcontented, who gave himſelf hopes to have her, but the hand of heaven hath predeſtined her for a far higher condition.

The *French* ambaſſadors who were ſent hither to conclude the buſineſs, having private audience of his Majeſty a little before his death, he told them pleaſantly, that he would make war againſt the Lady *Henrietta*, becauſe ſhe would not receive the two letters which were ſent her, one from himſelf and the other from his ſon, but ſent them to her mother, yet he thought he ſhould eaſily make peace with her, becauſe he underſtood ſhe had afterwards put the latter letter in her boſom, and the firſt in her cuſhionet; whereby he gathered, that ſhe intended to reſerve his ſon for her affection, and him for counſel.

The

The Bifhop of *Lucon*, now Cardinal *de Richelieu*, is . grown to be the fole favourite of the King of *France*, being brought in by the Queen-mother, he hath been very active in advancing the match ; but 'tis thought the wars will break out afrefh againft them of the religion, notwithftanding the ill fortune the King had before *Montauban* few years fince, where he loft above 500 of his nobles, whereof the Duke of *Main* was one ; and having lain in perfon before the town many months, and received fome affronts, as that infcription upon their gates fhews, *Roy fans foy, ville fans peu*: *A King without faith, a town without fear*, yet he was forced to raze his works and raife his fiege.

The letter which Mr. *Ellis Hicks* brought them of *Montauban* from *Rochel*, through fo much danger, and with fo much gallantry was an infinite advantage unto them ; for whereas, there was a politic report raifed in the King's army and blown to *Montauban*, that *Rochel* was yielded to the Count of *Soiffons* who lay then before her, this letter did inform the contrary, and that *Rochel* was in as good plight as ever ; whereupon, they made a fally the next day upon the King's forces, and did him a great deal of fpoil.

There be fummons out for a parliament, I pray God it may prove more profperous than the former.

I have been lately recommended to the Duke of *Buckingham* by fome noble friends of mine that have in-timacy with him ; about whom, though he hath three Secretaries already, I hope to have fome employment, for I am weary walking up and down fo idly upon *London* ftreets.

The plague begins to rage mightily. God avert his judgments that menace fo great a mortality, and turn not away his face from this poor ifland: fo, I kifs your. Lordfhip's hand in quality of

Your Lordfhip's moft humble fervitor,

London, Feb. 25. 1625.   J. H.

L E T-

LETTER XCVI.

To the Right Honourable my Lord of Carlingford, *after Earl of* Carberry, *at* Golden-Grove

My LORD,

WE have gallant news now abroad, for we are sure to have a new Queen before it be long; both the contract and marriage was lately solemnized in *France*, the one the second of this month in the *Louvre*, the other the eleventh day following in the great church of *Paris*, by the Cardinal of *Rochefoucault* : there was some clashing betwixt him and the Archbishop of *Paris*, who alleged it was his duty to officiate in that church; but the dignity of Cardinal and the quality of his office, being the King's great Almoner, which makes him chief Curate of the court, gave him the prerogative. I doubt not but your Lordship hath heard of the capitulations; but for better assurance, I will run them over briefly.

The King of *France* obliged himself to procure the dispensation; the marriage should be celebrated in the same form as that of Queen *Margaret*, and of the Dutchess of *Bar ;* her dowry should be 800,000 crowns, six shillings a-piece, the one moiety to be paid the day of the contract, the other twelve months after. The Queen shall have a chapel in all the King's royal houses, and any where else, where she shall reside within the dominions of his Majesty of *Great Britain*, with free exercise of the *Roman* religion, for herself, her officers, and all her houshold, for the celebration of the *mass*, the predication of the word, administration of the sacraments, and power to procure indulgences from the holy father. To this end she shall be allowed twenty-eight priests, or ecclesiastics in her house, and a Bishop in quality of Almoner, who shall have jurisdiction over all the rest; and that none of the King's officers shall have power over them, unless in case of treason; therefore all her ecclesiastics shall take the oath of fidelity to his Majesty of
Great

Great Britain : there fhall be a cemetery or church-yard clofed about to bury thofe of her family. That in confideration of this marriage all *Englifh* catholics, as well ecclefiaftics as lay, who fhall be in any prifon merely for religion, fince the laft edict, fhall be fet at liberty.

This is the eighth alliance we have had with *France* fince the conqueft ; and as it is the beft that could be made, in *chriftendom*, fo I hope it will prove the happieft. So, I kifs your hand, being

Your Lordfhip's moft humble fervant,

London, *March* 1. 1625.   J. H.

LETTER XCVII.

To the Honourable Sir THOMAS SAVAGE.

SIR,

I Converfed lately with a gentleman that came from *France*, who among other things difcourfed much of the favourite *Richelieu*, who is like to be an active man, and hath great defigns. The two firft things he did, was to make fure of *England* and the *Hollander :* he thinks to have us fafe enough by this marriage ; and *Holland,* by a late league, which was bought with a great fum of money ; for he hath furnifhed the States with 1,000000 of livres, at two fhillings a-piece in prefent, and 600,000 livres every year of thefe two that are to come, provided that the States repay thefe fums two years after they are in peace or truce. The King preffed much for liberty of confcience to *Roman catholics* among them, and the deputies promifed to do all they could with the States General about it ; they articled likewife for the *French* to be affociated with them in the trade to the *Indies*.

Monfieur is lately married to *Mary* of *Bourbon,* the Duke of *Montpenfier's* daughter ; he told her, *that he would be a better husband, than he had been a fuitor to her,* for he hung off a good while. This marriage was

made

made up by the King, and Monfieur hath for his appenage 100,000 livres annual rent from *Chartres* and *Blois*, 100,000 livres penfion, and 500,000 to be charged yearly upon the general receipts of *Orleans*, in all about 70,000 pounds. There was much ado before this match could be brought about ; for there were many oppofers, and there be dark whifpers, that there was a deep plot to confine the King to a monaftery, and that Monfieur fhould govern, and divers great ones have fuffered for it, and more are like to be difcovered. So, I take my leave for the prefent, and reft

Your very humble and ready fervant,

London, *March* 10. 1626.   J. H.

LETTER XCVIII.

To the Right Honourable, the Lord Clifford.

My LORD,

I Pray be pleafed to difpenfe with this flownefs of mine, in anfwering yours of the firft of this prefent.

Touching the domeftic occurrences, the gentleman who is bearer hereof, is more capable to give you account by *difcourfe* than I can in *paper*.

For foreign tidings, your Lordfhip may underftand, that the town of *Breda* hath been a good while making her laft will and teftament ; but now there is certain news come, that fhe hath yielded up the ghoft to *Spinola's* hands after a tough fiege of thirteen months, and a circumvallation of near upon twenty miles compafs.

My Lord *Southampton* and his eldeft fon fickened at the fiege, and died at *Berghen ;* the adventurous Earl *Henry* of *Oxford*, feeming to tax the Prince of *Orange* of flacknefs to fight, was fet upon a defperate work, where he melted his greafe, and fo being carried to the *Hague*, he died alfo. I doubt not but you have heard of Grave *Maurice's* death, which happened when the town was

R   paft

paſt cure ; which was his more than the the States : for
he was Marquis of *Breda*, and had near upon 30,000
dollars annual rent from her ; therefore he ſeemed in
a kind of ſympathy to ſicken with his town, and died
before her.   He had provided plentifully for his natural
children, but could not, though much importuned by
Dr. *Roſcus*, and other divines upon his death-bed, be
induced to make them legitimate by marrying the mother
of them : for the law there is, that if one hath got
children of any woman, though unmarried to her, yet if
he marry her never ſo little before his death, he makes
her honeſt, and them all legitimate.   But it ſeems the
Prince poſtponed the love he bore to this woman and
children, to that which he bore to his brother *Henry ;*
for had he made the children legitimate, it had prejudiced the brother in point of command and fortune ; yet,
he had provided plentifully for them and the mother.

Grave *Henry* hath ſucceeded him in all things, and is
a gallant gentleman, of a *French* education and temper :
he charged him at his death to marry a young Lady, the
Count of *Solme*'s daughter attending the Queen of *Bohemia*, whom he had long courted ; which is thought will
take ſpeedy effect.

When the ſiege before *Breda* had grown hot, Sir *Edward Vere* being one day attending Prince *Maurice*,
he pointed at a riſing place called *Terhay*, where the
enemy had built a fort, (which might have been prevented). Sir *Edward* told him, he feared that fort would be
the cauſe of the loſs of the town : the *Grave* ſputtered
and ſhook his head, ſaying, it was the greateſt error he
had committed ſince he knew what belonged to a ſoldier ;
as alſo, in managing the plot for ſurprizing the citadel of
Antwerp ; for he repented that he had not employed
Engliſh and *French* in lieu of the ſlow *Dutch*, who aimed
to have the ſole honour of it, and were not ſo fit inſtruments for ſuch a nimble piece of ſervice.   As ſoon as Sir
Charles Morgan gave up the town, *Spinola* cauſed a new
gate to be erected, with this inſcription in great golden
characters.

Philippo

Philippo *quarto regnante,*
Clarâ Eugreniâ Ifabellâ *gubernante,*
Ambrofio Spinolâ *obfidente,*
Quatuor regibus contra conantibus,
Breda *capta fuit idibus, &c.*

It is thought *Spinola* now, that he hath recovered
the honour he had loft before *Berghen-op-zoom* three
years fince, will not long ftay in *Flanders,* but retire.
No more now, but that I am refolved to continue ever

   Your Lordfhip's moft humble fervant

London, March 19. 1626.   J. H.

LETTER XCIX.

To Dr. FIELD, *Lord Bifhop of* Landaff.

My LORD,

I Send you my humble thanks for thofe worthy hofpitable favours you were pleafed to give me at your
lodgings at *Weftminfter.* I had yours of the fifteenth
of this prefent, by the hand of Mr. *Jonathan Field.*
The news which fills every corner of the town at this
time is the forry and unfuccefsful return that *Wimbledon's*
fleet hath made from *Spain.* It was a fleet that deferved
to have had a better deftiny, confidering the ftrength of it,
and the huge charge the crown was at : for, befides a
fquadron of fixteen *Hollanders,* whereof Count *William,*
one of Prince *Maurice's* natural fons was Admiral, there
were above eighty of ours, the greateft joint naval power
(of fhips without gallies) that ever fpread fail upon
falt-water ; which makes the world abroad to ftand a-
ftonifhed how fo huge a fleet could be fo fuddenly
made ready. The finking of the *Long Robin* with 176
fouls in her, in the bay of *Bifcay,* before fhe had gone
half the voyage, was no good augury ; and the critics
of the time fay, there were many other things that pro-

mifed

mifed no good fortune to this fleet; befides, they would
point at divers errors committed in the conduct of the
main defign: firft, the odd choice that was made of the
Admiral, who was a mere landman; which made the fea-
men much flight him; it belonging properly to Sir *Robert
Manfel*, Vice-Admiral of *England*, to have gone in cafe
the High-Admiral went not. Then they fpeak of the
uncertainty of the enterprize, and that no place was
pitched upon to be invaded, till they came to the height
of the South Cape, and in fight of fhore; where the Lord
Wimbledon firft called a council of war, wherein fome
would be for *Malaga*, others for *St. Mary-Port*, o-
thers for *Gibralter*, but moft for *Cales*; and while they
were thus confulting, the country had an alarm given
them.   Add hereunto the blazing abroad of this expedition before the fleet went out of the *Downs*; for
Mercurius Gallobelgicus had it in print, that it was for
the Streights-mouth. *Now it is a rule, that great defigns
of ftate fhould be myfteries till they come to the very act
of performance, and then they fhould turn to exploits.*
Moreover, when the local attempt was refolved on, there
were feven fhips (by the advice of one Capt. *Love*) fuffered to go up the river, which might have been eafily taken;
and being rich, it is thought they would have defrayed
well near the charge of our fleet; which fhips did much
infeft us afterwards with their ordnance, when we had
taken the fort of *Pontall.*   Moreover, the diforderly
carriage and excefs of our landmen (whereof there were
10,000) when they were put afhore, who broke into
the friers caves, and other cellars of fweet wines, where
many hundreds of them being furprized, and found dead
drunk, the *Spaniards* came and tore off their ears and
nofes, and plucked out their eyes; and I was told of one
merry fellow efcaping, that killed an afs for a buck.
Laftly, it is laid to the Admiral's charge, that my Lord *de
la Ware*'s fhip being infected, he fhould give orders that the
fick men fhould be fcattered into divers fhips; which difperfed the contagion exceedingly, fo that fome thoufands
died before the fleet returned, which was done in a confufed

fufed manner, without any obfervance of fea orders, yet I do not hear of any that will be punifhed for thefe mif-carriages, which will make the difhonour fall more foully upon the State; but the moft unfortunate paffage of all was, that though we did nothing by land that was con-fiderable, yet, if we had ftaid but a day or two longer, and fpent time at fea, the whole fleet of galleons from *Nova Hifpania* had fallen into our mouths, which came prefently in, clofe along the coaft of *Barbary;* and in all likelihood we might have had the opportunity to have taken the ticheft prize that ever was taken on falt-water. Add hereunto, that while we were thus mafters of thofe feas, a fleet of fifty fail of *Brafil* men got fafe into *Lisbon,* with four of the richeft *Caracks* that ever came from the *Eaft-Indies.*

I hear that my Lord *St. David*'s is to be remo-ved to *Bath* and *Wells,* and it were worth your Lordfhip's coming up to endeavour the fucceeding of him. So, I humbly reft

Your Lordfhip's moft ready fervant,

London, Nov. 20. 1626.   J. H.

LETTER C.

To my Lord Duke of Buckingham's *Grace, at New-Market.*

MAY it pleafe your Grace to perufe and pardon thefe few advertifements, which I would not dare to prefent, had I not hopes that the goodnefs which is concomitant with your greatnefs, would make them venial.

My Lord, a parliament is at hand; the laft was *boifte-rous,* God grant that this may prove more calm: a rumor runs that there are clouds already ingendered, which will break out into a ftorm in the *lower region,* and moft of the drops are like to fall upon your Grace. This, though

it

it be but vulgar aftrology, is not altogether to be contemned, though I believe that his Majefty's countenance
reflecting fo ftrongly upon your Grace with the bright-
nefs of your own innocency, may be able to difpel and
fcatter them to nothing.

My Lord, you are a great Prince, and all eyes are
upon your actions: this makes you more fubject to envy;
which like the fun-beams beats always upon rifing grounds.
I know your Grace hath many fage and folid heads, a-
bout you, yet I truft it will prove no offence, if out of
the late relation I have to your Grace, by the recommen-
dation of fuch noble perfonages, I put in alfo my mite.

My Lord, under favour, it were not amifs if your
Grace would be pleafed to part with fome of thofe places
you hold which have leaft relation to the court, and it
would take away the mutterings that run of multiplicity
of offices, and in my fhallow apprehenfion your Grace
might ftand more firm without an *anchor.* The office of
High-Admiral in thefe times of action requires one whole
man to execute it: your Grace hath another fea of bufinefs to wade through, and the voluntary refigning of this
office would fill all men, yea even your enemies, with
admiration and affection, and make you more a Prince,
than detract from your greatnefs. If any ill fucceffes
happen at fea, (as that of the Lord *Wimbledon*'s lately)
or if there be any murmurs for pay, your Grace will be
free from all imputation, befides, it will afford your
Grace more leifure to look into your own affairs, which
ly confufed and unfettled. Laftly, (which is not the
leaft thing) this act will be fo plaufible, that it may much
advantage his Majefty in point of fubfidy.

Secondly, it were expedient. (under correction) that
your Grace would be pleafed to allot fome fet hours
for audience and accefs of fuitors; and it would be
lefs cumber to yourfelf and your fervants, and give more
content to the world, which often mutters for difficulty
of accefs.

Laftly, it were not amifs that your Grace would fettle
a ftanding manfion-houfe and family, that fuitors may
know

know whither to repair conftantly; and that your fervants, every one in his place might know what belongs
to his place, and attend accordingly: for, though confufion in a great family carry a kind of a ftate with it, yet
order and regularity gains a greater opinion of virtue
and wifdom. I know your Grace doth not (nor needs
not) affect popularity: it is true, that the peoples love is
the ftrongeft citadel of a fovereign Prince, but to a great
fubject, it hath often proved fatal; for he who pulleth
off his *hat* to the people giveth his *head* to the Prince:
and it is remarkable what was faid of a late unfortunate
Earl, who a little before Queen *Elizabeth*'s death, had
drawn the ax upon his own neck, *That he was grown
fo popular, that he was too dangerous for the times, and
the times for him.*

My Lord, now that your Grace is threatened to be
heaved at, it fhould behove every one that oweth you
duty and good-will, to reach out his hand fome way or
other to ferve you: amongft thefe, I am one that pre-
fumes to do it in this poor impertinent paper; for which,
I implore pardon, becaufe I am

Your Grace's moft humble and faithful fervant,
London, Feb. 18. 1626. J. H.

L E T T E R CI.

To the Right Honourable the Earl R.

My LORD,

ACCORDING to promife, and that portion of o-
bedience I owe to your commands, I fend your
Lordfhip thefe few avifos, fome whereof I doubt not but
you have received before, and that by abler pens than
mine, yet your Lordfhip may happily find herein fomething which was omitted by others, or the former news
made clearer by circumftances.

I

I hear Count *Mansfelt* is in *Paris*, having now received three routings in *Germany*; 'tis thought the *French* King will piece him up again with new recruits. I was told, that as he was feeing the two queens one day at dinner, the Queen-mother faid, they fay, Count *Mansfelt* is here amongst this croud; I do not believe it quoth the Queen, for whensoever he feeth a *Spaniard* he runs away.

Matters go on untowardly on our fide in *Germany*, but the King of *Denmark* will be shortly in the field in perfon; and *Bethlem Gabor* hath been long expected to do fomething, but fome think he will prove but a bugbear. Sir *Charles Morgan* is to go to *Germany* with 6000 auxiliaries to join with the *Danish* army.

The parliament is adjourned to *Oxford*, by reafon of the ficknefs which increafeth exceedingly, and before the King went out of the town there died 1500 that very week, and two out of *Whitehall* itfelf.

There is high clafhing again betwixt my Lord Duke and the Earl of *Briftol*, they recriminate one another of divers things: the Earl accufeth him amongst other matters, of certain letters from *Rome*, of putting his Majefty upon that hazardous journey to *Spain*, and of fome mifcarriages at his being in that court: there be articles alfo againft Lord *Conway*, which I fend your Lordfhip here inclofed.

I am for *Oxford* the next week, and thence for *Wales*, to fetch my good old father's bleffing: at my return, if it fhall pleafe God to reprieve me in thefe dangerous times of contagion, I fhall continue my wonted fervice to your Lordfhip, if it may be done with fafety: fo, I reft

Your Lordfhip's moft humble fervitor,

Lond. March 15. 1626.   J. H.

LET-

L E T T E R CII.

To the Honourable the Lord Viscount C.

My Lord,

SIR *John North* delivered me one lately from your Lordship, and I send my humble thanks for the venison you intend me. I acquainted your Lordship as opportunity served, with the nimble pace the *French* match went on by the successful negotiation of the earls of *Carlisle*, and *Holland*, (who outwent the monsieurs themselves in courtship) and how in less than nine *moons* this great business was proposed, pursued and perfected; whereas the *sun* had leisure enough to finish his annual progress, from one end of the *Zodiac* to the other so many years, before that of *Spain* could come to any shape of perfection. This may serve to shew the difference betwixt the two nations, the *leaden-heeled* pace of the one, and the *quick-silvered* motions of the other. It shews also how the *French* is more generous in his proceedings, and not so full of scruples, reservations, and jealousies as the *Spaniard*, but deals more frankly, and with a greater confidence and gallantry.

The Lord Duke of *Buckingham* is now in *Paris* accompanied with the Earl of *Montgomery*, and he went in a very splendid equipage. The *Venetian* and *Hollander* with other states that are no friends to *Spain*, did some good offices to advance this alliance; and the new Pope propounded much towards it, but *Richelieu* the new favourite of *France* was the cardinal instrument in it.

This Pope *Urban* grows very active, not only in things present, but ripping up of old matters, for which there is a select committee appointed to examine accounts and errors past, not only in the time of his immediate predecessors, but others. And one told me of a merry pasquil lately in *Rome;* that whereas there are two great statues, one of *Peter*, the other of *Paul*, opposite one to the other upon a bridge, one had clapt a pair of spurs upon

upon St. *Peter*'s heels, and St. *Paul* afking him whither
he was bound, he anfwered, I apprehend fome danger
to ftay now in *Rome*, becaufe of this new commiffion,
for, I fear they will queftion me for denying my mafter.
Truly brother *Peter*, I fhall not ftay long after you, for I
have as much caufe to doubt that they will queftion me
for perfecuting the chriftians before I was converted. So,
I take my leave, and reft

Your Lordfhip's moft humble fervitor,
Lond. March 3. 1626.   J. H.

L E T T E R CIII.

To my Brother Mr. H U G H P E N R Y.

S I R,

I Thank you for your late letter, and the feveral good
tidings fent me from *Wales:* in requital, I can fend
you gallant news, for we have now a moft noble new
Queen of *England*, who in true beauty is beyond the
long wooed *Infanta:* for fhe was of a fading flaxen hair,
big lipped, and fomewhat heavy eyed; but this daughter
of *France*, this youngeft branch of *Bourbon* (being but
in her cradle when the great *Henry* her father was put
out of the world) is of a more lovely and lafting complexion, a dark brown; fhe hath eyes that fparkle like
ftars, and for her phyfiognomy fhe may be faid to be a
mirrour of perfection. She had a rough paffage in her
transfretation to *Dover* caftle; and in *Canterbury* the
King bedded firft with her: there were a goodly train of
choice ladies attended her coming upon the bowling-green
on *Barram* downs upon the way, who divided themfelves
into two rows, and they appeared like fo many conftellations; but, methought that the country ladies outfhined
the courtiers. She brought over with her 400,000
crowns in gold and filver, as half her portion, and the
other moiety is to be paid at the year's end. Her firft
                                                     fuit

fuit of fervants (by article) are to be *French*, and as they die *English* are to fucceed: fhe is alfo allowed twenty eight ecclefiaftics of any order except jefuits; a Bifhop for her Almoner, and to have private exercife of her religion.for her and her fervants.

I pray convey the inclofed to my father by the next convenience, and pray prefent my dear love to my fifter. I hope to fee you at *Dyvinnock* about *Michaelmas*, for I intend to wait upon my father, and take my mother in the way; I mean *Oxford*. In the interim, I reft

Your moft affectionate brother,

Lond. May 16. 1626.　　　　　　　　J. H.

LETTER CIV.

To my Uncle Sir SACKVILE TREVOR, *from* Oxford.

SIR,

I Am forry I muft write unto you the fad tidings of the diffolution of the parliament here; which was done fuddenly. Sir *John Elliot* was in the heat of a high fpeech againft the Duke of *Buckingham*, when the Ufher of the black-rod knocked at the door, and fignified the King's pleafure; which ftruck a kind of confternation in all the houfe. My Lord Keeper *Williams* hath parted with the broad-feal, becaufe as fome fay, he went about to cut down the fcale, by which he rofe, for fome it feems did ill offices betwixt the Duke and him. Sir *Thomas Coventry* hath it now: I pray God he be tender of the King's *confcience*, whereof he is keeper, rather than of the *feal*.

I am bound to-morrow upon a journey towards the mountains to fee fome friends in *Wales*, and to bring back my father's bleffing. For better affurance of lodging where I pafs, in regard of the plague, I have a poft warrant as far as St. *David's*; which is far enough you will fay, for the King hath no ground further on this

ifland.

ⁱſland. If the ſickneſs rage in ſuch extremity at *London*, the term will be held at *Reading*.

All your friends here are well, but many look blank becauſe of this ſudden rupture of the parliament. God almighty turn all to the beſt, and ſtay the fury of this contagion, and preſerve us from further judgment: ſo, I reſt

Your moſt affectionate nephew,
Oxford, Auguſt 6. 1626.　　　　　　　J. H.

LETTER CV.

To my FATHER, *from* London.

S I R,

I Was the fourth time at a dead ſtand in the courſe of my fortunes : for though I was recommended to the Duke, and received many noble reſpects from him, yet I was told by ſome who are neareſt him, that ſome body hath done me ill offices, by whiſpering in his ear I was too much *Digbyfied;* and ſo, they told me poſitively that I muſt never expect any employment about him of truſt. While I was in this ſuſpence, Maſter Secretary *Conway* ſent for me, and propoſed unto me that the King had occaſion to ſend a gentleman to *Italy*, in nature of a moving Agent, and though he might have choice of perſons of good quality that would undertake this employment, yet notwithſtanding, hearing of my breeding, he made the firſt proffer unto me, and that I ſhould go as the King's ſervant, and have allowance accordingly. I humbly thanked him for the good opinion he pleaſed to conceive of me being a ſtranger to him, and deſired ſome time to conſider of the propoſition, and of the nature of the employment; ſo he granted me four days to think upon it, and two of them are paſt already. If I may have a ſupport accordingly, I intend by God's grace (deſiring your conſent and bleſſing to go along) to apply myſelf to this
courſe ;

course; but before I part with *England*, I intend to send you further notice.

The sickness is miraculously decreased in this city and suburbs, for from 5200, which was the greatest number that died in one week, and that was some forty days since, they are now fallen to 300. It was the violentest fit of contagion that ever was for the time in this island, and such as no story can parallel; but the ebb of it was more swift than the tide. My brother is well, and so are all your friends here; for I do not know any of your acquaintance that is dead of this furious infection. Sir *John Walter* asked me lately how you did, and wished me to remember him to you. So, with my love to my brothers and sisters, and the rest of my friends which made so much of me lately in the country, I rest

Your dutiful son,

Lond. August 7. 1626. J. H.

LETTER CVI.

To the Right Honourable the Lord Conway, *principal Secretary of State to his Majesty,* at Hampton-Court.

Right Honourable,

SINCE I last attended your Lordship here, I summoned my thoughts to counsel, and canvased to and fro within myself the business you pleased to impart unto me, for going upon the King's service to *Italy.* I considered therein many particulars: first, the weight of the employment, and what maturity of judgment, discretion, and parts are required in him that will personate such a man: next, the difficulties of it; for one must send sometimes light out of darkness, and like the bee suck honey out of bad, as out of good flowers: thirdly, the danger which the undertaker must converse withal, and which may fall upon him by interception of letters or other cross casualties: lastly, the great expence it will require

S being

being not to remain fedentary in one place as other a-
gents, but to be often in itinerary motion.

Touching the firft, I refer myfelf to your honour's
favourable opinion, and the character which my Lord *S.*
and others fhall give of me: for the fecond, I hope to
overcome it: for the third, I weigh it not, fo that I
may merit of my King and country: for the laft, I crave
leave to deal plainly with your Lordfhip, that I am a
Cadet, and have no other patrimony or fupport but my
breeding, therefore I muft breathe by the employment;
and my Lord, I fhall not be able to perform what fhall
be expected at my hands under 100 *l.* a quarter, and to
have bills of credit according. Upon thefe terms, my
Lord, I fhall apply myfelf to this fervice, and by God's
bleffing hope to anfwer all expectations. So, referring
the premiffes to your noble confideration, I reft

My Lord, your very humble and ready fervitor,

London, Sept. 8. 1626. **J. H.**

LETTER CVII.

To my Brother, after Dr. HOWELL, *Bifhop of* Briftol.

My Brother,

NEXT to my father, 'tis fitting you fhould have
cognizance of my affairs and fortunes. You
heard how I was in agitation for an employment in *Italy,*
but my Lord *Conway* demurred upon the falary I propounded: I have now waved this courfe, yet I came off
fairly with my Lord; for, I have a ftable home-employ-
ment proffered me by my Lord *Scroop,* Lord Prefident
of the North, who fent for me lately to *Worcefter-
houfe,* though I never faw him before; and there the
bargain was quickly made, that I fhould go down with
him to *York* for Secretary; and his Lordfhip hath promifed me fairly. I will fee you at your houfe in *Horfley*

before

before I go, and leave the particular circumſtances of this busineſs till then.

The *French* that came over with her Majeſty, for their petulancy and ſome miſdemeanors, and impoſing ſome odd penances upon the Queen, are all caſhired this week, about the matter of ſixſcore; whereof the Biſhop of *Mende* was one, who had *ſtood* to be Steward of her Majeſty's courts; which office my Lord of *Holland* hath. It was a thing ſuddenly done; for about one o'clock as they were at dinner, my Lord *Conway* and Sir *Thomas Edmonds* came with an order from the King, that they muſt inſtantly away to *Somerſet-houſe*, for there were barges and coaches ſtaying for them; and there they ſhould have all their wages paid them to a penny, and they muſt be content to quit the kingdom. This ſudden undreamed of order ſtruck an aſtoniſhment into them all, both men and women; and running to complain to the Queen, his Majeſty had taken her before into his bed-chamber, and locked the doors upon them, until he had told her how matters ſtood: the Queen fell into a vio-lent paſſion, broke the glaſs-windows, and tore her hair, but ſhe was calmed afterwards. Juſt ſuch a deſtiny hap-pened in *France* ſome years ſince to the Queen's *Spaniſh* ſervants there, who were all diſmiſſed in like manner for ſome miſcarriages: the like was done in *Spain* to the *French*, therefore 'tis no new thing.

They are all now on their way to *Dover*, but I fear this will breed ill blood betwixt us and *France*, and may break out into an ill-favoured quarrel.

Mr. *Montague* is preparing to go to *Paris* as a meſ-ſenger of honour, to prepoſſeſs the King and council there with the truth of things So, with my very kind reſpects to my ſiſter, I reſt

Your loving brother,

London, *March* 15. 1626.   J. H.

LETTER CVIII.

To the Right Honourable the Lord S.

My LORD,

I Am bound shortly for *York*, where I am hopeful of a profitable employment. There is fearful news from *Germany*, that since Sir *Charles Morgan* went thither with 6000 men for the assistance of the King of *Denmark*, the King hath received an utter overthrow by *Tilly*: he had received a fall off a horse from a wall five yards high a little before, yet it did him little hurt.

Tilly pursueth his victory strongly, and is got over the *Elve* to *Holsteinland*, insomuch, that they write from *Hamburgh*, that *Denmark* is in danger to be utterly lost. The *Danes* and *Germans* seem to lay some fault upon our King, the King upon the parliament, that would not supply him with subsidies to assist his uncle, and Prince *Palsgrave*, both which was promised upon the rupture of the treaties with *Spain;* which was done by the advice of both houses.

This is the ground that his Majesty hath lately sent out privy-seals for loan monies, until a parliament be called, in regard that the King of *Denmark* is distressed, the *Sound* like to be lost, the *Eastland* trade and the staple at *Hamburgh* like to be destroyed, and the *English* garrison under Sir *Charles Morgan* at *Stoad* ready to be starved.

These loan monies keep a great noise, and they are imprisoned that deny to conform themselves.

I fear I shall have no more opportunity to send to your Lordship till I go to *York*, therefore I humbly take my leave, and kiss your hands, being ever,

> My Lord,
>
> *Your obedient and ready servitor,*
>
> J. H.

LET-

LETTER CIX.

To Mr. R. L. Merchant.

I Met lately with *J. Harris* in *London*, and I had not seen him two years before; and then I took him, and knew him to be a man of thirty, but now one would take him by his hair to be near threefcore, for he is all turned gray. I wondered at fuch a metamorphofis in fo fhort a time: he told me, 'twas for the death of his wife that nature had thus antedated his years. 'Tis true, that a weighty fettled forrow is of that force, that befides the contraction of the fpirits it will work upon the radical moifture, and dry it up, fo that the hair can have no moifture at the root. This made me remember a ftory that a *Spanifh* Advocate told me, which is a thing very remarkable.

When the Duke of *Alva* was in *Bruffels*, about the beginning of the tumults in the *Netherlands*, he had fat down before *Hulft* in *Flanders*, and there was a provoft - marfhal in his army who was a favourite of his; and this provoft had put fome to death by fecret commiffion from the Duke. There was one Captain *Bolea* in the army, who was an intimate friend of the provoft's; and one evening late, he went to the faid Captain's tent, and brought with him a *confeffor* and an *executioner*, as it was his cuftom, he told the Captain, that he came to execute his Excellency's commiffion and martial law upon him: the Captain ftarted up fuddenly, his hair ftanding at an end, and being ftruck with amazement afked him where-in he had offended the Duke: the provoft anfwered, Sir, I come not to expoftulate the bufinefs with you, but to execute my commiffion, therefore, I pray prepare your-felf, for there is your *ghoftly father* and *executioner*, fo he fell on his knees before the prieft, and having done, the *hangman* going to put the halter about his neck, the provoft threw it away, and breaking into a laughter, told him, there was no fuch thing, and that he had done this

to try his courage how he could bear the terror of
death.   The Captain looked ghaſtly upon him, and
ſaid, then ſir get you out of my tent, for you have done
me a very ill office.   The next morning the ſaid Captain *Bolea*, though a young man of about thirty had his
hair all turned gray, to the admiration of all the world,
and of the Duke of *Alva* himſelf, who queſtioned him
about it, but he would confeſs nothing.   The next year
the Duke was revoked, and in his journey to the court
of *Spain* he was to paſs by *Saragoſſa*, and this Captain
Bolea and the provoſt went along with him as his do-
meſtics.   The Duke being to repoſe ſome days in *Sara-*
goſa, the young old Captain *Bolea*, told him that there
was a thing in that town worthy to be ſeen by his Excellency; which was a *caſa de locos*, a bedlam-houſe, for
there was not the like in chriſtendom: well ſaid the
Duke, go and tell the *warden* I will be there to-morrow
in the afternoon, and wiſh him to be in the way.   The
Captain having obtained this, went to the *warden* and
told him, that the Duke would come to viſit the houſe
the next day; and the chiefeſt occaſion that moved him
to it, was, that he had an unruly provoſt about him,
who was ſubject oftentimes to fits of frenzy, and becauſe
he wiſhed him well, he had tried divers means to cure
him, but all would not do, therefore he would try whether keeping him cloſe in bedlam ſome days would do
him any good.   The next day the Duke came with a
ruffling train of captains after him; amongſt whom was
the ſaid provoſt, very ſhinning brave, being entered int
the houſe about the Duke's perſon, Captain *Bolea* tol
the *warden*, pointing at the provoſt, that's the man; ſ
he took him aſide into a dark lobby, where he had pla
ced ſome of his men, who muffled him in his cloak, ſeize
upon his gilt ſword with his hat and feather, and ſo hur
ried him down into a dungeon.   My provoſt had lain
there two nights and a day; and afterward, it happene
that a gentleman coming out of curioſity to ſee the houſe
peeped in at a ſmall grate where the provoſt was; th
provoſt conjured him as he was a chriſtian, to go an
te

tell the Duke of *Alva* his provoſt was there clapped up,
nor could he imagine why. The gentleman did the errand, whereat the Duke being aſtoniſhed, ſent for the
warden with his priſoner; ſo he brought my provoſt *en
cuerpo,* madman like, full of ſtraws and feathers before
the Duke, who at the firſt ſight of him, breaking out into laughter, aſked the *warden* why he made him his
priſoner, Sir, ſaid the *warden,* it was by virtue of your
Excellency's commiſſion brought me by Captain *Bolea.*
Bolea ſtept forth and told the Duke, Sir, you have aſked
me oft how theſe hairs of mine grew ſo ſuddenly gray?
I have not revealed it yet to any ſoul breathing, but now
I will tell your Excellency; and ſo fell a relating the
paſſage in *Flanders.* And Sir, I have been ever ſince
beating my brains how to get an equal revenge of him;
and, I thought no revenge to be more equal or corre-
ſponding, now that you ſee he hath made me old before
my time, than to make him mad if I could; and had he
ſtaid ſome days longer cloſe priſoner in the bedlam-houſe,
it might happily have wrought ſome impreſſions upon his
pericranium. The Duke was ſo well pleaſed with the
ſtory and the wittineſs of the revenge, that he made
them both friends; and the gentleman that told me this
paſſage, ſaid, that the ſaid Captain *Bolea* was yet alive,
ſo that he could not be leſs than ninety years of age.

I thank you a thouſand times for the *Cephalonia Muſ-
cadel* and *Botargo* you ſent me. I hope to be ſhortly
quit with you for all courteſies: in the interim, I am

Your obliged friend to ſerve you,

York, May 1. 1626. J. H.

P. S. I am ſorry to hear of the trick that Sir *John
Ayrs* put upon the company by the box of *Hailſhot,*
ſigned with the Ambaſſador's ſeal, that he had ſent ſo
ſolemnly from *Conſtantinople;* which, he made the world
believe to be full of *Chequins* and *Turky* gold.

L E T-

LETTER CX.

To Sir EDWARD SAVAGE, *Knight.*

SIR, It was no great matter to be a prophet, and to have foretold this rupture between us and *France* upon the sudden *renvoy* of her Majesty's servants; for many of them had 'sold their estates in *France*, given money for their places, and so thought to live and die in *England* in the Queen's service, and so have pitifully complained to that King; thereupon he hath arrested above 100 of our merchant-men that went to the vintage at *Bourdeaux*. We also take some stragglers of theirs, for there are letters of mart given on both sides.

There are writs issued out for a parliament, and the town of *Richmond* in *Richmondshire* hath made choice of me for their burgess, though Mr. *Christopher Wandesford*, and other powerful men, and more deserving than I, stood for it. I pray God send me fair weather in the house of commons, for there is much murmuring about the restraint of those that would not conform to *loan monies*. There is a great fleet preparing, and an army of landmen; but the design is uncertain, whether it be against *Spain* or *France*, for we are now in enmity with both those crowns. The *French* Cardinal hath been lately the other side the *Alps*, and settled the Duke of *Nevers* in the Dutchy of *Mantua*, notwithstanding the opposition of the King of *Spain* and the Emperor, who alledged, that he was to receive his investiture from him, and that was the chief ground of the war; but the *French* arms hath done the work, and come triumphantly back over the hills again. No more now, but that I am, as always

Your true friend,

March, 2. 1627.   J. H.

L E T T E R CXI.

To the Worshipful Mr. Alderman of the Town of
Richmond, *and the rest of the worthy Members of*
that antient Corporation.

S I R,

I Received a public inftrument from you lately, fub-
fcribed by yourfelf and divers others; wherein I find
that you have made choice of me to be one of your bur-
geffes for this now near approaching parliament. I
could have wifhed that you had not put by Mr. *Wandef-*
ford, and other worthy gentlemen that ftood fo earneftly
for it, who being your neighbours, had better means
and more abilities to ferve you. Yet, fince you have
caft thefe high refpects upon me, I will endeavour to acquit myfelf of the truft, and to anfwer your expectations
accordingly; and as I account this election an honour unto me, fo I efteem it a great advantage, that fo worthy
and well experienced a Knight as Sir *Talbot Bows* is to
be my collegue and fellow-burgefs. I fhall fteer by his
compafs, and follow his directions in any thing that may
conduce to the further benefit and advantage thereof;
and this I take to be the true duty of a parliamentary
burgefs, without roving at random to generals. I hope
to learn of Sir *Talbot* what is fitting to be done, and I
fhall apply myfelf accordingly to join with him to ferve
you with my beft abilities: fo, I reft

Your moft affectionate and ready friend to ferve you,

London, *March* 24. 1627. J. H.

L E T T E R CXII.

To the Right Hon. the Lord Clifford, *at* Knafbrugh.

My LORD,

THE news that fills all our mouths at prefent, is
the return of the Duke of *Buckingham* from the
ifle of *Ree,* or as fome call it, the ifle of *Rue,* for the
bitter

bitter fuccefs we had there: for we had but a tart entertainment in that *falt* ifland. Our firft invafion was mag-
nanimous and brave; whereat, near upon 200 *French*
gentlemen perifhed, and divers barons of quality. My
Lord *Newport* had ill luck to diforder our cavalry with
an unruly horfe he had. His brother Sir *Charles Rich*
was flain, and divers more upon the retreat; amongft
others, great Colonel *Gray* fell into a falt-pit, and being
ready to be drowned, he cried out, *Cent mille efcus pour
ma rançon*, a hundred thoufand crowns for my ranfom:
the *Frenchmen* hearing that, preferved him, though he
was not worth a hundred thoufand pence. Another merry paffage a Captain told me, that when they were riffling
the dead bodies of the *French* gentlemen after the firft
invafion, they found that many of them had their miftref-
fes favours tied about their genitories. The *French* do
much glory to have repelled us thus; and they have reafon, for the truth is, they comported themfeves gallantly, yet, they confefs our landing was a notable piece of
courage; and if our retreat had been anfwerable to the
invafion, we had loft no honour at all. A great number
of gentlemen fell on our fide, as Sir *John Heyden*, Sir
Jo. Burrowes, Sir *George Blundel*, Sir *Alexander Bret*,
with divers veteran commanders, who came from the
Netherlands to this fervice.

God fend us better fuccefs the next time, for there is
another fleet preparing to be fent under the command of
the Lord *Denbigh:* fo, I kifs your hand, and am

Your humble fervitor,

London, Sept. 24. 1627. J. H.

LETTER CXIII.

To the Right Honourable the Lord Scroop, *Earl of* Sunderland, *Lord Prefident of the North.*

My LORD,

MY Lord *Denbigh* is returned from attempting to relieve *Rochel*, which is reduced to extreme exigence; and now, the Duke is preparing to go again with as great power as was yet raifed, notwithſtanding that the parliament hath flown higher at him than ever; which makes the people here hardly wiſh any good ſuccefs to the expedition becaufe he is General. The *Spaniard* ſtands at a gaze all this while, hoping that we may do the work, otherwife I think he would find fome way to relieve the town; for there is nothing conduceth more to the uniting and ſtrengthening of the *French* monarchy than the reduction of *Rochel*. The King hath been there long in perfon with his Cardinal, and the ſtupendous works they have raifed by fea and land are beyond belief, as they fay. The fea-works and booms were traced out by Marquis *Spinola*, as he was paſſing that way for *Spain* from *Flanders*.

The parliament is prorogued till *Michaelmas* term: there were five fubfidies granted, the greateſt gifts that ever fubject gave their King at once; and it was in requital that his Majefty paſſed the petition of right, whereby the liberty of the freeborn fubject is fo ſtrongly and clearly vindicated, fo that there is a fair correfpondence like to be betwixt his Majefty and the two houfes. The Duke made a notable fpeech at the council-table in joy hereof: amongſt other paſſages one was, ‘ That here-‘ after his Majefty would pleafe to make the parliament ‘ his favourite, and he to have the honour to remain ſtill ‘ his fervant.’ No more now, but that I continue

Your Lordſhip's moſt dutiful fervant,

London, *Sept.* 25. 1627. J. H.

LET

LETTER CXIV.

To the Right Honourable the Lady Scroop, *Countess of* Sunderland, *from* Stamford.

Madam,

I Lay yeſternight at the poſt-houſe at *Stilton*, and this morning betimes the poſt-malter came to my bed's head, and told me the Duke of *Buckingham* was ſlain: my faith was not then ſtrong enough to believe it, till an hour ago I met in the way with my Lord of *Rutland* (your brother) riding poſt towards *London;* it pleaſed him to alight and ſhew me a letter, wherein there was an exact relation of all the circumſtances of this tragedy.

Upon *Saturday* laſt, which was but next before yeſterday, being *Bartholomew* eve, the Duke did riſe up in a well-diſpoſed humour out of his bed, and cut a caper or two, and being ready, and having been under the barber's hands, (where the murderer had thought to have done the deed, for he was leaning upon the window all the while) he went to breakfaſt attended by a great company of commanders, where Monſieur *Soubize* came unto him, and whiſpered him in the ear that *Rochel* was relieved: the Duke ſeemed to ſlight the news, which made ſome think that *Soubize* went away diſcontented. After breakfaſt the Duke going out, Colonel *Fryer* ſtept before him, and ſtopping him upon ſome buſineſs, one Lieutenant *Felton* being behind, made a thruſt with a common ten-penny knife over *Fryer's* arm at the Duke; which lighted ſo fatally, that he ſlit his heart in two, leaving the knife ſticking in the body. The Duke took out the knife and threw it away, and laying his hand on his ſword, and drawing it half out, ſaid, the villain hath killed me, (meaning as ſome think, Colonel *Fryer*) for there had been ſome difference betwixt them; ſo reeling againſt a chimney he fell down dead. The Dutcheſs being with child, hearing the noiſe below, came in her night-geers from her bed-chamber, which was in an upper-

per-room, to a kind of rail, and thence beheld him wel-
tering in his own blood. *Felton* had loft his hat in the
croud, wherein there was a paper fewed, wherein he
declared, that the reafon which moved him to this act
was no grudge of his own, though he had been far behind for his pay, and had been put by his Captain's place
twice, but in regard he thought the Duke an enemy to
the *State*, becaufe he was branded in parliament, therefore what he did was for the public good of his country.
Yet, he got clearly down, and fo might have gone to his
horfe which was tied to a hedge hard by, but he was fo
amazed that he miffed his way, and fo ftruck into the
paftery, where, though the cry went that fome *Frenchman* had done it, he thinking the word was *Felton*, he
boldly confeffed it was he that had done the deed; and
fo he was in their hands. *Jack Stamford* would have
run at him, but he was kept off by Mr. *Nicholas;* fo being carried up to a tower, Captain *Mince* tore off his
fpurs, and afking how he durft attempt fuch an act, making him believe the Duke was not dead, he anfwered
boldly that he knew he was difpatched, for it was not he,
but the hand of heaven that gave the ftroke, and though
his whole body had been covered over with armour of
proof he could not have avoided it. Captain *Charles
Price* went polt prefently to the King four miles off, who
being at prayers on his knees when it was told him, yet
he never ftirred, nor was he difturbed a whit till all divine fervice was done. This was the relation as far as
my memory could bear, in my Lord of *Rutland*'s letter,
who willed me to remember him unto your Ladyfhip,
and tell that he was going to comfort your niece (the
Dutchefs) as faft as he could; and fo, I have fent the
truth of this fad ftory to your Ladyfhip as faft as I could
by this poft, becaufe I cannot make that fpeed myfelf, in
regard of fome bufinefs I have to difpatch for my Lord
in the way: fo I humbly take my leave, and reft

Your Ladyfhip's moft dutiful fervant,

Stamford, Aug. 5. 1628.   J. H.

T   LET-

LETTER CXV.

To the Right Honourable Sir PETER WICHTS, *his*
Majesty's Ambassador at Conſtantinople.

My LORD,

YOURS of the 2d of *July* came ſafe to hand, and
I did all thoſe particular *recandos* you enjoined me
to do ſome of your friends here.

The town of *Rochel* hath been fatal and unfortunate
to *England*, for this is the third time that we have attempted to relieve her, but our fleets and forces returned without doing any thing. My Lord of *Lindſey* went
thither with the ſame fleet the Duke intended to go on,
but he is returned without doing any good: he made ſome
ſhots at the great boom, and other barricadoes at ſea, but
at ſuch a diſtance that they could do no hurt, inſomuch, that
the town is now given out for loſt, and to be paſt cure;
and they cry out, we have betrayed them. At the return of this fleet, two of the *Whelps* were caſt away, and
three ſhips more, and ſome five ſhips who had ſome of
thoſe great ſtones that were brought to build *Paul*'s, for
ballaſt, and for other uſes within them; which could promiſe no good ſucceſs, for I never heard of any thing that
proſpered which being once deſigned for the honour of
God was alienated from that uſe. The Queen inter-
poſeth for the releaſement of my Lord of *Newport* and
others who are priſoners of war. I hear that all the colours they took from us are hung up in the great church
of *Noſtre Dame*, as trophies in *Paris*. Since I began
this letter, there is news brought that *Rochel* hath yielded, and that the King hath diſmantled the town, and
razed all the fortifications landwards, but leaves thoſe
ſtanding which are toward the ſea. It is a mighty exploit the *French* King hath done, for *Rochel* was the
chiefeſt própugnacle of the proteſtants there; and now,
queſtionleſs all the reſt of their cautionary towns which
they kept for their own defence will yield, ſo that they
muſt

muſt depend upon the King's mere mercy. I hear of an overture of peace betwixt us and *Spain*, and that my Lord *Cottington* is to go thither, and *Don Carlos Coloma* to come to us. God grant it, for you know the ſaying in *Spaniſh*, *Nunca vi tan mala paz, que no fuera mejor, que la mejor guerra.* It was a bold thing in *England*, to fall out with the two greateſt monarchies of *chriſten-dom*, and to have them both her enemies at one time ; and as glorious a thing it was to bear up againſt them. God turn all to the beſt, and diſpoſe of things to his glory : ſo, I reſt

Your Lordſhip's ready ſervitor,

London, Sept. 1. 1628..   J. H.

LETTER CXVI.

To my Couſin Mr. St. Geon,- *at Chriſt-Church Col-lege in* Oxford.

COUSIN, though you want no incitements to go on in that fair road of virtue where you are now running your courſe, yet being lately in your noble fa-ther's company, he did intimate unto me that any thing which came from me would take with you very much. I hear ſo well of your proceedings, that I ſhould rather commend than encourage you. I know you were remo-ved to *Oxford* in full maturity ; you were a good Orator, a good Poet, and good Linguiſt for your time. I would not have that fate light upon you which uſeth to befal ſome, who from golden ſtudents, become ſilver batche-lors, and leaden maſters. I am far from entertaining any ſuch thought of you, that *Logic* with her *quiddities* and *que ca vel hipps*, can any way unpoliſh your human ſtu-dies. As *Logic* is clubfiſted and crabbed, ſo ſhe is ter-rible at firſt ſight ; ſhe is like a *Gorgon's* head to a young ſtudent, but after a twelvemonth's conſtancy and patience, this *Gorgon's* head will prove a mere bugbear : when you have devoured the *Organon*, you will find philoſophy far

T 2   more

more delightful and pleasing to your palate. In feeding the soul with knowledge, the understanding requireth the same consecutive acts which nature useth in nourishing the body. To the nutrition of the body, there are two essential conditions required, *assumption* and *retention;* then there follows two more πίψις and πρᾶψις concoction and agglutination or adhesion: so in feeding your soul with science, you must first assume and suck in the matter into your apprehension, then must the memory retain and keep it in; afterwards by disputation, discourse, and meditation, it must be well concocted; then must it be agglutinated and converted to nutriment. All this may be reduced to these two heads, *tenere fideliter, & uti feliciter;* which are two of the happiest properties in a student. There is another act required to good concoction, called the act of *expulsion,* wich puts off all that is unsound and noxious; so in study, there must be an expulsive virtue to shun all that is erroneous; and there is no science but is full of such stuff, which by direction or tutor, and choice of good books must be excerned. Do not confound yourself with multiplicity of authors, two is enough upon any science, provided they be plenary and orthodox: *Philosphy* should be your substantial food, *poetry* your banquetting-stuff. *Philosophy* hath more of reality in it than any knowledge; the *Philosopher* can fathom the deep, measure the mountains, reach the stars with a staff, and bless heaven with a girdle.

But amongst these studies, you must not forget the *unicam necessarius.* On *Sundays* and holidays, let *divinity* be the sole object of your speculation; in comparison whereof, other knowledge is but cobweb learning; *præqua quisquilia cætera.*

When you can make truce with study, I should be glad you would employ some superfluous hour or other to write unto me, for I much covet your good, because I am

Your affectionate cousin,

London, *Oct.* 25. 1627.   J. H.

L E T T E R CXVII.

To Sir SACKVILE TREVOR, *Knight.*

Noble Uncle,

I Send you my humble thanks for the curious fea-chest of glaffes you pleafed to beftow on me, which I fhall be very chary to keep as a monument of your love. I congratulate alfo the great honour you have got lately by taking away the fpirit of *France*, I mean, by taking the third great veffel of her *Sea-Trinity*, her *Holy Spirit*, which had been built in the mouth of the *Texel* for the fervice of her King. Without complimenting with you, it was one of the beft exploits that was performed fince the wars began; and befides the renown you have purchafed, I hope your reward will be accordingly from his Majefty, whom I remember you fo happily preferved from drowning in all probability at St. *Andera's* road in *Spain*. Though princes guerdons come flow, yet they come fure; and it is oftentimes the method of God almighty himfelf to be long both in his rewards and punifhments.

As you have bereft the *French* of their *Saint Efprit*, their *Holy Spirit*, fo there is news that the *Hollanders* have taken from *Spain* all her faints; I mean *todes los fantos*, which is one of the chiefeft ftaples of fugar in *Brafil*. No more, but that I wifh you all health, honour and heart's defire.

London, Oct. 26. 1625. J. H.

L E T T E R · CXVIII.

To Captain THO. B. *from* York.

NOBLE Captain, yours of the 1ft of *March* was delivered me by Sir *Richard Scot;* and I held it no profanation of this *Sunday* evening, confidering the

T 3 quality

quality of my fubject, and having (I thank God for it)
performed all church-duties, to employ fome hours to
meditate on you, and fend you this friendly falute,
though I confefs in an unufual monitory way. My dear
Captain, I love you perfectly well, I love both your perfon and parts, which are not vulgar: I am in love with
your difpofition which is generous; and I verily think
you were never guilty of any pufillanimous act in your
life: nor is this love of mine conferred upon you *gratis,*
but you may challenge it as your due, and by way of correfpondence, in regard of thofe thoufand convincing evidences you have given me of yours to me; which afcer-
tain me, that you take me for a true friend. Now I am
of the number of thofe that had rather commend the virtue of an enemy than footh the vices of a friend: for
your own particular, if your parts of virtue, and your
infirmities were caft into a balance, I know the firft would
much out-poife the other; yet give me leave to tell you,
that there is one frailty, or rather ill-favoured cuftom
that reigns in you, which weighs much, it is a humour
of *fwearing* in all your difcourfes; and they are not
flight, but deep, far fetched oaths that you are wont to
rap out, which you ufe as flowers of rhetoric to enforce a
faith upon the hearers, who believe you never the more;
and you ufe this in cold blood when you are not provo-
ked, which makes the humour far more dangerous. I
know many, (and I cannot fay I myfelf am free from it,
God forgive me) that being tranfported with choler, and
as it were made drunk with paffion by fome fudden pro-
voking accident, or extreme ill fortune at play, will let
fall oaths and deep proteftations; but to belch out, and
fend forth as it were whole vollies of oaths and curfes in
a calm humour to verify every trivial thing; is a thing
of horror. I knew a King that being croffed in his
game, would amongft his oaths fall on the ground, and
bite the very earth in the rough of his paffion. I heard
of another King (*Henry* IV. of *France*) that in his higheft
diftemper would fwear but *ventre de St. Gris; by the
belly of St. Gris.* I heard of an *Italian,* that having
been

been much accuſtomed to blaſpheme, was weaned from
it by a pretty wile; for having been one night at play, and
loſt all his money, after many execrable oaths, and having offered money to another to go out to deface heaven and defy God, he threw himſelf upon a bed hard
by, and there fell aſleep: the other gameſters played on
ſtill, and finding that he was faſt aſleep, they put out the
candles, and made ſemblance to play on ſtill; they fell a
wrangling, and ſpoke ſo loud that he awaked: he hearing them play on ſtill, fell a rubbing his eyes, and his
conſcience preſently prompted him that he was ſtruck
blind, and that God's judgment had deſervedly fallen
down upon him for his blaſphemies; and ſo he went to
ſigh and weep pitifully: a ghoſtly father was ſent for, who
undertook to do ſome acts of penance for him, if he
would make a vow never to play again or blaſpheme;
which he did, and ſo the candles were lighted again,
which he thought were burning all the while: ſo, he
became a perfect convert. I could wiſh this letter might
produce the ſame effect in you. There is a ſtrong text,
that the curſe of heaven hangs always over the dwelling
of the ſwearer; and you have more fearful examples of
miraculous judgments in this particular, than of any o-
ther ſin.

There is a little town in *Languedoc* in *France*, that
hath a multitude of the pictures of the virgin *Mary* up
and down, but ſhe is made to carry Chriſt in her right-
arm, contrary to the ordinary cuſtom; and the reaſon
they told me was this, that two gameſters being at play,
and one having loſt all his money, and bolted out many
blaſphemies, he gave a deep oath, that that whore upon
the wall, meaning the picture of the bleſſed Virgin, was
the cauſe of his ill luck: hereupon, the child removed
imperceptably from the left-arm to the right, and the
man fell ſtark dumb ever after: thus went the tradition
there. This makes me think upon the Lady *Southwel's*
news from *Utopia*, that he who ſweareth when he playeth
at dice, may challenge his damnation by way of purchaſe.
This infamous cuſtom of ſwearing, I obſerve, reigns in
England

England lately more than anywhere elfe; though a *Ger-man* in the higheft puff of paffion fwear a *hundred thou-fand facraments*, the *Italian* by the life of *God*, the *French* by his *death*, the *Spaniard* by his *flefh*, the *Welfhman* by his *fweat*, the *Irifhman* by his *five wounds;* though the *Scot* commonly bids the *devil hale his foul*, yet for variety of oaths the *Englifh* roarers put down all. Confider well what a dangerous thing it is to tear in pieces that dreadful name which makes the vaft fabric of the world to tremble; that holy name wherein the whole hierarchy of heaven doth triumph; that blifsful name, wherein confifts the fulnefs of all felicity. I know this cuftom in you yet, is but a light *difpofition*, 'tis no habit I hope: let me therefore conjure you by that power of friendfhip, by that holy league of love which is between us, that you would fupprefs it before it come to that; for I muft tell you, that thofe who could find in their hearts to love you for many other things, do difrefpect you for this; they hate your company, and give no credit to whatfoever you fay, it being one of the punifhments of a fwearer as well as of a liar, not to be believed when he fpeaks truth.

Excufe me that I am fo free with you: what I write proceeds from the clear current of a pure affection; and I fhall heartily thank you, and take it for an argument of love, if you tell me of my weakneffes, which are (God wot, too too many; for my body is but a cargazon of corrupt humours, and being not able to overcome them all at once, I do endeavour to do it by degrees, like *Ser-torius*'s foldier, who when he could not cut off the horfe tail with his fword at one blow, fell to pull out the hairs one by one. And touching this particular humour from which I diffuade you, it hath raged in me too often by contingent fits; but I thank God for it, I find it much a-bated and purged. Now the only phyfic I ufed was a precedent faft, and recourfe to the holy facrament the next day, of purpofe to implore pardon for what had paffed, and power for the future to quell thofe exorbi-tant motions, thofe ravings and feverifh fits of the foul,

in

in regard there are no infirmities more dangerous; for at the same instant they have being, they become impieties. And the greatest symptoms of amendment I find in me is, because, whensoever I hear the holy name of God blasphemed by any other, it makes my heart to tremble within my breast. Now it is a penitential rule, *that if sins present do not please thee, sins past will not hurt thee.* All other sins have for their object either pleasure or profit, or some aim and satisfaction to body or mind, but this hath none at all; therefore fy upon it, my dear Captain, try whether you can make a conquest of yourself in subduing this execrable custom. *Alexander* subdued the world, *Cæsar* his enemies, *Hercules* monsters; but he that overcomes himself is the true valiant Captain.

All your friends here are well, *Tom Young* excepted, who I fear hath not long to live amongst us: so, I rest

Your true friend,

York, August 1. 1628.   J. H.

L E T T E R CXIX.

To WILLIAM AUSTIN, *Esq;*

S I R,

I Have many thanks to give you for that excellent poem you sent me upon the passion of Christ; surely you were possessed with a very strong spirit when you penned it, you were become a true *enthusiast:* for, let me despair if I lie unto you, all the while I was perusing it, it committed holy rapes upon my soul: methought I felt my heart melting within my breast, and my thoughts transported me to a true *elysium* all the while, there were such flexanimous strong ravishing strains throughout it. To deal plainly with you, it were an injury to the public good, not to expose to open light such divine raptures; for they have an edifying power in them, and

may

may be termed the very quinteffence of devotion. You difcover in them what a rich talent you have; which fhould not be buried within the walls of a private ftudy, or pals through a few particular hands, but appear in publick view, and to the fight of the world, to the inriching of others, as they did me in reading them. Therefore I fhall long to fee them pafs from the bankfide to *Paul's* church-yard, with other precious pieces of yours, which you have pleafed to impart unto me.

Your moft affectionate fervitor,

Oxford, Auguft 20. 1628. **J. H.**

LETTER CXX.

To Sir J. S. *Knight.*

SIR,

YOU writ to me lately for a footman, and I think this bearer will fit you: I know he can run well, for he hath run away twice from me, but he knew the way back again; yet, though he hath a running head as well as running heels, (and who will expect a footman to be a ftayed man?) I would not part with him were I not to go poft to the North. There be fome things in him that anfwer for his waggeries: he will come when you call him, go when you bid him, and fhut the door after him; he is faithful and ftout, and a lover of his mafter. He is a great enemy to all dogs, if they bark at him in his running; for I have feen him confront a huge maftiff, and knock him-down. When you go a country journey, or have him run with you a-hunting, you muft fpirit him with liquor; you muft allow him alfo fomething extraordinary for focks, elfe you muft not have him to wait at your table; when his greafe melts in running hard, it is fubject to fall into his toes. I fend him you but for trial, if he be not for your turn, turn him over to me again when I come back.

The

The beſt news I can ſend you at this time, is, that we are like to have peace both with *France* and *Spain*, ſo that *Harwich* men your neighbours, ſhall not hereafter need to fear the name of *Spinola*, who ſtruck ſuch an apprehenſion into them lately, that I underſtand they begin to fortify.

I pray preſent my moſt humble ſervice to my good Lady; and at my return from the North I will be bold to kiſs her hands and yours: ſo, I am

Your moſt obliged ſervitor,

London, *May* 25. 1628.   J. H.

LETTER CXXI.

To my FATHER.

S I R,

OUR two younger brothers which you ſent hither are diſpoſed of: my brother Doctor hath placed the elder of the two with Mr. *Hawes,* a mercer in *Cheapſide,* and he took much pains in it; and I had placed my brother *Ned* with Mr. *Barrington,* a ſilkman in the ſame ſtreet; but afterwards for ſome inconveniencies, I removed him to one Mr. *Smith* at the *Flower-de-luce* in *Lombard-ſtreet,* a mercer alſo. Their maſters are both of them very well to paſs, and of good repute: I think it will prove ſome advantage to them hereafter, to be both of one trade, becauſe when they are out of their time they may join ſtocks together; ſo that I hope, Sir, they are well placed as any two youths in *London,* but you muſt not uſe to ſend them ſuch large tokens in money, for that may corrupt them. When I went to bind my brother *Ned* apprentice in *Drappers-hall,* caſting my eyes upon the chimney-piece of the great room, I ſpied a picture of an antient gentleman, and underneath *Thomas Howell.* I aſked the clerk about him, and he told me that he had been a *Spaniſh* merchant in *Henry* VIII's

time,

time, and coming home rich, and dying a batchellor, he gave that hall to the company of *Drapers*, with other things, fo that he is accounted one of their chiefeft benefactors. I told the clerk, that one of the fons of *Thomas Howell* came now thither to be bound; he anfwered, that if he be a right *Howell*, he may have when he is free, 300 pounds to help to fet up, and pay no intereft for five years. It may be hereafter we may make ufe of this. He told me alfo, that any maid that can prove her father to be a true *Howell*, may come and demand fifty pounds towards her portion, of the faid hall. I am to go poft towards *York* to-morrow, to my chaige, but hope, God willing, to be here again the next term: fo, with my love to my brother *Howell*, and my fifter his wife, I left

Your dutiful fon,

London, Sept. 30. 1629.　　　　**J. H.**

LETTER CXXII.

To my Father Mr. BEN. JOHNSON.

FATHER *Ben. Nullum fit magnum ingenium fine mixtura dementiæ,* there is no great wit without fome mixture of madnefs, fo faith the Philofopher: nor was he a fool who anfwered, *nec parvum fine mixtura ftultitiæ,* nor fmail wit without fome allay of foolifhnefs. Touching the firft, it is verified in you, for I find that you have been oftentimes mad; you were mad when you writ your *Fox,* and madder when you writ your *Alchimift;* you were mad when you writ your *Catilin,* and ftark mad when you writ *Sejanus;* but when you writ your *Epigrams,* and the *Magnetic Lady,* you were not fo mad, infomuch, that I perceive there be degrees of madnefs in you. Excufe me that I am fo free with you. The madnefs I mean, is that divine fury, that heating and heightening fpirit which *Ovid* fpeaks of.

Eß

Eſt deus in nobis, agitante caleſcimus illo: that true enthuſiaſm which tranſports, and elevates the ſouls of poets above the middle region of vulgar conception, and makes them ſoar up to heaven to touch the ſtars with their laurelled heads, to walk in the *Zodiac* with *Apollo* himſelf, and command *Mercury* upon their errand.

I cannot yet light upon Dr. *Davies*'s *Welſh* grammar; before *Chriſtmas* I am promiſed one: ſo, deſiring you to look better hereafter to your charcoal-fire and chimney; which I am glad to be one that preſerved from burning, this being the ſecond time that *Vulcan* hath threatened you, it may be becauſe you have ſpoken ill of his wife, and been too buſy with his horns. I reſt

Your ſon and contiguous neighbour,

Weſtminſter, June 27. 1629.　　　　　J. H.

LETTER CXXIII.

To R. S. *Eſq;*

SIR,

I Am one of them who value not a courteſy that hangs long betwixt the fingers. I love not thoſe *viſcoſa beneficia*, thoſe bird-limed kindneſſes which *Pliny* ſpeaks of; nor would I receive money in a dirty clout, if poſſibly I could be without it: therefore, I return you the courteſy by the ſame hand that brought it. It might have pleaſured me at firſt, but the expectation of it hath prejudiced me, and now, perhaps you may have more need of it than

Your humble ſervitor,

Weſtminſter, Auguſt 3. 1620.　　　　　J. H.

U　　　　　　　　　LET-

LETTER CXXIV.

To the Countess of Sunderland *at* York.

Madam,

MY Lord continues still in course of physic at Dr. *Napier's*. I wrote to him lately, that his Lordship would please to come to his own house here in St. *Martin's* lane, where there is a greater accommodation for the recovery of his health, Dr. *Mayern* being on the one side, and the King's Apothecary on the other; but I fear there be some mountebanks that carry him away, and, I hear he intends to remove to *Wickham*, to one *Atkinson* a mere Quacksalver that was once Dr. *Lopez's* man.

The little Knight that useth to draw up his breeches with a shoeing-horn, I mean, Sir *Posthumus Hobby*, flew high at him this parliament, and would have inserted his name in the scroll of recusants that is shortly to be presented to the King; but, I produced a certificate from *Linford* under the minister's hand, that he received the communion at *Easter* last, and so got his name out: besides, the Deputy-lieutenants of *Buckinghamshire* would have charged *Biggin* farm with a light-horse, but Sir *William Alford* and others joined with me to get it off.

Sir *Thomas Wentworth* and Mr. *Wansford*, are grown great courtiers lately, and come from *Westminster-hall* to *Whitehall*: (Sir *Jo. Savill* their countryman having shewn them the way with his white staff). The Lord *Weston* tampered with the one, and my Lord *Cottington* took pains with the other, to bring them about from their violence against the *prerogative;* and I am told, the first of them is promised my Lord's place at *York*, in case his sickness continues.

We are like to have peace with *Spain* and *France;* and for *Germany*, they say the *Swedes* are like to strike into her, to try whether they may have better fortunes than the *Danes*.

My

My Lady *Scroop* (my Lord's mother) hath laïn ſick a-good while, and is very weak. So I reſt, Madam,

Your humble and dutiful ſervitor,

Weſtminſter, Auguſt 4. 1629.　　　　J. H.

LETTER CXXV.

To the Right Honourable my Lady Scroop, *Counteſs of* Sunderland, *at* Langar.

Madam,

I Am newly returned from *Hunſdon*; from giving the rites of burial to my Lord's mother: ſhe made my Lord ſole executor of all. I have all her plate and houſhold-ſtuff in my cuſtody; and unleſs I had gone as I did, much had been embezzled. I have ſent herewith the copy of a letter the King wrote to my Lord upon the reſignation of his place, which is fitting to be preſerved for poſterity among the records of *Bolton* caſtle. His Majeſty expreſſeth therein that he was never better ſerved, nor with more exactneſs of fidelity and juſtice by any, therefore he intends to ſet a ſpecial mark of his favour upon him, when his health will ſerve him to come to court: my Lord *Carleton* delivered it me, and told me he never remembered that the King wrote a more gracious letter. I have lately bought in fee-farm, *Wanleſs* park of the King's commiſſioners for my Lord: I got it for 600*l.* doubling the old rent, and the next day I was offered 500*l.* for the bargain: there were divers that put in for it, and my Lord of *Angleſey* thought himſelf ſure of it, but I found means to fruſtrate them all. I alſo compounded with his Majeſty's commiſſioners for reſpite of homage for *Rabbi* caſtle; there was 120*l.* demanded, but I came off for forty ſhillings. My Lord *Wentworth* is made Lord Deputy of *Ireland*, and carries a mighty ſtroke at court. There have been ſome claſhings betwixt him and my Lord of *Pembroke* lately, with

　　　　　　　　others.

others at court, and divers in the North; and some, as Sir *David Fowler*, with others, have been crushed.

He pleased to give me the disposing of the next Attorney's place in *York;* and *John Lister* being lately dead, I went to make use of the favour, and was offered 300 *l.* for it, but some got betwixt me and home, so that I was forced to go away contented with 100 pieces Mr. *Ratcliff* delivered me in his chamber at *Grays-Inn,* and so to part with the legal instrument I had; which I did rather than contest.

The Dutchess your niece is well. I did what your Ladyship commanded me at *York* house. So I rest, Madam,

Your Ladyship's ready and faithful servant,

Westminster, July 1. 1629.　　　　　J. H.

LETTER CXXVI.

To the Right Honourable the Earl of Bristol *at* Sherburn *Castle.*

My LORD,

I Attended my Lord *Cottington* before he went on his journey towards *Spain,* and put him in mind of the old business against the Viceroy of *Sardinia,* to see whether any good can be done, and to learn whether the *Conde* or his son be solvent. He is to land at *Lisbon;* one of the King's ships attends him; and some merchant-men take the advantage of this convoy.

The news that keeps greatest noise now, is, that the Emperor hath made a favourable peace with the *Danes,* for *Tilly* had crossed the *Elve,* and entered deep into *Holstein* land, and in all probability might have carried all before him, yet that King had honourable terms given him, and a peace is concluded, (though without the privity of *England*). But I believe the King of *Denmark* fared the better, because he is grandchild to *Char-*

les

les the Emperor's fifter. Now it feems another fpirit is like to fall upon the Emperor; for, they write, that *Guftavus* King of *Swethland* is ftruck into *Germany*, and hath taken *Mecklenburgh*. The ground of this quarrel as I hear, is, that the Emperor would not acknowledge; much lefs give audience to his ambaffadors: he alfo gives out to come for the affiftance of his allies, the Dukes of *Pomerland* and *Mecklenburgh*; nor do I hear that he fpeaks any thing yet of the Prince *Palfegrave's* bufinefs. Don *Carlos Coloma* is expected here from *Flanders* about the fame time that my Lord *Cottington* fhall be arrived at the court of *Spain*. God fend us an honourable peace, for as the *Spaniard* fays, *Nunca vi tan mala pazque no fueffe mejor, que la mejor guerra.*

Your Lordfhip's moft humble and ready fervant,

1629. J. H.

LETTER CXXVII.

To my Coufin J. P. *at Mr.* CONRADUS'S.

Coufin,

A Letter of yours was lately delivered me, I made a fhift to read the fuperfcription, but within I wondered what language it might be in which it was written: at firft, I thought it was *Hebrew*, or fome of her dialects, and fo went from the liver to the heart, from the right hand to the left to read it, but could make nothing of it: then I thought it might be the *Chinefe's* language, and went to read the words perpendicular; and the lines were fo crooked and diftorted, that no coherence could be made. *Greek* I perceived it was not, nor *Latin* or *Englifh*; fo, I gave it for mere *gibberifh*, and your characters to be rather *hieroglyphicks* than *letters*. The beft is, you keep your lines at a good diftance, like thofe in chancery bills, who as a clerk faid, were made fo wide of purpofe, becaufe the clients fhould have room enough to walk between them without juftling one another; yet, this widenefs had been excufeable if your lines had been ftreight, but they were full of odd kind of undulations and windings. If you can write no otherways, one may read your thoughts as foon as your characters. It is fome excufe for you that you are but a young beginner: I pray let it appear in your next what a proficient you are, otherwife fome blame might light on me who placed you there. Let me receive no more *gibberifh* or *hiero-glyphicks* from you, but legible letters, that I may acquaint your friends accordingly of your good proceedings: fo, I reft

Your very loving coufin,

Weftminfter, Sept. 20. 1629.   J. H.

L E T T E R CXXVIII.

To the Lord Vifcount Wentworth, *Lord Prefident of* York.

My LORD,

MY laft was of the firft current, fince which, I received one from your Lordfhip, and your commands therein; which I fhall ever entertain with a great deal of chearfulnefs. The greateft news from abroad is, that the *French* King with his Cardinal are come again on this fidé the hills, having done his bufinefs in *Italy* and *Savoy*, and referved ftill *Pignerol* in his hands; which will ferve him as a key to enter *Italy* at pleafure. Upon the higheft mountain amongft the *Alps*, he left this oftentuous infcription upon a great pillar:

A la memoir eternelle de Louis *treiziefme,*
Roy de France *& de* Navarre,
Tres-Augufte, tres-victorreux, tres-heureux,
Conquerant, tres-jufte :

Lequel

Lequel âpres avoir vaicu toutes les nations
   de l'Europe,
Il a encore triumphe les elements
   Du ciel & de la terre,
Ayant paſſe deux fois cefmonts au mois
   De Mars *avec ſon armee,*
Victorieuſe pour remmettre les Princes
  · d'Italie *en leures eſtates,*
Defendre & proteger ſes alliez.

To the eternal memory of *Lewis* XIII. King of *France*
and *Navarre,* moſt gracious, moſt victorious, moſt happy, moſt juſt; a Conqueror, who having overcome all
the nations of *Europe:* he hath alſo triumphed over the
elements of heaven and earth, having twice paſſed over
theſe hills in the month of *March* with his victorious army, to reſtore the princes of *Italy* to their eſtates, and
to defend and protect his allies: ſo, I take my leave for
the preſent, and reſt

   Your Lordſhip's moſt humble and ready ſervitor,
Weſtminſter, Auguſt 5. 1629.   J. H.

LETTER CXXIX.

To Sir KENELM DIGBY *Knight.*

S I R,

GIVE me leave to congratulate your happy return
from the *Levant,* and the great honour you have
acquired by your gallant comportment in *Algier,* in re-
ſcuing ſo many *Engliſh* ſlaves ; by bearing up ſo bravely
againſt the *Venetian* fleet in the bay of *Scanderoon,* and
making the *Pantaloni* to know themſelves and *you* better.
I do not remember to have read or heard that thoſe huge
galeaſſes of *St. Mark* were beaten afore. I give you
the joy alſo, that you have born up againſt the *Venetian*
Ambaſſador here, and vindicated yourſelf of thoſe foul
                                  ſcandals

scandals he had caſt upon you in your abſence. Whereas you deſire me to join with Lord *Cottington* and others, to make *affidavit* touching *Bartholomew Spinola*, whether he be *Vezino de Madrid*, viz. *free Deniſon* of *Spain*: I am ready to ſerve you herein, or to do any other office that may right you, and tend to the making of your prize good. Yet, I am very ſorry that our *Alleppo* merchants ſuffered ſo much.

I ſhall be ſhortly in *London*, and I will make the greater ſpeed, becauſe I may ſerve you. So, I humbly kiſs my noble Lady's hand, and reſt

Your thrice aſſured ſervant,

Weſtminſt. Nov. 25. 1629.   J. H.

LETTER CXXX.

To the Right Honourable Sir PETER WICHT, *Ambaſſa-dor at* Conſtantinople.

SIR,

MR. *Simon Digby* delivered me one from your Lordſhip of the firſt of *June*; and I was extremely glad to have it, for I had received nothing from your Lordſhip a twelvemonth before. Maſter Controller Sir *Thomas Edmond* is lately returned from *France*, having renewed the peace which was made up to his hands before by the *Venetian* ambaſſadors, who had much laboured in it, and had concluded all things beyond the *Alps*, when the King of *France* was at *Suſa* to relieve *Caſal*. The *Monſieur* that was to fetch him from *St. Dennis* to *Paris*, put a kind of jeering compliment upon him, viz. that his Excellency ſhould not think it ſtrange, that he had ſo few *French* gentlemen to attend in this ſervice to accompany him to the court, *in regard there were ſo many killed at the iſle of* Rhee. The Marquis of *Chateauneuf* is here from *France*; and it was an odd ſpeech alſo from him, reflecting upon Maſter Controller,

that

that the King of Great Britain *used to send for his ambassadors from abroad to pluck capons at home.*

Mr. *Burlemach* is to go shortly to *Paris*, to recover the other moiety of her Majesty's portion ; whereof they say my Lord of *Holland* is to have a good share. The Lord Treasurer *Weston* is he who hath the greatest vogue now at court, but many great ones have clashed with him. He is so potent, that I hear his eldest son is to marry one of the blood-royal of *Scotland*, the Duke of *Lenox*'s sister, and that with his Majesty's consent.

Bishop *Laud* of *London* is also powerful in his way, for he sits at the helm of the church, and doth more than any of the two archbishops, or all the rest of his two and twenty brethren besides.

In your next I shall be glad your Lordship would do me the favour, as to write how the Grand Signior is like to speed before *Bagdat*, in this his *Persian* expedition. No more now, but that I always rest

Your Lordship's ready and most faithful servant,
Westminst. Jan. 1. 1629.   J. H.

LETTER CXXXI.

To my FATHER.

SIR,

SIR *Thomas Wentworth* hath been a good while Lord President of *York*, and since is sworn Privy-counsellor, and made Baron and Viscount ; the Duke of *Buckingham* himself flew not so high in so short a revolution of time. He was made Viscount with a great deal of high ceremony upon a *Sunday* in the afternoon at *Whitehall*. My Lord *Powis* (who affects him not so much) being told that the heralds had fetched his pedigree from the blood-royal, *viz.* from *John* of *Gaunt*, said, *dammy if ever he come to be King of* England, *I will turn rebel.*

rebel. · When I went firſt to give him · joy, he pleaſed to give me the diſpoſing of the next Attorney's place that falls void in *York*, which is valued at 300 *l.* I have no rea· ſon to leave my Lord of *Sunderland*, for I hope he will be noble unto me. The perquiſites of my place, taking the King's fee away, came far ſhort of what he promiſed me at my firſt coming to him, in regard of non-reſidence at *York* ; therefore I hope he will conſider it ſome' other way. This languiſhing ſickneſs ſtill hangs on him, and I fear will make an end of him. There is none cantell what to make of it, but he voided lately a ſtrange worm at *Wickham ;* but, I fear there is an impoſthume growing in him, for he told me a paſſage, how many years ago my Lord *Willowghby* and he, with ſo many of their ſervants (*de gayete de cœur*) played a match at foot-ball againſt ſuch a number of countrymen, where, my Lord of *Sunderland* being buſy about the ball, got a bruiſe in the breaſt ; which put him in a ſwoon for the preſent, but did not trouble him till three months after, when being at *Bever* caſtle (his brother-in-law's houſe) a qualm took him on a ſudden, which made him retire to his bed-chamber. My Lord of *Rutland* following him, put a pipe full of tobacco in his mouth ; he being not accuſtomed to tobacco, taking the ſmoke downwards, fell a caſting and vomiting up divers little impoſthumated bladders of congealed blood ; which ſaved his life then, and brought him to have a better conceit of tobacco ever after ; and I fear there is ſome of that clodded blood ſtill in his body.

Becauſe Mr. *Haws* of *Cheapſide* is lately dead, I have removed my brother *Griffith* to the hen and chickens in *Pater-noſter-row* to Mr. *Taylor's*, as genteel a ſhop as any in the city ; but I gave a piece of plate of twenty nobles price to his wife. I wiſh the *Yorkſhire* horſe may be fit for your turn, he was accounted the beſt ſaddle gelding about *York*, when I bought him of Captain *Philips* the Muſter-maſter ; and when he carried me firſt to *London*, there was twenty pounds offered for him by my Lady *Carliſle.*

Carifle. No more now, but defiring a continuance of
your blefling and prayers, I reft

Your dutiful fon,

London, Dec. 3. 1630   J. H.

LETTER CXXXII.

To the Lord Cottington, *Ambaffador Extraordinary for
his Majefty of* Great Britain *in the Court of* Spain.

My LORD,

I Received your Lordfhip's lately by *Harry Davies*
the *Correo Santo;* I return my humble thanks, that
you were pleafed to be mindful (among fo many high
negotiations) of the old bufinefs touching the Viceroy
of *Sardinia.* I have acquainted my Lord of *Briftol* accordingly; our eyes here look very greedily after your
Lordfhip, and the fuccefs of your embafly; we are glad
to hear the bufinefs is brought to fo good a pafs, and that
the capitulations are fo honourable (the high effects of
your wifdom).

For news, the *Swedes* do notable feats in *Germany;*
and we hope, they cutting the Emperor and *Bavarian*
fo much work to do, and the good offices we are to expect from *Spain* upon this redintegration of peace, will
be an advantage to the Prince *Palatine,* and facilitate
matters for reftoring him to his country.

There is little news at our court, but that there fell
an ill-favoured quarrel betwixt Sir *Kenelm Digby,* and
Mr. *Goring,* Mr. *Jermin,* and others at St. *James's*
lately, about Mrs. *Baker* the maid of honour, and duels
were like to grow of it, but that the bufinefs was taken
up by the Lord Treafurer, my Lord of *Dorfet,* and o-
thers appointed by the King. My Lord of *Sunderland*
is ftill indifpofed: he willed me to remember his hearty
fervice to your Lordfhip, and fo did Sir *Arthur Ingram,*

and

and my Lady: they all wifh you a happy and honourable
return, as doth

Your Lordfhip's moſt humble and ready fervitor,
London, March 1. 1630.   **J. H.**

L E T T E R CXXXIII.

To the Earl of Briftol.

My LORD,

I Doubt not but your Lordfhip hath had intelligence
from time to time what firm invafions the King of
Swedes hath made into *Germany,* and by what degrees
he hath mounted to this height, having but 6000 foot,
and 500 horfe when he entered firft to *Mecklenburgh,*
and taken that town while commiffioners ftood treating
on both fides in his tent: how thereby his army much
increafed, and fo rufhed further into the heart of the
country, but paffing near *Magdenbourg,* being diffident
of his own ftrength, he fuffered *Tilly* to take that great
town with fo much effufion of blood, becaufe they would
receive no quarters. Your Lordfhip hath alfo heard of
the battle of *Leipfick,* where *Tilly* notwithſtanding the
victory he had got over the Duke of *Saxony* a few days
before, received an utter difcomfiture; upon which victory the King fent Sir *Thomas Roe* a prefent of 2000 *l.*
and in his letter calls him his *ſtrenuum conſultorem,* he
being one of the firft who had advifed him to this *Ger-*
man war after he had made peace betwixt him and the
Polander. I prefume alfo your Lordfhip heard how he
met *Tilly* again near *Aufpurg,* and made him go upon a
wooden leg, whereof he died, and after foundly plundered the *Bavarian,* and made him flee from his own
houfe at *Munchen,* and rifled his very clofets.

Now, your Lordfhip fhall underſtand, that the faid
King is at *Mentz,* and keeps a court-there like an Em-
peror, there being above twelve ambaſſadors with him.
The

The King of *France* fent a great Marquis for his Ambaffador, to put him in mind of his articles, and to tell him, that his Chriftian Majefty wondered he would crofs the *Rhine* without his privity, and wondered more that he would invade the church-lands, meaning the Archbifhop of *Mentz*, who had put himfelf under the protection of *France*. The *Swede* anfwered, that he had not broke the leaft title of the articles agreed on; and touching the faid Archbifhop, he had not ftood neutral as was promifed, therefore he had juftly fet on his fkirts. The Ambaffador replied, in cafe of breach of articles, his mafter had 80,000 men to pierce *Germany* when he pleafed. The King anfwered, that he had but 20,000, and thofe would be fooner at the walls of *Paris*, than his 80,000 fhould be on the frontiers of *Germany*. If this new conqueror goes on with this violence, I believe it will caft the policy of all chriftendom into another mould, and beget new maxims of ftate; for none can foretel where his monftrous progrefs will terminate. Sir *Henry Vane* is ftill in *Germany* obferving his motions, and they write that they do not agree well: as I heard the King fhould tell him, that he fpoke nothing but *Spanifh* to him. Sir *Robert Anftruther* is alfo at *Vienna*, being gone thither from the diet at *Ratisbon*.

I hear the infante Cardinal is defigned to come Governor of the *Netherlands*, and paffeth by way of *Italy*, and fo through *Germany*: his brother *Don Carlos* is lately dead. So I humbly take my leave, and teft

Your Lordfhip's moft humble and ready fervitor,
Weftm. April 23. 1630.   J. H.

L E T T E R CXXXIV.
To my noble Lady, the Lady Cot.

Madam,

YOU fpoke to me for a cook who had feen the world abroad, and I think the bearer hereof will fit your Ladyfhip's turn. He can marinate fifh, and gellies; he

X   is

is excellent for a pickant fauce, and the haugou: befides, ·Madam, he is paffing good for an ollia.   He will
tell your Ladyfhip, that the reverend matron the *olla
podrida* hath intellectuals and *fenfes*; mutton, beef, and
bacon; are to her, as the will, underftanding, and memo-'
ry are to the foul.   Cabbage, turnips, archichocks, po-
tatoes and dates, are her five *fenfes*, and pepper the
common fenfe: fhe muft have marrow to keep life in her,
and fome birds to make her light; by all means lhe muft
go adorned with chains of fauceages.   He is alfo good
at larding of meat after the mode of *France.*   Madam,
you may make proof of him, and if your Ladyfhip find
him too ·faucy or wafteful, you may return him from
·whence you had him.   So, I reft, Madam,

Your Ladyfhip's moft humble fervitor,
Weftminfter, June 2. 163o.   ·   J. H.

L E T T E R CXXXV.

To Mr. E. D.

S I R,

YOU write to me, that *T. B.* defigns to give money for fuch a place; if he doth, I fear it will be
verified in him, that a *fool and his money is foon parted,*
for, I know he will never be able to execute it.   I heard
of a late Secretary of ftate that could not read the next
morning his own hand-writing; and I have heard of *Ca-
ligula's* horfe that was made Conful: therefore, I pray
tell him from me, (for I wifh him well) that if he thinks
he is fit for that office, he looks upon himfelf through a
falfe glafs: a trotting horfe is fit for a coach, but not
for a Lady's faddle, and an ambler is proper for a Lady's
faddle, but not for a coach.   If *Tom* undertakes this
place, he will be as an ambler in a coach, or a trotter
under a Lady's faddle.   When I come to town, I will
                                                              put

put him upon a far fitter and more feasible busines for him; and so, commend me to him, for I am his, and

Your true friend,

Westminster, June 5. 1630.   J. H.

LETTER CXXXVI.

To my FATHER.

S I R,

THERE are two ambasadors to go abroad shortly, the Earl of *Leicester*, and the Lord *Weston*: this latter goes to *France*, *Savoy*, *Venice*, and so returns by *Florence*; a pleasant journey, for he carrieth presents with him from the King and Queen. The Earl of *Liecester* is to go to the King of *Denmark*, and other princes of *Germany*. The main of the embassy is to condole the late death of the Lady *Sophia*, Queen Dowager of *Denmark*. She was the Duke of *Mecklenburgh*'s daughter, and her husband *Christian* III. dying young, her portion, which was 40,000*l.* was restored her; and living a widow forty four years, she grew to be so great a house-wife, setting near three or 400 hundred people at work, that she died worth near 2,000000 of dollars; so that she was reputed the richest Queen of christendom. By the constitutions of *Denmark* this estate is divisible amongst her children, whereof she had five; the King of *Denmark*, the Dutchess of *Saxony*, the Dutchess of *Brunswick*, Queen *Anne*, and the Dutchess of *Holstein*. The King being male, is to have two shares, our King and the Lady *Elizabeth*, is to have that which should have belonged to Queen *Anne*; so he is to return by the *Hague*. It pleased my Lord of *Leicester* to send for me to *Baynard*'s castle, and proffer me to go Secretary in this embasage, assuring me, that the journey shall tend to my profit and credit; so, I have accepted it, for I hear very nobly of my Lord, so that

X 2   I

I hope to make a boon voyage of it. I defire as hitherto your prayers and blefling may accompany me: fo,
with my love to my brothers and fifters, I reft

Your dutiful fon,

London, *May* 5. 1632.   J. H.

LETTER CXXXVII.

To the Right Honourable the Earl of Leicefter, *at*
Petworth.

My LORD,

SIR *John Pennington* is appointed to carry your Lordfhip and your company to *Germany*, and he intends
to take you up at *Margate*. I have been with Mr. *Bour-
lamack*, and received a bill of exchange from him for
10,000 dollars, payable in *Hamburgh*. I have alfo received 2000 *l.* of Sir *Paul Pinder* for your Lordfhip's
ufe, and he did me the favour to pay it me all in old
gold. Your allowance hath begun fince the 25th of
July laft, at eight pound *per diem*, and is to continue fo
till your Lordfhip return to his Majefty. I underftand
by fome merchants to-day upon the exchange, that the
King of *Denmark* is at *Luckftad*, and ftays there all this
fummer: if it be fo, it will fave half the voyage of going to *Copenhagen*, for in lieu of the *Sound*, we need go
no further than the river of *Elve*: fo, I reft

Your Lordfhip's moft humble
and faithful fervitor,

Weftminfter, Auguft 13. 1632.   J. H.

LET-

LETTER CXXXVIII.

To the Right Honourable the Lord Mohun.

My LORD,

THOUGH any command from your Lordſhip be welcome to me at all times, yet that which you enjoined me in yours of the 12th of *Auguſt*, that I ſhould inform your Lordſhip of what I know touching the *inquiſition*, is now a little unſeaſonable, becauſe I have much to do to prepare myſelf for this employment to *Germany*, therefore I cannot ſatisfy you in that fulneſs as I could do otherwiſe. The very name of the *inquiſition* is terrible all chriſtendom over, and the King of *Spain* himſelf with the chiefeſt of his grandees tremble at it. It was founded firſt by the catholick King *Ferdinand* (our *Henry* VIII's father-in-law), for he having got *Granada*, and ſubdued all the *Moors*, who had a firm footing in that kingdom about 700 years, yet he ſuffered them to live peaceably a while, in point of conſcience; but afterwards he ſent a ſolemn *mandamus* to the *Jacobin* friers, to endeavour the converſion of them by preaching, and all other means. They finding their pains did little good, (and that thoſe whom they had converted turned apoſtates) obtained power to make a reſearch; which afterwards was called *inquiſition:* and it was ratified by Pope *Sixtus*, that if they would not conform themſelves by fair means, they would be forced to do it. The *Jacobins* being found too ſevere herein, and for other abuſes beſides, this *inquiſition* was taken from them, and put into the hands of the moſt ſufficient eccleſiaſtics. So a council was eſtabliſhed, and officers appointed accordingly: whoſoever was found pendulous and brandling in his religion was brought by a ſerjeant called a *Familiar*, before the ſaid council of *inquiſition;* his accuſer or dilator ſtands behind a piece of tapeſtry to ſee whether he be the party, and if he be, then they put divers ſubtile and entrapping interrogatories unto him; and whether he

confeſs

confefs any thing or no, he is fent to prifon. When the faid *Familiar* goes to any houfe, though it be in the dead of the night, (and that is the time they commonly ufe to come, or in the dawn of the day) all doors, and trunks, and chefts, fly open to him, and the firft thing he doth he feizeth the party's breeches, fearcheth his pockets, and takes his keys, and fo rumageth all his clofets and trunks; and a public Notary whom he carrieth with him, takes an inventary of every thing; which is fequeftred and depofited in the hands of fome of his next neighbours. The party being hurried away in a clofe coach, and clapt in prifon, he is there eight days before he make his appearance; and then, they prefent unto him the crofs, and the miffal-book to fwear upon: if he refufeth to fwear, he convicteth himfelf, and though he fwear, yet he is remanded to prifon. This oath commonly is prefented before any accufation be produced. His goaler is ftrictly commanded to pry into his actions, his deportment, words, and countenance, and to fet fpies upon him; and whofoever of his fellow-prifoners, or others, can produce any thing againft him, he hath a reward for it. At laft, after divers appearances, examinations, and fcrutinies, the information againft him is read, but the witneffes names are concealed: then is he appointed a Rector and Advocate, but he muft not confer or advife with them privately, but in the face of the court. The King's Attorney is a party in it, and the accufers commonly the fole witneffes. Being to name his own lawyers, oftentimes others are difcovered, and fall into troubles: while he is thus in prifon, he is fo abhored and abandoned of all the world, that none will, at leaft dare not vifit him. Though one clear himfelf, yet he cannot be freed till an *act of faith* pafs; which is done feldom, but very folemnly. There are few who having fallen into the grips of the *inquifition* do efcape the rack, or the fambenito; which is a ftraight yellow coat without fleeves, having the pourtrait of the devil painted up and down in black; and upon their heads they carry a mitter of paper, with a man frying in the flames of hell upon
it:

it: they gag their mouths, and tie a great cord about their necks. The judges meet in some uncouth dark dungeon, and the executioner stands by, clad in a close dark garment, his face and head covered with a chaperon, out of which there are but two holes to look through, and a huge link burning in his hand. When the ecclesiastic inquisitors have pronounced the anathema against him, they transmit him to the secular judges to receive the sentence of death; for church-men must not have their hands imbrued in blood: the King can mitigate any punishment under death, nor is a nobleman subject to the rack.

I pray be pleased to pardon this rambling imperfect relation, and take in good part my conformity to your commands, for, I am

Your Lordship's most ready and faithful servitor,
Westminst. August 30. 1632.   J. H.

L E T T E R CXXXIX.

To P. W. *Esq; at the Signet-Office, from the* English *House in* Hamburgh.

WE are safely come to *Germany*, Sir *J. Pennington* took us aboard in one of his Majesty's ships at *Margate's*; and the wind stood so fair, that we were at the mouth of the *Elve* upon *Monday* following. It pleased my Lord I should land first with two footmen, to make haste to *Gluckstad*, to learn where the King of *Denmark* was; and he was at *Reinsburg*, some two days journey off, at a *richsdach*, an assembly that corresponds to our parliament. My Lord the next day landed at *Gluckstad*, where I had provided an accommodation for him, though he intended to have gone for *Hamburgh;* but I was bold to tell him, that in regard there were some umbrages, and not only so, but open and actual differences betwixt the King and that town, it might be

ill

ill taken if he went thither firſt, before he had attended
the King. So I left my Lord at *Gluckſtad;* and being
come hither to take up 8000 rich dollars upon Mr. *Bur-*
lamacks's bills, and fetch Mr. *Avery* our Agent here, I
return to-morrow to attend my Lord again. I find that
matters are much off the hinges betwixt the King of
Denmark and this town.

The King of *Sweden* is advancing apace to find out
Walleſtein, and *Walleſtein* him; and in all appearance
they will be ſhortly engaged.

No more now, for I am interpelled by many buſineſſes: when you write, deliver your letters to Mr. *Rail-*
ton, who will ſee them ſafely conveyed; for a little before my departure, I brought him acquainted with my
Lord, that he might negotiate ſome things at court. So,
with my ſervice and love to all at *Weſtminſter,* I reſt

Your faithful ſervitor,

Hamburgh, Oct. 23. 1632.   J. H.

L E T T E R   CXL.

To my Lord Viſcount S. *from* Hamburgh.

SINCE I was laſt in town, my Lord of *Leiceſter*
hath attended the King of *Denmark* at *Reinsburgh*
in *Holſteinland:* he was brought thither from *Gluckſtad*
in indifferent good equipage, both for coaches and waggons, but he ſtaid ſome days at *Reinsburgh* for audience:
we made a comely gallant ſhow in that kind, when we
went to court, for we were near upon a hundred all of
one piece in mourning. It pleaſed my Lord to make me
the orator; and ſo I made a long ſpeech, *alta voce,* to
the King in *Latin,* of the occaſion of this embaſſy, and
tending to the praiſe of the deceaſed Queen; and, I had
better luck than Secretary *Nanton* had ſome thirty years
ſince, with *Roger* Earl of *Rutland:* for at the beginning
of his ſpeech, when he had pronounced *ſereniſſime.Rex,*

he

he was dafhed out of countenance, and fo gravelled that he could go no further. I made another to *Chriftian* V. his eldeft fon, King elect of *Denmark*. For though that crown be purely elective, yet for thefe three laft kings, they wrought fo with the people, that they got their eldeft fons chofen, and declared before their death, and to affume the title of King's elect. At the fame audience, I made another fpeech to Prince *Frederick*, Archifhop of *Breme*, the King's third fon; and he hath but one more, (befides his natural iffue) which is Prince *Ulric*, now in wars with the Duke of *Sax ;* and they fay there is an alliance contracted already, betwixt *Chriftian* V. and the Duke of *Sax*'s daughter. This ceremony being performed, my Lord defired to find his own diet, and then he fell to divers bufineffes, which is not fitting for me to foreftal or impart to your Lordfhip now; fo we ftaid there near upon a month. The King feafted my Lord once; and it lafted from eleven o'clock, till towards the evening, during which time, the King began thirty five healths: the firft to the Emperor, the fecond to his nephew of *England ;* and fo went over all the kings and queens of chriftendom, but he never remembered the Prince *Palfegrave*'s health, or his niece's all the while. The King was taken away at laft in his chair, but my Lord of *Leicefter* bore up ftoutly all the while, fo that when there came two of the King's guard to take him by the arms as he was going down the ftairs, my Lord fhook them off and went alone.

The next morning I went to court for fome difpatches, but the King was gone a-hunting at break of day; but going to fome other of his officers, their fervants told me without any appearance of fhame, that their mafters were drunk over night, and fo it would be late before they would rife.

A few days after we went to *Gothorp* caftle in *Slefwickland*, to the Duke of *Holftein*'s court, where, at my firft audience, I made another *Latin* fpeech to the Duke, touching his grandmother's death. Our entertainment there was brave; (though a little fulfome): my

Lord

Lord was lodged in the Duke's caſtle, and parted with preſents ; which is more than the King of *Denmark* did. Thence we went to *Huſem* in *Ditzmarſh*, to the Dutcheſs of *Holſtein*'s court, (our Queen *Anne*'s youngeſt liſter) where he had alſo very full entertainment. I made a ſpeech to her alſo, about her mother's death; and when I named the Lady *Sophia*, the tears came down her cheeks. Thence we came back to *Reinsburgh*, and ſo to this town of *Hamburgh*, where my Lord intends to repoſe ſome days, after an abrupt odd journey we had through *Holſteinland;* but, I believe it will not be long, in regard Sir *John Pennington* ſtays for him upon the river. We expeἀt Sir *Robert Anſtruther* to come from *Vienna* hither, to take the advantage of the King's ſhip.

We underſtand that the imperial and the *Swediſh* armies have made near approaches one to another, and that ſome ſkirmiſhes and blows have been already betwixt them; which are the forerunners of a battle. So my good Lord, I reſt

Your moſt humble and faithful ſervitor,

Hamburgh, Oἀ. 9. 1632.   J. H.

L E T T E R CXLI.

To the Right Honourable the Earl R. *from* Hamburgh.

My Lord,

THOUGH your Lordſhip muſt needs, think, that in the employment I am in (which requires a whole man) my ſpirits muſt be diſtracted by multiplicity of buſineſſes ; yet becauſe I would not recede from my old method and firſt principles of travel, when I came to any great city, to couch in writing what is moſt obſervable, I ſequeſtered myſelf from other affairs, to ſend your Lordſhip what followeth touching this great *hanſe* town.

The

The *hanfe* or *hanfiatic league*, is very antient; fome would derive the word from *hand*, becaufe they of the fociety plight their faith by that action : others derive it from *hanfa*, which in the *Gothic* tongue is council : others would have it come from *hander-fee*, which fignifies near or upon the fea; and this paffeth for the beft etymology, becaufe their towns are all feated fo, or upon fome navigable river near the fea. The extent of the old *hanfe* was from *Nerve* in *Livonia* to the *Rhine*, and contained fixty-two great mercantile towns, which were divided into four precincts : the chiefeft of the firft precinct was *Lubeck*, where the archives of their antient records and their prime chancery is ftill, and this town is within that verge. *Cullen* is chief of the fecond precinct, *Brunfwick* of the third, and *Dantzick* of the fourth. The kings of *Poland* and *Sweden* have fued to be their Protector, but they refufed them becaufe they were not princes-of the empire ; they put off alfo the King of *Denmark* with a compliment, nor would they admit the King of *Spain* when he was molt potent in the *Netherlands*, though afterwards, when it was too late, they defired the help of the *ragged-ftaff;* nor of the Duke of *Anjou*, notwithftanding that the world thought he fhould have married cur Queen, who interceeded for him ; and fo it was probable that thereby they might recover their privileges in *England :* fo that I do not find they ever had any protector but the great Mafter of *Pruffia;* and their want of a protector did do them fome prejudice in that famous difference they had with our Queen.

The old *hanfe* had extraordinary immunities given them by our *Henry* III. becaufe they affifted him in his wars with fo many fhips ; and as they pretend, the King was not only to pay them for the fervice of the faid fhips, but for the veffels themfelves if they mifcarried : now, it happened that at their return to *Germany*, from ferving *Henry* III. there was a great fleet of them caft away; for which, according to covenant, they demanded reparation. Our King in lieu of money, among other acts

of

of grace, gave them a privilege to pay but one *per cent.* which continued till Queen *Mary*'s reign ; and she by the advice of King *Philip* her husband, as it was conceived, enhanced the one, to twenty *per, cent.* The *hanse* not only complained, but clamoured loudly for breach of their antient privileges, confirmed to them time out of mind by thirteen successive kings of *England;* which they pretended to have purchased with their money. King *Philip* undertook to accommodate the business ; but Queen *Mary* dying a little after, and he retiring, there could be nothing done. Complaint being made to Queen *Elizabeth,* she answered, *that as she would not innovate any thing, so she would maintain them still in the same condition she found them.* Hereupon the navigation and traffic ceased a while : whereupon the *English* tried what they could do themselves, and they thrived so well, that they took the whole trade into their own hands, and so divided themselves (though they be now but one) to *staplers;* and *merchant adventurers,* the one residing constant in one place, where they kept their magazine of wool, the other stirring, and adventuring to divers places abroad with cloth, and other manufactures ; which made the *hanse* endeavour to draw upon them all the malignancy they could from all nations. Moreover the *hanse* towns being a body-politic incorporated in the empire, complained hereof to the Emperor, who sent over persons of great quality to mediate an accommodation, but they could effect nothing. Then the Queen caused a proclamation to be published, that the *Easterlings* or *merchants* of the *hanse* should be treated and used as all other strangers were within her dominions, without any mark of difference in point of commerce. This nettled them more ; thereupon they bent their forces more eagerly, and in a diet at *Ratisbon* they procured that the *English* merchants who had associated themselves into *fraternities* in *Embden* and other places, should be declared *monopolists;* and so there was a *comitial edict* published against them, that they should be exterminated, and banished out of all parts of the empire ; and this was done by the

activity

activity of *Suderman* a great civilian. There was there for the Queen, *Gilpin*, as nimble à man as *Suderman*, and he had the Chancellor of *Embden* to second and countenance him ; but they could not stop the said *edict*, wherein the society of *English* merchant adventurers was pronounced to be a *monopoly ;* yet *Gilpin* plaid his game so well, that he wrought under-hand, that the said *imperial ban* should not be published till after the dissolution of the diet, and that in the *interim*, the Emperor should send ambassadors to *England*, to advertise the Queen of such a *ban* against her merchants. But this wrought so little impression upon the Queen, that the said *ban* grew rather ridiculous than formidable, for the town of *Embden* harboured our merchants notwithstanding, and afterwards *Stode ;* but they not being able to protect them so well from the *imperial ban*, they settled in this town of *Hamburgh*. After this the Queen commanded another proclamation to be divulged, that the *Easterlings* or *hansiatic* merchants should be allowed to trade in *England* upon the same conditions and payment of duties, as her own subjects, provided that the *English* merchants might have interchangeable privilege, 'to reside and trade peaceably in *Stode* or *Hamburgh*, or any where else, within the precinct of the *hanse*. This incensed them more ; thereupon they resolved to cut off *Stode* and *Hamburgh* from being members of the *hanse*, or of the empire ; but they suspended this design till they saw what success the great *Spanish* fleet should have, which was then preparing in the year eighty-eight : for they had not long before had recourse to the King of *Spain*, and made him their own, and he had done them some material good offices ; wherefore to this day the *Spanish* council is taxed of improvidence and imprudence, that there was no use made of the *hanse* towns in that expedition.

The Queen finding that they of the *hanse* would not be contended with that equality she had offered betwixt them and her own subjects, put out a proclamation, that they should carry neither corn, victuals, arms, timber, masts, cables, minerals, nor any other materials, or men

Y   to to *Spain* or *Portugal*. And after the Queen growing more redoubtable and famous by the overthrow of the fleet of eighty-eight, the *Easterlings* fell to despair of doing any good. Add hereunto another disaster that befel them, the taking of sixty sails of their Ships about the mouth of *Tagus* in *Portugal*, by the Queen's ships, that were laden with *ropas de contrabando*, viz. goods prohibited by her former proclamation into the dominions of *Spain* : and as these ships were upon point of being discharged, she had intelligence of a great assembly at *Lubeck*, which had met of purpose to consult of means to be revenged of her ; thereupon she staid and seized upon the said sixty ships, only two were freed to bring news what became of the rest. Hereupon the *Pole* sent an Ambassador to her, who spake in a high tone, but he was answered in a higher.

Ever since our merchants have beaten a peaceful and free uninterrupted trade into this town and elsewhere, within and without the *Sound*, with their manufactures of wool, and found the way also to the *White-sea*, to *Archangel* and *Mosco* : insomuch, that the premises being well considered, it was a happy thing for *England*, that that clashing fell out betwixt her and the *hanse* ; for it may be said to have been the chief ground of that shipping and merchandizing which she is now come to, and wherewith she has flourished ever since. But one thing is observable, that as the imperial or comitial *ban*, pronounced in the diet at *Ratisbon* against our merchants and manufactures of wool, incited them more to industry, so our proclamation upon Alderman *Cockein*'s project of transporting no white cloths, but dyed, and in their full manufacture, did cause both *Dutch* and *German* to turn necessity to a virtue, and made them far more ingenious to find ways not only to dye, but to make cloth, which hath much impaired our markets ever since ; for there hath not been the third part of our cloth sold since, either here or in *Holland*.

My Lord, I pray be pleased to dispense with the prolixity of this discourse, for I could not wind it up

closer,

clofer, nor on a leſſer bottom. I ſhall be careful to bring with me thoſe *furrs* I had inſtructions for. So, I am

Your Lordſhip's moſt humble ſervant,

Hamburgh, Oct. 20. 1632. J. H.

LETTER CXLII.

To Capt. J. SMITH, *at the* Hague.

Captain,

HAVING ſo wiſhful an opportunity as this noble gentleman Mr. *James Crofts*, who comes with a pacquet for the Lady *Elizabeth* from my Lord of *Leiceſter*, I could not but ſend you this friendly ſalute. We are like to make a ſpeedier return than we expected from this embaſſy; for we found the King of *Denmark* in *Holſtein*, which ſhortened our voyage from going to the *Sound :* the king was in an advantageous poſture to give audience, for there was a parliament then at *Reinsburgh*, where all the *Younkers* met. Among other things, I put myſelf to mark the carriage of the *Holſtein* gentlemen, as they were going in and out at the parliament-houſe; and obſerving well their phyſiognomies, their complexions and gaite, I thought verily I was in *England*, for they reſemble the *Engliſh* more than either *Welſh* or *Scot*, (though cohabiting upon the ſame iſland) or any other people, that ever I ſaw yet; which makes me verily believe, that the *Engliſh* nation came firſt from this lower circuit of *Saxony ;* and there is one thing that ſtrengtheneth me in this belief, that there is an antient town hard by called *Lunden*, and an iſland called *Angles ;* whence it may well be that our country came from *Britannia* to be *Anglia.*

This town of *Hamburgh* from a ſociety of *brewers*, is come to be a huge wealthy place, and her new town is al-

moſt

moſt as big as the old ; there is a ſhrewd jar betwixt her and her Protector, the King of *Denmark.*

My Lord of *Leiceſter* hath done ſome good offices to accommodate matters. She *chomps* extremely, that there ſhould be ſuch a *bit* put lately in her mouth, as the fort of *Luckſtadt,* which commands her river of *Elve,* and makes her pay what toll he pleaſes.

The King begins to fill his cheſts apace, which were ſo emptied in his late marches to *Germany :* he hath ſet a new toll upon all ſhips that paſs to this town ; and in the *Sound* alſo there be ſome extraordinary duties impoſed, whereat all nations begin to murmur, eſpecially the *Hollanders,* who ſay, that the old primitive toll of the *Sound* was but a roſe-noble for every ſhip, but by a new ſophiſtry, it is now interpreted for every ſail that ſhould paſs through, infomuch, that the *Hollander,* though he be a *low-countryman,* begins to ſpeake *High-Dutch* in this point, a rough language you know ; which made the *Italian* tell a *German* gentleman once, that *when God almighty thruſt* Adam *out of paradiſe, he ſpoke* Dutch ; but the *German* returned wittily, *then, Sir, if God ſpoke* Dutch *when* Adam *was ejected,* Eve *ſpoke* Italian *when* Adam *was ſeduced.*

I could be larger, but for a ſudden avocation to buſineſs; ſo I moſt affectionately ſend my kind reſpects to you, deſiring, when I am rendered to *London,* I may hear from you : ſo I am

Your faithful friend to ſerve you,

Hamburgh, Oct. 22. 1632.   J. H.

FAMILIAR
LETTERS.

PART II.

LETTER I.

To the Right Honourable the Earl of Br.

My Lord,

I Am newly returned from *Germany*, where there came lately two ambaffadors extraordinary in one of the fhips royal, the Earl of *Leicefter*, and Sir *Robert Anftruther* : the latter came from *Vienna*, and I know little of his negotiations'; but for my Lord of *Leicefter*, I believe there was never fo much bufinefs difpatched in fo fhort a compafs of time, by any Ambaffador, as your Lordfhip, who is beft able to judge, will find by this fhort relation. When my Lord was come to the King of *Denmark*'s court, which was then at *Reinsburgh*, a good way within *Holftein ;* the firft thing he did was to condole the late Queen Dowager's death, (our King's grandmother) which was done in fuch an equipage, that the *Danes* confeffed, there was never Queen of *Denmark* fo mourned for. This ceremony being paffed, my Lord fell to bufinefs ; and the firft thing which he propounded, was, that for preventing the further effufion of chriftian blood in *Germany*, and for facilitating a way to reftore peace to all chriftendom, his Majefty of *Denmark* would join with his nephew of *Great Britain*, to fend a folemn embaffy to the Emperor; and the King of *Sweden*, (the end of whofe proceedings were doubtful) to mediate an accommodation, and to appear for him who will be found moft conformable to reafon. To this, that

Y 3

King

King anfwered in writing, (for that was the way of proceeding) that the Emperor and the *Swede* were come to
that height and heat of war, and to fuch a violence, that
it is no time yet to fpeak to them of peace; but when. the
fury is a little paffed, and the times more proper, he
would take it for an honour to join with his nephew, and
contribute the beft means he could to bring about fo good
a work.

Then there was a computation made, what was due to
the King of *Great Britain* and Lady *Elizabeth*, out of
their grandmother's eftate; which was valued at near
upon two millions of dollars; and your Lordſhip muſt
think it was a hard taſk to liquidate fuch an accompt.
This being done, my Lord defired that part which was
due to his Majefty (our King) and the Lady his fifter;
which appeared to amount unto 160,000 *l. Sterl.* That
King anfwered, that he confeffed there was fo much money due, but his mother's eftate was yet in the hands of
commiſſioners; and neither he nor any of his fifters had
received their portions yet, and that his nephew of *England*, and his niece of *Holland*, ſhould receive theirs
with the firſt; but he did intimate befides, that there
were fome confiderable accompts betwixt him and the
crown of *England*, for ready monies he had lent his
brother King *James*, and for the 30,000 *l.* a month,
that was by covenant promifed him for the fupport of his
late army in *Germany*. Then my Lord propounded,
that his Majefty's fubjeſts of *Great Britain* were not
well ufed by his officers in the *Sound*: for, though that
was but a tranfitory paffage into the *Baltick* fea, and that
they neither bought nor fold any thing upon the place,
yet they were forced to ſtay there many days to take up
money at high intereft, to pay divers tolls for their
merchandize, before they have expofed them to vent:
therefore it was defired, that for the future what *Engliſh* merchants foever ſhould pafs through the *Sound*, it
ſhould be fufficient for him to regifter an invoice of his
cargazon in the cuftom-houfe book, and give his bond to
pay all duties at his return, when he had made his mar-

ket.

ket. To this my Lord had a fair anfwer, and fo procured a public inftrument under that King's hand and
feal, and figned by his counfellors, which he had
brought over, wherein the propofition was granted ;
which no Ambaffador could obtain before. Then it was
alledged, that the *Englifh* merchant adventurers who
trade into *Hamburgh*, have a new toll lately impofed
upon them at *Luckftadt;* which was defired to be taken
off: to this alfo, there was the like inftrument given, that
the faid toll fhould be levied no more. Laftly, my
Lord (in regard he was to pafs by the *Hague*) defired
that hereditary part, which belonged to the Lady *Elizabeth* out of her grandmother's eftate, becaufe his Majefty knew well what croffes and afflictions fhe had paffed,
and what a numerous iffue fhe had to maintain; and my
Lord of *Leicefter* would engage his honour, and all the
eftate he hath in the world, that this fhould no way prejudice the accompts he is to make with his Majefty of
Great Britain. The King of *Denmark* highly extolled
the noblenefs of this motion; but he protefted, that he
had been fo drained in the late wars, that his chefts are
yet very empty. Hereupon my Lord was feafted, and
fo departed.

He went to the Duke of *Holftein* to *Slefwick*, where
he found him at his caftle of *Gothorp;* and truly, I did
not think to have found fuch a magnificent building in
thefe bleak parts. There alfo my Lord did condole the
death of the late Queen, that Duke's grandmother; and
he received very princely entertainment.

Then we went to *Hufem*, where the like ceremony of
condolement was performed at the Dutchefs of *Holftein*'s court, his Majefty's (our King's) aunt.

Then he came to *Hamburgh*, where that inftrument
which my Lord had procured, for remitting of the new
toll at *Gluckftadt* was delivered to the company of our
merchant adventurers, and fome other good offices done
for that town, as matters ftood betwixt them and the
King of Denmark.

Then

Then we came to *Stode*, where *Lefly* was Governor, who carried his foot in a fcarf for a wound he had received at *Buckftobo*, and he kept that place for the King of *Sweden*; and fome bufinefs of confequence was done there alfo.

So we came to *Broomsbottle*, where we ftaid for a wind fome days; and in the mid-way of our voyage we met with a *Holland* fhip, who told us, the King of *Sweden* was flain: and fo, we returned to *London* in lefs than three months; and if this was not bufinefs enough for fuch a compafs of time, I leave your Lordfhip to judge. So craving your Lordfhip's pardon for this lame account, I relt

Your Lordfhip's moft humble and ready fervant,

London, *Oct.* 1. 1632. J. H.

LETTER II.

To my Brother Dr. HOWELL, *at his. Houfe in* Horfley.

My good Brother,

I Am fafely returned from *Germany*, thanks be to God; and the news which we heard at fea by a *Dutch* Skipper, about the midft of our voyage from *Hamburgh*, it feems proves too true; which was of the fall of the King of *Sweden*. One *Jerbire*, who fays that he was in the very action brought the firft news to this town, and every corner rings of it; yet fuch is the extravagancy of fome, that they will lay wagers he is not dead; and tha Exchange is full of fuch people. He was flain at *Lutzen* field battle, having made the imperial army give ground the day before; and being in purfuance of it, the next morning in a fudden fogg that fell, the cavalry on both fides being engaged, he was killed in the midft of the troops, and none knows who killed him, whether one of his own men, or the enemy; but, finding himfelf mortally hurt he told *Saxen Waymar*, *Coufin*, *I pray look to*

the

the troops, for I think I have enough. His body was not
only rescued, but his forces had the better of the day;
Papenheim being killed before him, whom he esteemed
the greatest Captain of all his enemies: for, he was used
to say, that.he had three men to deal withal, a *Pultrona*,
a *Jesuit*, and a *Soldier*; by the two first, he meant *Wat-
stein* and the Duke of *Bavaria;* by the last, *Papenheim*.

Questionless this *Gustavus* (whose anagram is *Augu-
stus*) was a great Captain, and a gallant man; and, had
he survived that last victory, he would have put the Emperor to such a plunge, that some think he would hardly
have been able to have made head against him to any purpose again. Yet his own allies confess, that none knew
the·bottom of his designs.

He was not much affected to the *English;* witness the
ill usage Marquis *Hamilton* had with his 6000 men,
whereof there returned not 600: the rest died of hun-
ger and sickness, having never seen the face of an enemy; witness also his harshness to our ambassadors, and
the rigid terms he would have tied the Prince *Palsegrave*
unto. So, with my affectionate respects to Mr. *Mous-
champ*, and kind commends to Mr. *Bridger*, I rest

Your loving brother,

Westminster, Dec. 5. 1632.   J. H.

LETTER III.

To the R. R. Dr. FIELD, *Lord Bishop of· St.* David's.

My LORD,

YOUR late letter affected me with two contrary
passions, with gladness and sorrow: the beginning
of it dilated my spirits with apprehensions of joy, that
you are so well recovered of your late sickness, which I
heartily congratulate; but the conclusion of your Lordship's letter contracted my spirits, and plunged them in a
deep sense of just sorrow, while you please to write me
the

the news of my dear father's death. *Permulfit initium, percufit finis.* Truly my Lord, it is the heavieſt news that ever was ſent me; but when I recolleƈt myſelf, and conſider the fairneſs and maturity of his age, and that it was rather a gentle diſſolution than a death. When I contemplate that infinite advantage he hath got by this change and tranſmigration, it much lightens the weight of my grief: for, if ever human ſoul entered heaven, ſurely his is there; ſuch was his conſtant piety to God, his rare indulgence to his children, his charity to his neighbours, and his candour in reconciling differences; ſuch was the gentleneſs of his diſpoſition, his unwearied courſe in aƈtions of virtue, that I wiſh my ſoul no other felicity when ſhe hath ſhaken off theſe rags of fleſh, than to aſcend to his, and co-enjoy the ſame bliſs.

Excuſe me, my Lord, that I take my leave at this time ſo abruptly of you. When this ſorrow is a little digeſted you ſhall hear further from me, for I am

Your Lordſhip's moſt true and humble ſerſitor,

Weſtminſter, May 1. 1633.　　　　　J. H.

L E T T E R IV.

To the Earl of Leiceſter, *at* Penſhurſt.

My LORD,

I Have delivered Maſter Secretary *Cook* an account of the whole legation, as your Lordſhip ordered me; which contained near upon twenty ſheets. I attended him alſo with the note of your extraordinaries, wherein I find him ſomething difficult and dilatory yet. The Governor of the *Eaſtland* company, Mr. Alderman *Clethero*, will attend your Lordſhip at your return to court, to acknowledge your favour unto them. I have delivered him a copy of the tranſaƈtions of things that concerned their company at *Reinsburgh.*

The

The news we heard at fea of the King of *Sweden*'s death is confirmed more and more, and by the computation I have been a little curious to make, I find that he was killed the fame day your Lordfhip fet out of *Hamburgh*. But there is other news come fince, of the death of the Prince *Palatine;* who, as they write, being returned from vifiting the Duke *de deux Ponts* to *Mentz*, was ftruck there with the contagion, yet by fpecial ways of cure, the malignity was expelled and great hopes of recovery, when the news came of the death of the King of *Sweden*, which made fuch impreffions in him, that he died a few days after, having overcome all difficulties concluding with the *Swede*, and the Governor of *Franckindale*, and being ready to enter into a repoffeffion of his country: a fad deftiny!

The *Swedes* bear up ftill, being fomented and fupported by the *French*, who will not fuffer them to leave *Germany* yet. A gentleman that came lately from *Italy*, told me, that there is no great joy in *Rome* for the death of the King of *Sweden*. The *Spaniards* up and down, will not ftick to call this Pope *Lutherano*, and that he had intelligence with the *Swede:* 'tis true, that he hath not been fo forward to affift the Emperor in this quarrel, and that in open confiftory, where there was fuch a *contrafto* betwixt the cardinals for a fupply from St. *Peter*, he declared, that he was well fatisfied that this war in *Germany* was no war of religion, which made him difmifs the imperial ambaffadors with this fhort anfwer, that the Emperor had drawn thefe mifchiefs upon himfelf; for at that time when he faw the *Swedes* upon the frontiers of *Germany*, if he had employed thofe men and monies which he confumed to trouble the peace of *Italy*, in making war againft the Duke of *Mantua*, againft them, he had not had now fo potent an enemy. So I take my leave for this time, being

Your Lordfhip's moft humble and obedient fervant,

Weftminfter, Jan. 3. 1632.   J. H.

L E T T E R   V.

To Mr. E. D.

S I R,

I Thank you a thoufand times for the noble entertainment you gave me at *Berry,* and the pains you took
in fhewing me the antiquities of that place.   In requital,
I can tell you of a ftrange thing I faw lately here; and I
believe it is true: as I paft by St. *Dunftan*'s in *Fleet-
ftreet* the laft *Saturday,* I ftept into a lapidary, or ftone-
cutter's fhop, to treat with the mafter for a ftone to be
put upon my father's tomb; and cafting my eyes up and
down, I fpied a huge marble with a large infcription upon
it; which was thus to my beft remembrance:

" Here lies *John Oxenham,* a goodly young man, in
" whofe chamber, as he was ftruggling with the
" pangs of death, a bird with a white breaft was feen
" fluttering about his bed, and fo vanifhed.

" Here lies alfo *Mary Oxenham,* the fifter of the faid
" *John,* who died the next day, and the fame appa-
" rition was feen in the room."   Then another fifter
is fpoken of.

Then, " Here lies hard by *James Oxenham* the fon of
" the faid *John,* who died a child in his cradle a little
" after, and fuch a bird was feen fluttering about his
" head a little before he expired, which vanifhed af-
" terwards."

At the bottom of the ftone there is:

" Here lies *Elizabeth Oxenham,* the mother of the faid
" *John,* who died fixteen years fince, when fuch a
" bird with a white breaft was feen about her bed be-
" fore her death."

To all thefe there be divers witneffes, both fquires
and ladies, whofe names are engraven upon the ftone.
                                                        This

This ſtone is to be ſent to a town hard by *Exeter* where this happened.

Were you here, I could raiſe a choice diſcourſe with you hereupon. So, hoping to ſee you the next term, to requite ſome of your favours, I reſt

Your true friend to ſerve you,

Weſtminſter, July 3. 1632.   J. H.

L E T T E R   VI.

To Sir ARTHUR INGRAM, *at* York.

S.I R,

OUR greateſt news here now, is, that we have a new Attorney-General, which is news indeed, conſidering the humour of the man, how he hath been always ready to entertain any cauſe whereby he might claſh with the *prerogative;* but now as judge *Richardſon* told him, his head is full of proclamations and devices how to bring money into the exchequer. He hath lately found out amongſt the old records of the *Tower,* ſome precedents for raiſing a tax called *ſhip-money* in all the port towns, when the kingdom is in danger. Whether we are in danger or no at preſent it were preſumption in me to judge ; that belongs to his Majeſty, and his privy-council, who have their choice inſtruments abroad for intelligence, yet one with half an eye may ſee we cannot be ſecure while ſuch huge fleets of men of war, both *Spaniſh, French, Dutch,* and *Dunkirkers,* ſome of them laden with ammunition, men, arms, and armies, do daily ſail on our ſeas, and confront the King's chambers, while we have only three or four ſhips abroad to guard our coaſt and kingdom, and to preſerve the faireſt flower of the crown, the dominions of the narrow-ſea ; which I hear the *French* Cardinal begins to queſtion : and, the *Hollander* lately, would not vail to one of his Majeſty's ſhips that brought over the Duke of *Lenox* and my Lord

Z   *Weſton*

Weston from *Bullen;* and indeed we are jeered abroad, that we send no more ships to guard our seas.

Touching my Lord Ambassador *Weston,* he had a brave journey of it, though it cost him dear: for, it is thought it will stand his Majesty 25,000 *l.* which makes some critics of the times to censure the Lord Treasurer, that now the King wanting money so much, he would send his son abroad to spend him such a sum, only for delivering of presents and compliments; but, I believe they were deceived, for there were matters of state also in the embassy.

The Lord *Weston* passing by *Paris,* intercepted, and opened a pacquet of my Lord of *Holland*'s, wherein there were some letters of her Majesty's: this my Lord of *Holland* takes in that scorn, that he defied him since his coming, and demanded a combate of him, for which he is confined to his house at *Kensington:* so, with my humble service to my noble Lady, I rest

Your most obliged servitor,

Westminst. April 1. 1633.　　　　　J. H.

L E T T E R VII.

To the Lord Viscount Wentworth, *Lord Deputy of* Ireland, *and Lord President of* York, *&c.*

My Lord,

I Was glad to apprehend the opportunity of this pacquet to convey my humble service to your Lordship.

There are odd doings in *France;* and it is no new thing for the *French* to be always a-doing, they have such a stirring genius. The Queen-mother hath made an escape to *Brussels,* and Monsieur to *Lorrain,* where they say, he courts very earnestly the Duke's sister, a young Lady under twenty: they say a contract is passed already, but the *French* Cardinal opposeth it; for they say, that *Lorrain milk seldom breeds good blood in* France.　Not

only

only the King, but the whole *Gallican* church hath protefted againft it in a folemn fynod, for, the heir apparent of the crown of *France* cannot marry without the royal confent. This aggravates a grudge the *French* King hath to the Duke, for fiding with the imperialifts, and for things reflecting upon the dutchy of *Bar;* for which he is homageable to the crown of *France,* as he is to the Emperor for *Lorrain.* A hard tafk it is to ferve two mafters; and an unhappy fituation it is to ly betwixt two puiffant monarchs, as the dukes of *Savoy* and *Lorrain* do : fo, I kifs your Lordfhip's hand, and reft, my Lord,

Your moft affectionate and ready fervitor,

Weftminfter, April 1.   J. H.

L E T T E R VIII.

To the Lord Clifford, *at* Knafburgh.

My Lord,

I Received your Lordfhip's of the laft of *June,* and I return you moft humble thanks for the choice nag you pleafed to fend me, which came in very good plight. Your Lordfhip defires me to lay down what in my travels abroad I obferved of the prefent condition of the *Jews,* once an elect people, but now grown contemptible, and ftrangely fquandered up and down the world. Though fuch a difcourfe exactly framed, might take up a volume, yet I will twift up what I know in this point, upon as narrow a bottom as may be fhut up within the compafs of this letter.

The firft country that expelled the *Jews* was *England.* *France* followed our example next, then *Spain,* and afterwards *Portugal :* nor were they exterminated thefe countries for religion, but for villanies and cheating, for clipping coins, poifoning of water, and counterfeiting of feals.

Thofe

Thofe countries they are permitted to live now moft in amongft chriftians, are *Germany, Holland, Bohemia* and *Italy*, but not in thofe parts where the King of *Spain* hath to do. In the *Levant* and *Turky* they fwarm moft; for their Grand Vizier, and all other great ba-fhaws, have commonly fome *Jew* for their counfellor or fpy, who inform them of the ftate of chriftian princes, poffefs them of a hatred of the religion, and fo incenfe them to a war againft them.

They are accounted the fubtileft and moft fubdolous people upon the earth : the reafon why they are thus de-generated from their primitive fimplicity and innocence, is their often captivities, their defperate fortunes, the neceffity and hatred to which they have been habituated; for, nothing depraves ingenious fpirits, and corrupts clear wits more than indigence. By their profeffion, they are for the moft part brokers, and lombardeers, yet by that bafe and fervile way of frippery trade, they grow rich wherefoever they neft themfelves; and this with their multiplication of children, they hold to be an argument that an extraordinary providence attends them ftill. Me-thinks that fo clear accomplifhments of the prophecies of our Saviour touching that people, fhould work upon them for their converfion, of the deftruction of their city and temple; that they fhould become defpicable, and the tail of all nations; that they fhould be vagabonds, and have no firm habitation.

Touching the firft, they know it came punctually to pafs, and fo have the other two : for they are the moft hateful race of men upon earth, infomuch, that in *Turky* where they are moft valued, if a *mufulman* come to any of their houfes, and leave his fhoes at the door, the *Jew* dare not come in all the while, till the *Turk* hath done what he will with his wife. For the laft, it is wonderful to fee in what confiderable numbers they are difperfed up and down the world; yet, they can never reduce themfelves to fuch a condition and unity as may make a republic, principality or kingdom.

They

They hold that the *Jews* of *Italy*, *Germany*, and the *Levant*, are of *Benjamin*'s tribe. Ten of the tribes at the deftruction of *Jeroboam*'s kingdom were led captives beyond *Euphrates;* whence they never returned, nor do they know what became of them ever after, yet they believe they never became apoftates and *Gentiles*: but the tribe of *Judah*, whence they expect their *Meffias*, of whom one fhall hear them difcourfe with fo much confidence, and felf-pleafing conceit, they fay is fettled in *Portugal;* where they give out to have thoufands of their race, whom they difpenfe withal to make a femblance of chriftianity, even to church degrees.

This makes them breed up their children in the *Lufi-tanian* language; which makes the *Spaniard* have an odd faying, that *el* Portuguez *fe crio del pedo de un Judio; a Portuguefe was engendered of a* Jew's *fart :* as the *Mahometans* have a paffage in their *alcoran, that a cat was made of a lion's breath.*

As they are the moft contemptible people, and have a kind of a fulfome fcent no better than a ftink, that diftinguifhes them from others, fo are they the moft timerous people on earth, and fo utterly incapable of arms ; for they are made neither foldiers nor failors : and this their pufilanimity and cowardice, as well as their cunning and craft, may be imputed to their various thraldoms; contempt and poverty, which hath cowed and daftardized their courage. Befides thefe properties, they are light and giddy-headed, much fymbolizing in fpirits with our apocalyptical zealots, and fiery inter-preters of *Daniel* and other prophets; whereby they often footh, or rather fool themfelves into fome illumination, which really proves but fome egregious dotage.

They much glory of their myfterious *cabal,* wherein they make the reality of things to depend upon letters and words ; but they fay that *Hebrew* only hath this privilege. This *cabal,* which is nought elfe but a tradition, they fay, being tranfmitted from one age to another, was in fome meafure a reparation of our knowledge loft in *Adam;* and they fay it was revealed four times :

firft

firſt to *Adam*, who being thruſt out of paradiſe, and ſitting one day very ſad, and ſorrowing for the loſs of the knowledge he had, of that dependance the creatures have with their Creator, the angel *Raguel* was ſent to comfort him, and inſtruct him, and repair his knowledge herein; and this they call the *cabal;* which was loſt the ſecond time by the flood and *Babel.* Then God diſcovered it to *Moſes* in the buſh; the third time to *Solomon* in a dream, whereby he came to know the beginning, mediety, and conſummation of times, and ſo wrote divers books, which were loſt in the grand captivity. The laſt time, they hold that God reſtored the *cabal* to *Eſdras*, (a book they value extraordinarily) who by God's command withdrew to the wildernefs forty days with five ſcribes, who in that ſpace wrote 204 books: the firſt 130 were to be read by all, but the other 70 were to paſs privately amongſt the *Levites;* and theſe they pretend to be *cabaliſtic*, and not yet all loſt.

There are this day three ſects of *Jews;* the *African* firſt, who beſides the holy ſcriptures, embrace the *Talmud* alſo for authentic; the ſecond receive only the ſcriptures; the third, which are called the *Samaritans,* (whereof there are but a few) admit only of the *Pentateuch*, the five books of *Moſes.*

The *Jews* in general drink no wine without a diſpenſation: when they kill any creature, they turn his face to the Eaſt, ſaying, *Be it ſanctified in the great name of God:* they cut the throat with a knife without a gap, which they hold very profane.

In their ſynagogues, they make one of the beſt ſort to read a chapter of *Moſes*, then ſome mean boy reads a piece of the prophets: in the midſt, there is a round place arched over, where one of their *Rabbies* walks up and down, and in *Portugueſe* magnifies the *Meſſias* to come, comforts their captivity, and rails at Chriſt.

They have a kind of cupboard to repreſent the tabernacle, wherein they lay the tables of the law, which now and then they take out and kiſs: they ſing many tunes, and *Adonai* they make the ordinary name of God. *Jehovah*

Jehovah is pronounced at high feſtivals: at circumciſion, boys are put to ſing ſome of *David*'s Pſalms ſo loud, as drowns the infant's cry. The ſynagogue is hung about with glaſs-lamps burning; every one at his entrance puts on a linen-cope, firſt killing it, elſe they uſe no manner of reverence all the while. Their elders ſometimes fall together by the ears in the very ſynagogue, and with the holy utenſils, as candleſticks, incenſe-pans, and ſuch like, break one another's pates.

Women are not allowed to enter the ſynagogue, but they ſit in a gallery without; for they hold they have not ſo divine a ſoul as men, and are of a lower creation, made only for ſenſual pleaſure and propogation.

Amongſt the *Mahometans* there is no *Jew* capable of a *Turkiſh* habit unleſs he acknowledge Chriſt as much as *Turks* do; which is to have been a great Prophet, whereof they hold there are three only, *Moſes*, *Chriſt*, and *Mahomet*.

Thus my Lord, to perform your commands, which are very prevalent with me, have I couched in this letter what I could of the condition of the *Jews*; and if it may give your Lordſhip any ſatisfaction, I have my reward abundantly. So, I reſt

Your Lordſhip's moſt humble and ready ſervitor,

Weſtminſter, *June* 3. 1633.   J. H.

L E T T E R IX.

To Mr. PHILIP WARRICK, *at* Paris.

S I R,

YOUR laſt unto me was in *French*, of the firſt current, and I am glad you are come ſo ſafe from *Swiſſarland* to *Paris*, as alſo, that you are grown ſo great a proficient in the language. I thank you for the variety of news you ſent me ſo handſomely couched and knit together.

To

To correspond with you, the greatest news we have here, is, that we have a gallant fleet-royal ready to set to sea, for the security of our coasts and commerce, and for the sovereignty of our seas. *Hanse* said the King of *England* was asleep all the while, but now he is awake; nor do I hear doth your *French* Cardinal tamper any longer with our King's title and right to the dominion of the narrow seas. These are brave fruits of the ship-monies.

I hear that the infante Cardinal having been long upon his way to *Brussels,* hath got a notable victory over the *Swedes,* at *Nordlinghen,* where 8000 were slain, *Gustavus Horn,* and other of the prime commanders taken prisoners: they write also that Monsieur's marriage with Madam of *Lorrain* was solemnly celebrated at *Brussels:* she had followed him from *Nancy* in page's apparel, because there were forces in the way. It must needs be a mighty charge to the King of *Spain,* to maintain mother, and son in this manner.

The court affords little news at present, but that there is a love called *platonic* love, which sways there of late. It is a love abstracted from all corporeal gross impressions and sensual appetites, but consists in contemplations and ideas of the mind, not in any carnal fruition. This love sets the wits of the town on work; and they say there will be a mask shortly of it, whereof her Majesty and her maids of honour will be part.

All your friends here in *Westminster* are very well, and very mindful of you, but none more often than

Your most affectionate servitor,

Westminster, June 3. 1634.　　　　　J. H.

L E T T E R X.

To my Brother, Mr. H. P.

Brother,

MY brain was overcaſt with a thick cloud of melancholy, I was become a lump of I know not what, I could ſcarce find any palpitation within me on the left ſide, when yours of the firſt of *September* was brought before me ; it had ſuch a virtue, that it begot new motions in me, like the loadſtone, which by its attractive occult quality moves the dull body of iron, and makes it active ; ſo dull was I then, and ſuch a magnetic property your letter had to quicken me.

There is ſome murmuring, againſt the *ſhip-money,* becauſe the tax is *indefinite,* as alſo, by reaſon that it is levied upon the country towns, as well as maritime ; and for that they ſay, *Noy* himſelf cannot ſhew any record. There are alſo divers patents granted, which are muttered at, as being no better than monopolies. Among others a *Scotſman* got one lately upon the ſtatute of levying twelve-pence for every oath, which the juſtices of peace and conſtables had power to raiſe, and have ſtill ; but this new patentee is to quicken and put more life in the law, and ſee it executed. He hath power to nominate one, or two, or three in ſome pariſhes, which are to have commiſſion from him for this public ſervice, and ſo they are to be exempt from bearing office, which muſt needs deſerve a gratuity ; and I believe this was the main drift of the *Scots* patentee, ſo that he intends to keep his office in the temple, and certainly he is like to be a mighty gainer by it ; for who would not give a good piece of money to be freed from bearing all cumberſome offices ? No more now, but that with my dear love to my ſiſter, I reſt

Your moſt affectionate brother,

Weſtminſter, Aug. 1. 1633.   J. H.

L E T-

LETTER XI.

To the Right Honourable the Lord Viscount SAVAGE *at* Long-Melford.

My LORD,

THE old steward of your courts, Master Atorney-General *Noy*, is lately dead, nor could *Tunbridge* waters do him any good : though he had good matter in his brain, he had, it seems, ill materials in his body; for his heart was shrivelled like a leather penny-purse when he was dissected, nor were his lungs found.

Being such a clerk in the law, all the world wonders he left such an odd will, which is short, and in *Latin :* the substance of it is, that he having bequeathed a few legacies, and left his second son 100 marks a-year, and 500 pounds in money, enough to bring him up in his father's profession, he concludes, *Reliqua meorum omnia primogenito meo* Eduardo, *dissipanda, nec melius unquam speravi ego :* I leave the rest of all my goods to my first-born *Edward*, to be consumed or scattered, for I never hoped better. A strange, and scarce a christian will, in my opinion, for it argues uncharitableness. Nor doth the world wonder less, that he should leave no legacy to some of your Lordship's children, considering what deep obligations he had to your Lordship ; for I am confident he had never been Attorney-General else.

The vintners drink carouses of joy that he is gone, for now they are in hopes to dress meat again, and sell tobacco, beer, sugar, and faggots ; which by a sullen *capricio* of his, he would have restrained them from. He had his humour as other men, but certainly he was a solid rational man; and though no great orator, yet a profound Lawyer, and no man better versed, in the records of the *Tower*. I heard your Lordship often say, with what infinite pains and indefatigable study he came to this knowlege ; and I never heard a more pertinent anagram than was made of his name, *William Noy, I moile in law.*

law. If an *s* be added, it may be applied to my country-man judge *Jones,* an excellent Lawyer too, and a far more genteel man *William Jones, I moile in laws.* No more now, but that I reſt

Your Lordſhip's moſt humble and obliged ſervant,

Weſtminſter, Oct. 1.   J. H.

LETTER XII.

To the Right Honourable the Counteſs of Sunderland.

Madam,

HERE incloſed I ſend your Ladyſhip a letter from the Lord-deputy of *Ireland,* wherein he declares, that the diſpoſing of the Attorneyſhip in *York,* which he paſſed over to me, had no relation to my Lord at all, but it was merely done out of a particular reſpect to me: your Ladyſhip may pleaſe to think of it accordingly touching the accounts.

It is now a good while the two *nephew princes* have been here, I mean the Prince Elector, and Prince *Robert.* The King of *Sweden*'s death, and the late blow at *Norlinghen* hath half blaſted their hopes to do any good for recovery of the *Palatinate* by land: therefore, I hear of ſome new deſigns by ſea, that the one ſhall go to *Madagaſcar,* a great iſland eighty miles long in the *Eaſt-Indies,* never yet colonized by any chriſtian, and Captain *Bond* is to be his Lieutenant; the other is to go with a conſiderable fleet to the *Weſt-Indies,* to ſeize upon ſome place there that may countervail the *Palatinate,* and Sir *Henry Mervin* to go with him: but I hear my Lady *Elizabeth* oppoſeth it, ſaying, that *ſhe will have none of her ſons to be Knights-errant.* There is now profeſſed actual enmity betwixt *France* and *Spain,* for there was a *Herald* at *Arms* ſent lately from *Paris* to *Flanders,* who by ſound of trumpet denounced and proclaimed open war againſt the King of *Spain* and all

his

his dominions : this. Herald 'left and fixed up the defiance in all the towns as-he paſſed ; ſo that whereas before, the war was but collateral and auxiliary, there is now proclaimed hoſtility between them, notwithſtanding that they have one another's filters in their beds every night. What the reaſon of this war is, truly, Madam I cannot tell, unleſs it be reaſon of ſtate, to prevent the further growth of the *Spaniſh* monarchy ; and there be a multitude of examples how preventive wars have been practiſed from all times. Howſoever, it is too ſure that abundance of chriſtian blood will be ſpilt. So, I humbly take my leave, and reſt, Madam,

Your Ladyſhip's moſt obedient and faithful ſervant,
Weſtminſter, June 4. 1635. J H.

LETTER XIII.

To the Earl of Leiceſter, *at* Penſhurſt.

My LORD,

I Am newly returned out of *France* from a flying journey as far as *Orleans*, which I made at the requeſt of Maſter Secretary *Windebank*, and I hope I ſhall receive ſome fruits of it hereafter. There is yet a great reſentment in many places in *France* for the beheading of *Montmorency*, whom *Henry* IV. was uſed to ſay to be the better gentleman than himſelf, for in his colours he carried this motto, *Dieu ayde le premier Chevalier de* France. God help the firſt Knight of *France*, he died upon a ſcaffold in *Tholouſe* in the flower of his years, at thirty-four, and hath left no iſſue behind, ſo that noble old family extinguiſhed in a ſnuff. His treaſon was very foul, having received particular commiſſions from the King to make an extraordinary levy of men and money in *Languedoc*, which he turned afterwards directly againſt the King ; againſt whoſe perſon he appeared armed in open
field,

field, and in a boftile pofture for foménting of Monfieut's rebellion.

The infante Cardinal is come to *Bruffels* at laft through many difficulties; and fome few days before, Monfieur made femblance to go a hawking, and fo fled to *France*, but left his mother behind, who fince the Archdutchefs death is not fo well looked on as formerly in that country.

Touching our bufinefs in the exchequer, Sir *Robert Pye* went with me this morning of purpofe to my Lord Treafurer about it, and told me with much earneftnefs and affurance, that there fhall be a fpeedy courfe taken for your Lordfhip's fatisfaction.

I delivered my Lord of *Lindfey* the manufcript he lent your Lordfhip of his father's embaffy to *Denmark;* and herewith I prefent your Lordfhip with a compleat diary of your own late legation, which hath coft me fome toil and labour. So, I reft always

Your Lordfhip's moft humble and ready ferviter,
Weftminft. June 19. 1635.   J. H.

LETTER XIV.

To my honoured Friend and Father, Mr. BEN. JOHNSON.

Father BEN.

BEING lately in *France,* and returning in a coach from *Paris* to *Rouen,* I lighted upon the fociety of a knowing gentleman who related unto me a choice ftory, whereof peradventure you may make fome ufe in your way.

Some hundred and odd years fince, there was in *France* one Captain *Coucy* a gallant gentleman of an antient extraction, and keeper of *Coucy* caftle, which is yet ftanding, and in good repair. He fell in love with a young gentlewoman, and courted her for his wife: there was a reciprocal love between them, but her parents underftanding

A a   derftanding

derſtanding of it, by way of prevention they ſhuffled up
a forced-match betwixt her and one Monſieur *Faiel*, who
was a great heir. Captain *Coucy* hereupon quitted *France*
in diſcontent, and went to the wars in *Hungary* againſt
the *Turb*, where he received a mortal wound, not far
from *Buda*. Being carried-to his lodging, he languiſhed
ſome days, but a little before his death he ſpoke to an
antient ſervant of his, that he had many proofs of-his fidelity and truth, but now he had a great buſineſs to en-
truſt him with, which he conjured him by all means to
do; which was, that after his death, he ſhould get his
body to be opened, and then to take his heart out of his
breaſt, and put it in an earthen-pot to be baked to powder, then to put the powder into a handſome box, with
that bracelet of hair he had worn long about his left
wriſt; which was a lock of Madamoiſelle *Faiel*'s hair,
and put it amongſt the powder together with a little note
he had written with his own blood to her; and, after he
had given him the rites of burial, to make all the ſpeed
he could to *France*, and deliver the ſaid box to Madamoiſelle *Faiel*. The old ſervant did as his maſter had
commanded him, and ſo went to *France;* and coming
one day to Monſieur *Faiel*'s houſe, he ſuddenly met with
that gentleman, who examined him, becauſe he knew
he was Captain *Coucy*'s ſervant; and finding him timerous
and faltering in his ſpeech, he ſearched him, and found
the ſaid box in his pocket, with the note which expreſſed
what was therein. He diſmiſſed the bearer with mena-
ces, that he ſhould come no more near his houſe. Monſieur *Faiel* going in, ſent for his cook, and delivered him
the powder, charging him to make a little well reliſhed
diſb of it, without loſing a jot of it, for it was a very
coſtly thing; and commanded him to bring it in himſelf,
after the laſt courſe at ſupper. The cook bringing in
the diſh accordingly, Monſieur *Faiel* commanded all to
void the room, and began a ſerious diſcourſe with his
wife, how ever ſince he had married her, he obſerved
ſhe was always melancholy, and he feared ſhe was inclining to a conſumption, therefore he had provided for her a

very precious cordial, which he was well affured would cure her: thereupon he made her eat up the whole difh, and afterward, much importuning him to know what it was, he told her at laft, fhe had eaten *Concy*'s heart, and fo drew the box out of his pocket, and fhewed her the note and bracelet; in a fudden exultation of joy, fhe with a far fetched figh faid, *This is precious indeed*, and fo licked the difh, faying, *It is fo precious, that it is pity to put ever any meat upon it.* So fhe went to bed, and in the morning fhe was found ftone dead.

This gentleman told me that this fad ftory is painted in *Coucy* caltle, and remains frefh to this day.

In my opinion, which vails to yours, this is choice and rich ftuff for you to put upon your loom, and make a curious web of.

I thank you for the laft *regalo* you gave me at your *mufeum*, and for the good company. I heard you cenfured lately at court, that you have lighted too foul upon Sir *Inigo*, and that you write with a *porcupine*'s quill dipped in too much gall. Excufe me that I am fo free with you; it is becaufe I am in no common way of friend-fhip.

Yours,

Weftminfter, May 3.   J. H.

LETTER XV.

To my Lord Vifcount S.

My LORD,

HIS Majefty is lately returned from *Scotland*, having given that nation fatisfaction to their long defires, to have him come hither to be crowned. I hear fome mutter at Bifhop *Laud*'s carriage there, that it was too haughty and pontifical.

Since the death of the King of *Sweden*, a great many *Scots* commanders are come over, and make a fhining fhew at court: what trade they will take hereafter I know not, having been fo inured to the wars. I pray God keep us from commotions at home, betwixt the two kingdoms, to find them work. I hear one Colonel *Lefly* is gone away difcontented, becaufe the King would not Lord him.

The old rotten Duke of *Bavaria*, for he hath divers iffues about his body, hath married one of the Emperor's fifters, a young lady little above twenty, and he near upon fourfcore. There is another remaining, who they fay, is intended for the King of *Poland*, notwithftanding his pretences to the young Lady *Elizabeth;* about which, Prince *Razevill* and other ambaffadors have been here lately, but that King being elective, muft marry as the eftates will have him. His mother was the Emperor's fifter, therefore fure he will not offer to marry his coufin-german; but it is no news for the houfe of *Auftria* to do fo, to ftrengthen their race. And if the *Bavarian* hath male-iffue of this young Lady, the fon is to fucceed him in the electorfhip, which may conduce much to ftrengthen the continuance of the empire in the *Auftrian* family. So, with a conftant perfervance of my hearty defires to ferve your Lordfhip, I reft, my Lord,

Your moft humble fervitor,

Weftminfter, Sept. 7. **J. H.**

LETTER XVI.

To my Coufin Mr. WILL. ST. GEON, *at* St. Omer.

Coufin,

I Was lately in your father's company, and I found him much difcontented at the courfe you take; which he not only protefts againft, but he vows never to give you his bleffing if you perfevere in it. I would wifh you to defcend into yourfelf, and ferioufly ponder what a weight a father's bleffing or curfe carries with it; for, there is **nothing**

nothing conduceth more to the happiness or infelicity of the child. Amongst the ten commandments in the *decalogue*, that which enjoins obedience from children to parents, hath only a benediction (of longevity) added to it. There be clouds of examples for this, but one I will instance in: when I was in *Valentia* in *Spain*, a gentleman told me of a miracle which happened in that town; which was, that a proper young man under twenty, was executed there for a crime, and before he was taken down from off the tree, there were many gray and white hairs had budded forth of his chin, as if he had been a man of sixty. It struck amazement in all men, but this interpretation was made of it, that the said young man might have lived to such an age, if he had been dutiful to his parents, unto whom, he had been barbarously disobedient all his life time.

There comes herewith a large letter to you from your father: let me advise you to conform your courses to his counsel, otherwise, it is an easy matter to be a Prophet what misfortunes will inevitably befal you; which by a timely obedience you may prevent, and I wish you may have grace to do it accordingly. So, I rest

Your loving well-wishing cousin,

Lond. May 1. 1634.   J. H.

LETTER XVII.

To the Lord Deputy of Ireland.

My LORD,

THE Earl of *Arundel* is lately returned from *Germany*, and his gallant comportment in that embassy deserved to have had better success. He found the Emperor conformable, but the old *Bavarian* froward, who will not part with any thing till he have monies reimbursed, which he spent in these wars, and for which he hath the upper *Palatinate in deposito;* insomuch, that in

A a 3   all

all probability all hopes are cut off of ever recovering that country, but by the fame means that it was taken away, which was by the fword: therefore, they write from *Holland* of a new army, which the Prince *Palatine* is like to have fhortly, to go up to *Germany*, and pufh on his fortunes with the *Swedes*.

The *French* King hath taken all *Nancy* and almoft all *Lorrain* lately, but he was forced to put a fox tail to the lion's fkin, which his Cardinal helped him to before he could do the work. The quarrel is, that the Duke fhould marry his fifter to Monfieur, contrary to promife; that he fided with the imperialifts againft his confederates in *Germany*, and that he neglected to do homage for the dutchy of *Bar*.

My Lord Vifcount *Savage* is lately dead, who is very much lamented by all that knew him, I could have wifhed had it pleafed God, that his father-in-law, who is riper for the other world had gone before him: fo, I reft

Your Lordfhip's moft humble and ready fervitor,

Weftminfter, April 6. **J. H.**

L E T T E R XVIII.

To the Right Honourable Sir PETER WICHTS, *Lord Ambaffador at* Conftantinople.

My LORD,

IT feems there is fome angry ftar that hath hung over this bufinefs of the *Palatinate* from the beginning of thefe *German* wars to this very day, which will too evidently appear, if one fhould mark and deduce matters from their firft rife.

You may remember how poorly *Prague* was loft: the Bifhop of *Halverftadt* and Count *Mansfelt* fhuffled up and down a good while, and did great matters, but all came to nothing at laft. You may remember how one
of

of the ſhips-royal was caſt away in carrying over the laſt, and the 12,000 men he had hence periſhed very miſerably, and he himſelf, as they write, died in a poor hoſtrey with one lacquey, as he was going to *Venice* to a bank of money he had ſtored up there for a dead lift. Your Lordſhip knows what ſucceſs the King of *Denmark* had, (and our 6000 men under Sir *Charles Morgan*) for while he thought to make new acqueſts, he was in hazard to loſe all that he had, had he not had favourable propoſitions tendered him. There were never poor chriſtians periſhed more lamentably than thoſe 6000 we ſent under M. *Hamilton* for the aſſiſtance of the King of *Sweden*, who did much, but you know what became of him at laſt; how diſaſterouſly the Prince *Palatine* himſelf fell, and in what an ill conjuncture of time, being upon the very point of being reſtored to his country.

But now we have as bad news as any we had yet, for the young Prince *Palatine*, and his brother Prince *Rupert*, having got a jolly conſiderable army in *Holland* to try their fortunes in *Germany* with the *Swedes*, they had advanced as far as *Munſterland* and *Weſtphalia*, and, having lain before *Lengua*, they were forced to raiſe the ſiege; and one General *Hatzfield* purſuing them, there was a ſore battle fought, wherein Prince *Rupert*, my Lord *Craven* and others were taken priſoners. The Prince *Palatine* himſelf, with Major *King*, thinking to get over the *Weſer* in a coach, the water being deep, and not fordable, he ſaved himſelf by the help of a willow, and ſo went a-foot all the way to *Munden*, the coach and the coachman being drowned in the river. There were near upon 2000 ſlain on the *Palſgrave*'s ſide, and ſcarce the twentieth part ſo many on *Hatzfield*'s. Major *Gœtus*, one of the chief commanders was killed.

I am ſorry I muſt write unto you this ſad ſtory; yet to countervail ſomething, *Saxon Waymar* thrives well, and is like to get *Briſac* by help of the *French* forces. All
your

your friends here are well, and remember your Lordſhip,, but none more oft than

Your moſt humble and ready ſervitor,.
London, *June* 5. 1635. J. H.

LETTER XIX.

To Sir SACKVIL C. *Knight.*.

SIR,

I Was as glad that you have lighted upon ſo excellent a Lady, as if an Aſtronomer by his optics had found out a new ſtar; and, if a wife be the beſt or worſt fortune of a man, certainly you are one of the fortunateſt men in this iſland.

The greateſt news I can write unto you, is of a bloody banquet that was lately at *Liege,* where a great faction was a fomenting betwixt the imperialiſts, and thoſe that were devoted to *France;* amongſt whom, one *Ruelle,* a popular Burgue-maſter was chief. The count of *War-ſuzee,* a vaſſal of the King of *Spain,* having fled thither for ſome offence, to ingratiate himſelf again into the King of *Spain's* favour, invited the ſaid *Ruelle* to a feaſt, and after brought him into a private chamber, where he had provided a ghoſtly father to confeſs him; and ſo ſome of the ſoldiers whom he had provided before to guard the houſe, diſpatched the Burgue-maſter. The town hearing this, broke into the houſe, cut to pieces the ſaid Count, with ſome of his ſoldiers, and dragged his body up and down the ſtreets. You know ſuch a fate befel *Walſtein* in *Germany* of late years, who having got all the Emperor's forces into his hands, was found to have intelligence with the *Swedes;* therefore the imperial ban was not only pronounced againſt him, but a reward promiſed to any that ſhould diſpatch him: ſome of the Emperor's ſoldiers at a great wedding in *Egra,* of which band of ſoldiers Colonel *Butler* an *Iriſhman* was chief.

chief, broke into his lodging when he was at dinner, killed him, with three commanders more that were at table with him, and threw his body out at a window into the ſtreets.

I hear *Butler* is made ſince Count of the empire: ſo, humbly kiſſing your noble Lady's hands, I reſt

Your faithful ſervitor,

London, Jan. 5.   J. H.

LETTER XX.

To Sir EDWARD B. *Knight.*

SIR,

I Received yours this *Maunday-Thurſday:* and whereas amongſt other paſſages, and high endearments of love, you deſire to know what method I obſerve in the exerciſe of my devotions, I thank you for your requeſt, which I have reaſon to believe doth proceed from an extraordinary reſpect unto me; and I will deal with you herein, as one ſhould do with his confeſſor.

'Tis true, though there be rules and rubrics in our *Liturgy* ſufficient to guide every one in the performance of all holy duties, yet I believe every one hath ſome mode and model or formulary of his own, ſpecially for private cubicular devotions.

I will begin with the laſt day of the week, and with the latter end of that day, I mean *Saturday* evening, on which, I have faſted ever ſince I was a youth in *Venice,* for being delivered from a very great danger. This year I uſe ſome extraordinary acts of devotion to uſher in the enſuing *Sunday* in hymns, and prayers of my own penning before I go to bed: On *Sunday* morning I riſe earlier than upon other days, to prepare myſelf for the ſanctifying of it: nor do I uſe barber, taylor, ſhoemaker, or any other mechanic that morning; and whatſoever diverſions, or lets may hinder me the week before, I

never

never mifs, but in cafe of ficknefs, to repair to God's holy houfe that day, where I come before prayers begin, to make myfelf fitter for the work by fome previous meditations, and take the whole fervice along with me: nor do I love to mingle fpeech with any in the interim, about news or worldly negotiations in God's holy houfe. I proftrate myfelf in the humbleft and decenteft way of genuflection I can imagine: nor do I believe there can be any excefs of exterior humility in that place; therefore I do not like thofe fquatting unfeemly bold poftures upon one's tail, or muffling the face in the hat, or thrufting it in fome hole, or covering it with one's hand; but with bended knee and an open confident face, I fix my eyes on the Eaft part of the church, and heaven. I endeavour to apply every title of the fervice to my own confcience and occafions; and I believe the want of this, with the huddling up, and carelefs reading of fome minifters, with the commonnefs of it, is the greateft caufe that many do undervalue and take a furfeit of our public fervice.

——For the reading and finging *pfalms*, whereas moft of them are either petitions or euchariftical ejaculations, I liften to them more attentively, and make them my own. When I ftand at the *Creed*, I think upon the cuftom they have in *Poland*, and elfewhere, for gentlemen to draw their fwords all the while, intimating thereby that they will defend it with their lives and blood. And for the *decalogue*, whereas others ufe to rife, and fit, I ever kneel at it in the humbleft and tremblingeft pofture of all, to crave remiffion for the breaches paft of any of God's holy commandments, (efpecially the week before) and future grace to obferve them.

I love a holy devout fermon, that firft checks, and then chears the confcience, that begins with the law, and ends with the gofpel: but I never prejudicate or cenfure any preacher, taking him as I find him.

And now that we are not only adulted, but antient chriftians, I believe the moft acceptable facrifice we can fend up to heaven, is *prayer* and *praife;* and that *fermons*

are

are not fo effential as either of them to the true practice
of devotion. The reft of the holy Sabbath, I fequefter my body and mind as much as I can from worldly affairs.

Upon *Monday* morning, as foon as the *Cinq-ports* are
open, I have a particular prayer of thanks, that I am
reprived to the beginning of that week; and every day
following, I knock thrice at heaven's gate, in the morning, in the evening, ard at night; befides prayers at
meals, and fome other occafional ejaculations, as upon
the putting on of a clean fhirt, wafhing my hands, and at
lighting of candles; which becaufe they are fudden, I do
in the the third perfon.

Tuefday morning I rife winter and fummer as foon
as I awake, and fend up a more particular facrifice for
fome reafons; and as I am difpofed, or have bufinefs,
I go to bed again.

Upon *Wednefday* night I always faft, and perform alfo
fome extraordinary acts of devotion, as alfo upon *Friday*
night; and *Saturday* morning, as foon as my fenfes are
unlocked, I get up. And in the fummer time, I am
oftentimes abroad in fome private field, to attend the
fun-rifing; and as I pray thrice every day, fo I faft thrice
every week, at leaft I eat but one meal upon *Wednefdays,*
Fridays, and *Saturdays,* in regard I am jealous with myfelf, to have more infirmities to anfwer for than others.

Before I go to bed I make a fcrutiny what peccant
humours have reigned in me that day, and fo I reconcile
myfelf to my Creator, and ftrike a *tally* in the *exchequer*
of heaven for my *quietus eft,* before I clofe my eyes, and
leave no burden upon my confcience.

Before I prefume to take the holy facrament, I ufe
fome extraordinary acts of humiliation to prepare myfelf fome days before, and by doing fome deeds of charity; and commonly I compofe fome new prayers, and
divers of them written in my own blood.

I ufe not to rufh rafhly into prayer without a trembling
precedent meditation; and if any odd thoughts intervene,
and grow upon me, I check myfelf, and recommence;
and

and this is incident to long prayers, which are more fubject to man's weaknefs and the devil's malice.

I thank God I have this fruit of my foreign travels,
that I can pray to him every day of the week in a feveral
language, and upon *Sunday* in feven, which in oraifons
of my own I punctually perform in my private pomeridian
devotions.

Et fic æternam contendo attingere vitam.

By thefe fteps I ftrive to climb up to heaven, and my
foul prompts me I fhall thither ; for there is no object in
the world delights me more than to caft up my eyes that
way, efpecially in a ftar-light night : and if my mind be
overcaft with any odd clouds of melancholy, when I
look up and behold that glorious fabrick, which I hope
fhall be my country hereafter, there are new fpirits begot
in me prefently, which makes me fcorn the world, and
the pleafures thereof, confidering the vanity of the one,
and the inanity of the other.

Thus my foul ftill moves *Eaftward*, as all the heavenly bodies do ; but I muft tell you, that as thofe bodies
are over-maftered, and fnatched away to the *Weft, raptu
primi mobilis*, by the general motion of the tenth fphere,
fo by thofe epidemical infirmities which are incident to
man, I am often fnatched away a clean contrary courfe,
yet my foul ftill perfifts in her own proper motion. I am
often at variance and angry with myfelf, (nor do I hold
this anger to be any breach of charity) when I confider
that as my Creator intended this body of mine, though
a lump of clay, to be a temple of his Holy Spirit, my affections fhould turn it often to a *brothel-houfe*, my paffions to a bedlam, and my exceffes to an hofpital.

Being of a lay profeffion, I humbly conform to the
conftitutions of the church, and my fpiritual fuperiors ;
and I hold this obedience to be an acceptable facrifice
to God.

Difference in opinion may work a difaffection in me,
but not a deteftation ; I rather pity than hate *Turb* or
infidel, for they are of the fame metal, and bear the fame
ftamp

ſtamp as I do, though the inſcriptions differ : if I hate any, 'it is thoſe ſchiſmaticks that puzzle the ſweet peace of our church, ſo that I could be content to ſee an *Anabaptiſt* go to hell on a *Browniſt*'s back.

Noble Knight, now that I have thus eviſcerated myſelf, and dealt clearly with you, I deſire by way of correſpondence that you would tell me, what way you take in your journey to heaven : for if my breaſt ly ſo open to you, it is not fitting yours ſhould be ſhut up to me ; therefore I pray let me hear from you when it may ſtand with your convenience.

So I wiſh you your heart's deſire here, and heaven hereafter, becauſe I am

Yours in no vulgar way of friendſhip,
London, July 25. 1635.   J. H.

LETTER XXI.

To SIMON DIGBY, *Eſq; at* Moſcow, *the Emperor of* Ruſſia'*s Court.*

S I R,

I Received yours by Mr. *Pickhurſt*, and I am glad to find that the rough clime of *Ruſſia* agrees ſo well with you ; ſo well, as you write, as the catholick air of *Madrid*, or the imperial air of *Vienna*, where you had ſuch honourable employments.

The greateſt news we have here is, that we have a Biſhop Lord Treaſurer ; and it is news indeed in theſe times, though it was no news you know in the times of old to have a Biſhop Lord Treaſurer of *England*. I believe he was merely paſſive in this buſineſs : the active inſtrument that put the white ſtaff in his hands, was the metropolitan at *Lambeth*.

I have other news alſo to tell you : we have a brave new ſhip, a royal galleon, the like they ſay did never ſpread ſail upon ſalt-water, take her true and well com-

B b   pacted

pacted symmetry, with all her dimensions together: for
her burden, she hath as many tons as there were years
since the incarnation, when she was built, which are 1636 :
she is in length 127 foot, her greatest breadth, with the
planks is 46 foot and six inches: her depth from the
breadth is 19 foot and four inches: she carrieth, 100
pieces of ordnance, wanting four, whereof she hath three
tyre: half a score of men may stand in her lanthorn: the
charges his Majesty hath been at in building of her, are
computed at 80,000 *l.* one whole year's ship-money. Sir
Robert Mansel launched her, and by his Majesty's command called her *the Sovereign of the sea.* Many would
have had her to be named the *Edgar;* who was one of
the most famous *Saxon* kings this island had, and the
most potent at sea. *Ranulphus Cestrensis* writes, that
the had 400 ships, which every year after *Easter* went
out in four fleets to scour the coasts. Another author
writes, that he had four kings to row him once upon the
Dee. But the title he gave himself, was a notable lofty
one; which was this, *Altitonantis Dei largeflua clementia
qui est Rex regum, ego* Edgardus *Anglorum Basilius, om-
nium regum, insularum, oceanique Britanniam circum-
jacentis, cunctarumque nationum quæ infra eam inclu-
duntur, Imperator & Dominus,* &c. I do not think
your grand Emperor of *Russia* hath a loftier title. I
confess the Sophy of *Persia* hath a higher one, though
profane and ridiculous, in comparison of this: for he
calls himself, *The star high and mighty, whose head is
covered with the sun, whose motion is comparable to the
æthereal firmament, Lord of the mountains* Caucasus
and Taurus, *of the four rivers* Euphrates, Tygris, Ara-
xis *and* Indus; *bud of honour, mirror of virtue, rose of
delight, and nutmeg of comfort.* It is a huge descent
methinks, to begin with a *star* and end in a *nutmeg.*

    All your friends here in court and city are well, and
often mindful of you, with a world of good wishes; and
you cannot be said to be out of *England,* as long as you
live in so many noble memories. Touching mine, you

have

have a large room in it, for you are one of my chief inmates. So, with my humble fervice to your Lady, I reſt

Your moſt faithful ſervitor,

Lond. *July* 1. 1635.   J. H.

LETTER XXII.

To Dr. THOMAS PRICHARD.

Dear Dr.

I Have now had too long a fuperfedeas from employment, having engaged myfelf to a fatal man at court,
(by his own feeking) who I hoped, and had reafon to
expect (for I waved all other ways) that he would have
been a *fcale* towards my rifing, but he hath rather proved an *inſtrument* to my ruin: it may be he will profper
accordingly.

I am fhortly bound for *Ireland*, and it may be the
ſtars will caſt a more benign aſpect upon me in the
Weſt; you know who got the *Perſian* empire by looking
that way for the firſt beams of the fun-rifing, rather than
towards the *Eaſt*.

My Lord Deputy hath made often profeſſions to do
me a pleaſure, and I intend now to put him upon it.

I purpofe to pafs by the *Bath* for a pain I have in my
arm, proceeding from a defluxion of rheum; and then I
will take *Brecknock* in my way, to comfort my fiſter
Penry, who I think hath loſt one of the beſt hufbands in
all the thirteen fhires of *Wales*.

So with apprecation of all happinefs to you, I reſt

Yours while,

London, *Feb.* 10. 1637.   J. H.

L E T T E R XXIII.

To Sir KENELM DIGBY *Knight, from* Bath.

S I R,

YOUR being then in the country, when I began my journey for *Ireland*, was the caufe I could not kifs your hands, therefore, I fhall do now from *Bath* what I fhould have done at *London*. ·

Being here for a diftillation of rheum that pains me in one of my arms, and having had about 3000 ftrokes of a pump upon me in the Queen's *bath;* and having been here now divers days, and viewed the feveral qualities of thefe waters, I fell to contemplate a little what fhould be the reafon of fuch extraordinary actual heat, and medicinal virtue in them. I have feen and read of divers *baths* abroad, as thofe of *Cadanel* and *Avinian*, in *Iagro Senenfi*, the *Grotta* in *Vicerbio*, thofe between *Naples* and *Puteolum* in *Campania;* and, I have been a little curious to know the reafon of thofe rare lymphatical properties in them above other waters. I find that fome impute it to wind, or air, or fome exhalations fhut up in the bowels of the earth; which either by their own nature, or by their violent motion and agitation, or attrition upon rocks, and narrow paffages do gather heat, and fo impart it to the waters.

⸰Others attribute this *balneal* heat unto the fun, whofe all-fearching beams penetrating the pores of the earth, do heat the waters.

Others think this heat to proceed from quick-lime, which by common experience we find to heat any waters caft upon it, and alfo to kindle any combuftible fubftance put upon it.

Laftly, there are fome that afcribe this heat to a fubterranean fire kindled in the bowels of the earth upon fulphury and bituminous matter.

'Tis true, all thefe may be general concurring caufes, but not the adequate, proper and peculiar reafon of *balneal*

neal heats; and herein, truly our learned countryman Dr. *Jorden* hath got the ſtart of any that ever wrote of this ſubject, and goes to work like a ſolid Philoſopher: for, having treated of the generation of minerals, he finds that they have their ſeminaries in the womb of the earth repleniſhed with active ſpirits; which meeting with apt matter and adjuvant cauſes, do proceed to the generation of ſeveral ſpecies; according to the nature of the efficient, and fitneſs of the matter. In this work of generation, as there is *generatio unius,* ſo there is *corruptio alterias;* and this cannot be done without a ſuperior power which by moiſture dilating itſelf, works upon the matter like a leavening and ferment, to bring it to its own purpoſe.

This motion betwixt the agent ſpirit, and patient matter, produceth an actual heat: *for motion is the fountain of heat,* which ſerves as an inſtrument to advance the work; for as cold dulls, ſo heat quickeneth all things. Now for the nature of this heat, it is not a deſtructive violent heat, as that of fire, but a generative gentle heat joined with moiſture, nor needs it air for eventilation. This natural heat is daily obſerved by digging in the mines; ſo then, while minerals are thus engendering, and *in ſolutis principiis,* in their liquid forms, and not conſolidated into hard bodies, (for then they have not that virtue) they impart heat to the neighbouring waters. So then it may be concluded, that this ſoil about the bath is a mineral vein of earth, and the fermenting gentle temper of generative heat that goes to the production of the ſaid minerals doth impart and actually communicate this *baltieal* virtue and medicinal heat to theſe waters.

This ſubject of *mineral waters* would afford an ocean of matter, were one to compile a ſolid diſcourſe of it; and I pray excuſe me, that I have preſumed in ſo narrow a compaſs as a letter to comprehend ſo much, which is nothing I think in compariſon of what you know already of this matter.

So I take my leave, and humbly kiſs your hands, being always

Your moſt faithful and ready ſervitor,

Bath, July 3. 1638. J. H.

LETTER XXIV.

To Sir EDWARD SAVAGE, *Knight, at* Towerhill.

SIR,

I Am come ſafely to *Dublin,* over an angry boiſterous ſea; whether it was my voyage on ſalt-water, or change of air, being now under another clime, which was the cauſe of it, I know not, but I am ſuddenly freed of the pain in my arm, when neither *bath,* nor plaiſters, and other remedies could do me good.

I delivered your letter to Mr. *James Dillon,* but nothing can be done in that buſineſs till your brother *Pain* comes to town. I met here with divers of my *Northern* friends, who I knew at *York.* Here is a moſt ſplendid court kept at the caſtle, and except that of the Viceroy of *Naples,* I have not ſeen the like in chriſtendom; and in one point of *grandeza,* the Lord Deputy here goes beyond him, for he can confer honours, and dub knights; which that Viceroy cannot, nor any other I know of. Traffick increaſeth here wonderfully, with all kind of bravery and building.

I made an humble motion to my Lord, that in regard buſineſſes of all ſorts did multiply here daily, and that there was but one Clerk of the council (Sir *Paul Davis*) who was able to diſpatch buſineſs, (Sir *William Uſher* his collegue being very aged and bedrid) his Lordſhip would pleaſe to think of me. My Lord gave me an anſwer full of good reſpeſt, to ſucceed Sir *William* after his death.

No more now, but with my moſt affeſtionate reſpeſts unto you, I reſt

Your faithful ſervitor,

Dublin, May 3. 1639. J. H.

LET-

LETTER XXV.

To Dr. Usher, *Lord Primate of* Ireland.

MAY it pleafe your Grace to accept of my moſt humble acknowledgment, for thoſe noble favours I received at *Drogheda;* and that you pleaſed to communicate unto me thoſe rare manuſcripts in ſo many languages, and divers choice authors in your library.

Your learned work, *De primordiis eccleſiarum Britannicarum,* which you pleaſed to ſend me, I have ſent to *England,* and ſo it ſhall be conveyed to *Jeſus College* in *Oxford,* as a gift from your Grace.

I hear that Cardinal *Barberino,* one of the Pope's nephews, is ſetting forth the works of *Faſtidius,* a *Britiſh* Biſhop called *De vita Chriſtiana.* It was written 300 years after our Saviour, and *Holſtenius* hath the care of the impreſſion.

I was lately looking for a word in *Suidas,* and I lighted upon a ſtrange paſſage in the name Ἰησῦς, that in the reign of *Juſtinian* the Emperor, one *Theodoſius* a *Jew,* a man of great authority, lived in *Jeruſalem,* with whom a rich goldſmith who was a chriſtian, was in much favour and very familiar, The goldſmith in private diſcourſe told him one day, that " he wondered, he being " a man of ſo great underſtanding did not turn chriſtian, " conſidering how he found all the prophecies of the " law ſo evidently accompliſhed in our Saviour, and our " Saviour's prophecies accompliſhed ſince." *Theodoſius* anſwered, " that it did not ſtand with his ſecurity and " continuance in authority to turn chriſtian, but he had " a long time a good opinion of that religion, and he " would diſcover a ſecret unto him, which was not yet " come to the knowledge of any chriſtian." It was, that when the temple was founded in *Jeruſalem,* there were twenty-two prieſts according to the number of the *Hebrew* letters, to officiate in the temple; and when any was choſen, his name, with his father's and mother's were

uſed

uſed to be regiſtered in a fair book. In the time of
Chriſt, a Prieſt died, and he was choſen in his place, but
when his name was to be entered, his father *Joſeph* being dead, his mother was ſent for, who being aſked who
was his father? She anſwered, that ſhe never knew man,
but that ſhe conceived by an angel: ſo his name was regiſtered in theſe words, JESUS CHRIST THE SON OF
GOD AND OF THE VIRGIN MARY. This record at
the deſtruction of the temple was preſerved, and is to be
ſeen in *Tiberias* to this day. I humbly deſire your Grace's
opinion hereof in your next.

They write to me from *England* of rare news in
France; which is, that the Queen is delivered of a
Dauphine, the wonderfulleſt thing of this kind that any
ſtory can parallel; for this is the twenty-third year ſince
ſhe was married, and hath continued childleſs all this
while, ſo that now Monſieur's cake is dough; and I believe he will be more quiet hereafter. So, I reſt

Your Grace's moſt devoted ſervitor,

Dublin, March 1. 1639.   J. H.

LETTER XXVI.

To my Lord Clifford, *from* Edinburgh.

My LORD,

I Have ſeen now all the King of *Great Britain's*
dominions; and he is a good traveller that hath ſeen
all his dominions. I was born in *Wales,* I have been in
all the four corners of *England:* I have traverſed the
diameter of *France* more than once, and now I am come
through *Ireland* into this kingdom of *Scotland.* This
town of *Edinburgh* is one of the faireſt ſtreets that ever
I ſaw, (excepting that of *Palermo* in *Sicily*) it is about a
mile long, coming ſloping down from the caſtle (called of
old the *Caſtle of Virgins,* and by *Pliny, Caſtrum ala-
tum*) to *Holyroodhouſe,* now the royal palace; and theſe

two

two begin and terminate the town. I am come hither
in a very convenient time, for here is a *national affembly*,
and a *parliament*, my Lord *Traquair* being his Majefty's
Commiffioner. The bifhops are all gone to wreck, and
they have had but a forry funeral: the very name is grown
fo contemptible that a black dog if he hath any white
marks about him, is called Bifhop. Our Lord of *Canterbury* is grown here fo odious, that they call him commonly in the pulpit, *the Prieft of* Baal, and *the fon of*
Belial.

I will tell your Lordfhip of a paffage which happened
lately in my lodging, which is a tavern. I had fent for
a fhoemaker to make me a pair of boots, and my land-
lord, who is a pert fmart man brought up a chopin of
white wine; and for this particular, there are better
French wines here than in *England* and cheaper, for
they are but a groat a quart; and it is a crime of a
high nature to mingle or fophifticate any wine here.
Over this chopin of white wine, my vintner and fhoemaker fell into a hot difpute about bifhops. The fhoemaker grew very furious, and called them the firebrands
of hell, the panders of the whore of *Babylon*, and the
inftruments of the devil; and that they were of his inftitution, not of God's. My vintner took him up fmartly
and faid, " Hold neighbour there, do you not know as
" well as I, that *Titus* and *Timothy* were hifhops? that
" our Saviour is intitled *the Bifhop of our fouls?* That
" the word *Bifhop* is as frequently mentioned in fcripture
" as the name *Paftor, Elder,* or *Deacon?* Then, why
" do you inveigh fo bitterly againft them." The fhoemaker anfwered, " I know the name and office to be
" good, but they have abufed it." My vintner replies,
" Well then, you are a fhoemaker by your profeffion,
" imagine that you, or a hundred, or a thoufand, or a
" hundred thoufand of your trade fhould play the knaves,
" and fell *calfskin-leather* boots for *neats-leather,* or
" do other cheats, muft we therefore go barefoot?
" Muft the gentle craft of fhoemakers fall therefore to
" the ground? It is the fault of the men not of the call-
" ing."

" ing." The fhoemaker was fo-gravelled at this, that he was put to his *laft;* for be had not a word more to fay, fo my vintner got the day.

There is a fair parliament houfe built here lately, and it was hoped his Majefty would have taken the maiden-head of it, and come hither to fit in perfon; and they did ill who advifed him otherwife.

I am to go hence fhortly back to *Dublin*, and fo to *London*, where I hope to find your Lordfhip, that according to my accuftomed boldnefs I may attend you. In the interim, I reft

Your Lordfhip's moft humble fervitor,

Edinburgh, 1639. **J. H.**

LETTER XXVII.

To Sir SACKVILL CROW, *his Majefty's Ambaffador at the Port of* Conftantinople.

Right Honourable Sir,

THE greateft news we have here now, is a notable naval fight that was lately betwixt the *Spaniard* and the *Hollander* in the *Downs;* but to make it more intelligible, I will deduce the bufinefs from the beginning. - The King of *Spain* had provided a great fleet of galleons, whereof the Vice-Admirals of *Naples* and *Portugal* were two, (whereof he had fent advice to *England* before). The defign was to meet with the *French* fleet, under the command of the Archbifhop of *Bourdeaux*, and in default of that, to land fome treafure at *Dunkirk*, with a recruit of *Spaniards* which were grown very thin in *Flanders*. Thefe recruits were got by an odd trick, for fome of the fleet being at *St. Andreas*, a report was blown up of purpofe that the *French* were upon the coafts: hereupon all the young men of the country came to the fea-fide, and fo a great number of them were tumbled a fhipboard, and fo they fet fail towards the coaft of *France;* but the Archbifhop

bifhop it feems had drawn in his fleet. Then ftriking into the narrow-feas, they met with a fleet of about fixteen
Hollanders, whereof they funk and took two, and the
reft got away to *Holland* to give an alarum to the States ;
who in lefs than a month got together a fleet of about
100 fail, and the wind being a long time eafterly, they
came into the *Downs*, where *Don Antonio d'Oquendo*
the *Spanifh* Admiral had ftaid for them all the while.
Sir *John Pennington* was then abroad with feven of his
Majefty's fhips ; and *Don Antonio* being daily warned
what forces were preparing in *Zealand* and *Holland*, and
fo advifed to get over to the *Flemifh* coafts. In the interim, with a haughty fpirit he anfwered, *Tengo de qued-*
arme aqui para caftigar eftos rebeldes: I will ftay here
to chaftife thefe rebels. There were ten more of his
Majefty's fhips appointed to go join with Sir *John Pen-*
nington to obferve the motions of thofe fleets, but the
wind continuing ftill Eaft, they could not get out of the
river.

The *Spanifh* fleet had frefh waters, victuals, and o-
ther neceffaries from our coafts for their money, according to the capitulations of peace, all this while. At laft,
being half furprized by a cloud of *Hollanders*, confifting
of 114 fhips, they launched out from our coafts, and a
moft furious fight began, our fhips having retired hard
by all the while. The Vice-Admiral of *Portugal*, a famous fea Captain, *Don Lope de Hozes*, was engaged in
clofe fight with the Vice-Admiral of *Holland;* and after many tough rencounters they were both blown up,
and burnt together. At laft, night came and parted the
reft, but fix *Spanifh* fhips were taken, aud about twenty
of the *Hollanders* perifhed. *Oquendo* then croffed over
to *Nardic*, and fo back to *Spain*, where he died before
he came to the court; and 'tis thought, had he lived,
he had been queftioned for fome mifcarriages: for if he
had fuffered the *Dunkirkers*, who are nimbler and more
fit for light, to have had the van, and dealt with the
Hollander, it is thought matters might have been better
　　　　　　　　　　　　　　　　　　　　　　　with

with him; but his ambition was, that the great *Spanish* galleons fhould get the glory of the day.

The *Spaniards* give out that they had the better, in regard they did the main work ; for *Oquendo* had conveyed all his recruits and treafure to *Flanders,* while he lay hovering on our coafts.

One thing is here very obfervable, what a mighty navigable power the *Hollander* is come to, that in fo fhort a compafs of time he could appear with fuch a numerous Fleet of 114 fails of men of war, in fuch a perfect equipage.

The times afford no more at prefent; therefore with a tender of my moft humble fervice to my noble Lady, and my thankful acknowledgment for thofe great favours, which my brother *Edward* writes to me he hath received from your Lordfhip in fo fingular a manner at that port; defiring you would ftill oblige me with a continuance of them, I reft, among thofe multitudes you have behind you in *England,*

Your Lordfhip's moft faithful fervant,

London, Aug. 31. 1639.   **J. H.**

LETTER XXVIII.

To SIMON DIGBY *Efq; at* Mofcow *in* Ruffia.

S I R,

I return you many thanks for your laft, of the firft of *June,* and that you acquaint me with the ftate of things in that country.

I doubt not but you have heard long finee of the revolt of *Catalonia* from the King of *Spain ;* it feems the fparkles of thofe fires are flown to *Portugal,* and put that country alfo in combuftion. The Duke of *Braganza,* whom you may well remember about the court of *Spain,* is now King of *Portugal,* by the name of *El Rey Don Juan ;* and he is generally obeyed, and quietly fettled,

as

as if he had been King thefe twenty years there ; for the whole country fell fuddenly to him, not one town ftanding out. When the King of *Spain* told *Olivares* of it firft, he flighted it, faying, *that he was but Rey de havat, a bean-cake King.* But it feems ftrange to me, and fo ftrange that it transformed me to wonder, that the *Spaniard* being accounted fo politic a nation, and fo full of precaution, could not forefee this ; efpecially there being divers intelligences given, and evident fymptoms of the general difcontentment of that kingdom, (becaufe they could not be protected againft the *Hollander* in *Brafil*) and of fome defigns a year before, when this Duke of *Braganza* was at *Madrid*. I wonder, I fay, they did not fecure his perfon, by engaging him to fome employment out of the way : truly, I thought the *Spaniard* was better fighted, and could fee further off than fo. You know what a huge limb the crown of *Portugal* was to the *Spanifh* monarchy, by the iflands in the *Altantick* fea, the towns in *Africk*, and all the *Eaft-Indies*, infomuch that the *Spaniard* hath nothing now left beyond the *Line*.

There is no offenfive war yet made by *Spain* againft King *John*, fhe only ftands upon the defenfive part, until the *Catalan* be reduced : and I believe, that will be a long winded bufinefs, for this *French* Cardinal ftirs all the devils of hell againft *Spain*, infomuch that moft men fay, that thefe formidable fires which are now raging in both thefe countries, were kindled at firft by a grenado hurled from his brain : nay, fome will not ftick to fay, that this breach betwixt us and *Scotland* is a reach of his.

There was a ruthful difafter happened lately at fea, which makes our merchants upon the *Exchange* hang down their heads very fadly. The fhip *Swan*, whereof one *Limery* was mafter, having been four years abroad about the *Streights*, was failing home with a cargazon valued at 800,000*l*. whereof 450,000 was in money, the reft in jewels and merchandize ; but being in fight of fhore, fhe fprung a leak, and being ballafted with falt, it choaked the pump, fo that the *Swan* could fwim no

C c   longer

longer: fixteen were drowned, and fome of them with ropes of pearl about their necks; the reft were faved by an *Hamburgher* not far off. The King of *Spain* lofeth little by it, (only his affairs in *Flanders* may fuffer) for his money was infured, and few of the principals, but the infurers only, who were moft of them *Genoefe* and *Hollanders*. A moft unfortunate chance! for had fhe come to fafe port, fhe had been the richeft fhip that ever came into the *Thames*, fo that *Neptune* had never fuch a morfel at one bit.

All your friends here are well, as you will underftand more particularly by thofe letters that go herewith. So I wifh you all health and comfort in that cold country, and defire that your love may continue ftill in the fame degree of heat towards

Your faithful fervitor,

Lond. March 5. 1639.   J. H.

L E T T E R XXIX.

To Sir K. D. *Knight.*

S I R,

IT was my fortune to be in a late communication, where a gentleman fpoke of a hideous thing that happened in *High Holborn*, how one *John Pennant* a young man of twenty-one being diffected after his death, there was a kind of ferpent with divers tails found in the left ventricle of his heart; which you know is the moft defended part, being thrice thicker than the right, and in the cell which holds the pureft and moft illuftrious liquor, the arterial blood and the vital fpirits. This ferpent was it feems three years engendering, for fo long a time he found himfelf indifpofed in the breaft; and it was obferved, that his eye in the interim grew more fharp and fiery, like the eye of a cock, which is next to a ferpent's eye in rednefs, fo that the fymptom of his inward dif-
eafe

case might have been told by certain exterior rays and signatures.

God preserve us from public calamities, for serpentine monsters have been often ill-favoured presages. I remember in the *Roman* story to have read, how when snakes or serpents were found near the statutes of their gods, as one time about *Jupiter*'s neck, another time about *Minerva*'s thigh, there followed bloody civil wars after it.

I remember also a few years since to have read the relation and deposition of the carrier of *Tewxbury*, who, with divers of his servants, passing a little before the dawn of the day with their packs over *Cots-hill*, saw most sensibly and very perspicuously in the air, musqueteers harnessed men, and horsemen, moving in battle array, and assaulting one another in divers furious postures. I doubt not but that you have heard of those fiery meteors and thunderbolts that have fallen upon sundry of our churches and done hurt. Unless God be pleased to make up these ruptures betwixt us and *Scotland*, we are like to have ill days. The Archbishop of *Canterbury* was lately outraged in his house by a pack of common people; and Captain *Mahun* was pitifully massacred by his own men lately, so that the common people it seems have strange principles infused into them, which may prove dangerous: for I am not of that Lord's mind who said, *That they who fear any popular insurrection in England, are like boys and women, that are afraid of a a turnip cut like a death's head with a candle in it.*

I am shortly for *France*, and I will receive your commands before I go. So I am

Your most humble servant,

Lond. May 2. 1640.   J. H.

LETTER XXX.

To the Honourable Sir P. M. *in* Dublin.

S I R,

I Am newly returned from *France*, and now that Sir *Edward Nicholas* is made Secretary of State, I am put in fair hopes, or rather assurances to succeed him in the clerkship of the council.

The Duke *de la Valette* is lately fled hither for sanctuary, having had ill luck in *Fontarabia*, they say his process was made, and that he was executed in effigy in *Paris*. 'Tis true, he could never square well with his eminency the Cardinal, (for this is a peculiar title be got long since from *Rome*, to distinguish him from all other) nor his father neither, the little old Duke of *Espernon*, the antientest soldier in the world, for he wants but one year of a hundred.

When I was last in *Paris*, I heard of a facetious passage betwixt him and the Archbishop of *Bourdeaux*, who in effect is Lord High Admiral of *France*, and it was thus: the Archbishop was to go General of a great fleet, and the Duke came to his house in *Bourdeaux* one morning to visit him: the Archbishop sent some of his gentlemen to desire him to have a little patience, *for he was dispatching away some sea-commanders*, and that he would wait on him presently. The little Duke took a pet at it, and went away to his house at *Cadillac*, some fifteen miles off. The next morning the Archbishop came to pay a visit, and to apologize for himself: being come in, and the Duke told of it, he sent his chaplain to tell him, *That he was newly fallen upon a chapter of St.* Austin*'s de civitate Dei*, and when he had read that chapter, he would come to him.

Some years before, I was told he was at *Paris*, and *Richelieu* came to visit him, he having notice of it, *Richelieu* found him in a Cardinal's cap, kneeling at a table

altar-

altar-wife, with his book and beads in his hand, and candles burning before him.

I hear the Earl of *Leicester* is to come shortly over, and so over to *Ireland* to be your Deputy. No more now, but that I am

Your most faithful servitor,

London, Sept. 7. 1641.   J. H.

L E T T E R XXXI.

To the Earl of B. *from the* Fleet.

My LORD,.

I Was lately come to *London* upon some occasions of mine own, and I had been divers times in *Westminster-hall*, where I conversed with many parliament men of my acquaintance; but one morning betimes there rushed into my chamber five armed men with swords, pistols, and bills, and told me they had a warrant from the parliament for me: I desired to see their warrant, they denied it: I desired to see the date of it, they denied it: I desired to see my name in the warrant, they denied all. At last one of them pulled a greasy paper out of his pocket, and shewed me only three or four names subscribed, and no more: so, they rushed presently into my closet, and seized on all my papers, and letters, and any thing that was manuscript; and many printed books they took also, and hurled all into a great hair trunk, which they carried away with them. I had taken a little physic that morning, and with very much ado, they suffered me to stay in my chamber with two guards upon me till the evening: at which time they brought me before the committee for examination, where I confess I found good respect; and being brought up to the close committee, I was ordered to be forth-coming till some papers of mine were perused, and Mr. *Corbet* was appointed to do it. Some days after, I came to Mr. *Cor-*

C c 3

bet

bet, and he told me he had perufed them, and could find nothing that might give offence. Hereunto, I defired him to make a report to the houfe, according to which (as I was told) he did very fairly; yet fuch was my hard hap, that I was committed to the *Fleet*, where I am now under clofe reftraint; and as far as I fee, I muft ly at dead anchor in this fleet a long time, unlefs fome gentle gale blow thence to make me launch out. God's will be done, and amend the times, and make up thefe ruptures which threaten fo much calamity. So, I am

Your Lordfhip's moft faithful,
(*though now afflicted*) *fervitor,*

Fleet, Nov. 20. 1642. J. H.

LETTER XXXII.

To Sir BEVIS THELWALL, *Knight*, (Petri ad vincula) *at* Peter-houfe *in* London.

SIR,

THOUGH we are not in the fame prifon, yet are we in the fame predicament of fufferance; therefore, I prefume you fubject to the like fits of melancholly as I. *The fruition of liberty is not fo pleafing, as a conceit of the want of it is irkfome,* fpecially to one of fuch free-born thoughts as you. Melancholly is a black noxious humour, and much annoys the whole inward man: if you would know what cordial I ufe againft it in this my fad condition, I will tell you, I pore fometimes on a book, and fo I make the *dead my companions;* and this is one of my chiefeft folaces. If the humour work upon me ftronger, I rouze my fpirits, and raife them up towards heaven, my future country; and one may be on his journey thither, though fhut up in prifon, and happily go a ftraighter way than if he were abroad. I confider, that my foul while fhe is cooped within thefe walls of flefh, is but in a perpetual kind of prifon: and now my
body

body correſponds with her in the ſame condition; my body is the priſon of the one, and theſe brick walls the priſon of the other. And let the *Engliſh*-people flatter themſelves as long as they will, that they are free, yet are they in effect but priſoners, as all other iſlanders are: for, being ſurrounded and incloſed about with ſalt-water, (as I am with theſe walls) they cannot go where they liſt unleſs they aſk the winds leave firſt, and *Neptune* muſt give them a paſs.

God almighty amend the times, and compoſe theſe woful diviſions, which menace nothing but public ruin, the thoughts whereof drown in me the ſenſe of mine own private affliction.

So wiſhing you courage (whereof you have enough, if you put it in practice) and patience in this ſad condition, I reſt

Your true ſervant and compatriot,

Fleet, Auguſt 2. 1643.   J. H.

LETTER XXXIII.

To Mr. E. P.

SIR,

I Saw ſuch prodigious things daily done theſe few years, that I had reſolved with myſelf to give over wonder-ing at any thing, yet a paſſage happened this week that forced me to wonder once more, becauſe it is without parallel. It was, that ſome odd fellows went ſculking up and down *London* ſtreets, and with figs and raiſins al-lured little children, and ſo purloined them away from their parents, and carried them a ſhip-board to tranſport them beyond ſea, where, by cutting their hair, and other devices, they ſo diſguiſe them that their parents could not know them. This made me think upon that miraculous paſ-ſage in *Hamelen*, a town in *Germany*, which I hoped to have paſſed through when I was in *Hamburgh*, had we

returned

returned by *Holland;* which was thus, (nor would I te-
late it unto you were there not some ground of truth for
it). The said town of *Hamelen* was annoyed with rats
and mice; and it chanced, that a pied-coated piper came
thither, who covenanted with the chief burghers for such
a reward, if he could free them quite from the said vermin, nor would he demand it till a twelvemonth and a
day after: The agreement being made, he began to
play on his pipes, and all the rats and the mice followed
him to a great loch hard by, where they all, perished,
so the town was infested no more. At the end of the
year, the pied-piper returned for his reward, the burghers put him off with slightings and neglects, offering him
some small matter; which he refusing, and staying some
days in the town, on *Sunday* morning at high mass when
most people were at church, he fell to play on his pipes,
and all the children up and down followed him out of the
town, to a great hill not far off, which rent in two, and
opened, and let him and the children in, and so closed
up again. This happened a matter of about 250 years
since; and in that town, they date their bills and bonds,
and other instruments in law, to this day, from the year
of the going out of their children: besides, there is a
great pillar of stone at the foot of the said hill, whereon
this story is engraven.

No more now, for this is enough in conscience for one
time: so, I am

Your most affectionate serviter,

Fleet, Oct. 1. 1643.   J. H.

LETTER XXXIV.

To my Lord G. D.

My LORD,

THERE be two weighty sayings in *Seneca, Nihil
est infelicius eo, cui nil unquam contigit adversi;
There is nothing more unhappy than he who never felt an
adversity.*

adverfity. The other is, *Nullum eft majus malum, quam non poffe ferre malum: There is no greater crofs, than not to be able to bear a crofs.* Touching the firft, I am not capable of that kind of unhappinefs, for I have had my fhare of adverfity: I have been hammered, and *dilated upon the anvil,* as our countryman *Breakfpear* (*Adrian* IV.) faid of himfelf, *I have been ftrained through the limbec of affliction.* Touching the fecond, I am alfo free of that crofs; for, I thank God for it, I have that portion of grace, and fo much philofophy as to be able to endure, and confront any mifery: it is not fo tedious to me as to others to be thus immured, becaufe I have been inured and habituated to troubles. That

* which finks deepeft in me, is the fenfe I have of the common calamities of this nation: there is a ftrange fpirit hath got in amongft us, which makes the idea of holinefs the formality of good, and the very faculty of reafon, to be quite differing from what it was. I remember to have read a tale of the ape in *Paris,* who having got a child out of the cradle, and carried him up to the top of the tiles, and there fat with him upon the ridge: the parents beholding this ruthful fpectacle, gave the ape fair and fmooth language, fo he gently brought the child down again and replaced him in the cradle. Our country is in the fame cafe this child was in, and I hope there will be fweet and gentle means ufed to preferve it from precipitation.

The city of *London* fticks conftantly to the parliament, and the common-council fways much, infomuch, that I believe, if the Lord Chancellor *Egerton* were now living, he would not be fo pleafant with them as he was once to a new Recorder of *London,* whom he had invited to a dinner to give him joy of his office, and having a great woodcock pye ferved in about the end of the repaft; which had been fent him from *Chefhire,* he faid, *Now, Mafter Recorder you are welcome to a common-council.*

There be many difcreet brave patriots in the city, and I hope they will think upon fome means to preferve us

and

and themfelves from ruin: fuch are the prayers early and late of

> *Your Lordſhip's moſt humble ſervitor,*

Fleet, Jan. 2. 1643.   I. H.

LETTER XXXV.

To Sir ALEXANDER R. *Knight.*

S I R,

SURELY God almighty is angry with *England*, and it is more fure, that God is never angry without caufe: now to know the caufe, the beft way is, for every one to lay his hand on his breaft and examine himfelf thoroughly, to fummon his thoughts, and winnow them, and fo call to remembrance how far he hath offended heaven; and then it will be found, that God is not angry with *England*, but with *Engliſhmen*. When that doleful change was pronounced againſt *Iſrael*, *Perditio ex te* Iſrael, it was meant of the *concrete*, (not the *abſtract*) *Oh! Iſraelites, your ruin comes from yourſelves.* When I make this ſcrutiny within myſelf, and enter into the clofeft cabinet of my foul, I find (God help me) that I have contributed as much to the drawing on of thefe judgments on *England* as any other. When I ranfack the three cells of my brain, I find that my *imagination* hath been vain and extravagant: my *memory* hath kept the bad, and let go the good, like a wide fieve that retains the bran and parts with the flour: my *underſtanding* hath been full of error and obliquities: my *will* hath been a rebel to reafon: my *reaſon* a rebel to faith, (which I thank God I have the grace to quell prefently with this caution) *Succumbat ratio fidei, & captive quieſcat.*

When I defcend to my heart, the center of all my affections, I find it hath fwelled often with tympanies of vanity, and tumors of wrath. When I take my whole self felf in a lump, I find that I am nothing elfe but a car-gazon of malignant humours, a rabble of unruly paffions, amongft which my poor foul is daïly crucified, as betwixt fo many thieves. Therefore, as I pray in general, that God would pleafe not to punifh this ifland for the fins of the people, fo more particularly I pray, that fhe fuffer not for me in particular; who, if one would go by way of indiction, would make one of the chiefeft inftances of the argument; and as I am thus confcious to myfelf of my own demerits, fo I hold it to be the duty of every one to complete himfelf this way, and to remember the faying of a noble *Englifh* Captain, who when the town of • *Calais* was loft (which was the laft footing we had in *France*) being jeered by a *Frenchman*, and afked, now *Englifhman*, when will you come back to *France ?* an-fwered, O Sir, mock not, when the fins of *France* are greater than the fins of *England*, then the *Englifhmen* will come again to *France.*

Before the fack of *Troy*, it was faid and fung up and down the ftreets :

> Iliacos *intra muros peccatur & extra.*

The verfe is as true for fenfe and feet :

> *Intra* Londini *muros peccatur & extra.*

> Without and eke within
> The walls of *London* there is fin.

The way to better the times is, for every one to mend one. I will conclude with this ferious invocation : I pray God avert thofe further judgments (of famine and pefti-lence) which are hovering over this populous and once flourifhing city, and difpofe of the brains and hearts of this people to feek and ferve him aright.

I thank you for your laft vifit, and for the poem you fent me fince : fo, I am

> *Your moft faithful fervitor,*

Fleet, June 3. J. H.

L E T-

LETTER XXXVI.

To Mr. JOHN BATTY, *Merchant.*

SIR,

I Received the printed difcourfe you pleafed to fend me, called *the merchant's remonftrance*, for which I re-turn you due and deferved thanks.

Truly Sir, it is one of the moft material and folid pieces I have read of this kind ; and, I difcover therein two things : firft, the affection you bear to your country, with the refentment you have of thefe woful diftractions: then the judgment and choice experience you have pur-chafed by your negotiations in *Spain* and *Germany*. In you may be verified the tenet they hold in *Italy*, that the merchant bred abroad, is the beft commonwealths-man, being properly applied : for my part, I do not know any profeffion of life (efpecially in an ifland) more to be cherifhed and countenanced with honourable em-ployments than the merchant-adventurer; (I do not mean only the ftaplers of *Hamburgh* and *Rotterdam*) for if valiant and dangerous actions do ennoble a man, and make him merit, furely the merchant-adventurer deferves more honour than any ; for he is to encounter not only with men of all tempers and humors, (as a *French* Coun-fellor hath it) but he contefts and tugs oft-times with all the elements: nor do I fee how fome of our country fquires, who fell calves and runts, and their wives per-haps cheefe and apples, fhould be held more genteel than the noble merchant-adventurer, who fells filks and lattins, tiffues and cloths of gold, diamonds and pearl, with filver and gold

In your difcourfe, you foretel the fudden calamities which are like to befal this poor ifland, if trade decay, and that this decay is inevitable, if thefe commotions laft: herein you are proved half a Prophet already, and I fear your prophecy will be fully accomplifhed if matters hold thus.   Good Lord ! was there ever people fo active to

draw

draw on their own ruin? Which is fo vifible, that a
pur-blind man may take a profpect of it. We all fee
this apparently, and hear it told us every minute; but we
are fallen to the condition of that foolifh people the Prophet fpeaks of, *who had eyes but would not fee, and
ears, but would not hear.* All men know there is nothing imports this ifland more than trade: it is that wheel
of induftry which fets all other a going: it is that which
preferves the chiefeft caftles and walls of this kingdom, I
mean the fhips; and how thefe are impaired within this
four years, I believe other nations (which owe us an invafion) obferve and know better than we: for truly, I
believe a million, (I mean of crowns) and I fpeak within
compafs, will not put the navy-royal in that ftrength it
was in four years fince, befides the decay of merchants
fhips. A little before *Athens* was overcome, the oracle
told one of the areopagites, that *Athens had feen her beft
days, for her wooden walls* (meaning her fhips) *were
decayed.* As I told you before, there is a nation or two
owe us an invafion.

No more now, but that with my moft kind and friendly
refpects unto you, I reft always

Yours to difpofe of,

Fleet, May 4. 1644. J. H.

L E T T E R XXXVII.

To my honoured Friend Mr. E. P.

S I R,

THE times are fo ticklifh, that I dare not adven-
ture to fend you any *London* intelligence, fhe being now a garrifon town, and you know as well as I,
what danger I may incur; but for foreign indifferent
news, you fhall underftand that Pope *Urban* VIII. is
dead, having fat in the chair above twenty years, a rare
thing; for it is obferved, that no Pope yet arrived to the

years of St. *Peter,* who, they fay, was Bifhop of *Rome*
twenty and five.   Cardinal *Pamfilio* a *Roman* born, a
knowing man, and a great lawyer is created Pope by af-
fumption of the name of *Innocent* X.   There was rough
canvafing for voices, and a great *contráfto* in the *con-
clave,* betwixt the *Spanifh* and *French* faction, who with
the *Barberino* ftood for *Sachetti,* but he was excluded,
as alfo another *Dominican.*   By thefe exclufions the *Spanifh* party, whereof the Cardinal of *Florence* was chief,
brought about *Barberino* to join with them for *Pamfilio,*
as being alfo a creature of the deceafed Pope.   He had
been *Nuncio* in *Spain* eight years, fo that it is conceived
he is much devoted to that crown, as his predeceffor was
to the *French,* who had been Legate there near upon
twenty years, and was godfather to the laft King; which
made him to be *fleurdelize,* to be flower-de-luced all
over.   This new Pope hath already paffed that number
of years which the Prophet affigns to man, for he goes
upon feventy-one, and is of a ftrong promifing conftitution to live fome years longer.   He hath but one nephew, who is but eighteen, and fo not capable of bufinefs: he hath therefore made choice of fome cardinals
more to be his coadjutors.   *Pancirellio* is his prime confident, and lodged in St. *Peter's.*   It is thought he will
prefently fet all wheels a going to meditate an univerfal
peace.   They write of one good augury among the reft;
that part of his arms is a *dove,* which hath been always
held for an emblem of peace ; but, I believe it will prove
one of the knottieft and difficulteft tafks that ever was attempted, as the cafe ftands betwixt the houfe of *Auftria*
and *France ;* and the rougheft and hardeft knot I hold
to be that of *Portugal,* for it cannot yet enter into any
man's imagination, how that may be accommodated,
though many politicians have beaten their brains about it.
God almighty grant, that the appealing of our civil wars
prove not fo intricate a work; and that we may at laft
take warning by the devaftations of other countries, before our own be paft cure.

They

They write from *Paris*, that Sir *Kenelm Digby* is to be employed to *Rome* from her Majesty, in quality of a high *Messenger of honour* to congratulate the new Pope, not of an Ambassador, as the vulgar give out: for, none can give that character to any, but a sovereign independant Prince; and all the world knows, that her Majesty is under *Covert Baron*, notwithstanding, that some cry her up for *Queen Regent of* England, as her sister is of *France*. The Lord *Aubigny* hath an abbacy of 1500, pistoles a year given him yearly there, and is fair for a Cardinal's cap.

I continue still under this heavy pressure of close restraint, nor do I see any hopes (God help me) of getting forth till the wind shift out of his unlucky hole. Howsoever, I am resolved, that if *innocence* cannot free my body, yet *patience* shall preserve my mind still in its *freeborn* thoughts: nor shall this storm slacken a whit that firm league of love, wherein I am eternally tied unto you. I will conclude with a distich, which I found amongst those excellent poems of the late Pope:

Quem valide strixit præstanti pollice virtus,
Nescius est solvi nodus amicitiæ.

Your *constant servitor*,

Fleet, Jan. 1. 1644. J. H.

LETTER XXXVIII.

To the Lord Bishop of London, *late Lord Treasurer of* England.

My LORD,

YOU are one of the miracles of these times, the greatest mirrour of moderation our age affords; and as heretofore when you carried the white staff, with such clean incorrupted hands, yet the *crosier* was still your chief care: nor was it perceived that that high all-obliging office did alter you a jot, or alienate you from

yourself,

yourſelf, but the ſame candour and countenance of meek-
neſs appeared ſtill in you. As whoſoever had occaſion to
make their addreſs to your gates, went away contented
whether they ſped in their buſineſs or not, (a gift your
predeceſſor was ſaid to want) ſo ſince the turbulency of
theſe times, the ſame moderation ſhines in you, notwithſtanding that the mitre is ſo trampled upon, and that
there be ſuch violent factions a-foot, infomuch, that you
live not only ſecure from outrages, but honoured by all
parties. 'Tis true, one thing fell out to your advantage, that you did not ſubſcribe to that petition which
proved ſo fatal to prelacy; but the chief ground of the
conſtant eſteem the diſtracted world hath ſtill of you, is
your wiſdom and moderation, paſſed and preſent. This
put me in mind of one of your predeceſſors (in your late
office) Marquis *Pawlet*, who it ſeems ſailed by the ſame
compaſs; for there being divers bandings, and factions at
court in his time, yet was he beloved by all parties;
and being aſked how he ſtood ſo right in the opinion of
all, he anſwered, *By being a willow, and not an oak.*

　I have many thanks to give your Lordſhip for the late
viſits I had; and when this cloud is ſcattered, that I may
reſpire free air, one of my journies ſhall be to kiſs your
Lordſhip's hands. In the interim, I reſt

　　　Your moſt devoted and ready ſervitor,

Fleet, Sept. 3. 1644.　　　　　　　　J. H.

LETTER XXXIX.

To PHIL. WARWICK, *Eſq;*

S I R,

THE earth doth not always produce roſes and lillies,
　　but ſhe brings forth alſo nettles and thiſtles; ſo
the world affords us not always contentments and plea-
ſures, but ſometimes affliction and troubles: *Ut illa tri-*
bulos, ſic iſte tribulationes producit. The ſea is not
more ſubject to contrary blaſts, nor the ſurges thereof to
　　　　　　　　　　　　　　　　　　　　　　　　toſſings

toffings and tumblings, as the actions of men are to in-cumbrances and croffes; the air is not fuller of meteors, than man's life is of miferies: but as we find that it is not a clear fky, but the clouds that drop fatnefs, as the holy text tells us, fo adverfity is far more fertile than profperity: it ufeth to water and mollify the heart, which is the centre of all our affections, and makes it produce excellent fruit; whereas the glaring fun-fhine of a con-tinual profperity would enharden and dry it up, and fo make it barren.

There is not a greater evidence of God's care and love to his creature than affliction; for a *French* author doth illuftrate it by a familiar example: if two boys fhould be feen to fight in the ftreets, and a ring of people about them, one of the ftanders by parting them, lets the one go untouched, but he falls a correcting the other, whereby the beholders will infer, that he is his child, or at leaft one whom he wifheth well unto: fo the ftrokes of adverfity which fall upon us from heaven, fhew that God is our Father as well as our Creator. This makes this bitter cup of affliction become *nectar*, and the bread I now eat, to be true *ambrofia* unto me. This makes me efteem thefe walls, wherein I have been immured thefe thirty months, to be no other than a college of in-ftruction unto me; and whereas *Varro* faid, that the great world was but the houfe of a little man, I hold this Fleet to be one of the beft lodgings in that houfe.

There is a people in *Spain* called *Los Patuecos*, who fome threefcore and odd years fince were difcovered by the flight of a hawk of the Duke of *Alva's*: this people, then all favage, (though they dwelt in the centre of *Spain*, not far from *Toledo*, and are yet held to be a part of thofe aborigines that *Tubál Cain* brought in) be-ing hemmed in, and imprifoned as it were, by a multi-tude of huge craggy mountains, thought that behind thofe mountains there was no more earth. I have been fo habituated to this prifon, and accuftomed to the walls thereof fo long, that I might well be brought to think, that there is no other world behind them. And in my

extravagant

extravagant imagination, I often compare this *Fleet* to *Noah*'s ark furrounded with a vaft fea, and huge deluge of calamities, which hath overwhelmed this poor ifland; nor, although I have been fo long aboard here, was I yet under hatches, for I have a cabin upon the upper deck, whence I breathe the beft air the place affords: add hereunto, that the fociety of Mr. *Hopkins* the warden is an advantage unto me, who is one of the knowingeft and moft civil gentlemen that I have converfed withal. Moreover, there are here fome choice gentlemen who are my co-martyrs; for a prifoner, and a martyr are the fame thing, fave *that the one is buried before his death, and the other after.*

God almighty amend thefe times, that make imprifonment to be preferred before liberty, it being more fafe and defirable by fome, though not by

Your affectionate fervitor,

Fleet, Nov. 3. 1643.   J. H.

LETTER XL.

To THOMAS YOUNG, *Efq;*

S I R,

I Received yours of the fifth of *March*, and it was as welcome to me as flowers in *May;* which are coming on apace. You feem to marvel I do not marry all this while, confidering that I am paft the meridian of my age, and that to your knowledge there have been overtures made me of parties above my degree. Truly in this point, I will deal with you as one fhould do with his confeffor: had I been difpofed to have married for wealth without affection, or for affection without wealth, I had been in bonds before now; but I did never caft my eyes upon any yet, that I thought I was born for, where both thefe concurred. It is the cuftom of fome (and it is a common cuftom) to chufe wives by the weight, that

is,

is, by their wealth. Others fall in love with light wives, I do not mean venerean lightness, but in reference to portion. The late Earl of *Salisbury* gives a caveat for this, *That beauty without a dowry,* (without that *unguentum indicum) is as a gilded shell without a kernel,* therefore he warns his son to be sure to have something with his wife, and his reason is, *because nothing can be bought in the market without money.* Indeed it is very fitting that he or she should have wherewith to support both according to their quality, at least to keep the wolf from the door, otherwise it were a meer madness to marry; but he who hath enough of his own to maintain a wife, and marrieth only for money, discovereth a poor sordid disposition. There is nothing that my nature disdains more, than to be a slave to silver or gold, for though they both carry the King's face, yet they shall never reign over me; and, I would I were free from all other infirmities as I am from this. I am none of those mammonists who adore white and red earth, and make their Princes picture their idol that way: such may be said to be under a perpetual eclipse, for the earth stands always betwixt them, and the fair face of heaven; yet my genius prompts me, that I was born under a planet, not to die in a lazaretto. I have upon occasion of a sudden distemper, sometimes a madman, sometimes a fool, sometimes a melancholy odd fellow to deal withal, I mean myself, for I have the humours within me that belongs to all three; therefore who would cast herself away upon such a one. Besides, I came tumbling out into the world a pure cadet, a true cosmopolite, not born to land, lease, house or office. It is true, I have purchased since, a small spot of ground upon *Parnassus;* which I hold in fee of the muses, and I have endeavoured to manure it as well as I could, though I confess it hath yielded me little fruit hitherto; and what woman would be so mad, as to take that only for her jointure.

But to come to the point of wiveing, I would have you know that I have, though never married, divers
children

children already, fome *French*, fome *Latin*, one *Italian*, and many *Englifh;* and though they be but poor brats of the brain, yet are they legitimate, and *Apollo* himfelf vouchfafed to co-operate in their production. I have expofed them to the wide world, to try their fortunes; and fome (out of compliment) would make me believe they are long-lived.

But to come at laft to your kind of wiveing, I acknowledge that marriage is an honourable condition, nor dare I think otherwife without profanenfs, for it is the epithet the holy text gives it: therefore it was a wild fpeech of the Philofopher to fay, that *if our converfation could be without women, angels would come down and dwell amongft us;* and a wilder fpeech it was of the *Cynic,* when paffing by a tree where a maid made herfelf away, wifhed, *that all trees might bear fuch fruit.* But to pafs from thefe moth-eaten philofophers, to a modern phyfician of our own, it was a moft unmanly thing in him, while he difplays his own religion, to wifh' that there were a way to propagate the world otherwife than by conjunction with women, (and *Parcelfus* undertakes to fhew him the way) whereby he feems to repine (though I underftand he was wived a little after) at the honourable degree of marriage; which I hold to be the prime link of human fociety, the chiefeft happinefs of mortals, and wherein heaven hath a fpecial hand.

But I wonder why you write to me of wiveing, when you know I have much ado to man or maintain myfelf, as I told you before; yet notwithftanding that the better part of my days are already threeded upon the ftring of time, I will not defpair, but I may have a wife at laft, that may perhaps enable me to build hofpitals: for, although nine luftres of years have long paffed over my head, and fome winters more, (for all my life, confidering the few fun-fhines I have had, may be called nothing but winters) yet, I thank God for it, I find no fymptom of decay either in body, fenfes, or intellectuals. But writing thus extravagantly methinks I hear you fay, that

this

this letter fhews I begin to dote and grow idle, therefore I will difplay myfelf no further unto you at this time.

To tell you the naked truth, my dear *Tom*, the higheft pitch of my aim is, that by fome condition or other, I may be enabled at laft (though I be put to fow, the time that others ufe to reap) to quit fcores with the world, but never to cancel that precious obligation, wherein I am indiffolubly bound to live and die

Your true conftant friend,

Fleet, April 28. 1645. J. H.

LETTER XLI.

To Mr. B. J.

F. *B.* The fangs of a bear, and the tufks of a wild boar, do not bite worfe, and make deeper gafhes than a goofe-quill fometimes ; oo not the badger himfelf, who is faid to be fo tenacious of his bite, that he will not give over his hold, till he feels his teeth meet, and the bone crack. Your quill hath proved fo to Mr. *Jones ;* but the pen wherewith you have fo gafhed him, it feems was made rather of a porcupine, than a goofe-quill, it is fo keen and firm : you know ;

Anfer, apis, vitulus, populos & regna gubernant.

The goofe, the bee, and the calf (meaning wax, parchment, and the pen) rule the world; but of the three, the pen is the moft predominant. I know you have a commanding one, but you muft not let it tyrannize in that manner, as you have done lately. Some give out there was a hair in it, or that your ink was too thick with gall, elfe it would not have fo befpattered and fhaken the reputation of a royal Architect; for reputation, you know, is like a fair ftructure, long time a rearing, but quickly ruined. If your fpirit will not let you retract, yet you fhall do well to reprefs any more copies

of

of the fatire ; for to deal plainly with you, you have loft
fome ground at court by it ; and, as I hear from a good
hand, the King who hath fo great a judgment in poetry
(as in all other things elfe) is not well pleafed therewith.
Difpenfe with this freedom of

Your refpectful S. and fervitor.

Weftminfter, July 3. 1635.   J. H.

LETTER XLII.

To T. D. *Efq;*

S I R,

I Had yours lately by a fafe hand : wherein I find you
open to me all the boxes of your breaft. I perceive
you are fore hurt, and whereas all other creatures run a-
way from the inftrument and hand that wounds them,
you feem to make more and more towards both.   I
confefs fuch is the nature of love, and which is worfe,
the nature of woman, is fuch, that like fhadows the more
you follow them, the fafter they flee from you. Nay,
fome females are of that odd humour, that to feed their
pride, they will famifh affection, they will ftarve thofe
natural paffions, which are owing from them to man.
I confefs coynefs becomes fome beauties, if handfomely
acted ; a frown from fome faces penetrates more, and
makes deeper impreffion than the fawning and foft glances
of a mincing fmile : yet, if this coynefs and thefe frowns
favour of pride, they are odious ; and it is a rule, that
where this kind of pride inhabits, honour fits not long
porter at the gate.   There are fome beauties fo ftrong,
that they are leauger-proof, they are fo barricadoed,
that no battery, no petard, or any kind of engine fapping
or mining, can do good upon them.   There are others
that are tenable a good while, and will endure the brunt
of a fiege, but will incline to parley at laft ; and you know
that fort and female which begins to parley, is half won ;
for

for my part, I think of beauties as *Philip* King of *Macedon* thought of cities, there is none fo inexpugnable, but an afs laden with gold may enter into them ; you know what the *Spaniard* faid, *davidos quebrantan pennas, prefents can rend rocks.* Pearls and golden bullets may do much upon the impregnablest beauty that is : it muft be partly your way. I remember a great Lord of this land fent a puppy with a rich collar of diamonds, to a rare *French* Lady, Madam St. *L.* that had come over hither with an Ambaffador ; fhe took the dog, but returned the collar. I will not tell you what effect it wrought afterwards. 'Tis a powerful fex, they were too ftrong for the firft, the ftrongeft, and wifeft man that was : they muft needs be ftrong when *one hair of a woman can draw more than a hundred pair of oxen;* yet for all their ftrength, in point of value, if you will believe the *Italian, A man of ftraw is worth a woman of gold:* therefore, if you find the thing perverfe, rather than to undervalue your fex (your manhood) retire handfomely, for there is as much honour to be won at an handfome retreat as at a hot onfet, it being the difficulteft piece of war. By this retreat you will get a greater victory than you are aware of, for thereby you will overcome yourfelf, which is the greateft conqueft that can be. Without feeking abroad, we have enemies enough within doors to practife our valour upon, we have tumultary and rebellious paffions, with whole bofts of humours within us. He who can difcomfit them is the greateft Captain, and may defy the devil. I pray recollect yourfelf, and think on this advice of ·

Your true and moft affectionate fervitor,

Weftminfter, Dec. 4. 1637. J. H.

LETTER XLIII.

To G. G. Eſq; at Rome.

SIR,

I Have more thanks to give you than can be folded up
in this narrow paper, though it were all wrote in the
cloſeſt kind of ſtenography, for the rich and accurate account you pleaſe to give me of that renowned city wherein you now ſojourn. I find you have moſt judiciouſly
pried into all matters both civil and clerical, eſpecially
the latter, by obſerving the poverty and pennances of
the frier, the policy and power of the jeſuit, the pomp
of the Prelate and Cardinal. Had it not been for the
two firſt, I believe the two laſt, and that See had been
at a low ebb by this time: for the learning, the pruden-
tial ſtate, knowledge and auſterity of the one, and the
venerable opinion the people have of the abſtemious and
rigid condition of the other, ſpecially of the mendicants,
ſeem to make ſome compenſation for the lux and magnificence of the two laſt: beſides, they are more beholding to the proteſtant than they are aware of, for unleſs
he had riſen up about the latter end of the laſt century
of years, which made them more circumſpect and warry
of their ways, life, and actions, to what an intolerable
high exceſs that court had come to by this time, you
may eaſily conjecture. But, out of my ſmall reading I
I have obſerved that no age ever ſince *Gregory the Great*
hath paſſed, wherein ſome or other have not repined and
murmured at the pontificial pomp of that court, yet for
my part I have been always ſo charitable as to think that
the religion of *Rome*, and the court of *Rome* were different things. The counterbuff that happened betwixt
Leo X. and *Francis* I. of *France* is very remarkable,
who being both met at *Bolonia*, the King ſeemed to give
a light touch at the Pope's pomp, ſaying, it was not uſed
to be ſo in former time. It may be ſo, ſaid *Leo*, but it
was then when the kings kept ſheep; (as we read in the

Old

Old Teſtament) no, the King replied, I ſpeak of times under the goſpel. Then rejoined the Pope, it was then when kings did viſit hoſpitals, hinting by thoſe words at St. *Lewis* who oft uſed to do ſo. It is memorable what is recorded in the life of *Robert Groſted* Biſhop of *Lincoln*, who lived in the time of one of the *Leo's*, that he feared the ſame ſin would overthrow *Leo*, as overthrew *Lucifer*.

For news hence, I know none of your friends but are as well as you left them, *hombres y lembras:* you are freſh and very frequent in their memory, and mentioned with a thouſand good wiſhes and benedictions. Amongſt others, you have a large room in the memory of my Lady *Elizabeth Cary;* and, I do not think all *Rome* can afford you a fairer lodging. I pray be cautious of your carriage under that meridian, it is a ſearching (inquiſitive) air: you have two eyes, and two ears, but one tongue; you know my meaning. This laſt you muſt impriſon, (as nature hath already done with a double fence of teeth and lips) or elſe ſhe may impriſon you, according to our countryman Mr. *Hoſkin's* advice when he was in the *Tower*.

Vincula da linguæ, vel tibi lingua dabit.

Have a care of your health, take heed of the ſyrens, of exceſs in fruit; and be ſure to mingle your wine well with water. No more now, but that in the large catalogue of friends you have left behind here, there is none who is more mindful of you than

Your moſt affectionate and faithful ſervitor,

J. H.

E e LET-

L E T T E R XLIV.

To Dr. T. P.

S I R,

I Had yours of the 10th current, wherein you write me tidings of our friend *Tom D.* and what his defires tend unto: in my opinion, they are fomewhat extravagant. I have read of one, that loving honey more than ordinary, feemed to complain againft nature, that fhe made not a bee as big as a bull, that we might have it in greater plenty. Another who was much given to fruit, wifhed that pears and plumbs were as big as pumpions. Thefe were but filly vulgar wifhes, for if a bee were as big as a bull, it muft have a fting proportionable; and what mifchiefs do you think fuch ftings would do, when we can hardly endure the fting of that fmall infected animal as now it is? And if pears and plumbs were as big as pumpions. it were dangerous walking in an orchard about the autumnal equinoctial, (at which time they are in their full maturity) for fear of being knocked on the head. Nature the handmaid of God almighty doth nothing but with good advice, if we make refearches into the true reafon of things. You know what anfwer the fox gave the ape, when he would have borrowed part of his tail to cover his pofteriors.

The wifhes you write that *T. D.* lately made, were almoft as extravagant in civil matters as the aforementioned were in natural: for, if he were partaker of them, they would draw more inconveniencies upon him than benefit, being nothing fortable either to his difpofition or breeding, and for other reafons befides, which I will referve till my coming up; and I pray let him know fo much from me, with my commendations. So, I reft

Yours in the perfecteft degree of friendfhip,

Weftminfter, Sept. 6. 1640. J. H.

L E T-

L E T T E R XLV.

To Doctor B.

S I R,

WHEREAS upon the large theorical difcourfe, and bandings of opinions we had lately at *Grefham* college, you defired I fhould couch in writing what I obferved abroad of the extent and amplitude of the chriftian commonwealth in reference to other religions: I obtained leave of myfelf to put pen to paper, rather to obey you, than oblige you with any thing that may add to your judgment, or inrich that rare knowledge I find you have already treafured up; but I muft begin with the fulfilling of your defire in a preambular way, for the fubject admits it.

'Tis a principle all the world over, except amongft atheifts, that *omne verum eft a Deo, omne falfum eft a diabolo, & omnis error ab homine: All truth is from God, all falfhood from the devil, and all error from man.* The laft goes always under the vifard of the firft, but the fecond confronts truth to the face, and ftands in open defiance of her: error and fin are contemporary, when one crept firft in at the fore-door, the other came in at the poftern. This made *Trifmegiftus* one of the great Lords of reafon to give this character of man, *Homo eft imaginatio quædam, & imaginatio eft fupremum mendacium: Man is nought elfe but a kind of i-maginatio, and imagination is the greateft lie.* Error therefore entering into the world with fin among us poor *Adamites,* may be faid to fpring from the tree of know-ledge itfelf, and from the rotten kernels of that fatal apple. This, befides the infirmities that attend the body, hath brought in perverfity of will, depravation of mind, and hath caft a kind of cloud upon all our intellectuals, that they cannot difcern the true effence of things with that clearnefs as the protoplaft our firft parent could; but we are involved in a mift, and grope as it were ever

E e 2. fince

since in the dark, as if truth were got into some dungeon, or as the old wizard said, into some deep pit which the shallow apprehension of men could not fathom. Hence comes it that the earth is rent into so many religions, and those religions torn into so many schisms, and various forms of devotion, as if the heavenly Majesty were delighted as much in diversities of worship as in diversities of works.

The first religion that ever was reduced to exact rules and ritual observances was that of the *Hebrews*, the antient people of God, called afterwards *Judaism*, the second *Christianity*, the third *Mahometism*, which is the youngest of all religions. Touching *Paganism*, an heathenish idolatry, they scarce deserve the name of religion; but for the former three, there is this analogy between them, that they all agree in the first person of the Trinity, and all his attributes. What kind of religion there was before the flood, it is in vain to make any researches, there having been no monuments at all left, (besides that little we find in *Moses* and the *Phœnician* story) but *Seth*'s pillars, and those so defaced, that nothing was legible upon them, though *Josephus* saith, that one was extant in his days: as also the oak under which *Abraham* feasted God almighty, which was 2000 years after. The religion (or cabal) of the *Hebrews* was transferred from the patriarchs to *Moses*, and from him to the prophets. It was honoured with the appearance and promulgation of God himself, specially the better part of it, I mean the decalogue containing the ten commandments; which being most of them moral and agreeing with the common notions of man, are in force all the world over. The *Jews* at this day are divided into three sects: the first, which is the greatest, are called the *Talmudists*, in regard that besides the holy Scriptures they embrace the *Talmud*, which is stuffed with the traditions of their rabbins and chacams: the second receive the Scriptures alone: the third the pentateuch only, *viz.* the five books of *Moses*, who are called *Samaritans*. Now touching what part of the earth is possessed by *Jews*, I
cannot

cannot find they have any at all peculiar to themfelves; but in regard of their murmurings, their frequent idolatries, defeftions, and that they crucified the Lord of life, this once feleft nation of God, and the inhabitants of the land flowing with milk and honey, is become now a fcorned fquandered people all the earth over, being ever fince incapable of any coalition or reducement into one body politic.. There where they are moft without mixture, is *Tiberias* in *Paleftine,* which *Amurath* gave *Mendez* the *Jew;* whither, and to *Jerufalem,* upon any conveniency, they convey the bones of their dead friends from all places to be reinterred. They are to be found in all mercantile towns and great marts, both in *Africa, Afia,* and *Europe,* the dominions of *England,* of the *Spaniard* and *French* excepted; and as their perfons, fo their profeffion is defpicable, being for the moft part but brokers every where. Among other places they are allowed to be in *Rome* herfelf near St. *Peter*'s chair; for they advance trade wherefoever they come, with their banks of money, and fo are permitted as neceffary evils. But put cafe the whole nation of the *Jews* now living were united into one colleftive body, yet according to the beft conjefture and exafteft computation that I could hear made by the knowingeft men, they would not be able to people a country bigger than the feventeen provinces. Thofe that are difperfed now in chriftendom and *Turky,* are the remnants only of the tribes of *Judah* and *Benjamin,* with fome *Levites* which returned from *Babylon* with *Zerubbabel.* The commmon opinion is, that the other ten are utterly loft; but they themfelves fancy that they are in *India,* a mighty nation, environed with ftony rivers, which always eeafe to run their courfe on their *Sabbath;* from whence they expeft their *Meffias,* who fhall in the fulnefs of time over-run the world with fire and fword, and re-eftablifh them in a temporal glorious eftate. But this opinion fways moft among the oriental *Jews,* whereas they of the *Weft* attend the coming of their *Meffias* from *Portugal;* which language is more common among them any other. And thus

much

much in brief of the *Jews*, as much as I could digeſt, and comprehend within the compaſs of this paper-ſheet; and let it ſerve for the accompliſhment of the firſt part of your deſire. In my next I ſhall give you the beſt ſatisfaction I can concerning the extent of chriſtianity up and down the globe of the earth; which I ſhall ſpeedily ſend: for, now that I have undertaken ſuch a taſk, my pen ſhall not reſt till I have finiſhed it. So, I am

Your moſt affectionate ready ſervitor,

Weſtminſt. Auguſt 1. 1635.　　　　　　J. H.

LETTER XLVI.

To Doctor B.

S I R,

HAVING in my laſt ſent you ſomething touching the ſtate of *Judaiſm* up and down the world, in this you ſhali receive what extent chriſtianity hath, which is the ſecond religion in ſucceſſion of time and truth: a religion *that makes not ſenſe ſo much ſubject to reaſon, as reaſon ſuccumbent to faith.* There is no religion ſo harſh and difficult to fleſh and blood, in regard of divers myſterious poſitions it conſiſts of; as the incarnation, reſurrection, the Trinity, &c. which, as one ſaid, *are bones to philoſophy, but milk to faith.* There is no religion ſo purely ſpiritual, and abſtracted from common natural ideas and ſenſual happineſs, as the chriſtian: no religion that excites men more to the love and practice of virtue, and hatred of vice, or that preſcribes greater rewards for the one, and puniſhments for the other: a religion that in a moſt miraculous manner did expand herſelf, and propagate by ſimplicity, humbleneſs, and by a meer paſſive way of fortitude, growing up like the palm-tree under the heavy weight of perſecution: for never any religion had more powerful oppoſition, by various kinds of puniſ.ments, oppreſſions and torture ; which may be

ſaid

said to have decked her with rubies in her very cradle; insomuch, that it is granted by her very enemies, that the christian in point of passive valour hath exceeded all other nations upon earth. And it is a thing of wonderment, how at her very first growth she flew over the heads of so many interjacent vast regions into this remote isle so soon, that her rays should shine upon the crown of a *British* King first of any; I mean King *Lucius,* the true proto-christian King in the days of *Eleutherius,* at which time she received her propagation; but for her plantation, she had it long before, by some of the apostles themselves. Now, as the christian religion hath the purest and most abstracted, the hardest and highest spiritual notions, so it hath been most subject to differences of opinions and distractions of conscience: the purer the wheat is, the more subject it is to tares, and the most precious gems to flaws. The first bone that the devil flung, was into the *Eastern* churches; then betwixt the *Greek* and the *Roman,* but it was rather for jurisdiction and power, than for the fundamentals of faith; and lately betwixt *Rome* and the *North West* churches. Now the extent of the *Eastern* church is larger far than that of the *Roman,* (excluding *America*) which makes some accuse her as well of uncharitableness as of arrogance, that she should positively damn so many millions of christian souls, who have the same common symbols of faith with her, because they are not within the close of her fold.

Of those *Eastern* and *South-East* churches, there are no less than eleven sects, whereof the three principallest are the *Grecian,* the *Jacobite,* and the *Nestorian,* with whom the rest have some dependance or conformity; and they acknowledge canonical obedience either to the Patriarch of *Constantinople,* of *Alexandria,* of *Jerusalem,* or *Antioch:* they concur with the *Western* reformed churches, in divers positions against *Rome;* as in denial of purgatory, in rejecting of extreme unction, and celebrating the sacrament under both kinds; in admitting their clergy to marry; in abhorring the use of massy statues, and celebrating

brating

brating their liturgy in the vulgar language : among
thefe, the *Ruſſe*, and the *Habaſſin* emperors are the
greateſt; but the latter is a *Jew* alſo from the girdle
downward, for he is both circumciſed and chriſtened,
having received the one from *Solomon*, and. the other
from the Apoſtle St. *Thomas*. They obſerve other rites
of the *Levitical* law : they have the croſs in that eſteem,
that they imprint the ſign of it upon ſome part of the
child's body when he is baptized : that day they take the
holy ſacrament they ſpit not till after ſun-ſet; and the
Emperor in his progreſſes, as ſoon as he comes to the ſight
of a church, lights off his camel, and foots it all along,
till he loſeth the ſight of it.

Now touching that proportion of ground that the
chriſtians have on the habitable earth, (which is the main
of our taſk) I find that all *Europe* with her adjacent iſles
is peopled with chriſtians, except that ruthful country of
Lapland, where idolaters yet inhabit : towards the *Eaſt*
alſo, that religion which lieth betwixt *Tanais* and *Boriſt-
henes*, the antient country of the *Goths*, is poſſeſſed by
Mahometan Tartars; but in theſe territories which the
Turk hath betwixt the *Danube* and the ſea, and betwixt
Raguſa and *Buda*, chriſtians are intermixed with *Mahometans;* yet in this cohabitation, chriſtians are computed
to make two third parts at leaſt : for here and elſewhere,
all the while they pay the *Turk* the quarter of their increaſe, and a ſultanin for every poll, and ſpeak nothing
in derogation of the *alcoran*, they are permitted to enjoy both their religion and lives ſecurely. In *Conſtantinople* herſelf, under the *Grand Signior*'s noſe, they
have twenty churches; in *Saloniche* (or *Theſſalonica*)
thirty. There are 150 churches under the metropolitan of *Philippi*, as many under him of *Athens*, and he of
Corinth hath about 100 ſuffragan biſhops under him.

But in *Afric*, (a thing which cannot be too much lamented) that huge extent of land which chriſtianity poſſeſſed of old betwixt the *Mediterranean* ſea, and the
mountain *Atlas*, yea as far as *Egypt*, with the large region of *Nubia*, the *Turks* have over-maſtered. We
read

read of 200 bishops met in synods in those parts; and in
that province where old *Carthage* stood, there were 164
bishops under one *Metropolitan;* but *Mahometism* hath
now overspread all thereabout, only the King of *Spain*
hath a few maritime towns under christian subjection, as
Septa, Tangier, Oran, and others. But through all the
huge continent of *Afric,* which is estimated to be thrice
bigger than *Europe,* there is not one region intirely christian, but *Habassia* or *Ethiopia :* besides, there is in *E-*
gypt a considerable number of them yet sojourning.
Now *Habassia,* according to the itineraries of the obser-
vingest travellers in those parts, is thought to be in re-
spective magnitude as big as *Germany, Spain, France,*
and *Italy* conjunctly: an estimate which comes nearer
truth than that which some make by stretching it from
one tropick to the other, *viz.* from the *Red-sea* to the
Western ocean. There are also divers isles upon the
coast of *Afric,* that are colonized with christians, as the
Madera, the *Canaries, Cape Verd,* and St. *Thomas's ;*
but on the *East* side there is none but *Zocotora.*

In *Asia* there is the empire of *Russia* that is purely
christian, and the mountain *Libanus* in *Syria.* In ether
parts they are mingled with *Mahometans,* who exceed
them one day more than another in numbers, especially
in those provinces (the more is the pity) where the gospel was first preached, as *Anatolia, Armenia, Syria,*
Mesopotamia, Palestina, Chaldea, Assyria, Persia, the
North of *Arabia,* and *South* of *India.* In some of
these parts, I say, especially in the four first, christians
are thick mixed with *Mahometans,* as also in *East-India,*
since the *Portugals* discovery of the passage by the *Cape*
of Good Hope, christians by God's goodness have multi-
plied in considerable numbers; as likewise in *Goa,* since
it was made an archbishoprick, and the court of a Viceroy. They speak also of a christian church in *Quinsay*
in *China,* the greatest of all earthly cities; but in the
islands thereabouts called the *Philippines,* which they say
are above 1100 in number, in thirty whereof the *Spa-*
niard hath taken firm footing, christianity hath made a
good

good progrefs, as alfo in *Japonia*. In the *North-Eaft* part of *Afia*, fome 400 years fince, chriftianity had taken deep root under the King of *Tenduc*, but he was utterly overthrown by *Chingis* one of his own vaffals, who came thereby to be the firft founder of the *Tartarian* empire: this King of *Tenduc* was the true *Prefter John*, not the *Ethiopian* King of the *Habaffines*, as *Scaliger* would have it; whofe opinion is as far diftant from truth in this point, as the *Southerneft* part of *Afric* from the *North-Eaft* part of *Afia*, or as a *Jacobite* is from a *Neftorian*. Thus far did chriftianity find entertainment in the old world: touching the new, I mean *America*, which is conjectured to equal, well near, the other three parts in magnitude, the *Spanifh* authors and merchants (with whom I have converfed) make report of a marvellous growth that chriftianity hath made in the kingdoms of *Mexico*, *Peru*, *Brafil*, and *Caftilia de loro;* as alfo in the greater iflands adjoining, as *Hifpaniola*, *Cuba*, *Portorico*, and others, infomuch that they write of one antient Prieft who had chriftened himfelf 700 *Savages* fome years after the firft difcovery; but there are fome who feeming to be no friends to *Spain*, report that they did not baptize half fo many as they have butchered.

Thus you have as compendioufly as an epiftle could make it, an account of that extenfion of ground which chriftians poffefs upon earth. My next fhall be one of the *Mahometan*, wherein I could wifh I had not occafion to be fo large as I muft be: fo, I am, Sir,

Your refpectful and humble fervant,

Weftminft. Auguft 9. 1635.   J. H.

L E T-

LETTER XLVII.

To Doctor B.

S I R,

MY two former were of *Judaism* and *chriftianity:* I come now to the *Mahometans,* the moderneft of all religions, and the moft mifchievous and deftructive to the church of Chrift; for this fatal fect hath juftled her out of divers large regions in *Afric,* in *Tartary* and other places, and attenuated their number in *Afia,* which they do wherefoever they come, having a more politic and pernicious way to do it than by fire and faggot: for, they having underftood well that the duft of martyrs were the thrivingeft feeds of chriftianity; and obferved that there reigns naturally in mankind, being compofed all of a lump, and carrying the fame ftamp, a general kind of compaffion and fympathy; which appears moft towards them who lay down their lives, and poftpone all worldly things for the prefervation of their confciences, (and never any died fo, but he drew followers after him) therefore the *Turk* goes a more cunning way to work: he meddles not with life and limb to prevent the fenfe of compaffion which may arife that way; but he grinds their faces with taxes, and makes them incapable of any offices either of authority, profit, or honour; by which means, he renders them defpicable to others, and makes their lives irkfome to themfelves. Yet the *Turks* have a high opinion of Chrift, " That he was a greater Pro-
" phet than *Mofes;* that he was the fon of a virgin,
" who conceived by the fmell of a rofe prefented to her
" by *Gabriel* the angel: they believe he never finned;
" nay, in their *alcoran,* they term him the breath and
" word of God: they punifh all that blafpheme him,
" and no *Jew* is capable to be a *Turk,* but he muft be
" firft an ABDULA, a chriftian." He muft eat hog's flefh, and do other things for three days, then he is
made

made a *Mahometan*, but by abjuring of Chrift to be a greater Prophet than *Mahomet*.

It is the *Alfange* that uſhers in the faith of *Mahomet* every where, nor can it grow in any place, unleſs it be planted and ſown with gunpowder intermixed: when planted, there are divers ways of policy to preſerve it: they have their *alcoran* in one only language, which is the *Arabic*, the mother-tongue of their Prophet. It is as bad as death for any to raiſe ſcruples of the *alcoran;* thereupon there is a reſtraint of the ſtudy of philoſophy, and other learning, becauſe the impoſtors of it may not be diſcerned. The *Mufti* is in as great reverence a-mongſt them as the Pope is among the *Romaniſts :* for, they hold it to be a true principle in divinity, *that no one thing preſerves and improves religion more than a venerable, high, pious eſteem of the chief miniſters.* They have no other guide or law both for temporal and church-affairs than the *alcoran;* which they hold to be the *rule of civil juſtice, as well as the divine charter of their ſalvation;* ſo that their judges are but expoſitors of that only: nor do they trouble themſelves or puzzle the plaintiff with any moth-eaten records, or precedents to entangle the buſineſs, but they immediately determine it, according to the freſh circumſtances of the action, & *ſecundum allegata, & probata,* by witneſſes. They have one extraordinary piece of humanity to be ſo ten-der of the rational ſoul, as not to put chriſtian, *Jew, Greek,* or any other to his oath, in regard that if, for ſome advantage of gain or occaſion of inconvenience and puniſhment any ſhould forſwear himſelf, they hold the impoſers of the oath to be acceſſory to the damnation of the perjured man. By theſe and divers other reaches of policy (beſide their arms) not practiſed elſewhere, they conſerve that huge bulk of the *Ottoman* empire, which extends without interruption (the *Helleſpont* only be-tween) in one continued piece of earth 3200 miles, from *Buda* in *Hungary* to a good way into *Perſia :* by theſe means, they keep alſo their religion from diſtracting opi-nions, from every vulgar fancy and ſchiſms in their church,

church, for there is no where fewer than here: the difference that is, is only with the *Perfian*, and that not in fundamentals of faith, but for priority of government in matters of religion. This fo univerfal, conformity in their religion, is afcribed as to other politic inftitutions, fo efpecially to the rigorous inhibition they have of raifing fcruples and difputes of the *alcoran* under pain of death, efpecially among the laity and common people; whofe *zeal commonly is ftronger than their judgment.*

That part of the world where *Mahomet* hath furtheft expanded himfelf, is *Afia;* which, as I faid before, exceeds *Africa* in greatnefs, and much more in people: he hath firm footing in *Perfia, Tartary,* (upon the latter of which the *Muffulman* empire is entailed) in *Turcomania* itfelf, and *Arabia,* four mighty kingdoms: the laft of thefe was the neft where that cockatrice egg was hatched, which hath diffufed its poifon fo far and near, through the veins of fo many regions: all the Southerly coafts of *Afia,* from the *Arabian* bay to the river of *Indus* is infected therewith, the vaft kingdom of *Cambaia* and *Bengala;* and about the South part, the inhabitants of *Malabar* have drank of this poifon, infomuch, that by no wrong computation it may well be faid, that *Mahometifm* hath difperfed itfelf over almoft one half of the huge continent of *Afia,* befides thofe multitudes of ifles efpecially feven, *Moldavia, Ceylon,* the fea-coaft of *Sumatra, Java, Sunda,* the ports of *Banda, Borneo,* with divers others, whereof there are many thoufands about *Afia,* who have entertained the *alcoran.* In *Europe* the *Mahometans* poffefs all the region betwixt *Don* and *Meper,* called of old *Tanais* and *Borifthenes,* being about the twentieth part of *Europe:* the King of *Poland* difpenfeth with fome of them in *Lithuania.* Touching *Greece, Macedon, Thracia, Bulgaria, Servia, Bofnia, Epire,* the greateft part of *Hungary* and *Dalmatia,* although they be wholly under *Turks* obedience, yet *Mahometans* fcarce make the third part of the inhabitants. In *Africa* this contagion is further fpread: it hath intoxicated all the fhore of *Ethiopia* as far as *Mofumbick,*

F f

bick, which lieth oppofite to *Madagafcar*.   It is worfe
with the firm land of *Africa* on the North and Weft parts :
for, from the *Mediterranean* fea to the great river *Ni-*
per, and along the banks of *Nile*, all *Egypt* and *Barbary*,
with *Lybia* and the *Negro*'s country, are tainted and tanned with this black religion.

The vaft propagation of this unhappy fect may be afcribed firft to the fword, for the *confcience commonly is apt*,
to follow the conqueror: then to the loofe reins it gives
to all fenfual liberty, as to have eight wives, and as many
concubines as one can maintain, with the affurance of
venerial delights in a far higher degree, to fucceed after,
death to the religious obfervers of it, as the fruition
of beautiful damfels, with large rolling eyes, whofe
virginity fhall renew after every act : their youth fhall laft
always with their luft, and love fhall be fatiated with only
one, where it fhall remain inalienable.   They concur,
with the chriftian but only in the acknowledgment of one
God, and in his attributes.   With the *Jew* they fymbo-
lize in many things more, as in circumcifion, in refrain-
ing from fwine's flefh, in deteftation of images, and
fomewhat in the quality of future happinefs; which, as
we faid before, they place in venerial pleafure, as the
Jew doth in feafting and banquetings, fo that neither of
their laws have punifhment enough to deter mankind from
wickednefs and vice, nor do they promife adequate rewards for virtue and piety : for, in the whole *alcoran*,
and through all the writings of *Mofes*, there is not a
word of angelical joys and eternity.   And herein chriftianity far excels both thefe religions, for fhe placeth
future happinefs in fpiritual, everlafting and unconceive-
able blifs, abftracted from the fading and faint grofsnefs
of fenfe.   The *Jew* and *Turk* alfo agree in their opinion of women, whom they hold to be of an inferior
creation to man; which makes the one to exclude them
from the mofques, and the other from his fynagogues.

Thus far have I rambled through the vaft *Ottoman*
empire, and taken a curfory furvey of *Mahomet*'s religion.   In my next I fhall take the beft view I can of
Pagans

Pagans and idolaters, with thofe who go for athiefts; and in this particular, it may be faid to be worfe than hell itfelf, and the kingdom of the devil, in regard there are no athiefts there: for the very damned fouls find and feel in the midft of their tortures, that there is a God by his juftice and punifhments; nay, the prince of darknefs himfelf and all the cacodæmons by an hiftorical faith believe there is a God, whereunto the poet alludes very divinely:

Nullus in inferno eft Atheus, *ante fuit.*

fo, I very affectionately kifs your hand, and reft·

Your faithful ready fervitor,.

Weftminfter, Auguft 14. 1635. J. H.

LETTER XLVIII.

To Doctor. B.

S I R,

HAVING in my three former letters wafhed my hands of the *Mahometan* and the *Jew*, and attended chriftianity up and down the earth, I come now to the *Pagan* idolater or *Heathen*, who (the more to be lamented) make the greateft part of mankind. *Europe* herfelf, though the beams of the crofs have fhined upon her above thefe fixteen ages, is not free from them, for they poffefs to this day *Lappia, Corelia, Biarmia, Scrifinnia*, and the North parts of *Finmark:* there are alfo fome fhreds of them to be found in divers places of *Lituania* and *Somogitia*, which make a region 900 miles in compafs.

But in *Africa* their numbers is incredible, for from *Cape Blanc*, the moft Wefterly point of *Africa*, all Southward to the *Cape of Good Hope*, and thence turning by the back of *Africa* to the *Cape of Mozambric*, all thefe coafts being about the one half of the circumference of

Africa, is peopled by idolaters, though in some places intermixed with *Mahometans* and christians, as in the kingdom of *Cong* and *Angola;* but, if we survey the inland territories of *Africa* between the river of *Nile*, and the West sea of *Ethiopia*, even all that country from about the North parallel of ten degrees, to the South parallel of six degrees, all is held by idolaters; besides, the kingdom of *Borno*, and a great part of *Nubia* and *Lybia*, continue still in their old *Paganism*, so that by this account we have above one half of that immense continent of *Africa* peopled by idolaters. But in *Asia*, which is far more spacious and more populous than *Africa*, *Pagan* idolaters, and *Gentiles*, swarm in great numbers, for from the river *Pechora* eastward to the ocean, and thence southward to the *Cape of Cincapura;* and from that point returning westward by the South coasts to the outlets of the river *Indus*, all that maritime tract, which makes a good deal more than half the circumference of *Asia*, is inhabited by idolaters: so are the inland parts. There are two mighty mountains that traverse all *Asia*, *Taurus* and *Imaus:* the first runs from the West to East, the other from North to South, and so quarter and cut that huge mass of earth into equal parts: this side those mountains most of the people are *Mahometans*, but the other side they are all idolaters. And as on the firm continent *Paganism* thus reigns, so in many thousand islands squandered in the vast ocean, on the East and South-east of *Asia*, idolatry overspreads all, except in some few islands that are possessed by *Spaniards* and *Arabs*.

Lastly, if one take a survey of *America*, (as none hath done yet exactly) which is estimated to be as big as all the old earth: idolaters there possess four parts of five. It is true some years after the first navigation thither, they were converted daily in great multitudes, but afterwards observing the licentious lives of the christians, their greediness for gold, and their cruelty, they came not in so fast; which made an *Indian* answer a *Spanish* frier who was discoursing with him of the joys of heaven,

and

and how all *Spaniards* went thither after this life. Then
said the *Pagan*, I do not defire to go thither if *Spaniards* be there, I had rather go to hell to be free of their
company. *America* differs from the reft of the earth in
this, that fhe hath neither *Jew* nor *Mahometan* in her,
but chriftians and *Gentiles* only. There are, befides
all thofe religions and people before mentioned, an irregular confufed nation in *Europe*, called the *Mordusts;*
which occupy the middle confines betwixt the *Tartars*
and the *Ruffe*, that are mingled in rites of religion with
all thofe that have been fore-fpoken: for from the
privy-members upward they are chriftian, in regard they
admit of baptifm: from the navel downward they are
Mahometans or *Jews*, for they are circumcifed; and
befides, they are given to the adoration of heathenifh
idols. In *Afia* there are the *Cardi*, which inhabit the
mountainous country about *Mozal*, between *Armenia*
and *Mefopotamia*, and the *Druci* in *Syria*, who are demi-
Mahometans and *chriftians*.

Now concerning *Pagans* and heathenifh idolaters,
whereof there are innumerable forts up and down the
furface of the earth. In my opinion, thofe are the ex-
cufeableft kind who adore the fun and moon, with the
hoft of heaven. And in *Ireland*, the *Kerns* of the
mountains, with fome of the *Scots* ifles, ufe a fafhion of
adoring the moon to this very day, praying, fhe would
leave them in as good health as fhe found them. This is
not fo grofs an idolatry as that of other heathens: for,
the adoration of thefe glorious celeftial bodies is more
excufeable than that of garlick and onions with the *E-
gyptian*, who fome think (with the *Sicynian*) was the
antienteft idolater upon earth; which he makes thrice
older than we do: for *Diodorus Siculus* reports that the
Egyptian had a religion and kings 18,000 years fince;
yet, for matter of philofophy and fcience, he had it
from the *Chaldean*, he from the *Gymnofophifts*, and
Brachmans of *India;* which country, as fhe is the next
neighbour to the rifing fun, in reference to this fide of
the hemifphere, fo the beams of learning did firft en-

lighten

lighten her. *Egypt* was the nurse of that famous *Hermes Trifmagiftus*, who having no other feale but that of natural reafon, mounted very-high towards heavens for he hath very many divine fayings, whereof I think it not impertinent to infert here a few, firft he faith, *That all human fins are venial with the gods, impiety excepted.* 2. *That goodnefs belongs to the gods, piety to men, revenge and wickednefs to the devils.* 3. *That the word is* lucens Dei filius, *the bright fon of God*, &c.

From *Egypt* theorical knowledge came down the *Nile*, and landed at fome of the *Greek* iflands; where, betwixt the 33d, 34th, and the 35th century of years after the creation, there flourifhed all thofe renowned philofophers that fway now in our fchools: *Plato* flew in the higheft divine notions, for fome call him another *Mofes* fpeaking *Athenian.* In one of his letters to a friend of his, he writes thus: " When I ferioufly falute thee, I begin my " letter with one God; when otherwife, with many." His fcholar *Ariftotle* commended himfelf at his death to the *Being of Beings;* and *Socrates* may be faid to be a martyr for the firft perfon of the Trinity. Thefe great fecretaries of nature, by ftudying the vaft volume of the world, came by main ftrength of reafon to the knowledge of one Deity, or *primus motor;* and of his attributes, they found by undeniable confequences that he was *infinite, eternal, ubiquitary, omnipotent, and not capable of any definition;* which made the philofopher being commanded of his King to define God, to afk the refpite of a day to meditate thereon, then two, then four: at laft, he ingenioufly confeffed, that the more he thought to dive into this myftery, the more he was *ingulphed in the fpeculation of it:* for the quiddity and effence of the incomprehenfible Creator, cannot imprint any formal conception upon the finite intellect of the creature. To this I might refer the altar which St. *Paul* found among the *Greeks* with this infcription, τῷ ἀγνώϛῳ Θιῳ, *To the unknown God*.

From the *Greek* ifles philofophy came to *Italy*, thence to this Weftern world among the *Druids*, whereof
                                                                    thofe

thofe of this ifle were moft celebrous; for, we read that
the *Gauls* (now the *French*) came to *Britany* in great
numbers to be inftructed by them. The *Romans* were
mighty great zealots in their idolatry; and their beft authors affirm, that they extended their monarchy fo far
and near, by a particular deference they had for their
gods, (which the *Spaniard* feems now to imitate) though
thofe gods of theirs were made of men, and of good fellows at firft: befides, in the courfe of their conquefts,
they adopted any ftrange gods to the fociety of theirs,
and brought them folemnly to *Rome;* and the reafon one
faith was, that they believed the more gods they had
the fafer they were, a few being not fufficient to con-
ferve and protect fo great an empire. The *Roman Gentiles* had their altars and facrifices, their arch-flamins and
veftal nuns: and it feems the fame genius reigns ftill in
them; for in the primitive church, that which the *Pagans* mifliked moft in chriftianity was, that it had not the
face and form of religion, in regard it had no oblations,
altars, and images; which may be a good reafon why
the facrifice of the mafs and other ceremonies were firft
inftituted to allure the *Gentiles* to chriftianity. But to
return a little further to our former fubject in the condition that mankind ftands now, if the globe of the earth
were divided into thirty parts, it is thought that idolaters, (with horror I fpeak it) having as I faid before,
the one half of *Afia* and *Africa*, both for the inland country and maritime coafts, with four parts of five in *America*, inhabit twenty parts of thofe regions that are already found out upon earth. Befides, in the opinion of
the knowing and moft inquifitive mathematicians, there
is toward the Southern clime as much land yet undifco-
vered, as may equal in dimenfion the late new world, in
regard, as they hold there muft be of neceffity fuch a
portion of earth to ballance the centre on all fides; and
it is more than probable, that the inhabitants there muft
be *Pagans.* Of all kinds of idolaters thofe are the hor-
rideft who adore the devil, whom they call *tantara*, who
appears often unto them, efpecially in a hurricane, though
he

he be not vifible to others. In fome places they worſhip
both God and the devil: the one, that he may do them
good, the other, that he may do them no hurt: the firſt
they call *tantum*, the other *fquantum*. It were prefumption beyond that of *Lucifer*'s or *Adam*'s, for man to
cenfure the juſtice of the Creator in this particular, why
he makes daily fuch innumerable veffels of diſhonour.
It is a wifer and fafer courfe far, to fit down in an humble
admiration, and cry out, Oh, the profound infcrutable
judgments of God! his ways are paſt finding out; and
fo to acknowledge with the divine Philofopher, *Quod oc-*
culus vefpertilionis ad folem, idem eſt omnis intelleĉtus
humanus ad Deum: what the eye of a bat is to the fun,.
the fame is all human underſtanding to God wards.

Now to draw to a conclufion, touching the refpeĉtive
largenefs of chriſtianity and *Mahometanifm* upon the
earth, I find the firſt to exceed, taking the new world
with the old, confidering the fpacious plantations of the
Spaniard in *America*, the colonies the *Englifh* have
there in *Virginia*, *New-England* and *Caribbee* iſlands,.
with thofe of the *French* in *Canada*, and of the *Hollan-*
der in *Eaſt-India:* nor do I find that there is any region.
purely *Mahometans* without intermixtures, as chriſtianity
hath many; which makes me to be of a differing opinion
to that gentleman, ·who held, that chriſtianity added
little to the general religion of mankind.

Now touching the latitude of chriſtian faith in reference
to the differing profeffors therof, as in my former I ſhewed that the Eaſtern churches were more fpacious than
the *Latin* or *Roman* (excepting the two *Indies*) fo they
who have fallen off from her in the Weſtern parts are·
not fo far inferior to her in *Europe* as fome would make
one believe; which will appear, if we caſt them in counterbalance.

Among the *Roman* catholicks, there is the Emperor,
and in him the King of *Hungary*, the three kings of
Spain France, and *Poland*; *Italy*, the dukes of *Savoy*,
Bavaria, and *Lorain*, the three fpiritual eleĉtors, with·
fome few more. Touching them who have renounced:
all

all obedience to *Rome*, there are the three kings of *Great Britain*, *Denmark*, and *Swethland*, the Duke of *Saxon*, *Holstein*, and *Wittemberg*: the Marquis of *Brandenburg*, and *Baden*, the Landgrave of *Hesse*, most of the *Han-siatic* towns, which are eighty-eight in number, some wherof are equal to republics, the (almost seven) provinces the *Hollander* hath. The five cantons of *Swiss* and *Geneva*; they of *France* who are reputed the fifth part of the kingdom; the Prince of *Transylvania*; they of *Hungary*, and of the large kingdom of *Bohemia*, of the marquisates of *Lusatia*, *Moravia*, and the dukedom of *Silesia*; as also they have the huge kingdom of *Poland*, wherein protestants are diffus'd through all quarters in great numbers, having in every province their public churches and congregations orderly severed and bounded with diocesses, whence are sent some of the chiefest and most principal men of worth, unto their general synods: for although there are divers sorts of these *Polonian* protestants, some embracing the *Waldensian* or the *Bohemic*, others the *Augustane*, and some the *Helvetian* confession; yet they all concur in opposition to the *Roman* church, as also they of the *Anglican*, *Scotican*, *Gallic*, *Argentine*, *Saxonick*, *Wirtenbergick*, *Palatine* and *Belgick* confessions. They also harmoniously symbolize in the principal articles of faith, and which mainly concern eternal salvation; in the full sufficiency of the scriptures, divine essence, and unity of the everlasting Godhead, the sacred trinity of the three glorious persons, the blessed incarnation of Christ, the omnipotent presence of God, the absolute supreme head of the church, Christ himself, justification by faith through his merits, and touching the nature of lively faith, repentance, regeneration, and sanctification, the difference between the law and the gospel, touching free-will, sin, and good works, the sacraments, their number, use and efficacy, the marks of the church, the resurrection and state of souls deceased. It may seem a rambling wild speech at first view, of one who said, that to make one a complete christian, he must have the ' works of a papist, the words

' of

‘ of a puritan, and the faith of a proteſtant;’ yet this
wiſh if well expounded ‘may bear a good ſenſe, which
were unfitting for me to give, you being better able to
put a gloſs upon it yourſelf.

Thus learned Sir, have I exerciſed my pen, according
to my ſmall proportion of knowledge, and converſation
with books, men, and maps, to obey your deſire, though
in compariſon of your ſpacious literature, I have held all
this while but a candle to the ſun, yet by the light of
this ſmall candle you may ſee how ready I am to ſhew
myſelf

Your very humble and affeƈtionate ſervitor,
Weſtminſter, Aug. 25. 1635.　　　　　　　　J. H.

L E T T E R XLIX.

To Sir Tho. Hawk, *Knight.*

S I R,

I Was invited yeſternight to a ſolemn ſopper by *B J.*
where you were deeply remembered, there was good
company, excellent cheer, choice wines, and jovial welcome: one thing interveened, which almoſt ſpoiled the
reliſh of the reſt, that *B.* began to engroſs all the diſcourſe, to vapour extremely of himſelf, and by villifying
others to magnify his own muſe. *T. C.* buzzed me in
the ear, that though *Ben* had barrelled up a great deal
of knowledge, yet it ſeems he had not read the ethics;
which among other precepts of morality forbid ſeif-com-
mendation, declaring it to be an ill-favoured ſoleciſm in
in good manners. It made me think upon the lady, (not
very young) who having a good while given her gueſts
neat entertainment, a capon being brought upon the
table, inſtead of a ſpoon ſhe took a mouthful of claret
and ſpouted it into the poop of the hollow bird: ſuch
an accident happened in this entertainment, you know—
Proprio

Proprio laus sordet in ore: Be a man's breath never so
sweet, yet it makes one's praise stink, if he makes his
own mouth the conduit-pipe of it. But for my part, I
am content to dispense with the *Roman* infirmity of *B.*
now that time hath snowed upon his pericranium. You
know *Ovid* and (your) *Horace* were subject to his humour, the first bursting out into

> *Jamq; exegi quod nec Jovis ira nec ignis,* &c.

The other into,

> *Exegi monumentum ære perennius,* &c.

As also *Cicero*, while he forced himself into this exa-
meter, *O fortunatum natum, me consule, Romam!* there
is another reason that excuseth *B.* which is, that if one
be allowed to love the natural issue of his body, why not
that of the brain, which is of a spiritual and more noble
extraction? I preserve your manuscripts safe for you till
you return to *London :* what news the times afford, this
bearer will impart unto you. So, I am, Sir,

Your very humble and most faithful servitor,

Westminster, April 5. 1636. J. H.

LETTER L.

To my Cousin Mr. J. P. *at* Gravesend.

COUSIN,

GOD send you a good passage to *Holland*, and the
world to your mind when you are there. Now,
that you intend to trail a pike, and make profession of
arms, let me give you this caveat, that nothing must be
more precious to you than your reputation. As I know
you have not a spirit to receive wrong, so you must be
careful not to offer any, for the one is as base as the
other: your pulse will be quickly felt, and trial made
what mettle you are made of after your coming. If you
get

get but once handfomely off, you are made ever after, for you will be free from all baffles and affronts. *He that hath once got the name of early rifing may ly till noon;* therefore be wondrous warry of your firft comportments, get once a good name, and be very tender of it afterwards, for it is like *Venice glafs, quickly cracked, never to be mended, patched it may be.* To this purpofe take along with you this fable : it happened that fire, water, and fame, went to travel together, (as you are going now) they confulted, that if they loft one another, how they might be retrieved and meet again : fire faid, where you fee fmoke, there you fhall find me : water faid, where you fee marfh and moorifh low ground, there you fhall find me : but fame faid, take heed you do not lofe me, for if you do, you will run a great hazard never to meet me again, there is no retrieving of me.

It imports you alfo to conform yourfelf to your commanders, and fo you may more confidently demand obedience, when you come to command yourfelf, as I doubt not but you may do in a fmall time. The *Hogen Mogen* are very exact in their polemical government, their pay is fure, though fmall, four fhillings a week being too little a hire, as one faid, to kill men. At your return, I hope you will give a better account of your doings than he who being afked what exploits he had done in the *Low-Countries,* anfwered, that he had cut off a *Spaniard's* legs : reply being made, that that was no great matter, it had been fomething if he had cut off his head; O, faid he, you muft confider his head was off before. Excufe me that I take my leave of you fo pleafantly, but I know you will take any thing in good part from him who is fo much

Your truly affectionate Coufin,

Weftminfter, Aug. 3. 1634.　　　　　　　　.J. H.

LET-

LETTER LI.

To the Lord C.

My LORD,

THERE are two fayings which are fathered upon Secretary *Walfingham*, and Secretary *Cecil*, a pair of the beft weighed ftatefmen this ifland hath bred: one was ufed to fay at the Council-table, ' My lords, ftay a ' little, and we fhall make an end the fooner:' the other would oft-times fpeak of himfelf, ' It fhall never be faid ' of me, that I will defer till to-morrow what I can do ' to-day.' At firft view thefe fayings feem to clafh' with one another, and to be diametrically oppofite, but being rightly underftood, they may very well be reconciled. Touching the firft, it is true, that hafte and choler are enemies to all great actions: for, as it is a principle in chymiftry, that *omni feftinatio eft a diabolo;* all hafte comes from hell: fo in the confultations, contrivings, and conduct of any bufinefs of ftate, all rafhnefs and precipitation comes from an ill fpirit. There cannot be a better pattern for a grave and confiderate way of deliberation than the antient courfe of our high-court of parliament, who, when a law is to be made which concerns the welfare of fo many thoufands of men, after a mature debate and long difcuffion of the point beforehand, caufe the bill to be read folemnly three times in, the houfe before it be tranfmitted to the lords; and there alfo, it is fo many times canvaffed, and then prefented to the Prince. That which muft ftand for law, muft be long ftood upon, becaufe it impofeth an univerfal obedience, and is like to be everlafting, according to the *Ciceronian* maxim, *deliberandum eft diu quod ftatuendum eft femel.* Such a kind of cunctation, advifednefs, and procraftination is allowable alfo in all councils of ftate and war: for the day following may be able commonly to be mafter to the day paffed, fuch a world of contingencies human actions are fubject unto. Yet, under favour,

G g I

I believe this firſt ſaying to be meant of matters while
they are in agitation, and upon the anvil; but when they
have received form and are reſolved upon, I believe then,
nothing is ſo advantageous as ſpeed. And at this, I am
of opinion, the ſecond ſaying aims; for when the
weights that uſe to hang to all great buſineſſes are taken
away, it is good then to put wings unto them, and to
take the ball before the bound, for expedition is the life
of action; otherwiſe, time may ſhew his bald *occiput*,
and ſhake his poſteriors at them in deriſion. Among o-
ther nations, the *Spaniard* is obſerved to have much
phlegm, and to be moſt dilatory in his proceedings; yet
they who have pried narrowly into the ſequel and ſucceſs
of his actions, do find that this gravity, reſervedneſs and
tergiverſations of his, have turned rather to his prejudice
than advantage, take one with another. The two laſt
matrimonial treaties we had with him continued long,
the firſt, betwixt *Ferdinand* and *Henry* VII. for *Catha-
rine* of *Arragon* for ſeven years; that betwixt King
James and the now *Philip* IV. for *Mary* of *Auſtria*,
laſted eleven years, (and ſeven and eleven is eighteen);
the firſt took effect for Prince *Arthur*, the latter miſcar-
tied for Prince *Charles;* and the *Spaniard* may thank
himſelf and his own ſlow pace for it, for had he mended
his pace to perfect the work, I believe his monarchy had
not received ſo many ill-favoured ſhocks ſince. The
late revolt of *Portugal* was foreſeen and might have been
prevented, if the *Spaniard* had not been too ſlow in his
purpoſe to have ſent the Duke of *Braganza* out of the
way upon ſome employment as was projected.

Now will I reconcile the former ſayings of thoſe two
renowned ſecretaries, with the gallant compariſon of
Charles the Emperor, (and he was of a more temperate
mould than a *Spaniard*, being a *Fleming* born) he was
uſed to ſay, that while any great buſineſs of ſtate was
yet in conſultation, we ſhould obſerve the motion of *Sa-
turn*, which is plumbeous, long, and heavy; but when it
is abſolutely reſolved upon, then we ſhould obſerve the
motion of *Mercury*, the nimbleſt of all the planets: *Ubi
deſinit*

definit Saturnus, *ibi incipiat* Mercurius. Whereunto, I will add, that we should imitate the mulberry, who of all trees casts out her buds latest, for she doth it not till all the cold weather be passed, and then she is sure they cannot be nipped, but then she shoots them all out * in one night; so though she be one way the slowest, she is another way the nimblest of all trees.

Thus have I obeyed your Lordship's command in expounding the sense of these two sayings, according to my mean apprehension; but this exposition relates only to public affairs, and political negotiations, wherein your Lordship is so excellently versed. I shall most willingly conform to any other instructions of your Lordship's, and esteem them always as favours, while I am

Westminster, Sept. 5. 1633. J. H.

LETTER LII.

To Sir J. Brown, *Knight.*

`SIR;`

ONE would think that the utter falling off of *Catalonia* and *Portugal* in so short a compass of time should much lessen the *Spaniard*, the people of both these kingdoms being from subjects become enemies against him, and in actual hostility: without doubt it hath done so, yet not so much as the world imagines. It is true, in point of regal power, and divers brave subordinate commands for his servants, he is a great deal lessened thereby; but though he be less powerful, he is not a penny poorer thereby, for there comes not a farthing less every year into his exchequer, in regard that those countries were rather a charge than benefit unto him, all their revenue being drunk up in pensions, and payment of officers and garrisons: for, if the King of *Spain* had lost all except the *West-Indies,* and all *Spain* except *Castile* herself,

G g 2

* Quodum cum strepitu. PLIN.

felf, it would little diminifh his treafury.   Touching *Catalonia* and *Portugal*, efpecially the latter, it is true, they were mighty members of the *Caftilian* Monarchy; but, I believe they will fooner want *Caftile*, than *Caftile* them becaufe fhe filled them with treafure : now that *Barcelona* and *Lisbon* hath fhaken hands with *Sevil*, I do not think that either of them hath the tithe of that treafure they had before, in regard the one was the feale whereby the King of *Spain* fent his money to *Italy;* the other, becaufe all her *Eaft-India* commodities were bartered commonly in *Andaluzia* and elfewhere for *bullion*. *Catalonia* is fed with money from *France*, but for *Portugal*, fhe hath little or none ; therefore I do not fee how fhe could fup· port a war long to any purpofe if *Caftile* were quiet, unlefs foldiers would be contented to take *cloves* and *pepper-corns* for *pattacons* and *piftoles*. You know money is the finew and foul of war.   This makes me think on that blunt anfwer which Capt. *Talbot* returned *Henry* VIII. from *Calais*, who having received fpecial command from the King to erect a new fort at the water-gate, and to fee the town well fortified, fent him word, *that he could neither fortify nor fiftify without money.*   There is no news at all ftirring here now, and I am of the *Italian*'s mind that faid, *nulla nuova buona nuova ;* no news good news.   But it were great news to fee you here, whence you have been an alien fo long to

Your moft affectionate friend,

Holborn, June 3. 1640.   J. H.

L E T T E R LIII.

To Captain C. PRICE.

COUSIN,

YOU have put me upon fuch an odd intricate piece of bufinefs, that I think there was never the like of it.   I am more puzzled and entangled with it than oft-
times

times I ufe to be with my bandftrings when I go haftily
to bed, and want fuch a fair female hand as you have to
untie them. I muft impute all this to the peevifh humour
of the people I dealt withal. I find it true now, that
one of the greateft tortures that can be in the negotiation
of the world is, to have to do with perverfe irrational
half-witted men, and to be worded to death by non-
fenfe; befides, as much brain as they have is as full of
fcruples, as a bur is of prickles; which is a quality incident to all thofe that have their heads lightly hallafted,
for they are like buoys in a barred port, waving perpetually up and down. The father is fcrupulous of the fon,
the fon of the fifters, and all three of me, to whofe a-
ward they referred the bufinefs three feveral times. It
is as hard a tafk to reconcile the fanes of St. *Sepulcher*'s
fteeple, which never look all four upon one point of the
heavens, as to reduce them to any conformity of reafon.
I never remember to have met with father and children,
or children among themfelves, of a more differing genius
and contrariety of humours; infomuch that there cannot be a more pregnant inftance to prove that human
fouls come not *ex traduce*, and by feminal production
from the parents. For my part, I intend to fpend my
breath no longer upon them, but to wafh my hands
quite of the bufinefs; and fo I would wifh you to do, unlefs you love to walk in a labyrinth of briers. So expecting with impatience your return to *London*, I reft.

Your moft faithful fervitor,

Weftminfter, April 27. 1632.   J. H.

LETTER LIV.

To Sir J. B.

Noble Sir,

THAT odd opinion the *Jew* and *Turk* have of women, that they are of an inferior creation to man,
and therefore exclude them, the one from their fynagogues,

nagogues, the other from their mofques, is in my judgment not only partial, but profane : for the image of the Creator fhines as clearly in the one, as in the other ; and I believe, there are as many female faints in heaven as male, unlefs you could make me adhere to the opinion that women muft be all mafculine before they be capable to be made angels of. Add hereunto, that there went better and more refined ftuff to the creation of woman than man. It is true, it was a weak part in *Eve* to yield to the feducement of *Satan* ; but it was a weaker thing in *Adam* to fuffer himfelf to be tempted by *Eve*, being the weaker veffel.

The antient philofophers had a better opinion of that fex, for they afcribed all fciences to the *mufes*, all fweetnefs and morality to the *graces*, and prophetic infpirations to the *Sybils*. In my fmall revolving of authors, I find as high examples of virtue in women as in men ; I could produce here a whole regiment of them, but that a letter is too narrow a field to mufter them in. I muft confefs, there are alfo counter inftances of this kind : if Queen *Zenobia* was fuch a precife pattern of continency, that after the act of conception, fhe would know her hufband no more all the time of her pregnancy till fhe had been delivered : there is another example of a *Roman* Emprefs, that when fhe found the veffel fraughted, would take in all paffengers ; when the barn was full any one might threfh in the haggard, but not till then, for fear the right father fhould be difcovered by the countenance of the child. But what need I go fo far off, to rake the afhes of the dead ? There are living examples enough *pro* and *con* of both fexes ; yet woman being (as I faid before) the weaker veffel, her failings are more venial than thofe of man ; though man indeed being more converfant with the world, and meeting more opportunities abroad (and opportunity is the greateft bawd) of falling into infirmities, as he follows his worldly negotiations, may on the other fide be judged the more excufeable.

But you are fitter than I to difcourfe of this fubject, being better verfed in the theory of women, having had

a moſt virtuous Lady of your own before, and being now
linked to another. · I wiſh a thouſand benedictions may
fall upon this your ſecond choice, and that——*tam bona
ſit quam bona prima fuit.* This option ſhall be my concluſion for the preſent, whereunto I add, that I am in
no vulgar degree of affection

Your moſt humble and faithful ſervitor,
Weſtminſter, Aug. 5. 1632. J. H.

LETTER LV.
To Mr. P. W.

S I R,

THERE are two things which add moſt to the merit
of courteſies, viz. *chearfulneſs* and *ſpeed*, and the
contraries of theſe leſſen the value of them; that which
hangs long betwixt the fingers, and is done with difficulty and a ſullen ſupercilious look, makes the obligation of
the receivers nothing ſo ſtrong, or the memory of the
kindneſs half ſo grateful. The beſt thing the gods themſelves liked of in the entertainments they received of
theſe poor wretches *Baucis* and *Philemon,* was open
hearty looks.

——*Super omnia vultus,*
Acceſſere boni.——

A clear unclouded countenance makes a cottage appear like a caſtle in point of hoſpitality; but a beetle-
browed ſullen face makes a palace as ſmoaky as an *Iriſh*
hut. There is a *mode* in giving entertainment, and doing any courteſy elſe, which trebly binds the receiver
to an acknowledgment, and makes the remembrance of
it more acceptable. I have known two lord high treaſur-
ers of *England* of quite contrary humours, one ſuccef-
ſively after the other; the one, though he did the ſuitors
buſineſs, yet he went murmuring; the other, though
he

he did it not, was ufed to difmifs the party with fome
fatisfaction.   It is true, money is welcome though it be
in a dirty clout, but it is far more acceptable if it come
in a clean handkerchief.

Sir, you may fit in the chair, and read lectures of morality to all mankind in this point, you have fuch a dexterous difcreet way to handle fuitors in that troublefome
office of yours ; wherein as you have already purchafed
much, I wifh you all increafe of honour and happinefs.

Your humble and obliged fervitor,

J. H.

LETTER LVI.

To Mr. F. COLL. *at* Naples.

S I R,

IT is confeffed I have offended by my over-long filence,
and abufed our maiden friendfhip : I appear before
you now in this white fheet to do penance : I pray in
your next to me, fend an abfolution.   Abfolutions, they
fay, are as cheap in that town as courtefans, whereof it
was faid there were 20,000 on the common lift, when
I was there ; at which time I remember one told me a
tale of a *Calabrian* who had buggered a goat ; and having bought an abfolution of his confeffor, he was afked
by a friend what it coft him ; he anfwered, I procured
it for four piftoles, and for the other odd one, I think I
might have had a difpenfation to have married the beaft.

I thank you for the exact relation you fent me of the
fearful earthquakes and fires which happened lately in
that country, and particularly about *Vefuvius*.   It feems
the huge giant, who the poets fay, was hurled under
the vaft mountain by the gods for thinking to fcale heaven, had a mind to turn from one fide to the other,
which he ufeth to do at the revolution of every hundred
years ; and ftirring his body by that action, he was taken
with

with a fit of the cough, which made the hill fhake, and
belch out fire in this hideous manner. But to repay you
in the like coin, they fend us ftranger news from *Lisbon ;*
for they write of a fpick and fpan-new ifland, that hath
peeped up out of the *Atalantick* fea, near the *Terceras,*
which never appeared before fince the creation, and begins to be peopled already : methinks the King of *Spain*
needs no more countries, he hath too many already, unlefs they were better united.   All your friends here are
well, and mind you often in town and country, as doth

Your true conftant fervitor,

Weftminfter, *April* 7. 1629.   J. H.

LETTER LVII.

To Mr. G. C. at Dublin.

S I R,

THE news of this week have been like the waves
of that boifterous fea, through which this letter
is to pafs over to you. Divers reports for peace have
fwoln high for the time, but they fuddenly fell low and
flat again.   Our relations here, are like a peal of bells in
windy bluftering weather ; fometimes the found is ftrong
on this fide, fometimes on that fide of the fteeple ; fo
our relations found diverfly, as the air of affection carries
them ; and fometimes in a whole volley of news, we fhall
not find one true report.

There was in a *Dunkirk* fhip, taken fome months ago,
hard by *Arundel* caftle, among other things, a large
picture feized upon, and carried to *Weftminfter-ball,* and
put in the *Star-chamber* to be publickly feen : it was the
legend of *Conanus* a *Britifh* Prince in the time of *Gra-
tian* the Emperor, who having married *Urfula,* the
King of *Cornwall*'s daughter, was embarked with 11,000
virgins for *Britany* in *France* to colonize that part with
chriftians ; but being by diftrefs of weather beaten upon
                                                    the

the *Rhine*, becaufe they would not yield to the luſt of the infidels, after the example of *Urſula* they were all ſlain, their bodies were carried to *Colen*, where there ſtands to this day a ſtately church built for them.   This is the ſtory of that picture ; yet the common people here take *Conanus* for our King, and *Urſula* for the Queen, and the Biſhop which ſtands hard by to be the Pope, and ſo ſtare upon it accordingly, notwithſtanding that the Prince there repreſented, hath ſandals on his feet after the old faſhion, that the coronets on their heads reſemble thoſe of dukes and earls : as alſo, that there are rays about them which never uſe to be applied to living perſons, with divers other incongruities : yet it cannot be beaten out of the belief of thouſands here, but that it was intended to repreſent our King and Queen ; which makes me conclude with this interjection of wonder, Oh the ignorance of the common people !

Your faithful friend at command,

Weſtminſter, Aug. 12. 1644.   **J. H.**

L E T T E R LVIII.
To the Right honourable the Lord R.

My LORD,

SURE there is ſome angry planet hath lowred long upon the catholic King ; and though one of his titles to *Pagan* princes be, that he wears the ſun for his helmet, becauſe it never ſets upon all his dominions, in regard ſome part of them lies on the other ſide of the hemiſphere among the *Antipodes*, yet methinks that neither that great ſtar, or any of the reſt are now propitious unto him : they caſt, it ſeems, more benign influences upon the *flower-de-luce*, which thrives wonderfully ; but how long theſe favourable aſpects will laſt, I will not preſume to judge.   This, among divers others of late, hath been a fatal year to the ſaid King ; for Weſtward he hath loſt *Dunkirk*. *Dunkirk*, which was the terror of

this

this part of the world, the fcourge of the oecidental feas, whofe name was grown to be a bugbear for fo many years, hath now changed her mafter, and thrown away the *ragged-ftaff;* doubtlefs a great exploit it was to take this town : but whether this be advantageous to *Holland,* (as I am fure it is not to *England*) time will fhew. It is more than probable that it may make him carelefs at fea, and in the building, and arming of his fhips, having now no enemy near him ; befides, I believe it cannot much benefit *Hans,* to have the *French* fo contiguous to him : the old faying was, *Ayez le* François *pour ton amy, non pas pour ton voifon ;* have the *Frenchman* for thy friend, not for thy neighbour.

Touching *England,* I believe thefe diftractions of ours have been one of the greateft advantages that could befall *France ;* and they happened in the moft favourable conjuncture of time that might be, elfe I believe he would never have as much as attempted *Dunkirk :* for *England,* in true reafon of ftate, had reafon to prevent nothing more, in regard no one place could have added more to the naval power of *France ;* this will make his fails fwell bigger, and I fear make him claim in time as much regality in thefe narrow feas as *England* herfelf.

In *Italy* the *Spaniard* hath alfo had ill fuccefles at *Piombino* and *Porto-longone :* befides, they write that he hath loft *il Prete, & il Medico,* the Prieft and the Phyfician ; to wit, the Pope, and the Duke of *Florence,* (the houfe of *Medici*) who appear rather for the *French* than for him.

Add to thefe difafters, that he hath loft within the revolution of the fame year the Prince of *Spain* his unic-fon, in the very flower of his age, being but feventeen years old. Thefe with the falling off of *Catalonia* and *Portugal,* with the death of his Queen not above forty, are heavy loffes to the catholic King, and muft needs much infeeble the great bulk of his monarchy, falling in fo fhort a compafs of time, one upon the neck of ano-ther ; and we are not to enter into the fecret counfels of God almighty for a reafon. I have read it was the
fenfuality

fenfuality of the flefh that drove the Kings out of _Rome_,
the _French_ out of _Sicily_, and brought the _Moors_ into
Spain, where they kept firm footing above 700 years.
I could tell you how not long before her death, the late
Queen of _Spain_ took off one of her chapines and clowt-
ed _Olivares_ about the noddle with it, becaufe he had accompanied the King to a Lady of pleafure ; telling him,
that he fhould know, fhe was fifter to a King of _France_,
as well as wife to a King of _Spain_.' For my part, _France_
and _Spain_ is all one to me in point of affection ; I am one
of thofe indifferent men that would have the fcale of power
in _Europe_ kept even: I am alfo a _philerenus_, a lover
of peace, and I could wifh the _French_ were more inclinable to it, now that the common enemy hath invaded
the territories of _St. Mark_. Nor can I but admire, that
at the fame time the _French_ fhould affail _Italy_ at one fide,
when the _Turk_ was doing it on the other. But had that
great naval power of chriftians, which were this fummer
upon the coafts of _Tufcany_, gone againft the _Mahometan_
fleet, which was the fame time fetting upon _Candy_, they
might in all likelihood have atchieved a glorious exploit,
and driven the _Turk_ into the _Hellefpont_. Nor is poor
chriftendom torn thus in pieces by the _German_, _Spaniard_,
French, and _Swedes_, but our three kingdoms have alfo
moft pitifully fcratched her face, wafted her fpirits, and
let out fome of her illuftrious blood, by our late horrid
diftractions ; whereby it may be inferred, that the Mufti
and the Pope feem to thrive in their devotion one way,
a chief part of the prayers of the one being, that dif-
cord fhould ftill continue betwixt chriftian princes ; of
the other, that divifion fhould ftill increafe among the
proteftants. This poor ifland is a woful example thereof.

I hear the peace betwixt _Spain_ and _Holland_ is abfolutely concluded by the plenipotentiary minifters at
Munfter, who have beat their heads fo many years about
it : but they write that the _French_ and _Swede_ do mainly
endeavour, and fet all the wheels of policy a going to
puzzle and prevent it If it take effect, I do not fee
how

how the *Hollander* in common honefty can evade it.
I hope it will conduce much to an univerfal peace ; which
God grant, for war is a *fire ftruct in the devil's tinder-
box.* No more now, but that I am,   my Lord,

   Your moft humble fervant,

Fleet, Dec. 1. 1643.   J. H.

L E T T E R LVIII.

To Mr. S. B. *Merchant, at his Houfe in the* Old-Jewry.

S I R,

I Return you thofe two famous fpeeches of the late Queen
Elizabeth, with the addition of another from *Baudius*
at an embaffy here from *Holland.* It is with languages
as it is with liquors, which by transfufion ufe to take wind
from one veffei to another ; fo, things tranflated into another tongue, lofe of their primitive vigour and ftrength,
unlefs a paraphraftical verfion be permitted; and then,
the traduct may exceed the original, not otherwife,
though the verfion be never fo punctual, efpecially in thefe
orations which are framed with fuch art, that like *Vi-
truvius's* palace, there is no place left to add one ftone
more without defaceing, or to take any out without hazard of deftroying the whole fabric.

Certainly fhe was a Princefs of rare endowments for
learning and languages : fhe was bleffed with a long life,
and triumphant reign, attended with various forts of admirable fucceffes, which will be taken for fome romance
a thoufand winters hence, if the world laft fo long. She
freed the *Scot* from the *French,* and gave her fucceffor
a royal penfion to maintain his court : fhe helped to fettle
the crown on *Henry the Great's* head : fhe gave effence
to the State of *Holland:* fhe civilzed *Ireland,* and fuppreffed divers infurrections there : fhe preferved the dominion of the narrow feas in greater glory than ever :
fhe maintained open war againft *Spain,* when *Spain* was

in her higheſt flouriſh, for divers years together ; yet, ſhe
left a mighty treaſure behind ; which ſhews that ſhe was a
notable good houſewife. Yet, I have read divers cenſures
of her abroad ; that ſhe was ingrateful to her brother of
Spain, who had been the chiefeſt inſtrument under God
to preſerve her from the block, and had left her all
Queen *Mary*'s Jewels without diminution ; accuſing her,
that afterwards ſhe ſhould firſt infringe the peace with
him, by intercepting his treaſure in the narrow ſeas, by
ſuffering her *Drake* to ſwim to his *Indies,* and rob him
there ; by fomenting and ſupporting his *Belgic* ſubjeſts
againſt him then, when he had an Ambaſſador reſident at
her court. But this was the cenſure of a *Spaniſh* author ;
and, *Spain* had little reaſon to ſpeak well of her. The
French handle her worſe, by terming her, among other
contumlies, *l'Haquenee de ſes propres vaſſaux.*

Sir, I muſt much value the frequent reſpeſts you have
ſhewn me, and am very covetous of the improvement of
this acquaintance : for, I do not remember at home or a-
broad to have ſeen in the perſon of any, a gentleman and
a merchant ſo equally met, as in you ; which makes me
ſtyle myſelf

Your moſt affeſtionate friend to ſerve you,

Fleet, May 3. 1645.　　　　　　　　　　　J. H.

LETTER LIX.

To my honourable Friend, Sir S. C.

S I R,

I Was upon point of going abroad to ſteal a ſolitary
walk, when yours of the 12th current came to hand,
the high reſearches and choice abſtraſted notions I found
therein, ſeemed to heighten my ſpirits, and make my
fancy fitter for my intended retirement and meditation.
Add hereunto, that the countenance of the weather invited me : for it was a ſtill evening, it was alſo a clear open
ſky,

ſky, not a ſpeck or the leaſt wrinkle appeared in the whole face of heaven, it was ſuch a pure deep azure all the hemiſphere over, that I wondered what was become of the three regions of the air with their meteors. So having got into a cloſe field, I caſt my face upwards, and fell to conſider what a rare prerogative the optic virtue of the eye hath, much more the intuitive virtue of the thought, that the one in a moment can reach heaven, and the other go beyond it: therefore, ſure that Philoſopher was but a kind of frantic fool, that would have plucked out both his eyes becauſe they were a hindrance to his ſpeculations. Moreover, I began to contemplate, as I was in this poſture, the vaſt magnitude of the univorſe, and what proportion this poor globe of earth might bear with it: for, if thoſe numberleſs bodies which ſtick in the vaſt roof of heaven, though they appear to us but as ſpangles, be ſome of them thouſands of times bigger than the earth, take the ſea with it to boot, for they both make but one ſphere, ſurely the aſtronomers had reaſon to term this ſphere an inviſible point, and a thing of no dimenſion at all, being compared to the whole world. I fell then to think, that at the ſecond general deſtruction, it is no more for God almighty to fire this earth, than for us to blow up one ſmall ſquib, or rather one ſmall grain of gunpowder. As I was muſing thus, I ſpied a ſwarm of gnats waving up and down the air about me; which I knew to be part of the univerſe as well as I: and methought, it was a ſtrange opinion of our *Ariſtotle* to hold, that the leaſt of thoſe ſmall infected ephemerans ſhould be more noble than the ſun, becauſe it had a ſenſitive ſoul in it. I fell to think, that the ſame proportion which thoſe animalillios bore with me in point of bigneſs, the ſame I held with thoſe glorious ſpirits which are near the throne of the Almighty. What then ſhould we think of the magnitude of the Creator himſelf? Doubtleſs, it is beyond the reach of any human imagination to conceive it. In my private devotions, I preſume to compare him to a great mountain of light, and my ſoul ſeems to diſcern ſome glorious form therein;

but

but fuddenly as fhe would fix her eyes upon the object, her fight is prefently dazled and difgregated with the refulgency and corufcations thereof.

Walking a little further, I fpied a young boifterous bull breaking over hedge and ditch to a herd of kine in the next pafture; which made me think, that if that fierce ftrong animal, with others of that kind knew their own ftrength, they would never fuffer man to be their mafter. Then looking upon them quietly grazing up and down, I fell to confider that the flefh that is daily difhed upon our tables is but concocted grafs, which is recarnified in our ftomachs, and tranfmuted to another flefh. I fell alfo to think what advantage thofe innocent animals had of man, who, as foon as nature caft them into the world, find their meat dreffed, the cloth laid, and the table covered: they find their drink brewed, and the buttery open, their beds made, and their clothes ready. And though man hath the faculty of reafon to make him a compenfation for the want of thofe advantages, yet this reafon brings with it a thoufand perturbations of mind, and perplexities of fpirit, gripping cares, and anguifhes of thought, which thofe harmlefs filly creatures were exempted from. Going on, I came to repofe myfelf upon the trunk of a tree, and I fell to confider further what advantage that dull vegetable had of thofe feeding animals, as not to be fo troublefome and beholding to nature, nor to be fubject to ftarving, to difeafes, to the inclemency of the weather, and to be far longer lived. Then I fpied a great ftone, and fitting a while upon it, I fell to weigh in my thoughts that that ftone was in a happier condition in fome refpects, than either thofe fenfitive creatures or vegetables I faw before, in regard that that ftone which propagates by affimilation, as the philofophers fay, needed neither grafs nor hay, or any aliment for reftoration of nature, nor water to refrefh its roots, or the heat of the fun to attract the moifture upwards, to increafe growth, as the other did. As I directed my path homeward, I fpied a kite foaring high in the air, and gently gliding up and down the clear

region

region fo far above my head, I fell to envy the bird extremely, and repine at his happinefs, that he fhould have a privilege to make a nearer approach to heaven than I.

Excufe me that I trouble you thus with thefe rambling meditations, they are to correfpond with you in fome part for thofe accurate fancies of yours you lately fent me. So, I reft

Your intire and true fervitor;

Holborn, March 17. 1639. J. H.

LETTER LX.

To the Right Honourable the Lord CLIFF.

My LORD,

SINCE among other paffages of entertainment we had lately at the *Italian* ordinary, (where your Lordfhip was pleafed to honour us with your prefence) there happened a large difcourfe of wines, and of other drinks that were ufed by feveral nations of the earth, and that your Lordfhip defired me to deliver what I obferved therein abroad, I am bold now to confirm and amplify in this letter what I then let drop *extempore* from me, having made a recollection of myfelf for that purpofe.

It is without controverfy, that in the nonage of the world, men and beafts had but one buttery, which was the fountain and river: nor do we read of any vines or wines till 200 years after the flood. But now, I do not know or hear of any nation that hath water only for their drink, except the *Japonois*, and they drink it hot too; but we may fay, that what beverage foever we make, either by brewing, by diftillation, decoction, percollation or preffing, it is but water at firft: nay, wine itfelf is but water fublimed, being nothing elfe but that moifture and fap which is caufed either by rain or other kind of irrigations about the roots of the vine, and drawn up to

H h 3 the

the branches and berries by the virtual attractive heat of the fun, the bowels of the earth ferving as a limbec to that end; which made the *Italian* vineyard-man (after a long drought, and an extreme hot fummer, which had parched up all his grapes) to complain, that *per manca mento d'acqua bevo dell' acqua fe io haveffi acqua, beverei el vino;* for want of water, I am forced to drink water; if I had water, I would drink wine. It may be alfo applied to the miller when he had no water to drive his mills.

The vine doth fo abhor cold, that it cannot grow beyond the forty-ninth degree to any purpofe: therefore God and nature hath furnifhed the Northweft nations with other inventions of beverage. In this ifland the old drink was ale, noble ale, than which, as I heard a great Doctor affirm, there is no liquor that more increafeth the radical moifture, and preferves the natural heat; which are the two pillars that fupport the life of man: but fince beer hath hopped in amongft us, ale is thought to be much adulterated, and nothing fo good as Sir *John Oldcaftle* and *Smug* the fmith was ufed to drink. Befides ale and beer, the natural drink of part of this ifle may be faid to be metheglin, braggot, and mead, which differ in ftrength according to the three degrees of comparifon. The firft of the three, which is ftrong in the fuperlative, if taken immoderately, doth ftupify more than any other liquor, and keeps a humming in the brain; which made one fay, that he loved not metheglin, becaufe he was ufed to fpeak too much of the houfe he came from, meaning the hive. Cyder and perry are alfo the natural drinks of part of this ifle: but, I have read in fome old authors of a famous drink the antient nation of the *Picts*, who lived betwixt *Trent* and *Tweed*, and weie utterly extinguifhed by the overpowering of the *Scot*, were ufed to make of decoction of flowers, the receipt wherof they kept as a fecret, and a thing facred to themfelves, fo it perifhed with them: thefe are the common drinks of this Ifle, and of *Ireland* alfo, where they are more given to milk and ftrong waters of all kinds:

the

the prime is *ufquebagh* which cannot be made any where in that perfection; and whereas we drink it here in *aqua-vitæ* meafures, it goes down there by beer glafs-fulls being more natural to the nation.

In the feventeen provinces hard by, and all *Low-Germany*, beer is the common natural drink, and nothing elfe: fo is it in *Weftphalia*, and all the lower circuit of *Saxony*, in *Denmark*, *Swethland* and *Norway*. The *Pruffe* hath a beer as thick as honey. In the Duke of *Saxe*'s country, there is beer as yellow as gold, made of wheat, and it inebriates as foon as fack. In fome parts of *Germany* they ufed to fpice their beer, which will keep many years, fo that at fome weddings there will be a but of beer drunk out as old as the bride. *Poland* alfo is a beer country; but in *Ruffia*, *Mofcovy* and *Tartary*, they ufe *Mead*, which is the naturalleft drink of the country, being made of the decoction of water and honey: this is that which the antients called *hydromel*. Mare's milk is a great drink with the *Tartar*, which may be a caufe why they are bigger than ordinary: for the phyficians hold, that milk enlargeth the bones, beer ftrengtheneth the nerves, and wine breeds blood fooner than any other liquor. The *Turk* when he hath his tripe full of pelaw, or of mutton and rice, will go to nature's cellar; either to the next well or river to drink water, which is his natural common drink: for *Mahomet* taught them, that there was a devil in every berry of the grape, and fo made a ftrict inhibition to all his fect from drinking of wine as a thing profane. He had alfo a reach of policy therein, becaufe they fhould not be incumbered with luggage when they went to war, as other nations do, who are fo troubled with the carriage of their wine and beverages; yet hath the *Turk* peculiar drinks to himfelf befides, as *fherbet*, made of the juice of limon, fugar, amber, and other ingredients: he hath alfo a drink called *cauphe*, which is made of a brown berry; and it may be called their clubing drink between meals, which though it be not very guftful to the palate, yet it is very comfortable to the ftomach, and good

for

for the fight: but notwithftanding their Prophet's anathema, thoufands of them will venture to drink wine,
and they will make a precedent prayer to their fouls to
depart from their bodies in the interim, for fear fhe partake of the fame pollution. Nay, the laft *Turk* died of
excefs of wine, for he had at one time fwallowed thirty-
three okes; which is a meafure near upon the bignefs of
our quart; and that which brought him to this, was the
company of a *Perfian* Lord that had given him his daughter for a prefent, and came with him from *Bagdat*: befides, one accident that happened to him was, that he
had an eunuch who was ufed to be drunk, and whom he
had commanded twice upon pain of life to refrain, fwearing by *Mahomet* that he would caufe him to be ftrangled
if he found him the third time fo, yet the eunuch ftill
continued in his drunkennefs: hereupon the *Turk* concei-
ving with himfelf that there muft needs be fome extraordinary delight in drunkennefs, becaufe this man preferred
it before his life, fell to it himfelf, and fo drunk himfelf
to death.

In *Afia* there is no beer drunk at all, but water, wine,
and an incredible variety of other drinks made of dates,
dried raifons, rice, divers forts of nuts, fruits, and roots.
In the Oriental countries, as *Cambia*, *Calicut*, *Narfingha*,
there is a drink called banque, which is rare and precious; and it is the height of entertainment they give their
guefts before they go to fleep, like that *nepenthe* which
the poets fpeak fo much of, for it provokes pleafing
dreams, and delightful phantafies: it will accommodate
itfelf to the humour of the fleeper, as if he be a foldier,
he will dream of victories and taking of towns: if he be
in love, he will think to enjoy his miftrefs: if he be covetous, he will dream of mountains of gold, &c. In the
Moluccas and *Philippines*, there is a curious drink called
tampoy, made of a kind of gilliflowers; and another drink
called *otraqua*, that comes from a nut, and is the more
general drink. In *China*, they have a holy kind of liquor made of fuch fort of flowers for ratifying and binding of bargains; and having drunk thereof, they hold it

no lefs than perjury to break what they promife : as they write of a river in *Bithynia*, whofe water hath a peculiar virtue to difcover a perjurer, for if he drink thereof, it will prefently boil in his ftomach, and put him to vifible tortures. This makes me think of the river *Styx* among the poets, which the gods were ufed to fwear by; and it was the greateft oath for the performance of any thing.

Nubila promiſſi Styx *mihi teſtis erit.*

It put me in mind alfo of that which fome write of the river of *Rhine* for trying the legitimation of a child being thrown in, if he be a baftard he will fink, if other-wife he will not.

In *China* they fpeak of a tree called *maguais*, which affords not only good drink being pierced, but all things elfe that belong to the fubfiftence of man : they bore the tree with an awger, and there iffueth out fweet potable liquor; betwixt the rind and the tree there is a cotton or hempy kind of mofs, which they wear for their cloath-ing : it bears huge nuts, which have excellent food in them : it fhoots out hard prickles above a fathom long; and thofe arm them, with the bark they make tents, and the dotard trees ferve for firing.

Africa alfo hath a great diverfity of drinks, as having more need of them, being a hotter country far. In *Guiney*, or the lower *Ethiopia*, there is a kind of drink called *mingol;* which iffueth out of a tree much like the palm, being bored: but in the upper *Ethiopia*, or the *Habaſſines* country, they drink *mead*, decofted in a dif-ferent manner : there is alfo much wine there. The common drink of *Barbary* after water, is that which is made of dates; but in *Egypt* in times paft there was beer drunk called *zichus* in *Latin;* which was no other than a decoftion of barley and water. They had alfo a famous compofition (and they ufe it to this day) called *chiffi*, made of divers cordials and provocative ingredients, which they throw into water to make it guftful : they ufe it alfo for fumigation. But now, the general drink of *Egypt* is *Nile* water; which of all water may be faid to be the beſt, infomuch that *Pindar's* words might be more applicable to that than to any other, Ἀριϛὸν μὲν ὕδωρ. It doth not only fertilize, and extremely fatten the ſoil which it covers, but it helps to impregnate barren wo- men ; for there is no place on earth where people increaſe and multiply faſter : it is yellowiſh and thick, but if one caſt a few almonds into a potful of it, it will become as clear as rock water : it is alſo in a degree of lukewarm- neſs as *Martial's* boy:

Tolle puer calices tepidique toreumata Nili.

In the new world they have a world of drinks : for there is no root, flower, fruit, or pulſe, but is reducible to a potable liquor ; as in the *Barbado* iſland, the com- mon drink among the *Engliſh*, is *mobbi*, made of pota- toe roots. In *Mexico* and *Peru*, which is the great con- tinent of *America*, with other parts, it is prohibited to make wines under great penalties, for fear of ſtarving of trade, ſo that all the wines they have are ſent from *Spain*.

Now for the pure wine countries, *Greece* with all her iſlands, *Italy*. *Spain*, *France*, one part of four of *Ger- many*, *Hungary*, with divers countries thereabouts, all the iſlands in the *Mediterranean* and *Atlantic* ſea, are wine countries.

The moſt generous wines of *Spain*, grow in the mid- land parts of the continent, and *St. Martin* bears the bell, which is near the court. Now, as in *Spain*, ſo in all other wine countries, one cannot paſs a day's journey but he will find a differing race of wine. Thoſe kinds that our merchants carry over are thoſe only that grow upon the ſea-ſide, as *Malaga*, *Sherries*, *Tents*, and *Ali- cants :* of this laſt there is little comes over right, there- fore the vintners make *tent*, (which is a name for all the wines in *Spain*, except white) to ſupply the place of it. There is a gentle kind of white wine grows among the mountains of *Galicia*, but not of body enough to bear the ſea, called *Rabidavia*. *Portugal* affords no wines worth the tranſporting : they have an old ſtone we call *yef*, which they ufe to throw into their wines, which clarifieth it, and makes it more lafting. There is alfo a drink in *Spain*, called *alofha*, which they drink between meals in hot weather; and it is a *hydromel* made of water and honey, much of the tafte of our *mead*. In the court of *Spain* there is a *German* or two that brew beer; but for that antient drink of *Spain* which *Pliny* fpeaks of, compofed of flowers, the receipt thereof is utterly loft.

In *Greece* there are no wines that have bodies enough to bear the fea for long voyages: fome few mufcadels, and malmfies are brought over in fmall cafks. Nor is there in *Italy* any wine tranfported to *England* but in bottles, as *Verde* and others; for the length of the voyage makes them fubject to pricking, and fo lofe colour by reafon of their delicacy.

France participating of the climes of all the countries about her, affords wines of quality accordingly: as towards the *Alps* and *Italy*, fhe hath a lufcious rich wine called *florentine*. In the country of *Provence* towards the *Pyrenees* in *Languedoc*, there are wines concuftable with thofe of *Spain*: one of the prime fort of white wines is that of *Beaume*; and of clarets, that of *Orleans*, though it be interdicted to wine the King's cellar with it, in refpect of the corrofivenefs it carries with it. As in *France*, fo in all other wine countries, the white is called the *female*, and the claret or red wine is called the *male*, becaufe commonly it hath more fulphur, body, and heat in it. The wines that our merchants bring over grow upon the river of *Garon* near *Bordeaux* in *Gafcony*; which is the greateft mart for wines in all *France*. The *Scot* becaufe he hath always been an ufeful confederate to *France* againft *England*, hath (among other privileges) the right of pre-emption or firft choice of wines in *Bordeaux*: he is alfo permitted to carry his ordnance to the very walls of the town, whereas the *English* are forced to leave them at *Blay*, a good way diftant, down the river. There is a hard green wine that grows about *Rochel*, and the iflands thereabouts, which

the

the cunning *Hollander* sometime used to fetch; and he hath a trick to put a bag of herbs, or some other infu- sions into it, (as he doth brimstone in *rhenish*) to give it a white tincture and more sweetness: then they reimbark it for *England*, where it passeth for *Bachrag;* and this is called stooming of wines. In *Normandy* there is little or no wine at all grows, therefore the common drink of that country is cyder, especially in low *Normandy.* There are also many beer-houses in *Paris,* and else- where; but though their barley and water be better than ours, or that of *Germany*, and though they have *Eng- lish* and *Dutch* brewers among them, yet they cannot make beer in that perfection.

The prime wines of *Germany* grow about the *Rhine,* especially in the *Psalts* or *Lower-Palatinate* about *Bach- rag;* which hath its etymology from *Bachiara:* for in antient times there was an altar erected there to the ho- nour of *Bacchus,* in regard of the richness of the wines here and all *France* over. It is held a great part of in- civility for maidens to drink wine until they are married, as it is in *Spain* for them to wear high shoes, or to paint till then. The *German* mothers, to make their sons fall into hatred of wine, do use when they are little to put some owl's eggs into a cup of *rhenish*, and some- times a little living eel; which twingling in the wine while the child is drinking, so feares him, that many come to abhor, and have an antipathy to wine all their lives after. From *Bachrag,* the first stock of vines which grow now in the grand *Canary* island were brought; which with the heat of the sun and the soil, is grown now to that height of perfection, that the wine which they afford are accounted the richest, the most firm, the best bodied, and lastingest wine, and the most defecated from all earthly grosness of any other whatsoever: it hath little or no sulphur at all in it, and leaves less dregs behind, though one drink it to excess. *French* wines may be said but to pickle meat in the stomachs, but this is the wine that digests, and doth not only breed good blood, but it nutrifieth also, being a glutinous subſtantial liquor. Of this wine, if of any other, may be verified that merry induction, that good wine makes good blood, good blood cauſeth good humours, good humours cauſe good thoughts, good thoughts bring forth good works, good works carry a man to heaven; *ergo*, good wine carrieth a man to heaven. If this be true, ſurely more *Engliſh* go to heaven this way than any other; for, I think there is more *Canary* brought into *England* than to all the world beſides. I think alſo there is a hundred times more drunk under the name of *Canary* wine than there is brought in; for *Sherries* and *Malagas* well mingled paſs for *Canaries* in moſt taverns, more often than *Canary* itſelf, elſe I do not ſee how it were poſſible for the vintner to ſave by it, or to live by his calling, unleſs he were permitted ſometimes to be a brewer. When *Sacks* and *Canaries* were brought in firſt among us, they were uſed to be drunk in *aquavitæ* meaſures; and it was held fit only for thoſe to drink of them who were uſed to carry their legs in their hands, their eyes upon their noſes, and an almanack in their bones: but now, they go down every one's throat, both young and old, like milk.

The countries that are freeſt from exceſs of drinking, are *Spain* and *Italy*: if a woman can prove her buſband to have been thrice drunk, by the antient laws of *Spain* ſhe may plead a divorce from him. Nor indeed can the *Spaniard*, being hot brained, bear much drink; yet, I have heard that *Gondamer* was once too hard for the King of *Denmark*, when he was here in *England*. But the *Spaniſh* ſoldiers that have been in the wars of *Flanders*, will take their cups freely, and the *Italian* alſo. When I lived on the other ſide the *Alps*, a gentleman told me a merry tale of a *Ligurian* ſoldier who had got drunk in *Genoa*; and Prince *Doria* going a horſeback to take the round one night, the ſoldier took his horſe by the bridle, and aſked what the price of him was, for he wanted a horſe: the Prince ſeeing in what humour he was, cauſed him to be taken into a houſe and put to ſleep: in the

morning

morning he fent for him, and afked him what he would
give for his horfe. Sir, faid the recovered foldier, the
merchant that would have bought him yefternight of your
Highnefs, went away betimes in the morning. The
boonefl companions for drinking, are the *Greeks* and *Germans;* but the *Greek* is the merrier of the two, for he
will fing and dance and kifs his next companions; but
the other will drink as deep as he. If the *Greek* will
drink as many glaffes as there be letters in his miftrefs's
name, the other will drink the number of her years; and
though he be not apt to break out into finging, being not
of fo airy a conftitution, yet he will drink often mufically
a health to every one of thefe fix notes, *Ut, Re, Mi,
Fa, Sol, La;* which, for this reafon, are all comprehended in this hexameter:

Ut Relevet Miferum Fatum Solitofque Labores.

The fewest draughts he drinks are three; the firft to
quench the thirft paft, the fecond to quench the prefent
thirft, the third to prevent the future. I heard of a
company of *Low-Dutchmen* that had drunk fo deep,
that beginning to ftagger, and their heads turning round,
they thought verily they were at fea, and that the upper-
chamber where they were was a fhip; infomuch that it
being foul windy weather, they fell to throw the ftools,
and other things out of the window, to lighten the veffel for fear of fuffering fhipwreck.

Thus have I fent your Lordfhip a dry difcourfe upon
a fluent fubject, yet I hope your Lordfhip will pleafe to
take all in good part, becaufe it proceeds from

Your moft humble and ready fervant,

Weftminfter, Oct. 7. 1634.　　　　　J. H.

LETTER LXI.

To the Right Honourable the Earl R:

My LORD,

YOUR defires have been always to me as commands, and your commands as binding as acts of parliament: nor do I take pleafure to employ head or hand in any thing more than in the exact performance of them. Therefore if in this crabbed difficult tafk, you have been pleafed to impofe upon me about languages, I come fhort of your Lordfhip's expectation, I hope my obedience will apologize for my difability. But whereas your Lordfhip defires to know what were the original mothertongues of the countries of *Europe*, and how thefe modern fpeeches that are now in ufe were firft introduced, I may anfwer hereunto, that it is almoft as eafy a thing to difcover the fource of *Nile*, as to find out the original of fome languages; yet, I will attempt it as well as I can; and I will take my firft rife in thefe iflands of *Great Britain* and *Ireland:* for to be curious and eagle-eyed abroad, and to be blind and ignorant at home, (as many of our travellers are now a days) is a curiofity that carrieth with it more of affectation than any thing elfe.

Touching the ifle of *Albion*, or *Great Britan*, the *Cambrian* or *Cymraccan* tongue, commonly called *Welfh*, (and *Italian* alfo is fo called by the *Dutch*) is without controverfy the prime maternal tongue of this ifland, and connatural with it: nor could any of the four conquefts that have been made of it by the *Roman*, *Saxon*, *Done*, or *Norman*, ever extinguifh her; but fhe remains ftill pure and incorrupt: of which language, there is as exact and methodical a grammar, with as regular precepts, rules, and inftitutions both for profe and verfe, compiled by Dr. *David Rice*, as I have read in any tongue whatfoever. Some of the authentickeft annalifts report that the old *Gauls*, (now the *French*) and the *Britons* underftood one another: for they came thence very frequently

to be inſtructed here by the *Britiſh* druids; which were
the philoſophers and divines of thoſe times: and this was
long before the *Latin* tongue came on this ſide the *Alps*,
or books written; and there is no meaner man than *Cæſar*
himſelf records this.

This is one of the fourteen *vernacular* and independ-
dant tongues of *Europe*, and ſhe hath divers dialects: the
firſt is the *Corniſh*, the ſecond the *Armoricans*, or the
inhabitants of *Britany* in *France*, whither a colony was
ſent over hence in the time of the *Romans*. There was
alſo another dialect of the *Britiſh* language among the
Picts, who kept in the North parts, in *Northumberland*,
Weſtmorland, *Cumberland*, and ſome parts beyond *Tweed*,
until the whole nation of the *Scots* poured upon them
with ſuch multitudes, that they utterly extinguiſhed both
them and their language. There are ſome which have
been curious in the compariſon of tongues, who believe
that the *Iriſh* is but a dialect of the antient *Britiſh*; and
the learnedeſt of that nation, in a private diſcourſe I happened to have with him, ſeemed to incline to this opinion: but this I can aſſure your Lordſhip of, that at my
being in that country, I obſerved by a private collection
which I made, that a great multitude of their radical
words are the ſame with the *Welſh*, both for ſenſe and
ſound; the tone alſo of both the nations is conſonant:
for, when I firſt walked up and down *Dublin* markets,
methought verily I was in *Wales*, when I liſtened unto
their ſpeech; but, I found that the *Iriſh* tone is a little
more querulous and whining than the *Britiſh*, which I
conjectured with myſelf proceeded from their often being
ſubjugated by the *Engliſh*. But, my Lord, you would
think it ſtrange, that divers pure *Welſh* words ſhould be
found in the new-found world in the *Weſt-Indies*; yet it
is verified by ſome navigators, as *grando* (hark), *nef*
(heaven), *lluynog* (a fox), *pergwin* (a bird with a white
head), with ſundry others, which are pure *Britiſh*: nay,
I have read a *Welſh* epitaph which was found there upon
one *Madoc* a *Britiſh* Prince, who ſome years before the
Norman conqueſt, not agreeing with his brother, then

Prince

Prince of *South-Wales*, went to try his fortunes at sea, embarking himself at *Milford-haven*, and so tarried on those coasts. This if well proved, might well intitle our crown to *America*, if first discovery may claim a right to any country.

The *Romans*, though they continued here constantly above 300 years, yet could they not do as they did in *France*, *Spain*, and other provinces, plant their language as a mark of conquest; but the *Saxons* did, coming in far greater numbers under *Hengist* from *Holsteinland* in the lower circuit of *Saxony*; which people resemble the *English* more than any people upon earth, so that it is more than probable that they came from thence: besides, there is a town there called *Lunden*, and another place named *Angles*, whence it may be presumed that they took their new denomination here. Now the *English*, though as *Saxons*, (by which name the *Welsh* and *Irish* call them to this day) they and their language is antient, yet in reference to this island they are the modernest nation in *Europe*, both for habitation, speech, and denomination; which makes me smile at Mr. *Fox's* error in the very front of his epistle before the book of martyrs, where he calls *Constantine* the first christian Emperor, the son of *Helen* an *English* woman; whereas, she was purely *British*, and that there was no such nation upon earth called *English* at that time, nor above 100 years after, till *Hengist* invaded this island, and settling himself in it, the *Saxons* who came with him, took the appellation of *Englishmen*. Now the *English* speech, though it be rich, copious, and significant, and that there be divers dictionaries of it, yet under favour, I cannot call it a regular language, in regard though often attempted by some choice wits, there could never any grammar of exact syntaxis be made of it; yet hath she divers subdialects, as the Western and Northern *English*, but her chiefest is the *Scotick*, which took footing beyond *Tweed* about the last conquest; but the antient language of *Scotland* is *Irish*, which the mountaineers and divers of the plain, retain to this day. Thus, my

Lord,

Lord, according to my fmall model of obfervation, have I endeavoured to fatisfy you in part: I fhall in my next go on, for in the purfuance of any command from your Lordfhip, my mind is like a ftone thrown into a deep water, which never refts till it goes to the bottom: fo for this time, and always, I reft, my Lord,

Your *moft humble and ready fervitor,*
Weftminfter, Aug. 9. 1630. J. H.

LETTER LXII.

To the Right honourable the Earl R.

My LORD,

IN my laft I fulfilled your Lordfhip's commands, as far as my reading and knowledge could extend, to inform you what were the radical primitive languages of thofe dominions that belong to the crown of *Great Britain,* and how the *Englifh,* which is now predominant, entered in firft: I will now hoift fail for the *Netherlands,* whofe dialect is the fame with the *Englifh,* and was fo from the beginning, being both of them derived from the *High-Dutch.* The *Danifh* alfo is but a branch of the fame tree, no more is the *Swedifh,* and the fpeech of them of *Norway* and *Iceland.* Now the *High-Dutch,* or *Teutonick* tongue, is one of the prime and moft fpacious maternal languages of *Europe:* for, befides the vaft extent of *Germany* itfelf, with the countries and kingdoms before mentioned, whereof *England* and *Scotland* are two, it was the language of the *Goths* and *Vandals,* and continueth yet of the greateft part of *Poland* and *Hungary,* who have a dialect of hers for their vulgar tongue; yet though fo many dialects and fubdialects be derived from her, fhe remains a ftrong finewy language, pure and incorrupt in her firft centre, towards the heart of *Germany.* Some of her writers would make the world believe that fhe was the language fpoken in paradife; for

ε i i   they

they produce many words and proper names in the five
books of *Moses*, which fetch their etymology from her:
as also in *Perfia to* this day divers radical words are the
same with her, *fader, moeder, broder, ftar;* and a *German* gentleman, speaking hereof one day to an *Italian,*
that she was the language of paradise, *sure,* said the *Italian,* (alluding to her roughness) *then it was the tongue
that God almighty chid* Adam *in.* It *may be so,* replied
the *German, but the devil had tempted* Eve *in* Italian *before.* A full-mouthed language she is, and pronounced
with that strength as if one had bones in his tongue instead of nerves.

, Those countries that border upon *Germany,* as *Bohemia, Silefia, Poland,* and those vast countries North-
Eastward, as *Ruffia* and *Mufcovy,* speak the *Sclavonic*
language; and it is incredible what I have heard some
travellers report of the vast extent of that language; for
beside *Sclavonia* itself, which properly is *Dalmatia* and
Liburnia, it is the vulgar speech of the *Macedonians,* E-
*pirots, Bofnians, Servians, Bulgarians, Moldavians,
Rœfcians,* and *Podolians:* nay, she spreads herself over
all the Eastern parts of *Europe,* (*Hungary* and *Wallachia*
excepted) as far as *Conftantinople,* and is frequently spoken in the seraglio among the *Janizaries:* nor doth she
rest there, but crossing the *Hellefpont* divers nations in
Afia have her for their popular tongue, as the *Circaffians,
Mongrelians,* and *Gazarites* Southward: Neither in *Europe* nor in *Afia* doth she extend herself further North
than to the parallel of forty degrees. But those nations
which celebrate divine service after the *Greek* ceremony,
and profess obedience to the Patriarch of *Conftantinople,*
as the *Rufs,* the *Mufcovite,* the *Moldavian, Rœfcian,
Bofnian, Servian,* and *Bulgarian,* with divers others
Eastern, and North-East people that speak *Sclavonic,*
have her in a different character from the *Dalmatian,
Croatian, Iftrian, Polonian, Bohemian, Silefian,* and
other nations towards the West. These last have the *Illyrian* character, and the invention of it is attributed to
St. *Jerom;* the other is of *Cyril's* devising, and is called
the

the *Servian* character. Now, although there be above
fixty feveral nations that have this vaft extended language
for their vulgar fpeech, yet the pure primitive *Sclavonic*
dialect is fpoken only in *Dalmatia*, *Croatia*, *Liburnia*,
and the countries adjacent, where the antient *Sclavonians* yet dwell; and they muft needs be very antient, for
there is in a church in *Prague* an old charter yet extant given them by *Alexander the Great*, which I thought
not amifs to infert here. ' We *Alexander the Great*,
' fon of King *Philip*, founder of the *Grecian* empire,
' conqueror of the *Perfians*, *Medes*, &c. and of the whole
' world from Eaft to Weft, from North to South, fon of
' great *Jupiter* by, &c. fo called: to you the noble ftock
' of *Sclavonians*, and to your language, becaufe you have
' been unto us a help, true in faith, and valiant in war,
' we confirm all that tract of earth from the North to the
' South of *Italy*, from us and our fucceffors, to you, and
' your pofterity for ever; and if any other nation be
' found there, let them be your flaves. Dated at *Alex-
' andria* the 12th of the goddefs *Minerva*, witnefs *Eth-
' ra*, and the eleven princes whom we appoint our fuc-
' ceffors.' With this rare, and one of the antienteft records in *Europe*, I will put a period to this fecond account I fend your Lordfhip touching languages. My
next fhall be of *Greece*, *Italy*, *France*, and *Spain*, and
fo I fhall fhake hands with *Europe*; till when, I humbly
kifs your hand, and reft, my Lord,

Your moft obliged fervitor,

Weftminfter, *Aug.* 2. 1630. 　　　　J. H.

' LETTER LXIII. '

To the Right Honourable the Earl R.

My LORD,

HAVING in my laft rambled through high and
low *Germany*, *Bohemia*, *Denmark*, *Poland*, *Ruffia*, and thofe vaft North-Eaft regions, and given your
Lordfhip

Lordſhip a touch of their languages, (for it was no treatiſe I intended at firſt, but a curſory ſbort literal account)
I will now paſs to *Greece*, and ſpeak ſomething, of that
large and learned language; for it is ſhe indeed upon
whom the beams of all ſcientifical knowledge did firſt
ſhine in *Europe*, which ſhe afterwards diffuſed through
all the Weſtern world.

The *Greek* tongue was firſt peculiar to *Hellas* alone,
but in tract of time the kingdom of *Macedon*, and *Epire*
had her: then ſhe arrived on the iſles of the *Egean* ſea,
which are interjacent and divide *Aſia* and *Europe* that
way: then ſhe got into the fifty-three iſles of the *Cycla-
des* that ly betwixt *Negropont* and *Candy*, and ſo got up
to the *Helleſpont* to *Conſtantinople*: ſhe then croſſed o-
ver to *Anatolia*, where, though ſhe prevailed by intro-
ducing multitudes of colonies, yet ſhe came not to be
the ſole vulgar ſpeech anywhere there, ſo far as to ex-
tinguiſh the former languages. Now *Anatolia* is the
moſt populous part in the whole earth; for *Strabo* ſpeaks
of ſixteen ſeveral nations that ſlept in her boſom, and it
is thought the twenty-two languages which *Mithridates*
the great *Polyglot* King of *Pontus* did ſpeak, were all
within the circumference of *Anatolia*, in regard his dominions extended but a little farther. She glided then
along the maritime coaſts of *Thrace*, and paſſing *Byzantium*, got into the out-lets of *Danube*, and beyond her
alſo to *Zaurica*, yea, beyond that to the river *Phaſis*;
and thence compaſſing to *Trebizond*, ſhe took footing on
all the circumference of the *Euxine* ſea. This was her
courſe from Eaſt to Noith; whence we will return to
Candy, *Cyprus*, and *Sicily*; thence croſſing the *Phare* of
Meſſina, ſhe got all along the maritime coaſts of the
Tyrrhene ſea to *Calabria*: ſhe reſted herſelf alſo a great
while in *Apuleia*. There was a populous colony of
Greeks alſo in *Marſeilles* in *France*, and along the ſea-
coaſts of *Savoy*. In *Africa* likewiſe, *Cyrene*, *Alexandria*, and *Egypt*, with divers others were peopled with
Greeks; and three cauſes may be alleged why the *Greek*
tongue did ſo expand herſelf. Firſt, it may be imputed
to

to the conquefts of *Alexander the Great*, and the captains he left behind him for fucceffors: then the love the people had to the fciences, fpeculative learning and civility, whereof the *Greeks* accounted themfelves to be the grand mafters, accounting all other nations *Barbarians* befides themfelves.   Thirdly, the natural inclination and dexterity the *Greeks* had to commerce, wherein they employed themfelves more than any other nations, except the *Phænician* and *Armenian;* which may be a reafon why in all places moft commonly they colonized the maritime parts; for I do not find they did penetrate far into the bowels of any country; but lived on the fea-fide in obvious mercantile places, and acceffible ports.

Now many ages fince, the *Greek* tongue is not only impaired, and pitifully degenerated in her purity and eloquence, but extremely decayed in her amplitude and vulgarnefs.   For firft, there is no trace at all left of her in *France* or *Italy*, the *Sclavonic* tongue hath abolifhed her in *Epire* and *Macedon*, the *Turkifh* hath outed her from moft parts of *Anatolia*, and the *Arabian* hath extinguifhed her in *Syria*, *Paleftine*, *Egypt*, and fundry other places.   Now touching her degeneration from her primitive fuavity and elegance, it is not altogether fo much as the deviation and declenfion of the *Italian* from the *Latin;* yet it is fo far that I could fet foot on no place, nor hear of any people, where either the *Attick*, *Doric*, *Aeolic*, or *Bæotic*, antient *Greek* is vulgarly fpoken; only in fome places near *Heraclia* in *Anatolia* and *Peloponnefus*, (now called the *Morea*) they fpeak o fome towns called the *Lacones*, which retain yet, and vulgarly fpeak the old *Greek*, but incongruoufly: ye though they cannot themfelves fpeak according to rules they underftand thofe that do.   Nor is this corruption happened to the *Greek* language, as it ufeth to happen to others, either by the law of the conqueror, or inundation of ftrangers; but it is infenfibly crept in by their own fupine negligence and fantafticknefs, efpecially by that common fatality and changes which attend time, and all other fublunary things.   Nor is this antient fcientifi cal language decayed only, but the nation of the *Greeks* itself is as it were mouldered away, and brought in a manner to the same condition, and to as contemptible a pass as the *Jew* is: infomuch that there cannot be two more pregnant instances of the lubricity and inftableness of mankind, than the decay of these two antient nations; the one the select people of God, the other the moft famous that ever was for arts, arms, civility and government: fo that *in ftatu quonunc*, they who termed all the world *Barbarians* in comparifon of themfelves in former times, may be now termed (more than any other) *Barbarians* themfelves, as having quite loft not only all inclination and afpiring to knowledge and virtue, but likewife all courage and bravery of mind to recover their antient freedom and honour.

Thus have you, my Lord, as much of the *Greek* tongue as I could comprehend within the bounds of a letter; a tongue that both for knowledge, for commerce, and for copioufnefs, was the principalleft that ever was. In my next I will return near home, and give your Lordfhip account of the *Latin* tongue, and of her three daughters, the *French, Italian* and *Spanifh*. In the interim you find I am ftill, my Lord,

Your moft obedient fervitor,

Weftminfter, July 25. 1630. J. H.

LETTER LXIV.

To the Right Honourable the Earl R.

My LORD,

MY laft was a purfuit of my endeavours to comply with your Lordfhip's defires touching languages; and I fpent more oil and labour than ordinary in difplaying the *Greek* tongue, becaufe we are more beholden to her for all philofophical and theoric knowledge, as alfo for rules of commerce and commutative juftice, than to

any

any other. I will now proceed to the *Latin* tongue, which had her fource in *Italy*, in *Latium*, called now *Compagna di Roma*, and received her growth with the monftrous increafe of the city and empire. Touching the one, fhe came from poor mud-walls at mount *Pala-tine*, which were fcarce a mile about at firft, to be-after-wards fifty miles compafs, (as fhe was in the 'reign' of *Aurelianus*) and her territories, which were hardly a day's journey extent, came by favourable fuccefles and fortune of war, to be above 3000 in length, from the banks of the *Rhine*, or rather from the fhores of this ifland to *Euphrates*, and fometimes to the river *Tigris*. With this vaft expanfion of *Roman* territories, the tongue alfo did fpread ; yet I do not find by thofe refearches I have made into antiquity, that fhe was vulgarly fpoke by any nation, or any intire country, but in *Italy* itfelf ; for notwithftanding that it was the practice of the *Roman* with his lance to ufher in his laws and language as marks of conqueft, yet I believe his tongue never took fuch firm impreffion any where, as to become the vulgar epi-demic fpeech of any people elfe, or that fhe was able to null and extinguifh the native languages fhe found in thofe places where fhe planted her ftandard : nor can I there be a more pregnant inftance hereof than this ifland, for notwithftanding that fhe remained a *Roman* province 400 years together, yet the *Latin* tongue could never have the vogue here fo far as to abolifh the *Britifh* or *Cam-brian* tongue.

It is true, that in *France* and *Spain* fhe made deep-er impreffions, the reafon may be in regard there were far more *Roman* colonies planted there ; for whereas there were but four in this ifle, there were twenty-nine in *France*, and fifty-feven in *Spain*, and the greateft entertainment the *Latin* tongue found out of *Itay* her-felf, was in thefe two kingdoms ; yet I am of opinion that the pure congruous grammatical *Latin* was never fpoken in either of them as a vulgar vernacular language, common amongft women and children ; no, nor in all *Italy* itfelf, except *Latium* : in *Africa*, though there were

were fixty *Roman* colonies difperfed upon that continent, yet the *Latin* tongue made not fuch deep impreffions there, nor in *Afia* neither ; nor is it to be thought, that in thofe colonies themfelves did the common foldiers fpeak in that congruity as the flamens, the judges,· the magiftrates and chief commanders did.   When the *Romans* fent legions and planted colonies abroad,· it was for divers political confiderations, partly to fecure their new acquefts, partly to abate the fuperfluous numbers and redundancy of *Rome*. Then by this way they found means to employ and reward men of worth, and to heighten their minds ; for the *Roman* fpirit did rife up, and take growth with his good fucceffes, conquefts, commands, and employments.

But the reafon that the *Latin* tongue found not fuch entertainment in the Oriental parts, was, that the *Greek* had fore-ftalled her ; which was of more efteem among them, becaufe of the learning that was couched in her, and that fhe was more ufeful for negotiation and traffic ; whereunto the *Greeks* were more addicted than any people : therefore, though the *Romans* had an ambition to make thofe foreign nations that were under their yokè to fpeak, as well as to do what pleafed them, and that all orders, edicts, letters, and laws themfelves, civil as well as martial, were publifhed and executed in *Latin ;* yet I believe the *Latin* was fpoken no otherwife among thofe nations, than the *Spanifh* or *Caftilian* tongue is now in the *Netherlands*, in *Sicily*, *Sardinia*, *Naples*, the two *Indies* and other provincial countries which are under that King. Nor did the pure *Latin* tongue continue long at a ftand of perfection in *Rome* and *Latium* itfelf among all forts of people, but fhe received changes and corruption : neither do I believe that fhe was born a perfect language at firft, but fhe received nutriment, and degrees of perfection with time, which matures, refines, and finifheth all things. The verfes of the *Salii* compofed by *Numa Pompilius* were fcarce intelligible by the flamins, and judges, themfelves in the wane of the *Roman* commonwealth, nor the laws of the *Decemviri*. And

if

if that *Latin* wherein were couched the capitulations of
peace betwixt *Rome* and *Carthage* a little after the expulfion of the kings, which are yet extant upon a pillar in *Rome*,
were compared with that which was fpoken in *Cæfar's*
reign, 140 years after, at which time the *Latin* tongue
was mounted to the meridian of her perfection, fhe
would be found as differing as *Spanifh* now differeth from
the *Latin*. After *Cæfar* and *Cicero's* time, the *Latin*
tongue continued in *Rome* and *Italy* in her purity 400
years together, until the *Goths* rufhed into *Italy* firft
under *Alaric;* then the *Huns* under *Attilia;* then the
Vandals under *Genfericus;* and the *Heruli* under *Odoacer*,
who was proclaimed King of *Italy;* but the *Goths* a little
after, under *Theodoric* thruft out the *Heruli;* which *Theodoric* was by *Zeno* the Emperor formally invefted King of
Italy, who with his fucceffors reigned there peaceably
fixty years and upwards ; fo that in all probability the
Goths cohabiting fo long among the *Italians* muft adul-
terate their language, as well as their women.

The laft barbarous people that invaded *Italy* about
the year 570 were the *Lombards*, who having taken
firm rooting in the very bowels of the country above 200
years without interruption, during the reign of twenty
kings, muft of neceffity alter and deprave the general
fpeech of the natural inhabitants; and among others, one
argument may be, that the beft and midland part of
Italy changed its name, and took its appellation from thefe
laft invaders, calling itfelf *Lombardy*, which name it retains to this' day : yet before the intrufions of thefe
wandering and warlike people into *Italy*, there may be a
precedent caufe of fome corruption that might creep into the *Latin* tongue in point of vulgarity : firft, the incredible confluence of foreigners that came daily far and
near, from the colonized provinces to *Rome;* then, the
infinite number of flaves which furpaffed the number of
free citizens, might much impair the purity of the *Latin*
tongue ; and laftly, thofe inconftancies and humour of
novelty, which is naturally inherent in man, who according to thofe frail elementary principles and ingredients
whereof

whereof he is compofed, is fubject to infenfible alterations, and apt to receive impreffions of any change.

Thus, my Lord, as fuccinctly as I could digeft it into the narrow bounds of an epiftle, I have fent your
Lordfhip this fmall furvey of the *Latin*, or firft *Roman*
tongue : in my next I fhall fall aboard of her three
daughters, *viz.* the *Italian*, the *Spanifh*, and the *French*,
with a diligent inveftigation what might be the original
native languages of thofe countries from the beginning,
before the *Latin* gave them the law. In the interim, I
crave a candid interpretation of what is paffed, and of
my ftudioufnefs in executing your Lordfhip's injunctions ;
I am, my Lord,

Your moft humble and obedient fervant,
Weftminfter, July 16. 1630.   J. H.

L E T T E R LXV.
To the Right Honourable, the E. R.

My LORD,

MY laft was a difcourfe on the *Latin* or primitive
Roman tongue, which may be faid to be expired
in the *market*, though living yet in the *fchools;* I mean,
fhe may be faid to be defunct in point of vulgarity, any
time thefe 1000 years paffed. Out of her ruin have
fprung up the *Italian*, the *Spanifh*, and the *French*,
whereof I am now to treat ; but I think it not improper
to make a refearch firft what the radical prime mother-
tongues of thefe countries were before the *Roman* eagle
planted her talons upon them.

Concerning *Italy*, doubtlefs there were divers before
the *Latin* did fpread all over the country, the *Calabrian*
and *Apulian* fpoke *Greek*, whereof fome reliques are
to be found to this day, but it was an adventitious, no
mother-language to them. It is confeffed that *Latium*
itfelf, and all the territories about *Rome* had the *Latin*
forits maternal and common firft vernacular tongue ; but

Tuscany and *Liguria*, had others quite difcrepant, *viz.*
the *Hetruscane* and *Mefapian*, whereof though there
be fome records yet extant, yet there are none alive
can underftand them : the *Oscan*, the *Sabin* and *Tuscu-
lan*, are thought to be but dialects of thefe.

Now the *Latin* tongue with the coincidence of the
Goths language, and other Northern people, who like
waves tumbled off one another, did more in *Italy* than
anywhere elfe, for fhe utterly abolifhed (upon that part
of the continent) all other maternal tongues as antient
as herfelf, and thereby their eldeft daughter the *Italian*
came to be the vulgar univerfal tongue to the whole
country ; yet the *Latin* tongue had not the fole hand in
doing this, but the *Goths* and other feptentrional nations
who rufhed into the *Roman* ftate, had a fhare in it as
I faid before, and pegged in fome words which have
been ever fince irremoveable, not only in the *Italian*,
but alfo in her two younger fifters, the *Spanish* and
the *French*, who felt alfo the fury of thofe people.
Now the *Italian* is the fmootheft and fofteft running
language that is, for there is not a word except fome few
monofyllables, conjunctions and propofitions, that ends
with a confonant in the whole language : nor is there
any vulgar fpeech which hath more fubdialects in fo fmall
a tract of ground, for *Italy* itfelf affords above eight.
There you have the *Roman*, the *Tuscan*, the *Venetian*,
the *Milanez*, the *Neapolitan*, the *Calabreffe* the *Genoefe*, the *Picmontez ;* you have the *Corfican*, *Sicilian*,
with divers other neighbouring iflands ; and as the caufe
why, from the beginning there were fo many different
dialects in the *Greek* tongue, was becaufe it was fliced
into fo many iflands ; fo, the reafon why there be fo
many fubdialects in the *Italian*, is the diverfity of go-
vernments that the country is fquandered into ; their being in *Italy* at this day two kingdoms, *viz.* that of
Naples and *Calabria ;* three republicks, *Venice*, *Genoa* and *Lucca*, and divers other abfolute princes.

Concerning the original language of *Spain*, it was
without any controverfy the *Bafcuence* or *Cantabrian :*
which

which tongue and territory neither *Roman*, *Goth*, (whence this King hath his pedigree, with divers of the nobles) or *Moor*, could ever conquer, though they had over-run and taken firm footing in all the rest for many ages; therefore, as the remnant of the old *Britons* here, so are the *Bifcayneers* accounted the antienteft and unqueftionableft gentry in *Spain*; infomuch that when any of them is to be dubbed Knight, there is no need of any fcrutiny to be made whether he be of the blood of the *Morifcos*, who had mingled and incorporated with the reft of the *Spaniards* about 700 years. And as the *Arcadians*, and *Attiques* in *Greece*, for their immemorial antiquity are faid to vaunt of themfelves, that the one are Πρσσέλυνοι, before the moon; the other αὐτόχθονες, iffued of the earth itfelf; fo the *Bifcayneer* hath fuch like rodomontadoes.

The *Spanifh* or *Caftilian* language hath few fubdialects, the *Portugueze* is moft confiderable: touching the *Catalan*, and *Valencian*, they are rather dialects of the *French*, *Gafcon*, or *Aquitarian*. The pureft dialect of the *Caftilian* tongue is held to be in the town of *Toledo*; which above other cities of *Spain* hath this privilege, to be arbitrefs in the decifion of any controverfy that may arife touching the interpretation of any *Caftilian* word.

It is an infallible rule to find out the mother and antienteft tongue of any country, to go among thofe who inhabit the barreneft and moft mountainous places, which are pofts of fecurity and faftnefs; whereof divers inftances could be produced: but, let the *Bifcayneer* in *Spain*, the *Welfh* in *Great Britain*, and the mountaineers in *Epire* ferve the turn, who yet retain their antient unmixt mothertongues, being extinguifhed in all the country befides.

Touching *France*, it is not only doubtful, but left yet undecided, what the true *Gallic* tongue was: fome would have it to be the *German*, fome the *Greek*, fome the old *Britifh* or *Welfh*; and the laft opinion carrieth away with it the moft judicious antiquaries. Now all *Gallia* is not meant by it, but the country of the *Celtæ* that inhabit the middle part of *France*, who are the true *Gauls*. *Cæfar* and *Tacitus* tells us, that thefe *Celtæ*,

K k 3   and

and the old *Britons*, (whereof I gave a touch in my firſt letter) did mutually underſtand one another; and ſome do hold that this iſland was tied to *France*, as *Sicily* was to *Calabria*, and *Denmark* to *Germany*, by an iſthmus of land betwixt *Dover* and *Bullen*: for if one do well obſerve the rocks of the one, and the cliffs of the other, he will judge them to be one homogeneous piece, and that they were cut and ſhivered aſunder by ſome act of violence.

The *French* or *Gallic* tongue hath divers dialects; the *Picard*, that of *Jerſey* and *Guernſey*, (appendixes once to the dutchy of *Normandy*) the *Provenſal*, the *Gaſcon*, or ſpeech of *Languedoc*, which *Scaliger* would etymologize from *Langue do'uy*, whereas it comes rather from *Langue de got;* for the *Saracens* and *Goths*, by their incurſions and long ſtay in *Aquitain*, corrupted the language of that part of *Gallia*. Touching the *Britan* and they of *Bearn*, the one is a dialect of the *Welſh*, the other of the *Baſcuence*. The *Walloon* who is under the King of *Spain*, and the *Liegois*, is alſo a dialect of the *French;* which in their own country they call *Roman*. The *Spaniard* alſo terms his *Caſtillian*, *Roman;* whence it may be inferred that the firſt riſe and derivation of the *Spaniſh* and *French* were from the *Roman* tongue, not from the *Latin;* which makes me think that the language of *Rome* might be degenerated, and become a dialect to her own mother-tongue (the *Latin*) before ſhe brought her language to *France* and *Spain*.

There is beſides theſe ſubdialects of the *Italian*, *Spaniſh* and *French*, another ſpeech that hath a great ſtroke in *Greece* and *Turky*, called *Franco*, which may be ſaid to be compoſed of all the three, and is at this day the greateſt language of commerce and negotiation in the *Levant*.

Thus have I given your Lordſhip the beſt account I could of the ſiſter-dialects of the *Italian*, *Spaniſh*, and *French*. In my next I ſhall croſs the *Mediterranean* to *Africa*, and the *Helleſpont* to *Aſia*, where I ſhall obſerve the generalleſt languages of thoſe vaſt continents where ſuch numberleſs ſwarms and differing ſorts

.of

of nations do crawl up and down this earthly globe; there·
fore, it cannot be expected that I fhould be fo punctual
there as in *Europe:* fo, I am ftill, my Lord,

Your obedient fervitor,

Weftminfter, July 7. 1630.   J. H.

L E T T E R LXVI.
To the Right Honourable the Earl R.

My LORD,

HAVING in my former letters made a flying progrefs through the *European* world, and taken a
view of the feveral languages, dialects and fubdialects
whereby people converfe one with another, and being
now wind-bound for *Africa,* I held it not altogether
fupervacaneous to take a review of them, and inform
your Lordfhip what languages are original independant
mother-tongues of chriftendom, and what are dialects,
derivations, or degenerations from their originals.

The mother-tongues of *Europe* are thirteen, though
Scaliger would have but eleven: there is 1. the *Greek,*
2. the *Latin,* 3. the *Dutch,* 4. the *Sclavonic,* 5. the
Welfh or *Cambrian,* 6. the *Bafcuence* or *Cantabrian,*
7. the *Irifh,* 8. the *Albanian* in the mountains of *Epire,*
9. the *Tartarian,* 10. the old *Illyrian,* remaining yet in
Liburnia, 11. the *Jazygian,* on the North of *Hungary,*
12. the *Chauchian* in *Eaft-Friezeland,* 13. the *Finnic;*
which I put laft with good reafon, becaufe they are the
only heathens of *Europe:* all which were known to be
in *Europe* in the time of the *Roman* empire. There is a
learned antiquary that makes the *Arabic* to be one of
the mother-tongues in *Europe,* becaufe it was fpoken in
fome of the mountains of South *Spain.* It is true, it was
fpoken for divers hundred years all *Spain* over, after the
conqueft of the *Moors;* but yet it could not be called a
mother-tongue, but an adventitious tongue in reference
to that part of *Europe.*

And

And now that I am to paſs to *Africa*, which is far
bigger than *Europe;* and to *Aſia*, which is far bigger than
Africa; and to *America*, which is thought to be as big
as all the three: if *Europe* herſelf hath ſo many mother-
languages, quite diſcrepant one from the other, beſides
ſecondary tongues and dialeⅽts, which exceed the number of their mothers, what ſhall we think of the other
three huge continents in point of differing languages?
Your Lordſhip knows that there be divers meridians and
climes in the heavens, whence influxes of differing qualities fall upon the inhabitants of the earth; and as they
make men to differ in the ideas and conceptions of the
mind, ſo in the motion of the tongue, in the tune and
tones of the voice, they come to differ one from the o-
ther. Now, all languages were at firſt imperfeⅽt 'confuſed ſounds, then came they to be ſyllables, then words,
then ſpeeches and ſentences; which by praⅽtice, by tradition, and a kind of natural inſtinⅽt from parents to children, grew to be fixed. Now to attempt a ſurvey of all
the languages in the other three parts of the habitable
earth, were rather a madneſs than a preſumption, it being a thing of impoſſibility, and not only above the capacity, but beyond the ſearch of the aⅽtiveſt, and know-
ingeſt man upon earth: let it therefore ſuffice, while I
behold thoſe nations that read and write from right to
left, from the liver to the heart, I mean the *Africans*
and *Aſians*, that I take a ſhort view of the *Arabic* in the
one, and the *Hebrew* or *Syriac* in the other: for touching the *Turkiſh* language, it is but a dialeⅽt of the *Tartarian*, though it have received a late mixture of the
Armenian, the *Perſian*, and *Greek* tongues, but ſpecially of the *Arabic*, which was the mother-tongue of
their Prophet, and is now the ſole language of their *alcoran*, it being ſtriⅽtly inhibited, and held to be a profaneneſs to tranſlate it to any other; which, they ſay,
preſerves them from the encroachment of ſchiſms.

Now the *Arabic* is a tongue of vaſt expanſion; for
beſides the three *Arabias*, it is become the vulgar ſpeech
of *Syria*, *Meſopotamia*, *Paleſtine*, and *Egypt;* from
whence

whence fhe ftretch'eth herfelf to the ftreight of *Gibraltar*, through all that vaft tract of earth which lieth betwixt the mountain *Atlas* and the *Mediterranean* fea, which is now called *Barbary*, where chriftianity and the *Latin* tongue, with divers famous bifhops flourifhed. She is fpoken likewife in all the Northern parts of the *Turkifh* empire, as alfo in petty *Tartary;* and fhe, above all other, hath reafon to learn *Arabic*, for fhe is in hope one day to have the *Crefcent*, and the whole *Ottoman* empire; it being entailed upon her, in cafe the prefent race fhould fail, which is now in more danger than ever. In fine, wherefoever the *Mahometan* religion is profeffed, the *Arabic* is either fpoken or taught.

My laft view fhall be of the firft language of the earth, the antient language of paradife, the language wherein God almighty himfelf pleafed to pronounce and publifh the tables of the law, the language that had a benediction promifed her, becaufe fhe would not confent to the building of the *Babylonifh* tower: yet this holy tongue hath had alfo her eclipfes, and is now degenerated to many dialects, nor is fhe fpoken purely by any nation upon earth; a fate alfo which is befallen the *Greek* and *Latin*. The moft fpacious dialect of the *Hebrew* is the *Syriac*, which had her beginning in the time of the captivity of the *Jews* at *Babylon*, while they cohabited and were mingled with the *Chaldeans*; in which tract of feventy years time, the vulgar fort of *Jews* neglecting their own maternal tongue, (the *Hebrew*) began to fpeak the *Chaldee;* but not having the right accent of it, and fafhioning that new learned language to their own innovation of points, affixes, and conjugations, out of that intermixture of *Hebrew* and *Chaldee*, refulted a third language called the *Syriac;* which alfo after the time of our Saviour, began to be more adulterated by admiffion of *Greek*, *Roman*, and *Arabic*. In this language is the *talmud* and *targum* couched; and all their rabbins, as Rabbi *Jonathan*, and Rabbi *Onkelos*, with others, have written in it; infomuch that, as I faid before, the antient *Hebrew* had the fame fortune that the *Greek* and

Latin

Latin tongues had, to fall from their being naturally spoken anywhere, to lose their general communicableness and vulgarity, and to become only school and book-languages.

Thus we see, that as all other sublunary things are subject to corruption and decay, as the potenteft monarchies, the proudest republicks, the opulenteft cities have their growth, declinings, and periods: as all other elementary bodies likewise by reason of the frailty of their principles, come by insensible degrees to alter and perish, and cannot continue long at a stand of perfection; so the learnedeft and moft eloquent languages, are not free from this common fatality, but they are liable to those alterations and revolutions, to those fits of inconstancy, and other destructive contingencies which are unavoidably incident to all earthly things.

Thus, my noble Lord, have I eviscerated myself, and stretched all my sinews: I have put all my small knowledge, observations, and reading, upon the tenter, to satisfy your Lordship's desires touching this subject. I it afford you any contentment. I have hit the white I aimed at, and hold myself abundantly rewarded for my oil and labour: so, I am, my Lord,

Your moft humble and ever obedient servitor,

Weftminfter, July 1. 1630.   J. H.

L E T T E R LXVII.

To the Honourable Mr. CAR. RA.

S I R,

YOURS of the 7th current was brought me, whereby I find that you did put yourself to the penance of perusing some epistles that go imprinted lately in my name. I am bound to you for your pains and patience, (for you write you read them all thorough) much more for your candid opinion of them, being right glad that
they

they fhould give entertainment to fuch a choice and judicious gentleman as yourfelf. But whereas you feem to except againft fomething in one letter that reflects upon Sir *Walter Rawleigh*'s voyage to *Guinea*, becaufe I term the gold mine he went to difcover, an *airy and fuppofitious mine*, and fo infer that it toucheth his honour: truly, Sir, I will deal clearly with you in that point, that I never harboured in my brain the leaft thought to expofe to the world any thing that might prejudice, much lefs traduce in the leaft degree that could be, that rare and renowned Knight, whofe fame fhall contend in longevity with this ifland itfelf, yea, with that great world which he hiftorifeth fo gallantly. I was a youth about the town when he undertook that expedition, and I remember moft men fufpected that mine then, to be but an imaginary politic thing; but at his return, and miffing of the enterprize, thefe fufpicions turned in moft, to real beliefs that it was no other. And King *James* in that declaration which he commanded to be publifhed and printed afterwards touching the circumftances of this action, (upon which my letter is grounded, and which I have ftill by me) terms it no lefs: and if we may not give faith to fuch public regal inftruments, what fhall we credit? Befides, there goes another printed kind of remonftrance annexed to that declaration which intimates as much; and there is a worthy Captain in this town, who was a co-adventurer in that expedition, who, upon the ftorming of *St. Thomas* heard young Mr. *Rawleigh* encouraging his men in thefe words, ' Come on my noble hearts, ' this is the mine we come for, and they who think there ' is any other are fools.' Add hereunto, that Sir *Richard Baker* in his laft hiftorical collections intimates fo much: therefore, it was far from being any opinion broached by myfelf, or bottomed upon weak grounds; for I was careful of nothing more, than that thofe letters, being to breathe open air, fhould relate nothing but what fhould be derived from good fountains. And truly, Sir, touching that apology of Sir *Walter Rawleigh*'s you write of, I never faw it; and I am very forry I did not, for it had

had let in more light upon me of the carriage of that
great action, and then you might have been assured that
I would have done that noble Knight all the right that
could be.

· But Sir, the several arguments that you urge in your
letters are of that strength, I confess, that they are able
to rectify any indifferent man in this point, and induce
him to believe that it was no chimera, but a real mine:
for you write of divers pieces of gold brought thence by
Sir *Walter* himself, and Captain *Kemys*, and of some
ingots that were found in the Governor's closet at *St.
Thomas*, with divers crucibles, and other refining instruments; yet, under favour, that might be, and the benefit not countervail the charge, for the richest mines that
the King of *Spain* hath upon the whole continent of *A-
merica*, which are the mines of *Potosi*, yield him but six
in the hundred, all expences defrayed. You write how
King *James* sent privately to Sir *Walter*, being yet in the
Tower, to intreat and command him, that he would impart his whole design unto him under his hand, promising
upon the word of a King to keep it secret; which being done accordingly by Sir *Walter Rawleigh*, that very
original paper was found in the said *Spanish* Governor's
closet at *St. Thomas*: whereat, as you have just cause
to wonder and admire the activeness of the *Spanish* agents
about our court at that time, so I wonder no less at the
miscarriage of some of his late Majesty's ministers, who,
notwithstanding that he had passed his royal word to the
contrary, yet they did help Count *Gondomar* to that paper; so that the reproach lieth more upon the *English*
than the *Spanish* ministers in this particular. Whereas
you allege, that the dangerous sickness of Sir *Walter*, being arrived near the place, and the death of (that rare
spark of courage) your brother upon the first landing,
with other circumstances discouraged Captain *Kemys* from
discovering the mine, but to reserve it for another time.
I am content to give as much credit to this as any man
can; as also that Sir *Walter*, if the rest of the fleet according to his earnest motion had gone with him to re-

victual in *Virginia*, (a country where he had reason to be welcome unto, being of his own discovery) he had a purpose to return unto *Guyana* the spring following to pursue his first design. I am also very willing to believe, that it cost Sir *Walter Rawleigh* much more to put himself in equipage for that long intended voyage, than would have paid for his liberty, if he had gone about to purchase it for reward of money at home; though I am not ignorant that many of the coadventurers made large contributions, and the fortunes of some of them suffer for it at this very day. But although *Gondomar*, as my letter mentions, calls Sir *Walter* pirate, I for my part am far from thinking so, because, as you give an unanswerable reason, the plundering of *St. Thomas*, was an act beyond the equator, where the articles of peace betwixt the two kings do not extend. Yet, under favour, though he broke not the peace, he was said to break his patent by exceeding the bounds of his commission, as the foresaid declaration relates: for King *James* had made strong promises to Count *Gondomar*, that this fleet should commit no outrages upon the King of *Spain*'s subjects by land, unless they began first; and I believe that was the main cause of his death, though I think, if they had proceeded that way against him in a legal course of trial, he might have defended himself well enough.

Whereas you allege, that if that action had succeeded, and afterwards been well prosecuted, it might have brought *Gondomar*'s great catholic Master to have been begged for at the church-doors by friers, as he was once brought in the latter end of Queen *Elizabeth*'s days: I believe it had much damnified him, and interrupted him in the possession of his *West-Indies*, but not brought him, under favour, to so low an ebb. I have observed, that it is an ordinary thing in your popish countries for princes to borrow from the altar, when they are reduced to any straits; for they say, ' the riches of the church are to ' serve as anchors in time of a storm.' Divers of our kings have done worse, by pawning their plate and jewels. Whereas, my letter makes mention that Sir *Wal-*

ter

ter Rawleigh mainly laboured for his pardon before he
went, but could not compass it: this is also a paſſage in
the foreſaid printed relation; but I could have wiſhed
with all my heart he had obtained it, for I believe, that
neither the tranſgreſſion of his commiſſion, nor any thing
that he did beyond the *Line*, could have ſhortened the
line of his life otherwiſe; but in all probability we might
have been happy in him to this very day, having ſuch an
heroic heart as he had, and other rare helps, by his
knowledge, for the great preſervation of health. I believe without any ſcruple what you write, that Sir *William St. Geon* made an overture unto him of procuring
his pardon for 1500*l.* but whether he could have ef-
fected it I doubt a little, when he had come to negotiate
it really. But I extremely wonder how that old ſentence which had lain dormant above ſixteen years againſt
Sir *Walter Rawleigh*, could have been made uſe of to
take off his head afterwards, conſidering that the Lord
Chancellor *Verulam*, as you write, told him poſitively
(as Sir *Walter* was acquainting him with that proffer of
Sir *William St. Geon* for a pecuniary pardon) in theſe
words, ' Sir, the knee-timber of your voyage is money,
' ſpare your purſe in this particular, for upon my life you
' have a ſufficient pardon for all that is paſſed already,
' the King having under his broad-ſeal made you Admi-
' ral of your fleet, and given you power of the martial-
' law over your officers and ſoldiers.' One would think
by this royal patent, which gave him power of life and
death over the King's liege people, Sir *Walter Rawleigh*
ſhould become *rectus in curia*, and free from all old
convictions; but, Sir, to tell you the plain truth, Count
Gondomar at that time had a great ſtroke in our court,
becauſe there was more than a mere overture of a match
with *Spain;* which makes me apt to believe that that
great wiſe Knight being ſuch an *Anti-Spaniard*, was
made a ſacrifice to advance the matrimonial treaty. But
I muſt needs wonder, as you juſtly do, that one and the
ſame man ſhould be condemned for being a friend to the
Spaniard, (which was the ground of his firſt condemnation)

nation) and afterwards lofe his head for being their enemy by the fame fentence. Touching his return, I muft confefs I was utterly ignorant that thofe two noble earls, *Thomas* of *Arundel*, and *William* of *Pembroke*, were engaged for him in this particular; nor doth the printed relation make any mention of them at all, therefore I muft fay, that envy herfelf muft pronounce that return of his, for the acquitting of his fiduciary pledges, to be a moft noble act; and waving that of King *Alphonfo's* moor, I may more properly compare it to the act of that famous *Roman* commander, (*Regulus*, as I take it) who to keep his promife and faith, returned to his enemies where he had been prifoner, though he knew he went to an inevitable death. But well did that faithlefs cunning Knight who betrayed Sir *Walter Rawleigh* in his intended efcape, being come afhore, fall to that contemptible end, as to die a poor diftracted beggar in the ifle of *Lundey*, having for a bag of money falfified his faith, confirmed by the tie of the holy facrament, as you write; as alfo before the year came about, to be found clipping the fame coin in the King's own houfe at *Whitehall*, which he had received as a reward for his perfidioufnefs; for which being condemned to be hanged, he was driven to fell himfelf to his fhirt, to purchafe his pardon, of two knights.

And now, Sir, let that glorious and gallant cavalier Sir *Walter Rawleigh*, (*who lived long enough for his own honour, though not for his country*, as it was faid of a *Roman* Conful) reft quietly in his grave, and his virtues live in his pofterity, as I find they do ftrongly, and very eminently in you. I have heard his enemies confefs, that he was one of the weightieft and wifeft men that this ifland ever bred. Mr. *Nath. Carpenter*, a learned and judicious author, was not in the wrong when he gave this difcreet character of him: ‘ Who ‘ hath not known or read of this prodigy of wit and ‘ fortune, Sir *Walter Rawleigh*, a man unfortunate in ‘ nothing elfe but in the greatnefs of his wit and advance- ‘ ment; whofe eminent worth was fuch both in dome-

‘ ftic

‘ ftic policy, foreign expeditions, and difcoveries in arts
‘ and literature, both practic and contemplative, that it
‘ might feem at once to conquer example and imitation.’

Now, Sir, hoping to be rectified in your judgment
touching my opinion of that illuftrious Knight your father, give me leave to kifs your hands very affectionately
for the refpectful mention you pleafe to make of my brother, once your neighbour: he fuffers good foul, as well
as I, though in a differing manner. I alfo much value
that favourable cenfure you give of thofe rambling letters
of mine, which indeed are nought elfe than a legend of
the cumberfome life and various fortunes of a cadet.
But whereas you pleafe to fay, ‘ That! the world of
‘ learned men is much beholden to me for them, and
‘ that fome of them are freighted with many excellent
‘ and quaint paffages, delivered in a mafculine and folid
‘ ftyle, adorned with much eloquence, and ftuck with
‘ choiceft flowers picked from the mufes garden.’ Whereas you alfo pleafe to write, ‘ That you admire my great
‘ travels, my ftrenuous endeavours, at all times and in
‘ all places, to accumulate knowledge, my active laying
‘ hold upon all occafions, and on every handle that might
‘ (with reputation) advantage either my wit or fortune.’
Thefe high gallant ftrains of expreffions, I confefs, tran-
fcend my merit, and are a garment too gaudy for me to
put on; yet I will lay it up among my beft. reliques,
whereof I have divers fent me of this kind. And whereas in publifhing thefe epiftles at this time you pleafe to
fay, ‘ That I have done like *Hezekiah* when he fhewed
‘ his treafures to the *Babylonians*, that I have difcovered
‘ my riches to thieves, who will bind me faft and fhare
‘ my goods.’ To this I anfwer, that if thofe innocent
letters (for I know none of them but is fuch), fall among
fuch thieves, they will have no great prize to carry a-
way, it will be but petty larceny. I am already, God
wot, bound faft enough, having been a long time cooped
up between thefe walls, bereft of all my means of fubfiftence and employment: nor do I know wherefore I am
here, unlefs it be for my fins: for, I bear as upright a

heart

heart to my King and country, I am as conformable and well affected to the government of this land, especially to the high court of parliament, as any one whatsoever that breathes under this meridian, I will except none; and for my religion, I defy any creature betwixt heaven and earth, that will say that I am not a true *English* protestant.. I have from time to time employed divers of my best friends to get my liberty, at leastwise leave to go abroad upon bail, (for I do not expect, as you please also to believe in your letter, to be delivered hence, as St. *Peter* was, by miracle) but nothing will yet prevail.

To conclude, I do acknowledge in the highest way of recognition, the free and noble proffer you please to make me of your endeavours to pull me out of this doleful sepulchre, wherein you say I am entombed alive. I am no less obliged to you for the opinion I find you have of my weak abilities, which you pleased to wish heartily may be no longer eclipsed. I am not in despair, but a day will shine, that may afford me opportunity to improve this good opinion of yours, (which I value at a high rate) and let the world know how much I am, Sir,

Your real and ready servitor;

Fleet, May 5. 1645. J. H.

LETTER LXVIII.

To Mr. T. V. *at* Brussels.

My dear TOM,

WHO would have thought poor *England* had been brought to this pass? Could it ever have entered into the imagination of man, that the scheme and whole frame of so antient and well-moulded a government should be so suddenly struck off the hinges, quite out of joint, and tumbled into such a horrid confusion? Who would have held it possible, that to fly from *Babylon*, we should fall into such a *Babel?* That to avoid superstition, some

people fhould be brought to belch out fuch a horrid profanenefs, as to call the temples of God, the tabernacles of fatan; the Lord's fupper, a two-penny ordinary; to make the communion-table a manger, and the font a trough to water their horfes in; to term the white decent robe of the Prefbyter, the whore's fmock; the pipes through which nothing came · but anthems and holy hymns, the devil's bagpipes; the liturgy of the church, though extracted moft of it out of the facred text, called by fome another kind of *alcoran*, by others raw porridge, by fome a piece forged in hell? Who would have thought to have feen in *England*, the churches fhut and the fhops open upon *Chriftmas* day? Could any foul have imagined that this ifle would have produced fuch monfters, as to rejoice at the *Turks* good fucceffes againft chriftians, and wifh he were in the midft of *Rome?* Who would have dreamed ten years fince, when Archhifhop *Laud* did ride in ftate through *London* ftreets, accompanying my Lord of *London* to be fworn Lord High-Treafurer of *England*, that the mitre fhould have now come to fuch a fcorn, to fuch a national kind of hatred, as to put the whole ifland in a combuftion; which makes me call to memory a faying of the Earl of *Kildare* in *Ireland* in the reign of *Henry* VIII. which Earl, having deadly feud with the Bifhop of *Caffiles*, burnt a church belonging to that diocefe; and being afked upon his examination before the Lord-Deputy at the caftle of *Dublin*, why he had committed fuch a horrid facrilege as to burn God's church? He anfwered, ' I had never burnt ' the church unlefs I had thought the Bifhop had been in ' it.' Laftly, who would have imagined that the excife would have taken footing here? A word I remember in the laft parliament fave one, fo odious, that when Sir *D. Carleton*, then Secretary of State, did but name it in the houfe of commons, he was like to be fent to the *Tower;* although he named it to no ill fenfe, but to fhew what advantage of happinefs the people of *England* had over other nations, having neither the gabels of *Italy*, the tallies of *France*, or the excife of *Holland* laid upon them;
yet

yet upon this he was suddenly interrupted, and called to the bar.. Such a strange metamorphosis poor *England* is now come unto, and I am afraid our miseries are not come to their height, but the longest shadows stay till the evening.

The freshest news that I can write unto you is, that the *Kentish* Knight of your acquaintance, whom I wrote in my last had an *apostacy* in his brain, died suddenly this week of an *imposthume* in his breast, as he was reading a pamphlet of his own that came from the press, wherein he shewed a great mind to be nibling with my trees; but he only shewed his teeth, for he could not bite them to any purpose.

William Roe is returned from the wars, but he is grown lame in one of his arms, so he hath no mind to bear arms any more: he confesseth himself to be an egregious fool to leave his mercership, and go to be a musqueteer. It made me think upon the tale of the *Gallego* in *Spain*, who in the civil wars against *Arragon*, being in the field he was shot in the forehead, and being carried away to a tent, the Surgeon searched his wound and found it mortal: so he advised him to send for his confessor, for he was no man for this world, in regard the brain was touched. The soldier wished him to search it again, which he did, and told him, that he found he was hurt in the brain, and could not possibly scape: whereupon the *Gallego* fell into a chafe, and said he lied; for he had no brain at all, *por que se tuviera sesso, nunca huniera venido esta guerra;* for if I had had any brain, I would never have come to this war. All your friends here are well, except the maimed soldier, and remember you often, especially Sir *J. Brown* a good gallant gentleman, who never forgets any who deserved to have a place in his memory. Farewel my dear *Tom*, and God send you better days than we have here; for I wish you as much happiness as possibly man can have: I wish your mornings may be good, your noons better, your evenings and nights best of all: I wish your sorrows may be short, your joys lasting, and all your desires end in success. Let me

me hear once more from you before you remove thence,
and tell me how the fquares go in *Flanders :* fo, I reft &c.

Your entirely affectionate fervitor,

Fleet, Auguft 3. 1644. **J. H.**

LETTER LXIX.

To his Majefty at Oxon.

SIR,

I Proftrate this paper at your Majefty's feet, hoping
it may find way thence to your eyes, and fo defcend
to your royal heart.

The foreign Minifter of Sa﹍te, by whofe conveyance
this comes, did lately intimate unto me, that among
divers things which go abroad under my name reflecting
upon the times, there are fome which are not fo well
taken, your Majefty being informed that they difcover
a fpirit of indifferency, and lukewarmnefs in the author.
This added much to the weight of my prefent fufferances,
and exceedingly imbittered the fenfe of them unto me,
being no other than a corrofive to one already in a hectiç
condition. I muft confefs that fome of them were more
moderate than others ; yet (moft humbly under favour)
there were none of them but difplayed the heart of a
conftant true loyal fubject ; and as divers of thofe who
are moft zealous to your Majefty's fervice told me,
they had the good fuccefs to rectify multitudes of people
in their opinion of fome things: infomuch that I am not
only confcious, but moft confident that none of them
could tend to your Majefty's difservice any way imagin-
able : therefore I humbly befeech, that your Majefty
would vouchfafe to conceive of me accordingly, and of
one who by this reclufe paffive condition hath his fhare of
this hideous ftorm : yet he is in affurance, rather than
hopes, that though divers crofs winds have blown, thefe
times will bring in better at laft. There have been
divers

divers of your royal progenitors who have had as fhrewd fhocks; and it is well known, how the next tranfmarine kings have been brought to lower ebbs: at this very day he of *Spain* is in a far worfe condition, being in the midft of two forts of people, (the *Catalan* and *Portuguefe*) which were lately his vaffals, but now have torn his feals, renounced all bonds of allegiance, and are in actual hoftility againft him. This great city, I may fay, is like a chefsboard chequered, inlaid with white and black fpots, though I believe the white are more in number; and your Majefty's countenance, by returning to your great council and your court at *Whitehall* would quickly turn them all white. That almighty Majefty who ufeth to draw light out of darknefs, and ftrength out of weaknefs, making man's extremity his opportunity, preferve and profper your Majefty according to the prayers early and late of your Majefty's moft loyal fubject, fervant, and martyr,

Fleet, Sept. 3. 1644. HOWELL.

L E T T E R LXX.

To Sir R. GR. *Knight and Baronet.*

S I R,

I Had yours upon *Maunday-Thurfday* late; and the reafon that fufpended my anfwer till now, was, that the feafon engaged me to fequefter my thoughts from my wonted negotiations, to contemplate the great work of man's redemption, fo great, that were it caft in counterbalance with his creation, it would outpoize it far. I fummoned all my intellectuals to meditate upon thofe paffions, upon thofe pangs, upon that defpicable and moft dolorous death, upon that crofs whereon my Saviour fuffered, which was the firft chriftian altar that ever was; and I doubt that he will never have benefit of the facrifice, who hates the harmlefs refemblance of the altar
whereon

whereon it was offered. I applied my memory to fasten
upon it, my underſtanding to comprehend it, my will to
embrace it. From theſe three faculties, methought I
found by the mediation of the fancy, ſome beams of love
gently gliding down from the head to the heart, and in-
flaming all my affections. If the human ſoul had far
more powers than the philoſophers afford her, if ſhe had
as many faculties within the head as there be hairs without, the ſpeculation of this myſtery would find work e-
nough for them all. Truly the more I ſcrew up my ſpirits to reach it, the more I am ſwallowed in a gulph of
admiration, and of a thouſand imperfect notions; which
makes me ever and anon to quarrel my ſoul that ſhe cannot lay hold on her Saviour, much more my heart, that
my pureſt affections cannot hug him as much as I would.

They have a cuſtom beyond the ſeas, (and I could wiſh
it were the worſt cuſtom they had) that during the *Paſſion* week divers of their greateſt princes and ladies will
betake themſelves to ſome convent or recluſed houſe, to
wean themſelves from all worldly incumbrances, and converſe only with heaven, with performance of ſome kind
of penances all the week long. A worthy gentleman
that came lately from *Italy*, told me that the Count of
Byron, now Marſhal of *France*, having been long perſe-
cuted by Cardinal *Richlieu*, put himſelf into a monaſtery,
and the next day news was brought him of the Cardinal's
death; which I believe made him ſpend the reſt of the
week with the more devotion in that way. *France* brags
that our Saviour had his face turned towards her when
he was upon the croſs: there is more cauſe to think that
it was towards this iſland, in regard the rays of chriſtianity firſt reverberated upon her, her King being chriſtian
400 years before him of *France*, (as all hiſtorians concur)
notwithſtanding that he arrogates to himſelf the title of
the firſt ſon of the church.

Let this ſerve for part of my apology. The Day following, my Saviour being in the grave, I had no liſt to
look much abroad, but continued my retiredneſs: there
was another reaſon alſo why, becauſe I intended to take
the

the holy sacrament the *Sunday* ensuing; which is an act
of the greatest consolation, and consequence, that possibly
a christian can be capable of: it imports him so much,
that he is made or marred by it: it tends to his damnation or salvation, to help him up to heaven, or tumble
him headlong to hell. Therefore, it behoves a man to
prepare and recollect himself, to winnow his thoughts
from the chaff and tares of the world beforehand. This
then took up a good part of that day to provide myself a
wedding-garment, that I might be a fit guest at so precious a banquet, so precious, that manna and angels food
are but coarse viands in comparison of it.

I hope that this excuse will be of such validity, that it
may procure my pardon for not corresponding with you
last week. I am now as freely as formerly,

Your most ready and humble servitor,

Fleet, April 30. 1647.   J. H.

LETTER LXXI.

To my honourable Friend Mr. E. P. at Paris.

S I R,

LET me never sally hence from among these disconsolate walls, if the literal correspondence you please
to hold so punctually with me, be not one of the greatest
solaces I have had in this sad condition: for I find so
much salt, such endearments and flourishes, such a gallantry and neatness in your lines, that you may give the
law of lettering to all the world. I had this week a twin
of yours, of the 10th and 15th current: I am sorry to
hear of your achaques, and so often indisposition there;
it may be very well (as you say) that the air of that
dirty town doth not agree with you, because you speak
Spanish; which language you know is used to be breathed out under a clearer clime, I am sure it agrees not with
the sweet breezes of peace, for it is you there that would

keep

keep poor christendom in perpetual whirlwinds of wars;
but I fear, that while *France* sets all wheels a-going,
and stirs all the cacodæmons of hell to pull down the
house of *Austria*, she may chance at last to pull it down
upon her own head. I am sorry to understand what they
write from *Venice* this week, that there is a discovery
made in *Italy*, how *France* had a hand to invade the territories of *St. Mark*, and puzzle the peace of *Italy*. I
want faith to believe it yet, nor can I entertain in my
breast any such conceit of the most *Christian King*, and
first son of the church, as he terms himself: yet I pray
in your next to pull this thorn out of my thoughts, and
tell me whether one may give any credit to this report.

We are now *Scot* free as touching the Northern army,
for our dear brethren have trussed up their baggage, and
put the *Tweed* betwixt us and them once again: dear
indeed, for they have cost us first and last above
1,900,000 *l. Sterling*, which amounts to near 8,00000
of crowns with you there. Yet if reports be true, they
left behind them more than they lost, if you go to number of men; which will be a brave race of *Mestizos* hereafter, who may chance meet their fathers in the field,
and kill them unwittingly: he will be a wise child that
knows his right father. Here we are like to have
twenty-four seas emptied shortly, and some do hope to
find abundance of treasure in the bottom of them, as no
doubt they will, but many doubt that it will prove but
aurum tolosanum to the finders. God grant that from
Aereans we turn not to be *Arians*: the Earl of *Straf-
ford* was accounted by his very enemies to have an extraordinary talent of judgment and parts, (though they say
he wanted moderation) and one of the prime precepts he
left upon the scaffold to his son was, that he should not
*meddle with church-lands, for they would prove a can-
ker to his estate.* Here are started up some great knowing men lately, that can shew the very track by which
our Saviour went to hell: they will tell you precisely
whose names are written in the book of life, whose not.
God deliver us from spiritual pride, which of all sorts is
the

the moſt dangerous. Here are alſo notable ſtar-gazers, who obtrude to the world ſuch confident bold predictions, and are ſo familiar with heavenly bodies, that *Ptolemy*, and *Tycho Brache* were but ninnies to them. We have likewiſe a multitude of witches among us, for in *Eſſex* and *Suffolk* there were above 200 indicted within theſe two years, and above the one half of them executed: more, I may well ſay, than ever this iſland bred ſince the creation, I ſpeak it with horror. God guard us from the devil, for I think he was never ſo buſy upon any part of the earth that was enlightened with the beams of chriſtianity; nor do I wonder at it, for there is never a croſs left to fright him away. *Edinburgh* I hear is fallen into a relapſe of the plague: the laſt they had raged ſo violently, that the fortieth man or woman lives not of thoſe that dwelt there four years ſince, but it is all peopled with new faces. *Don* and *Hans*, I hear, are abſolutely accorded; nor do I believe that all the arti-fices of policy that you uſe there can hinder the peace, though they may puzzle it for a while: if it be ſo, the people which button their doublets upward, will be bet-ter able to deal with you there.

Much notice is taken that you go on there too faſt in your acqueſts; and now that the eagle's wings are pretty well clipped, it is time to look that your *flower-de-luce* grow not too rank, and ſpread too wide. Whereas you deſire to know how it fares with your maſter, I muſt tell you, that like the glorious ſun, he is ſtill in his own orb, though clouded for a time that he cannot ſhoot the beams of majeſty with that luſtre he was wont to do: never did cavalier woo fair Lady as he wooes the parlia-ment to a peace; it is much the head ſhould ſo ſtoop to the members.

Farewel my noble friend, chear up, and reſerve your-ſelf for better days; take your royal maſter for your pat-tern, who for his longanimity, patience, courage, and conſtancy, is admired of all the world, and in a paſſive way of fortitude hath outgone all the nine worthies If the cedar be ſo weather-beaten, we poor ſhrubs muſt not

murmur

murmur to bear part of the ftorm.   I have had my fhare, and I know you want not yours: the ftars may change their afpects, and we may live to fee the fun again in his full meridian.   In the interim come what will, I am

.·*Entirely yours,*

Fleet, Feb. 3. 1646.   J. H.·

LETTER LXXII.

To the Rt. Hon. EDWARD *Earl of* Dorfet, (*Lord Cham-berlain of his Majefty's Houfhold,* &c.) *at* Knowles.

My LORD,

HAVING fo advantageous a hand as Dr. *S. Tur-ner,* I am bold to fend your Lordfhip a new tract of *French* philofophy, called *L'ufage de paffions,* which is cried up to be a choice piece.   It is a moral difcourfe of the right ufe of paffions, the conduct whereof as it is the principal employment of virtue, fo the conqueft of them is the difficulteft part of valour: to *know* one's felf is much, but to *conquer* one's felf is more.   We need not pick quarrels and feck enemies without doors, we have too many inmates at home to exercife our prowefs upon; and there is no man, let him have his humours never fo well balanced, and in fub-jection unto him, but like *Mufcovia* wives, they will oftentimes infult, unlefs they be checked; yet we fhould make them our fervants, not our flaves.   Touching the occurrences of the times, fince the King was fnatched a-way from the parliament, the army they fay, ufe him with more civility and freedom; but for the main **work** of reftoring him, he is yet, as one may fay, but tanta-·lized, being brought often within the fight of *London,* and fo off again.   There are hopes that fomething **will** be done to his advantage fpeedily, becaufe the *Gregorian* foldiers and grofs of the army is well affected to him, though fome of the chiefeft commanders be ftill averfe.

For

For foreign news, they fay *St. Mark* bears up ſtoutly againſt *Mahomet* both by land and ſea: in *Dalmatia* he hath of late ſhaken him by the turban ill-favouredly. I could heartily wiſh that our army were there to help the republick, and combate the common enemy, for then one might be ſure to die in the bed of honour. The commotions in *Sicily* are quaſhed, but thoſe of *Naples* increaſe; and it is like to be a more raging and voracious fire than *Veſuvius*, or any of the ſulphureous mountains about her did ever belch out. The *Catalan* and *Portuguéſe* bait the *Spaniard* on both ſides, but the firſt hath ſhrewder teeth than the other; and the *French* and *Hollander* find him work in *Flanders*. And now, my Lord, to take all nations in a lump, I think God almighty hath a quarrel lately with all mankind, and given the reins to the ill ſpirit to compaſs the whole earth; for within theſe twelve years there have the ſtrangeſt revolutions, and horrideſt things happened not only in *Europe*, but all the world over, that have befallen mankind, I dare boldly ſay, ſince *Adam* fell, in ſo ſhort a revolution of time. There is a kind of popular planet reigns everywhere: I will begin with the hotteſt parts, with *Africa*, where the Emperor of *Ethiopia* (with two of his ſons) was encountered and killed in open field by the groom of his camels and dromedaries, who had levied an army out of the dregs of the people againſt him, and is like to hold that antient empire in *Aſia*. The *Tartar* broke over the 400 miled wall, and ruſhed into the heart of *China*, as far as *Quinzay*, and belaguered the very palace of the Emperor, who rather than become captive to the baſe *Tartar* burnt his caſtle, and did make away himſelf, his thirty wives and children. The great *Turk* hath been lately ſtrangled in the ſeraglio, his own houſe. The Emperor of *Muſcovia* going in a ſolemn proceſſion upon the *Sabbath* day, the rabble broke in, knocked down and cut in pieces divers of his chiefeſt counſellors, favourites, and officers before his face; and dragging their bodies to the mercat-place, their heads were chopped off, into veſſels of hot water, and ſo ſet upon poles to burn

more

more bright before the court-gate. In *Naples* a common fruiterer hath raifed fuch an infurrection, that they fay above fixty men have been flain already upon the ftreets of that city alone. *Catalonia* and *Portugal* have quite revolted from *Spain*. Your Lordfhip knows what knocks have been betwixt the Pope and *Parma :* the *Pole* and the *Cofacks* are hard at it, *Venice* wreftleth with the *Turk*, and is like to lofe her maidenhead unto him, unlefs other chriftian princes look to it in time. And touching thefe three kingdoms, there is none more capable than your Lordfhip to judge what monftrous things have happened; fo that it feems the whole earth is off the hinges; and (which is the more wonderful) all thefe prodigious paffages have fallen out in lefs than the compafs of twelve years. But now that all the world is together by the ears, the States of *Holland* would be quiet, for advice is come that the peace is concluded, and interchangeably ratified betwixt them and *Spain;* but they defer the publifhing of it yet; till they have collected all the contribution-money for the army. The *Spaniard* hopes that one day this peace may tend to his advantage more than all his wars have done thefe fourfcore years, relying upon the old prophecy: *Marte triumphabis,* Batavia, Pace *peribis.*

The King of *Denmark* hath buried lately his eldeft fon *Chriftian,* fo that he hath now but one living, *viz. Frederick,* who is Archbifhop of *Breme,* and is fhortly to be King elect.

My Lord, this letter runs upon univerfals, becaufe I know your Lordfhip hath a public great foul, and a fpacious underftanding, which comprehends the whole world: fo in a due pofture of humility I kifs your hands, being my Lord,

Your moft obedient and moft faithful fervitor,

Fleet, Jan. 20. 1646.   J. H.

LET.

LETTER LXXIII.

To Master W. B.

S I R,

I Had yours of the laſt week, and by reaſon of ſome ſudden incumbrances I could not correſpond with you by that carrier. As for your deſire to know the pedigree and firſt riſe of thoſe we call preſbyterians, I find that your motion hath as much of piety as curioſity in it; but I muſt tell you it is a ſubject fitter for a treatiſe than a letter, yet I will endeavour to ſatisfy you in ſome part.

Touching the word Πρεσβύτερος, it is as antient as chriſtianity itſelf; and every churchman compleated in holy orders was called Preſbyter, as being the chiefeſt name of the function; and ſo it is uſed in all churches both Ealtern and Occidental to this day. We by contraction call him Prieſt, ſo that all biſhops and archbiſhops are prieſts though not *vice verſa.* Theſe holy titles of Biſhop and Prieſt are now grown odious among ſuch poor ſciolilts, who ſcarce know the hoties of things, becauſe they ſavour of antiquity: though their Miniſter that officiates in their church be the ſame thing as Prieſt, and their Superintendent the ſame thing as Biſhop; but becauſe they are lovers of novelties, they change old *Greek* words for new *Latin* ones. The firſt broacher of the preſbyterian religion, and who made it differ from that of *Rome,* and *Luther,* was *Calvin;* who being once baniſhed *Geneva,* was revoked, at which time, he no leſs petulantly than profanely applied to himſelf that text of the holy Prophet which was meaned of Chriſt, *The ſtone which the builders refuſed, is made the head-ſtone of the corner,* &c. Thus *Geneva* lake ſwallowed up the epiſcopal ſea, and church-lands were made ſecular; which was the white they levelled at. This *Geneva* bird flew thence to *France,* and hatched the *Hugonots,* which make about the tenth part of that people. It took wing

alſo

alfo to *Bohemia* and *Germany* high and low, as the *Palatinate*, the land of *Heſſe*, and the confederate provinces of the States of *Holland*, whence it took flight to *Scotland* and *England*. It took firſt footing in *Scotland*, when King *James* was a child in his cradle; but when he came to underſtand himſelf, and was manumitted from *Buchanan*, he grew cold in it; and being come to *England*, he utterly diſclaimed it, terming it, in a public ſpeech of his to the parliament, a ſect, rather than a religion. To this ſect may be imputed all the ſciſſures that have happened in chriſtianity, with moſt of the wars that have lacerated poor *Europe* ever ſince; and it may be called the ſouree of the civil diſtractions that now afflict this poor iſland.

Thus have I endeavoured to fulfil your deſires in part: I ſhall enlarge myſelf further when I ſhall be made happy with your converſation here, till when, and always, I reſt

Your moſt affectionate to love and ſerve you,

Fleet, Nov. 29. 1647.   J. H.

L E T T E R LXXIV.

To HENRY HOPKINS, *Eſq;*

S I R,

TO uſher in again old *Janus*, I ſend you a parcel of *Indian* perfume, which the *Spaniard* calls the holy herb, in regard of the various virtues it hath, but we call it tobacco: I will not ſay it grew under the King of *Spain*'s window, but I am told it was gathered near his gold mines of *Potoſi*, (where they report, that in ſome places there is more of that ore than earth) therefore it muſt needs be precious ſtuff: if moderately and ſeaſonably taken, (as I find you always do) it is good for many things: it helps digeſtion taken a while after meat, it makes one void rheum, break wind, and keeps

the

the body open: a leaf or two being fteeped over night in a little white wine is a vomit that never fails in its operation: it is a good companion to one that converfeth with dead men, for if one hath been poring long upon a book, or is toiled with the pen, and ftupified with ftudy, it quickeneth him, and difpels thofe clouds that ufually overfet the brain. The fmoke of it is one of the wholefomeft fcents that is, againft all contagious airs, for it over-matters all other fmells, as King *James* they fay found true, when being once a hunting, a fhower of rain drove him into a pig-fty, for fhelter, where he caufed a pipefull to be taken of purpofe: it cannot endure a fpider, or a flea, with fuch like vermin; and if your hawk be troubled with any fuch, being blown into his feathers it frees him: it is good to fortify and preferve the fight, the fmoke being let in round about the balls of the eyes once a week, and frees them from all rheums, driving them back by way of repercuffion; being taken backward, it is excéllent good againft the cholic, and taken into the ftomach, it will heat and cleanfe it; for I could inftance in a great Lord, (my Lord of *Sunderland*, Prefident of *York*) who told me, that he taking it downward into his ftomach, it made him caft up an impofthume, bag and all, which had been a long time engendering out of a bruife he had received at foot-ball, and fo preferved his life for many years. Now to defcend from the fubftance of the fmoke, to the afhes, it is well known that the medicinal virtues thereof are very many; but they are fo common, that I will fpare the inferting of them here: but if one would try a pretty conclufion, how much fmoke there is in a pound of tobacco, the afhes will tell him; for let a pound be exactly weighed, and the afhes kept charily and weighed afterwards, what wants in a pound weight in the afhes cannot be denied to have been fmoke, which evaporated in the air. I have been told that Sir *Walter Rawleigh* won a wager of Queen *Elizabeth* upon this nicety.

The *Spaniards* and *Irifh* take it moft in powder or fnutchin, and it mightily refrefhes the brain; and I believe

lieve there is as much taken this way in *Ireland*, as there is in pipes in *England*: one shall commonly see the serving-maid upon the washing-block, and the swain upon the plough-share, when they are tired with labour, take out their boxes of snutchin and draw it into their nostrils with a quill, and it will beget new spirits in them with a fresh vigour to fall to their work again. In *Barbary* and other parts of *Africa*, it is wonderful what a small pill of tobacco will do; for those who use to ride post through the sandy deserts, where they meet not with any thing that is potable or edible, sometimes three days together, they use to carry small balls or pills of tobacco, which being put under the tongue, it affords them a perpetual moisture, and takes off the edge of the appetite for some days.

If you desire to read with pleasure all the virtues of this modern herb, you must read Dr. *Thorius*'s Pætologis, an accurate piece couched in a strenuous heroic verse, full of matter, and continuing its strength from first to last; insomuch that for the bigness it may be compared to any piece of antiquity, and in my opinion is beyond βάτραχομυομαχία, or γαλεωμυομαχία.

So I conclude these rambling notions, presuming you will accept this small argument of my great respects unto you. If you want paper to light your pipe, this letter may serve the turn; and if it be true what the poets frequently sing, that *affection is fire*, you shall need no other than the clear flames of the donor's love to make ignition, which is comprehended in this distich:

> *Ignis amor fi fit, tobaccum accendere nostrum,*
> *Nulla petenda tibi fax nisi dantis amor.*

> *If love be fire, to light this* Indian *weed,*
> *The donor's love of fire may stand instead.*

So I wish you, as to myself, a most happy new year: may the beginning be good, the middle better, and the end best of all.

Your most faithful and truly affectionate servitor,

Fleet, Jan. 1. 1646. J. H.

LETTER LXXV.

To the Right Honourable my Lord of D.

My LORD,

THE subject of this letter may peradventure seem a paradox to some, but not, I know, to your Lordship, when you have pleased to weigh well the reasons. Learning is a thing that hath been much cried up, and coveted in all ages, especially in this last century of years, by people of all sorts, though never so mean and mechanical; every man strains his fortunes to keep his children at school; the cobler will clout it till midnight, the porter will carry burdens till his bones crack again, the ploughman will pinch both back and belly to give his son learning; and I find that this ambition reigns nowhere so much as in this island. But under favour, this word, *learning*, is taken in a narrower sense among us than among other nations, we seem to restrain it only to the book, whereas indeed, any artisan whatsoever (if he know the secret and mystery of his trade) may be called a learned man. A good mason, a good shoemaker that can manage St. *Crispin*'s lance handsomely, a skillful yeoman, a good shipwright, &c. may be called learned men, and indeed the usefullest sort of learned men, for without the two first, we might go barefooted, and ly abroad as beasts, having no other canopy than the wild air, and without the two last we might starve for bread, have no commerce with other nations, or ever be able to trade upon a continent: these, with such like dexterous artisans, may be termed learned men, and the more behoveful for the subsistence of a country than those polymathists, that stands poring all day in a corner upon a moth-eaten author, and converse only with dead men. The *Chinese* (who are the next neighbours to the rising sun on this part of the hemisphere, and consequently acutest) have a wholesome piece of policy, *that the son is always of the father's trade*, and it is all the learning he aims

at;

at ; which makes them admirable artifans, for, befides
the dexteroufnefs and propenfity of the child, being defcended lineally from fo many of the fame trade, the
father is more careful to inftruct him, and to difcover to
him all the myftery thereof.   This general cuftom or
law, keeps their heads from running at random after
book-learning and other vocations.   I have read a tale
of *Robert Grofthead* Bifhop of *Lincoln*, that being come
to his greatnefs he had a brother who was a hufbandman,
and expected great matters from him in point of preferment, but the Bifhop told him, that if he wanted money
to mend his plow or his cart, or to buy tacklings for
horfes with other things belonging to his hufbandry, he
fhould not want what was fitting ; but he *wifhed him to
aim no higher, for a husbandman he found him, and a
husbandman he would leave him.*

The extravagant humor of our country is not to be
altogether commended, that all men fhould afpire to
book-learning : there is not a fimpler animal, and a more
fuperfluous member of a ftate, than a mere fcholar, than
only a felf-pleafing ftudent, he is, ——*Telluris inutile
pondus.*

The *Goths* forbore to deftroy the libraries of the
Greeks and *Italians*, becaufe books fhould keep them
ftill foft, fimple or too cautious in warlike affairs.   *Ar-
chimedes* though an excellent engineer when *Syracufe*
was loft, was found at his book in his ftudy, intoxicated
with fpeuclations.   Who would not have thought another
great learned Philofopher to be a fool or frantic, when
being in a bath he leaped out naked among the people
and cried, *I have found it, I have found it*, having hit
then upon an extraordinary conclufion in geometry ?
There is a famous tale of *Thomas Aquinas*, the angelical Doctor, and of *Bonaventure* the feraphical Doctor,
of whom *Alexander Hales* (our countryman and his
mafter) reports, whether it appeared not in him that
Adam had finned.   Both thefe great clerks being invited
to dinner by the *French* King, of purpofe to obferve
their humours, and being brought to the room where the
table

table was laid, the firſt fell a eating of bread as hard as
he could drive, at laſt breaking out of a brown ſtudy, he
cried out, *Conclusum eſt contra manichæos,* the other
fell a gazing upon the Queen, and the King aſked him
how he liked her, *Oh, Sir, if an earthly Queen be ſo
beautiful, what ſhall we think of the Queen of heaven?*
The latter was the better courtier of the two. Hence
we may infer, that your mere book-men, your deep
clerks, whom we call the only learned men, are not
always the civilleſt or beſt moral men: nor is too great a
number of them convenient for any ſtate, leading a ſoft
ſedentary life, eſpecially thoſe who feed their own fancies upon the public ſtock. Therefore it were to be
wiſhed that there reigned not among the people of this
land ſuch a general itching after book-learning; and I believe ſo many free-ſchools do rather hurt than good: nor
did the art of printing much avail the chriſtian commonwealth, but may be ſaid to be well near as fatal as gunpowder, which came up in the ſame age: for, under
correction, to this may be partly aſcribed that ſpiritual
pride, that variety of dogmatiſts which ſwarm among us.
Add hereunto, that the exceſſive number of thoſe which
converſe only with books, and whoſe profeſſion conſiſts
in them, is ſuch, that one cannot live for another, according to the dignity of the calling: a phyſician cannot
live for the phyſicians, a lawyer (civil and common)
cannot live for lawyers, nor a divine for divines. Moreover, the multitudes that profeſs theſe three beſt vocations, eſpecially the laſt, make them of far leſs eſteem.
There is an odd opinion among us, that he who is a contemplative man, a man who weds himſelf to ſtudy, and
ſwallows many books, muſt needs be a profound ſchol-
lar, and a great learned man, though in reality he be
ſuch a dolt, that he hath neither a retentive faculty to
keep what he hath read, nor wit to make any uſeful application of it in common diſcourſe; what he draws in
lieth upon dead lees, and never grows fit to be broached.
Beſides, he may want judgment in the choice of his authors, and knows not how to turn his hand either in
weighing

weighing .or winnowing the foundeſt opinions. ., There
are divers who are cried up for great clerks, who want
diſcretion.   Others though they wade deep into the
cauſes and knowledge of things, yet they are ſubject to
ſcrew up their wits, and ſoar ſo high, that they loſe
themſelves in their own ſpeculations ; for thinking to
tranſcend the ordinary pitch of reaſon, they come to in-
volve the common principles of philoſophy in a miſt : inſtead of illuſtrating things, they render them more ob-
ſcure : inſtead of a plainer and ſhorter way to the palace
of knowledge, they lead us through briery odd uncouth
paths, and ſo fall into the fallacy called *notum per igno-
tius.* Some have the hap to be termed learned men,
though they have gathered up but the ſcraps of knowledge here and there, though they be but ſmatterers and
mere ſcioliſts, ſcarce knowing the hoties of things ; yet
like empty caſks, if they can make a ſound, and have a
gift to vent with confidence what they have ſucked in,
they are accounted great ſcholars.   Amongſt all book-
learned men, except the divine, to whom all learned
men ſhould be lacqueys, the Philoſopher who hath waded through all the mathematicks, who hath dived into
the ſecrets of the elementary world, and converſeth alſo with celeſtial bodies, may be termed a learned man :
the critical hiſtorian and antiquary, may be called alſo a learned man, who hath converſed with our forefathers, and obſerved the carriage and contingencies of
matters paſſed, whence he draws inſtances and cautions
for the benefit of the times he lives in : the civilian may
be called likewiſe a learned man, if the revolving of huge
volumes may intitle one ſo ; but touching the authors of
the common law, which is peculiar only to this meridian, they *may be all carried in a wheel-barrow,* as my
countryman Dr. *Gwyn* told Judge *Finch :* the phyſician
muſt needs be a learned man, for he knows thimſelf inward and outward, being well verſed in autology, in that
leſſon *noſce teipſum ;* and as *Adrian* VI. ſaid, he is very
neceſſary for a populous country, for ' were it not for
' the phyſician, men would live ſo long and grow ſo
                                        ' thick,

' thick, that one could not live for the other; and he
' makes the earth cover all his faults.'

But what Dr. *Gwyn* said of the common law-books,
and Pope *Adrian* of the phyſician, was ſpoken, I conceive, in merriment: for my part, I honour thoſe two
worthy profeſſions in a high degree. Laſtly, a polyglot, or good linguiſt, may be alſo termed an uſeful learned man, eſpecially if verſed in ſchool-languages.

My Lord, I know none of this age more capable to
ſit in the chair, and cenſure what is true learning and
what is not, than yourſelf: therefore in ſpeaking of this
ſubject to your Lordſhip, I fear to have committed the
ſame error as *Phormio* did in diſcourſing of war before
Hannibal. No more now, but that I am, my Lord,

Your moſt humble and obedient ſervant,

J. H.

LETTER LXXVI.

To Doctor J. D.

S I R,

I Have many ſorts of civilities to thank you for, but a-
mong the reſt, I thank you a thouſand times (twice
told) for that delightful fit of ſociety, and conference of
notes we had lately in this *Fleet* cabin of mine upon divers problems, and upon ſome which are exploded, (and
that by thoſe who ſeem to ſway moſt in the commonwealth of learning) for paradoxes, merely by an implicit
faith, without diving at all into the reaſon of the aſſert-
ors. And whereas you promiſed a further expreſſion of
yourſelf by way of a diſcourſive letter, what you thought
of *Copernicus*'s opinion touching the movement of the
earth, which hath ſtirred all our modern wits; and
whereof Sir *J. Brown* pleaſed to oblige himſelf to do
the like touching the philoſopher's ſtone, the powder of
projection, and potable gold, provided that I would do

the

the fame concerning a peopled country, and a fpecies of
moving creatures in the concave of the moon; which I
willingly undertook upon thofe conditions.   To acquit
myfelf of this obligation, and to draw on your performances the fooner, I have adventured to fend you this
following difcourfe (fuch as it is) touching the lunary
world.

I believe it is a principle which not many will offer to controvert, that as *antiquity cannot privilege an*
error, fo novelty cannot prejudice truth.   **Now,** truth
hath her degrees of growing and expanding herfelf, as
all other things have; and as time begets her, fo he doth
the obftetricious office of of a midwife **to bring her** forth.
Many truths are but embrios or problems: **nay,** fome
of them feem to be mere paradoxes at firft.   The opinion that there were *Antipodes,* was exploded when it was
firft broached: it was held abfurd and ridiculous, and the
thing itfelf to be as impoffible as it was for men to go
upon their heads, with their heels upwards: nay, it was
adjudged to be fo dangerous a tenet, that you know well
the Bifhop's name, who in the primitive church was by
fentence of condemnation fent out of this world without
a head, to go and dwell amongft his *Antipodes,* becaufe
he firft hatched and held that opinion.   But now our
late navigators, and *Eaft-India* mariners, who ufe to
crofs the equator and tropicks fo often, will **tell** you,
that it is as grofs a paradox to hold there are **no** *Anti-*
podes, and that the negative is now as abfurd as the affirmative feemed at firft.   For men to walk upon the ocean
when the furges were at the higheft, and to make a
heavy dull piece of wood to fwim, nay, fly upon the
water, was held as impoffible a thing at firft, as it is now
thought impoffible for men to fly in the air: fails were
held then as uncouth, as if one fhould attempt to make
himfelf wings to mount up to heaven *à la volle.*   Two
hundred and odd years ago, he would have been taken
for fome frantic fool that would undertake to batter and
blow up a caftle with a few barrels of a fmall contemptible
black powder.

The great Architect of the world hath been obſerved not to throw down all gifts and knowledge to mankind confuſedly at once; but in a regular parſimonions method, to diſperſe them by certain degrees, periods, and progreſs of time, leaving man to make induſtrious reſearches and inveſtigations after truth: *He left the world to the diſputations of men,* as the wiſeſt of men ſaith, who in the acquiſition of natural truths went from the hyſſop to the cedar. *One day certifieth another,* and one age rectifieth another: the morrow hath more experience than the precedent day, and is oft-times able to be his ſcoolmaſter: the grandchild laughs at ſome things that were done in his grandſire's days; inſomuch, that hence it may well be inferred, that natural human knowledge is not yet mounted to its meridian, and higheſt point of elevation. I confeſs it cannot be denied without groſs ingratitude, but we are infinitely obliged to our forefathers for the fundamentals of ſciences; and as the herald hath a rule, *Mallem cum patribus quam cum fratribus errare; I had rather err with my fathers than brothers:* ſo it holds in other kinds of knowledge. But thoſe times which we term vulgarly the *old world,* was indeed the youth or adoleſcence of it; and though if reſpect be had to the particular and perſonal acts of generation, and to the relation of father and ſon, they who forelived and preceded us, may be called our anceſtors, yet if you go to the age of the world in general, and to the true length and longevity of things, we are more properly the older coſmopolites: in this reſpect the cadet may be termed more antient than his elder brother, becauſe the world was older when he entered into it. Moreover, beſides truth, time hath alſo another daughter, which is experience, who holds in her hands the great looking-glaſs of wiſdom and knowledge.

But now to the intended talk, touching an habitable world, and a ſpecies of living creatures in the orb of the moon, which may bear ſome analogy with thoſe of this elementary world: although it be not my purpoſe to maintain and abſolutely aſſert this problem, yet I will ſay

this,

this, that whofoever crieth it down for a new neoterical opinion, as divers do, commit a groffer error than the opinion may be in its own nature: for it is almoft as antient as philofophy herfelf; I am fure, it is as old as *Orpheus*, who fings of divers fair cities and caftles within the circle of the moon. Moreover, the profoundeft clerks and moft renowned philofophers in all ages have affirmed it. Towards the firft age of learning, among others, *Pythagoras* and *Plato* avouched it; the firft of whom was pronounced the wifeft of men by the *Pagan* oracle, as our *Solomon* is by holy write. In the middle age of learning *Plutarch* fpeaks of it; and in thefe modern times, the moft fpeculative and fcientificalleft men, both in *Germany* and *Italy* feem to adhere to it, fubinuating that not only the fphere of the moon is peopled with *Selenites* or lunary men, but that likewife every ftar in heaven is a peculiar world of itfelf, which is colonized and replenifhed with *Aftrean* inhabitants, as the earth, fea, and air, are with elementary; the body of the fun not excepted, who hath alfo his *Solar* creatures, and they are accounted the moft fublime, the moft pure, and perfecteft of all. The elementary creatures are held the groffeft of all, having more matter than form in them: the *Solar* have more form than matter; the *Selenites* with other *Aftrean* inhabitants, are of a mixed nature, and the nearer they approach the body of the fun, the more pure and fpiritual they are: were it fo, there were fome ground for his fpeculation, who thought that human fouls, be they never fo pious and pure, afcend not immediately after the diffolution from the corrupt mafs of the flefh before the glorious prefence of God, prefently to behold the beatifical vifion, but firft into the body of the moon, or fome other ftar, according to their degrees of goodnefs, and actuate fome bodies there of a purer compofition: when they are refined there, they afcend to fome higher ftar, and fo to fome higher than that, till at laft by thefe degrees they be made capable to behold the luftre of that glorious Majefty, in whofe fight no impurity can ftand. This is illuftrated

by

by a comparison, that if one after he hath been kept close in a dark dungeon a long time, should be taken out, and brought suddenly to look upon the sun in the meridian, it would endanger him to be struck stark blind; so no human soul suddenly sallying out of a dirty prison, as the body is, would be possibly able to appear before the incomprehensible Majesty of God, or be susceptible of the brightness of his all-glorious countenance, unless he be fitted thereunto beforehand by certain degrees, which might be done by passing from one star to another, who, we are taught differ one from the other in glory and splendor.

Among our modern authors that would furbish this old opinion of lunary creatures, and plant colonies in the orb of the moon with the rest of the celestial bodies, *Gasper Galileo Galilei* is one, who by artificial prospectives hath brought us to a nearer commerce with heaven, by drawing it sixteen times nearer earth than it was before in ocular appearance, by the advantage of the said optic instrument.

Among other arguments which the assertors of *Astrean* inhabitants do produce for proof of this high point, one is, that it is neither repugnant to reason or religion to think, that the almighty Fabricator of the universe, who doth nothing in vain, nor suffers his handmaid nature to do so, when he created the cratic and fixed stars, he did not make those huge immense bodies, whereof most are bigger than the earth and sea, though conglobated, to twinkle only, and to be an ornament to the roof of heaven; but he placed in the convex of every one of those vast capacious spheres some living creatures to glorify his name, among whom, there is in every one of them one supereminent, like man upon earth, to be Lord paramount of all the rest. To this haply may allude the old opinion, that there is a peculiar *intelligence* which guides and governs every orb in heaven.

They that would thus colonize the stars with inhabitants, do place in the body of the sun, as was said before, the purest, the most immaterial and refinedest in-

tellectual

tellectual creatures, whence the Almighty calls thofe he will have to be immediately about his perfon, and to be admitted to the hierarchy of angels. This is far diffo-nant from the opinion of the *Turk*, who holds that the fun is a great burning globe defigned for the damned.

They who are tranfported with this high fpeculation that there are manfions and habitable conveniencies for creatures to live within the bodies of the celeftial orbs, feem to tax man of a high prefumption, that he fhould think all things were principally created for him; that the fun and ftars are ferviceable to him in chief, *viz.* to meafure his days, to diftinguifh his feafons, to direct him in his navigations, and pour wholefome influences upon him.

No doubt they were created to be partly ufeful and comfortable to him; but to imagine that they are folely and chiefly for him, is a thought that may be faid to be above the pride of *Lucifer*: they may be beneficial unto him in the generation and increafe of all elementary crea-tures, and yet have peculiar inhabitants of their own be-fides, to concur with the reft of the world in the fervice of the Creator. It is a fair prerogative for man to be Lord of all terreftrial, aquatic, and airy creatures; that with his harping-iron he can draw afhore the great levia-than; that he can make the camel and huge dromedary, to kneel unto him, and take up his burden; that he can make the fierce bull though ten times ftronger than him-felf, to endure his yoke; that he can fetch down the eagle from his neft, with fuch privileges. But let him not prefume too far in comparing himfelf with heavenly bodies, while he is no other thing than a worm crawling upon the furface of this earth. Now the earth is the bafeft creature which God hath made, therefore it is called his *footftool;* and though fome take it to be the centre, yet it is the very fediment of the elementary world, as they fay the moon is of the celeftial: it is the very fink of all corruption and frailty; which made *Trif-megiftus* fay that *terra non mundus, eft nequitiæ locus;* the earth, not the world is the feat of wickednefs: and though,

though, it is true, she be fufceptible of light, yet the light terminates only in her fuperfices, being not able to enlighten any thing elfe, as the ftars can do.

Thus have I proportioned my fhort difcourfe upon this fpacious problem to the fize of an epiftle: I referve the fulnefs of my opinion in this point, till I receive yours touching *Copernicus*.

It hath been always my practice in the fearch and e-ventilation of natural verities, to keep to myfelf a philofophical freedom, as not to make any one's opinion fo magifterial and binding, but that I might be at liberty to recede from it upon more pregnant and powerful reafons. For as in theological tenets it is a rule; *Quicquid non defcendit a monte fcripturæ, eadem authoritate contemnitur; qua approbatur;* whatfoever defcends not from the mount of holy fcripture, may be by the fame authority rejected as well as received: fo in the difquifitions and winnowing of phyfical truths; *Quicquid non defcendit a monte rationis*, &c. whatfoever defcends not from the mount of reafon, may be as well rejected as approved of.

So longing after an opportunity to purfue this point by mixture of oral difcourfe, which hath more elbow room than a letter. I reft with all candour and cordial af-fection,

Your faithful fervant,

Fleet, Nov. 2. 1647.   J. H.

LETTER LXXVII.

To Mr. EN. P. *at Paris.*

S I R,

THAT which the plots of the jefuits in their dark cells, and the policy of the greateft roman catholic princes have driven at thefe many years, is now done to their hands, which was to divide and break the ftrength of thefe three kingdoms, becaufe they held it

to

to be too great a glory and power to be in one heretical Prince's hands, (as they efteemed the King of *Great Britain*) becaufe he was in a capacity to be umpire, if not arbiter of this part of the world, as many of our kings have been.

You write thence, that in regard of the fad condition of our Queen, their countrywoman, they are fenfible of our calamities; but I believe, it is the populace only, who fee no further than the rind of things: your cabinet-council rather rejoiceth at it, who, or I am much deceived, contributed much in the time of the late fanguine Cardinal, to fet a-foot thefe diftractions, beginning firft with *Scotland*, who, you know, hath always ferved that nation for a brand to fet *England* a-fire for the advancement of their own ends. I am afraid we have feen our beft days; we knew not when we were well; fo that the *Italian* faying may be well applied to poor *England*, I was well, I would be better, I took phyfic and died. No more now, but that I reft ftill

Yours entirely to ferve you,

Fleet, Jan. 20. 1647. J. H.

LETTER LXXVIII.

To Mr. W. B.

HOW glad was I, my choice and precious nephew, to receive yours of the 24th current; wherein I was forry, though fatisfied in point of belief, to find the ill fortune of interception which hefel my laft unto you.

Touching the condition of things here, you fhall underftand, that our miferies lengthen with our days; for though the fun and the fpring advance nearer us, yet our times are not grown a whit the more comfortable. I am afraid this city hath fooled herfelf into flavery: the army, though forbidden to come within ten miles of her by order of parliament, quarters now in the bowels
of

of her: they threaten to break her percullies, posts, and
chains, to make her pervious upon all occasions: they
have secured also the *Tower*, with addition of strength
for themselves: besides, a famine doth insensibly creep
upon us, and the mint is starved for want of bullion.
Trade, which was ever the sinew of this island, doth visibly decay, and the insurance of ships is risen from two
to ten in the hundred: our gold is ingrossed in private
hands, or gone beyond sea to travel without licence;
and much I believe of it is returned to the earth (whence
it first came) to be buried where our late nephews may
chance to find it a thousand years hence, if the world
lasts so long; so that the exchanging of white earth into
red, (I mean silver into gold) is now above six in the
hundred; and all these, with many more, are the dis-
mal effects and concomitants of a civil war.   It is true,
we have had many such black days in *England* in former
ages; but those paralelled to the present, are as the sha-
dow of a mountain compared to the eclipse of the moon.
My prayers early and late are, that God almighty would
please not to turn away his face quite, but chear us again
with the light of his countenance.   And I am well af-
sured you will join with me in the same orison to heaven's gate: in which confidence I rest

Yours most affectionately to serve you,

Fleet, Dec. 10. 1647.   J. H.

LETTER LXXIX.

To Dr. W. TURNER.

SIR,

I Return you my most thankful acknowledgments, for
that collection, or farrago of prophecies, as you
call them, (and that very properly, in regard there is a
mixture of good and bad) you pleased to send me lately,
especially that of *Nostredamus*, which I shall be very
chary

chary to preferve for you. I could requite you with divers predictions more, and of fome of the *Britifh* bards, which were they tranflated to *Englifh* would transform the world to wonder.

They fing of a *red* parliament and *white* King, of a race of people which fhould be called *Pengruns*, of the fall of the church, and divers other things which glance upon thefe times. But I am none of thofe that afford much faith to rambling prophecies, which (as we faid elfewhere) are like fo many odd grains fown in the vaft field of time, whereof not one in a thoufand comes to grow up again and appear above ground. But that I may correfpond with you in fome part for the like courtefy, I fend you thefe following prophetic verfes of *Whitehall*, which were made above twenty years ago, to my knowledge, upon a book called *Balaam*'s afs that confifted of fome invectives againft King *James* and the court *in ftatu quo tunc:* it was compofed by one Mr. *Williams* a Counfellor of the *Temple*, but a roman catholic, who was hanged, drawn, and quartered at *Charing-Crofs* for it; and I believe there be hundreds that have copies of thefe verfes ever fince that time about town yet living. They were thefe:

> Some feven years fince Chrift rid to court,
> And there he left his afs,
> The courtiers kicked him out of doors,
> Becaufe they had no * grafs.   * grace.
> The afs went mourning up and down,
> And thus I heard him bray,
> If that they could not give me grafs,
> They might have given me hay:
> But fixteen hundred forty three,
> Whofoe'er fhall fee that day;
> Will nothing find within that court,
> But only grafs and hay, &c.

which was found to happen true in *Whitehall*, till the foldiers coming to quarter there trampled it down.

Truly,

Truly Sir, I find all things conspire to make strange mutations in this miserable island: I fear we shall fall from under the sceptre to be under the sword; and since we speak of prophecies, I am afraid among others that which was made since the reformation will be verified, *The churchman was, the lawyer is, the soldier shall be.* Welcome be the will of God, who transvolves kingdoms, and tumbles down monarchies as mole-hills at his pleasure. So I rest, my dear Doctor,

Your most faithful servant,

Fleet, Aug. 9. 1648. J. H.

LETTER LXXX.

To the Honourable Sir EDWARD SPENCER *Knight, at his House near* Branceford.

S I R,

WE are not so bare of intelligence between these walls, but we can hear of your doings in *Branceford:* that so general applause whereby you were cried up Knight of the shire for *Middlesex,* sounded round about us upon *London* streets, and ecchoed in every corner of the town; nor do I mingle speech with any, though half affected to you, but highly approves of and congratulates the election, being glad that a gentleman of such extraordinary parts and probity, as also of such a mature judgment, should be chosen to serve the public,

I return you the manuscript you lent me of *Dæmonology,* but the author thereof and I are two in point of opinion that way; for he seems to be on the negative part, and truly, he writes as much as can be produced for his purpose. But there are some men that are of a mere negative genius, like *Johannes ad oppositum,* who will deny, or at least cross and puzzle any thing though never so clear in itself, with their *but, yet, if,* &c. they will slap the lie in truth's teeth though she visibly stand

before

before their face without any vizard: such perverfe crofs-
grained fpirits are not to be dealt withal by arguments,
but palpable proofs; as if one fhould deny that the fire
burns, or that he hath a nofe on his face: there is no
way to deal with him, but to pull him by the tip of the
one, and put his finger into the other. I will not fay
that this gentleman is fo perverfe; but to deny there are
any witches, to deny that there are ill fpirits which
feduce, tamper and converfe in divers fhapes with human
creatures, and impel them to actions of malice: I fay,
that he who denies there are fuch bufy fpirits, and fuch
poor paffive creatures upon whom they work, which commonly are called witches: I fay again, that he who denies there are fuch fpirits, fhews that he himfelf hath a
fpirit of contradiction in him, oppofing the current and
confentient opinion of all antiquity. We read that both
Jews and *Romans*, with all other nations of chriftendom,
and our anceftors here in *England*, enacted laws againft
witches: fure they were not fo filly as to wafte their
brains about chimeras, againft *non entia*, or fuch as
Plato's *Kterifmata*'s were. The judicial law is apparent
in the holy codex, *Thou fhalt not fuffer a witch to live:*
the *Roman* law which the *Decemviri* made, is yet extant
in the twelve tables, *Qui fruges incantaffent pœnis dan-
to;* They who fhall inchant the fruit of the earth let
them be punifhed. The imperial law is known by every
civilian; *Hi cum hoftes naturæ fint, fupplicio affician-
tur;* Thefe, meaning witches, becaufe they are enemies
to nature, let them be punifhed. And the acts of parliament in *England* are againft thofe ‘ that invoke ill fpi-
‘ rits, that take up any dead man, woman, or child, or
‘ take the fkin or bone of any dead body, to employ it
‘ to forcery or charm, whereby any one is lamed or made
‘ to pine away, *&c.* fuch fhall be guilty of flat felony,
‘ and not capable of clergy or fanctuary, *&c.*'
   What a multitude of examples are here in good authentic authors of divers kinds of fafcinations, incantati-
ons, preftigiations, of philtres, fpells, charms, forceries,
characters, and fuch like; as alfo of magic, necromancy,
and

and divinatiõs? Surely the witch of *Endor* is no fable;
the burning *Joan d'Arc* the maid of *Orleans* in *Rouen*;
and of the Marchionefs *d'Ancre* of late years in *Paris*, are no fables: the execution of *Noftredamus* for a
kind of witch, fome fourfcore years fince, is but a modern ftory, who among other things foretold, *Le fenat
de* Londres *tuera fon Roy;* The fenate of *London* fhall
kill their King.   The beft hiftorians have it upon record,
how *Charlemain's* miftrefs inchanted him with a ring,
which as long as fhe had about her, he would not fuffer
her dead carcafe to be carried out of his chamber to be
buried; and a Bifhop taking it out of her mouth, the
Emperor grew to be as much bewitched with the Bifhop;
but he being cloyed with his excefs of favour, threw it
into a pond, where the Emperor's chiefeft pleafure was
to walk till his dying day.   The ftory tells us, how the
Waldenfes in *France* were by folemn arreft of parliament
accufed and condemned of witchcraft.   The *Maltefes*
took St. *Paul* for a witch.   St. *Auguftin* fpeaks of women who could turn men to horfes, and make them carry
their burdens.   *Danaus* writes of an inchanted ftaff,
which the devil, fummoner like, was ufed to deliver
fome mercat-women to ride upon.   In fome of the
Northern countries, it is as ordinary to buy and fell
winds, as it is to do wines in other parts; and hereof, I
could inftance in fome examples of my own knowledge.
Every one knows what *Olaus Magnus* writes of *Erich*
(King of *Swethland's*) cornered cap, who could make
the wind fhift to any point of the compafs, according as
he turned it about.

Touching diviners of things to come, which is held a
fpecies of witchcraft, we may read they were frequent
among the *Romans;* yea, they had colleges for their augurs and arufpices, who ufed to make their predictions
fometimes by fire, fometimes by flying of fowls, fometimes by infpection into entrails of beafts, or invoking the
dead, but moft frequently by confulting with the oracles,
to whom all nations had recourfe except the *Jews*.   But
you will fay, that fince chriftianity difplayed her banners,

O o   the

the crofs hath feared away the devil, and ftruck the oracles dumb: as *Plutarch* reports a notable paffage of *Thamus* an *Italian* pilot, who, a little after the birth of Chrift, failing along the coafts of *Calabria* in a ftill filent night, all his paffengers being afleep, an airy cold voice came to his ears, faying, *Thamus, Thamus, Thamus, The great god* Pan *is dead*, who was the chiefeft oracle of that country. Yet though the light of the gofpel chafed away thofe great owls, there be fome bats and little night-birds that fly ftill abroad, I mean petty fpirits, that by fecret pactions, which are made always without witnefs, enable men and women to do evil. In fuch compacts beyond the feas, the party muft *firft renounce Chrift, and the extended woman, meaning the bleffed Virgin; he muft contemn the facrament, tread on the crofs, fpit at the hoft*, &c. There is a famous ftory of fuch a paction, which Frier *Louis* made fome half a hundred years ago with the devil in *Marfeilles*, who appeared to him in fhape of a goat, and promifed him the enjoyment of any woman whom he fancied, with other pleafures, for 41 years; but the devil being too cunning for him put the figure of 1 before, and made it 14 years in the contract, (which is to be feen to this day, with the devil's claw to it) at which time the Frier was detected for witchcraft, and burnt; and all thofe children whom he had chriftened during that term of fourteen years, were rebaptized: the gentlewomen whom he had abufed, put themfelves into a nunnery by themfelves. Hereunto may be added the great rich widow that was burned in *Lions*, becaufe it was proved the devil had lain with her; as alfo the biftory of Lieutenant *Jaquette*, which ftands upon record with the former; but, if I fhould infert them here at large, it would make this letter fwell too much.

But we need not crofs the fea for examples of this kind, we have too many (God wot) at home. King *James* a great while was loth to believe there were witches; but that which happened to my Lord *Francis* of *Rutland*'s children, convinced him, who were bewitched

witched by an old woman that was fervant at *Belvoir* caftle; but being difpleafed, fhe contracted with the devil, (who converfed with her in form of a cat, whom fhe called *rutterkin*) to make away thofe children out of mere malignity and thirft of revenge.

But fince the beginning of thefe unnatural wars, there may be a cloud of witneffes produced for the proof of this black tenet: for within the compafs of two years near upon 300 witches were arraigned, and the major part executed in *Effex* and *Suffolk* only: *Scotland* fwarms with them now more than ever, and perfons of good quality are executed daily.

Thus Sir, have I huddled together a few arguments touching this fubject, becaufe in my laft communication with you, methought I found you fomewhat unfatisfied, and ftaggering in your opinion touching the affirmative part of this thefis, the difcuffing whereof is far fitter for an elaborate large treatife than a loofe letter.

Touching the new commonwealth you intend to eftablifh now, that you have affigned me my part among fo many choice legiflators: fomething I fhall do to comply with your defires; which fhall be always to me as commands, and your commands as laws; becaufe I love and honour you in a very high degree for thofe gallant freeborn thoughts, and fundry parts of virtue which I have difcerned in you; which makes me intitle myfelf

Your moft humble and affectionate faithful fervant,

Eleet, Feb. 20. 1647. J. H.

LETTER LXXXI.

To R. K. *Efq; at St.* Giles.

S. I R,

DIFFERENCE in opinion, no more than a differing complexion, can be caufe enough for me to hate any. A differing fancy is no more to me than a

differing

differing face.   If another hath a fair countenance,
though mine be black; or if I have a fair opinion,
though another have a hard-favoured one, yet it shall
not break that common league of humanity, which should
be betwixt rational creatures, provided he corresponds
with me in the general offices of morality and civil up-
rightness: this may admit him to my acquaintance, and
conversation, though I never concur with him in opinion:
he bears the image of *Adam,* and the image of the Almighty as well as I: he had God for his father, though
he hath not the same church for his mother.   The om-
niscient Creator, as he is only kardiognostic, so he is the
sole Lord of the whole inward man: it is he who reigns
over the faculties of the soul, and the affections of the
heart: it is he who regulates the will, and rectifies all
obliquities in the understanding by special illuminations,
and oftentimes reconciles men as opposite in opinions, as
meridians and parallels are in point of extension, whereof the one draws from East to West, the other from
North to South.

Some of the *Pagan* philosophers, especially *Themi-
stius* who was Prætor of *Byzantium,* maintained an opinion, that as the pulchritude and preservation of the
world consisted in varieties and dissimilitudes, (as also in
eccentric and contrary motions) that as it was replenished
with such numberless sorts of several species, and that
the individuals of those species differed so much one
from the other, especially mankind, amongst whom one
shall hardly find two in ten thousand' that hath exactly
(though twins) the same tone of voice, similitude of
face, or ideas of mind; therefore, the *God of Nature*
ordained from the beginning, that he should be worship-
ped in various and sundry forms of adorations, which
nevertheless like so many lines should tend all to the
same centre.   But christian religion prescribes another
rule, *viz.* that there is but *una via, una veritas,* there
is but one true way to heaven, and that but a narrow
one; whereas there be huge roads that lead to hell.

God

' God almighty guide us in the firſt, and guard us from
the ſecond,' as alſo ' from all croſs and uncouth by-paths,
which uſe to lead ſuch giddy brains that follow them to
a confuſed labyrinth of errors; where being intangled,
the devil, as they ſtand gaping for new lights to lead
them out, takes his advantage to ſeize on them for their
ſpiritual pride,' and inſobriety in 'the ſearch of more
knowledge.'

Your moſt faithful ſervant,

July 28. 1648. J. H.

LETTER LXXXII.

To Mr. T. MORGAN.

SIR,

I Received two of yours upon *Tueſday* laſt, one to
your brother, the other to me; but the ſuperſcrip-
tions were miſtaken, which makes me think upon that
famous civilian Dr. *Dale*, who being employed to *Flanders* by Queen *Elizabeth*, ſent in a pacquet to the Secretary of State two letters, one to the Queen, the other
to his wife; but that which was meant for the Queen
was ſuperſcribed, *To his dear wife;* and that for his
wife, *To her moſt excellent Majeſty:* ſo that the Queen
having opened his letters, ſhe found it beginning with
ſweet heart, and afterwards with my *dear,* and *dear
love,* with ſuch expreſſions, acquainting her with the ſtate
of his body, and that he began to want money. You
may eaſily gueſs what motions of mirth this miſtake
raiſed, but the Doctor by this overſight (or cunningneſs
rather) got a ſupply of money. This perchance may be
your policy, to indorſe me your brother, thereby to endear me the more unto you; but you needed not to have
done that, for the name friend goes ſometimes further
than brother; and there be more examples of friends
that did ſacrifice their lives for one another, than of bro-

thers;

thers; which the writer doth think he fhould do for you, if the cafe required. But fince I am fallen upon Dr. *Dale,* who was a witty kind of drole, I will tell you inftead of news, (for there is little good ftirring now) of two other facetious tales of his; and familiar tales may become *familiar letters* well enough: when Queen *Elizabeth* did firft propofe to him that foreign employment to *Flanders,* among other encouragements, fhe told him, that he fhould have 20 s. *per diem* for his expences; then Madam, faid he, I will fpend 19 s. a day. What will you do with the odd fhilling, the Queen replied? I will referve that for my *Kate,* and for *Tom* and *Dick,* meaning his wife and children: this induced the Queen to enlarge his allowance. But this that comes laft is the beft of all, and may be called the fuperlative of the three; which was, when at the overture of the treaty, the other ambaffadors came to propofe in what language they fhould treat, the *Spanifh* Ambaffador anfwered, that the *French* was the moft proper, becaufe his miftrefs intitled herfelf *Queen of* France: nay then, faid Dr. *Dale,* let us treat in *Hebrew,* for your mafter calls himfelf King of *Jerufalem.*

I performed the civilities you enjoined me to your friends here, who return you the like contuplicated, and fo doth.

Your intire friend,

May 12.   J. H.

LETTER LXXXIII.

To the Lord Marquis of Hartford.

My LORD,

I Received your Lordfhip's of the 11th current, with the commands it carried, whereof I fhall give an account in my next. Foreign parts afford not much matter of intelligence, it being now the dead of winter, and

the

the feafon unfit for action; but we need not go abroad
for news, there is ftore enough at home. We fee daily
mighty things, and they are marvellous in our eyes;
but the greateft marvel is, that nothing fhould now be
marvelled at, for we are fo habituated to wonders, that
they are grown familiar unto us.

Poor *England* may be faid to be like a fhip toffed up
and down the furges of a turbulent fea, having loft her
old pilot; and God knows when fhe can get into fafe
harbour again: yet doubtlefs this tempeft, according to
the ufual operations of nature, and the fucceffion of
mundane effects by contrary agents, will turn at laft into
a calm, though many who are yet in their nonage may
not live to fee it. Your Lordfhip knows that this κόσμος,
this fair frame of the univerfe came out of a chaos, an
indigefted lump; and that this elementary world was
made of millions of ingredients repugnant to themfelves
in nature; and the whole is ftill preferved by the reluctancy and reftlefs combatings of thefe principles. We
fee how the fhipwright doth make ufe of knee-timber,
and other crofs-grained pieces as well as of ftraight and
even, for framing a goodly veffel to ride on *Neptune*'s
back. The printer ufeth many contrary characters in
his art, to put forth a fair volume; as d is a p reverfed,
and n is an u turned upward, with other differing letters,
which yet concur all to the perfection of the whole work.
There go many and various diffonant tones to make an
harmonious confort: this puts me in mind of an excellent paffage which a noble fpeculative Knight (Sir *P.
Herbert*) hath in his late conceptions to his fon: how a
holy anchoret being in a wildernefs, among other contemplations he fell to admire the method of providence,
how out of caufes which feem bad to us he often produceth good effects: how he fuffers virtuous, loyal and
religious men to be oppreffed, and others to profper.
As he was tranfported with thefe ideas, a goodly young
man appeared to him, and told him, ' Father, I know
' your thoughts are diftracted, and I am fent to quiet
' them; therefore if you will accompany me a few days,
' you

' you ſhall return very well. ſatisfied of thoſe doubts
' that now incumber your mind.' So going along with
him, they were to paſs over a deep river, whereon there
was a narrow bridge; and meeting there with another
paſſenger, the young man juſtled him into the water, and
ſo drowned him. The old anchoret being much aſtoniſhed hereat, would have left him, but his guide ſaid,
' Father, be not amazed, becauſe I ſhall give you good
' reaſons for what I do, and you ſhall ſee ſtranger things
' than this before you and I part, but at laſt I ſhall ſettle
' your judgment, and put your mind in full repoſe.' So
going that night to lodge in an inn where there was a
crew of banditti, and debauched ruffians, the young man
ſtruck into their company, and revelled with them till the
morning, while the anchoret ſpent moſt of the night in
numbering his beads; but as ſoon as they were departed
thence, they met with ſome officers who went to apprehend that crew of banditti they had left behind them.
The next day they came to a gentleman's houſe, which
was a fair palace, where they received all the courteous
hoſpitality which could be; but in the morning as they
parted, there was a child in a cradle, which was the only
ſon of the gentleman; and the young man ſpying his
opportunity, ſtrangled the child, and ſo got away. The
third day they came to another inn, where the man of
the houſe treated them with all the civility that could be,
and *gratis*; yet the young man embezzled a ſilver goblet, and carried it away in his pocket, which ſtill in-
creaſed the amazement of the anchoret. The fourth
day in the evening they came to lodge at another inn,
where the hoſt was very ſullen, and uncivil to them, ex-
acting much more than the value of what they had ſpent;
yet at parting, the young man beſtowed upon him the
ſilver goblet he had ſtoln from that hoſt who had uſed
them ſo kindly. The fifth day they made towards a
great rich town; but ſome miles before they came at it,
they met with a merchant at the cloſe of the day, who
had a great charge of money about him; and aſking the
next paſſage to the town, the young man put him in a
clean

clean contrary way. The anchoret and his guide being come to the town, at the gate they spied a devil, which lay as it were centinel, but he was asleep: they found also both men and women at sundry kinds of sports, some dancing, others singing, with divers sorts of revellings. They went afterwards to a convent of capuchins, where, about the gate they found legions of devils, laying siege to that monastery, yet they got in and lodged there that night. Being awaked the next morning, the young man came to that cell where the anchoret was lodged, and told him, ' I know your heart is full of horror, and your
' head full of confusion, astonishments, and doubts for
' what you have seen since the first time of our associati-
' on. But know, that I am an angel sent from heaven
' to rectify your judgment; as also to correct a little
' your curiosity in the researches of the ways and acts of
' providence too far: for though separately, they seem
' strange to the shallow apprehension of man, yet con-
' junctly they all tend to produce good effects.

' That man which I tumbled into the river, was an
' act of providence, for he was going upon a most mis-
' chievous design, that would have dammified not only
' his own soul, but destroyed the party against whom it
' was intended; therefore I prevented it.

' The cause why I conversed all night with that crew
' of rogues, was also an act of providence, for they in-
' tended to go a robbing all that night, but I kept them
' there purposely till the next morning, that the hand of
' justice might seize upon them.

' Touching the kind host from whom I took the silver
' goblet, and the clownish or knavish host to whom I gave
' it, let this demonstrate unto you, that good men are
' liable to crosses and losses, whereof bad men often-
' times reap the benefit; but it commonly produceth pa-
' tience in the one, and pride in the other.

' Concerning that noble gentleman whose child I
' strangled after so courteous entertainment, know, that
' that also was an act of providence; for the gentleman
' was

‘ was fo indulgent and doting on that child, that it
‘ leffened his love to heaven, fo I took away the
‘ caufe.

‘ Touching the merchant whom I mifguided in his
‘ way, it was likewife an act of providence; for had he
‘ gone the direct way to this town, he had been robbed,
‘ and his throat cut, therefore I preferved him by that
‘ deviation.

‘ Now concerning this great luxurious city, whereas
‘ we fpied but one devil which lay afleep without the
‘ gate, there being fo many about this poor convent, you
‘ muft confider, that *Lucifer* being already affured of
‘ that riotous town by corrupting their manners every
‘ day more and more, he needs but one fingle centinel
‘ to fecure it: but for this holy place of retirement, this
‘ monaftery inhabited by fo many devout fouls, who fpend
‘ their whole lives in acts of mortification, as exercifes
‘ of piety and penance, he hath brought fo many legions
‘ to belaguer them, yet he can do no good upon them,
‘ for they bear up againft him moft undauntedly, maugre
‘ all his infernal power and ftratagems.’ So the young
man or divine meffenger, fuddenly difappeared and vanifhed; yet leaving his fellow-traveller in good hands.

My Lord, I crave your pardon for this extravagancy,
and the tedioufnefs thereof; but I hope the fublimity of
the matter will make fome compenfation, which if I am
not deceived, will well fute with your genius; for I
know your contemplations to be as high as your condition, and as much above the vulgar. This figurative
ftory fhews that the ways of providence are infcrutable,
his intention and method of operation not conformable
oftentimes to human judgment, the plummets and line
whereof is infinitely too fhort to fathom the depth of his
defigns; therefore let us acquiefce in an humble admiration, and with this confidence that all things co-operate
to the beft at laft, as they relate to his glory, and the
general good of his creatures, though fometimes they
appear to us, by uncouth circumftances, and crofs me-
diums.

So in a due distance and posture of humility, I kiss your Lordship's hands, as being, my most highly honoured Lord,

Your-thrice obedient, and obliged servitor, J. H.

LETTER LXXXIV.

To Sir EDWARD SPENCER *Knight.*

SIR,

I Find by your last of the first current, that your thoughts are much busied in forming your new commonwealth : and whereas the province that is allotted to me is to treat of a right way to govern the female sex, I hold my lot to be fallen upon a fair ground, and I will endeavour to husband it accordingly. I find also, that for the establishment of this new republic, you have culled out the choicest wits in all faculties, therefore I account it an honour that you have put me in the list, though the least of them.

In every species of government, and indeed among all societies of mankind, (reclufed orders, and other regulars excepted) there must be a special care had of the female kind ; for nothing can conduce more to the propagation, and perpetuity of a republic, than the well managing of that gentle and useful sex ; for though they be accounted the weaker vessels, yet are they those in whom the whole mass of mankind is moulded, therefore they must not be used like saffron bags, or verde bottles which are thrown into some by-corner when the wine and spice are taken out of them.

It was an opinion truly befitting a *Jew* to hold, that woman is of an inferior creation to man, being made only for multiplication and pleasure ; therefore hath she no admittance into the body of the synagogue. Such another opinion was that of the *Pagan* poet who stuttered out
this

this verfe, that there are but two good hours of any
woman.

Τὴν μίαν ἰν θαλάμω, τὴν μίαν ἰν θανάτῳ: *Unam in thalamo,
alteram in tumulo;* one hour in bed, the other in the
grave.   Moreover, I hold alfo that of the orator to be
a wild extravagant fpeech, when he faid, that if *women
were not conterranean and mingled with men, angels
would defcend and dwell amongft us.*   But a far wilder
fpeech was that of the *Dog* philofopher, who termed
women, *neceffary evils.*   Of this cynical fect, it feems
was he, .ho would needs make *orcus* to be the anagram
of *uxor*, by contracting *c s* into an *x*, *uxor & orcus——
idem.*

Yet I confefs, that among this fex, as among men,
there are fome good, fome bad, fome virtuous, fome
vicious, and fome of an indifferent nature in whom virtue
makes a compenfation for vice.   If there was an Emprefs
in *Rome* fo cunning in her luft, that fhe would take in no
paffenger until the veffel was freighted, (for fear the te-
femblance of the child might difcover the true father):
there was a *Zenobia* in *Afia* who would not fuffer her
hufband to know her carnally no longer when once fhe
found herfelf quick.   If there was a Queen of *France*
that poifoned her King, there was a Queen in *England*,
who when her hufband had been fhot with an envenom-
ed arrow in the *Holy-Land*, fucked out the poifon with
her own mouth, when none elfe would do it.   If the
Lady *Barbara* wife to *Sigifmond* the Emperor, being
advifed by her ghoftly father after his death to live like
a *turtle*, having loft fuch a mate that the world had not
the like, made this wanton anfwer, *Father, fince you
would have me to lead the life of a bird, why not of a
fparrow, as well as a turtle?* which fhe did afterwards,
I fay, if there were fuch a Lady *Barbara*, there was the
Lady *Beatrix*, who after *Henry* her Emperor's death
lived after like a *dove*, and immurred herfelf in a monaftic
cell.   But what fhall I fay of Queen *Artemifia* who had
an urnful of her bufband *Maufolus*'s afhes in her clofet,
whereof fhe would take down a dram every morning
next

next her heart, faying, that her body was the fitteft place to be a fepulchre to her dear bufband, notwithftanding that fhe had erected fuch a tomb for the reftof his body, that to this day is one of the wonders of the world?

Moreover, it cannot be denied, but fome females are of a high and barfh nature; witnefs thofe two that of our greateft clerks for law and learning (Lord *B.* and *C.*) did meet withal, one of whom was faid to have brought back her hufband to his horn-book again: as alfo *Mofes* and *Socrates*'s wives, who were *Zipporah* and *Xantippe:* you may guefs at the humour of one in the holy code. The hiftory of the other is alfo well known.

But a thoufand fuch inftances are not able to make me a mifogenes, a female foe; therefore towards the polifh-ing and perpetuating of this your new republic, there muft be fome fpecial rules for regulating of marriage, for a wife is the beft or worft fortune that can betide a man throughout the whole train of his life. *Plato*'s pro-mifcuus concubitus or copulation is more proper for beafts than rational creatures. That inceftuous cuftom they have in *China*, that one fhould marry his own fifter, and in default of one, the next a kin, I utterly diflike: nor do I approve of that goatifh latitude of luft which the *alchoran* allows, for one man to have eight wives, and as many concubines as he can well maintain; nor of ano-ther branch of their law, that a man fhould marry after fuch an age under pain of mortal fin, (for then what would become of me?) No, I would have every man left at liberty in this point, for there are men enough be-fides to people the earth.

But that opinion of a poor fhallow-brained puppy, who upon any caufe of difaffection, would have men to have a privilege to change their wives, or repudiate them, de-ferves to be hiffed at rather then confuted; for nothing can tend more to ufher in all confufion and beggary throughout the world: therefore that wifeacre deferves of all others to wear a toting horn. In this republic one man fhould be contented with one wife, and he may have work enough to do with her; but whereas in other

common-

commonwealths men use to wear invisible horns, it would
be a wholesome constitution, that they who upon too much
jealousy and restraint, or ill usage of their wives; or, indeed not knowing how to use and man them aright, (which
is one of the prime points of masculine discretion,) as also
they who according to that barbarous custom in *Russia* do
use to beat their wives duly once a week ; but especially
they who in their absence coop them up and secure their bodies with locks : I say, it would be a very fitting ordinance
in this new moulded commonwealth, that all such who impel their wives by these means to do bad things, should
wear plain visible horns, that all passengers may beware
of them as they go along, and give warning to others,
——*Cornu ferit ille, caveto.* For indeed nothing doth
incite the mass of blood, and muster up libidinous thoughts
more than diffidence, and restraint.

Moreover, in coupling women by way of matrimony
it would be a good law, and consentaneous to reason, if
out of all dowries exceeding 100 *l.* there should be two
out of every *cent.* deducted and put into a common trea-
sury for putting off hard-favoured and poor maids.

Touching virginity and the vestal fire I could wish it
were the worst custom the *Roman* church had, when
gentle souls to endear themselves the more unto their
creator, do immure their bodies within perpetual bounds
of chastity, dieting themselves and using austerities accordingly; whereby, bidding a farewel, and dying unto the world, they bury themselves alive, as it were,
and so pass their time in constant exercises of piety, and
penance night and day, or in some other employments of
virtue, holding idleness to be a mortal sin. Were this
cloistered course of life merely spontaneous and unforced,
I could well be contented that it were practised in your
new republic.

But there are other kinds of cloyiers in some commonwealths, and among those who are accounted the
wisest and best policied, which cloisters are of a clean contrary nature to the former : these they call the courtesan
cloister. And as in others, some females shut up themselves

felves to keep the facred fire of pudicity and continence, fo in thefe latter there are fome of the handfomeft forts of females who are connived at to quench the flames of irregular luft, left they fhould break into the lawful married bed. It is true, nature hath poured more active, and hotter blood into the veins of fome men wherein there are ftronger appetites and motions, which motions were not given by nature to be a torment to man, but to be turned into delight, health and propagation. Therefore they to whom the gift of continence is denied, and have not the conveniency to have *debita vafa*, and lawful coolers of their own by way of wedlock, ufe to extinguifh their fires in thefe venerean cloifters, rather then abufe their neighbours wives, and break into other mens inclofures. But whether fuch a cuftom may be connived at in this your republick, and that fuch a common may be allowed to them who have no inclofures of their own, I leave to wifer legiflators than myfelf to determine, efpecially in South-Eaft countries where venerean titillation (which *Scaliger* held to be a fixed outward fenfe, but ridiculoufly) is in a ftronger degree, I fay, I leave others to judge whether fuch a rendezvous to be connived at in hotter climes, where both air, and food, and the blood of the grape do all concur to make one more libidinous, But it is a vulgar error to think that the heat of the clime is the caufe of luft: it proceeds rather from aduft choler and melancholy that predominate, which humours carry with them a falt and fharp itching quality.

The dull *Hollander* (with other North-Weft nations, whofe blood may be faid to be as butter-milk in their veins) is not fo frequently fubject to fuch fits of luft, therefore he hath no fuch cloifters or houfes for ladies of pleafure: witnefs the tale of *Hans Boobikin*, a rich boor's fon, whom his father had fent abroad a *fryaring*, that is, fhroving in our language, and fo put him in an equipage accordingly, having a new fword and fcarf, with a gold hatband, and money in his purfe to vifit handfome ladies; but *Hans* not knowing where to go elfe, went to his grandmother's houfe, where he fell a courting and feasting of her; but his father questioning him at his return where he had been a *fryaring*, and he answering that he had been at his grandmother's: the boor replied, God's sacrament, I hope thou haft not lain with my mother! yes, said *Boobikin*, why should not I ly with your mother, as you have lain with mine?

Thus in conformity to your desires, and the task imposed upon me, have I scribled out this piece of drollery, which is the way as I take it, that your design drives at: I reserve some things till I see what others have done in the several provinces they have undertaken towards the settlement of your new republic. So with a thousand thanks for your last hospitable favours, I rest as I have reason, and as you know me to be

Your own true servant,

London, *Jan.* 24.   J. H.

LETTER LXXXV.

To J. SUTTON, *Esq;*

S I R,

WHEREAS you desire my opinion of the late history translated by Mr. *Wad.* of the civil wars of *Spain*, in the beginning of *Charles* the Emperor's reign, I cannot chuse but tell you, that it is a faithful and pure maiden story, never blown upon before in any language but in *Spanish*, therefore very worthy your perusal: for among those various kinds of studies that your contemplative soul delights in, I hold history to be most fitting to your quality.

Now among those sundry advantages which accrue to a reader of history, one is, that no modern accident can seem strange unto him, much less astonish him: he will leave off wondering at any thing, in regard he may remember to have read of the same, or much like the same that happened in former times; therefore he doth
not

not ftand ftaring like a child at every unufual fpectacle, like that fimple *American*, who the firft time he faw a *Spaniard* on horfeback, thought the man and the beaft to be but one creature, and that the horfe did chew the rings of his bit, and eat them.

Now, indeed, not to be an hiftorian, that is, not to know what foreign nations, and our forefathers did, *Hoc eft femper effe puer*, as *Cicero* hath it, this is ftill to be a child who gazeth at every thing. Whence may be inferred, there is no knowledge that ripeneth the judgment, and puts one out of his nonage fooner than hiftory.

If I had not formerly read the barons wars in *England*, I had more admired that of the ligners in *France:* he who had read the near upon fourfcore years wars in *Low-Germany*, I believe he never wondered at the late wars in *High-Germany*. I had wondered more that *Richard* of *Bordeaux* was knocked down with halbards, had I not read formerly that *Edward* of *Carnarvon* was made away by a hot iron thruft up his fundament. It was ftrange that *Murat* the great *Ottoman* Emperor fhould be lately ftrangled in his own court at *Conftantinople*; yet confidering that *Ofman* his predeceffor had been knocked down by one of his ordinary flaves not many years before, it was not ftrange at all. The blazing ftar in *Virgo* thirty-four years fince did not feem ftrange to him who had read of that which appeared in *Caffiopeia* and other conftellations fome years before. Hence may be inferred, that hiftory is the great lookingglafs through which we may behold with anceftral eyes, not only the various actions of ages paffed, and the odd accidents that attend time, but alfo difcern the different humours of men, and feel the pulfe of former times.

This hiftory will difplay the very intrinficals of the *Caftilian*, who goes for the prime *Spaniard;* and make the opinion a paradox, which cries him up to be fo conftant to his principles, fo loyal to his prince, and fo conformable to government, for it will difcover as much levity, and tumultuary paffions in him as in other nations.

Among divers other examples which could be produced out of this ftory, I will inftance in one: when *Juan de Padillia* an infamous fellow, and of bafe extraction, was made General of the people, among others there was a Prieft, that being a great zealot for him, ufed to pray for him publickly in the church, ‘ Let us pray ‘ for the holy commonalty, and his majefty Don' *Juan* ‘ *de Padillia*, and for the Lady Donna *Maria Pachecho* ‘ his wife, *&c.*' But a little after fome of *Juan de Padillia*'s foldiers having quartered in his houfe, and pitifully plundered him, the next *Sunday* the fame Prieft faid in the church, ‘ Beloved chriftians, you know how ‘ *Juan de Padillia* paffing this way, fome of his brigade ‘ were billotted in my houfe: truly they have not left ‘ me one chicken, they have drunk up a whole barrel of ‘ wine, devoured my bacon, and taken away my *Catalina*, my maid *Kate;* I charge you therefore pray no ‘ more for him.' Divers fuch traverfes as thefe may be read in that ftory, which may be the reafon why it was fuppreffed in *Spain*, that it fhould not crofs the feas, or clamber over the *Pyreneans* to acquaint other nations with their foolery and bafenefs: yet Mr. *Simon Digby*, a gentleman of much worth, got a copy, which he brought over with him, out of which this tranflation is derived though I muft tell you by the by, that fome paffages were commanded to be omitted, becaufe they had too near an analogy with our times.

So in a ferious way of true friendfhip, I profefs myfelf,

Your moft affectionate fervant,

London Jan. 15.   J. H.

LETTER LXXXVI.

To the Lord Marquis of Dorcheſter.

My LORD,

THERE is a ſentence that carrieth a high ſenſe
with it, *viz. Ingenia principium fata temporum;*
The fancy of the Prince is the fate of the times: ſo in
point of peace or war, oppreſſion or juſtice, virtue or
vice, profaneneſs or devotion: for *Regis ad exemplum.*
But there is another ſaying which is as true, *viz. Genius
plebis eſt fatum Principis;* The happineſs of the Prince
depends upon the humour of the people. There cannot
be a more pregnant example hereof, than in that ſucceſs-
ful and long-lived Queen, Queen-*Elizabeth*, who having
come as it were from the ſcaffold to the throne, enjoyed
a wonderful calm, (excepting ſome ſhort guſts of inſur-
rection that happened in the beginning) for near upon
forty-five years together. But this, my Lord, may be
imputed to the temper of the people, who had had a
boiſterous King not long before, with ſo many revolutions in religion, and a minor King afterward, which made
them to be governed by their fellow-ſubjects. And the
fire and faggot being frequent among them in Queen
Mary's days, the humours of the common people were
pretty well ſpent, and ſo were willing to conform to any
government that might preſerve them and their eſtates in
quietneſs. Yet in the reign of that ſo popular and well-
beloved Queen, there were many traverſes which trench-
ed as much if not more upon the privileges of parliament, and the liberties of the people, than any that happened in the reign of the two laſt kings, yet it was not
their fate to be ſo popular. Touching the firſt, *viz.* parliament: in one of hers, there was a motion made in the
houſe of commons, that there ſhould be a lecture in the
morning ſome days of the week before they ſat, whereunto the houſe was very inclinable: the Queen hearing
of it ſent them a meſſage, that ſhe much wondered at
their

their rafhnefs, that they fhould offer to introduce fuch an innovation.

Another parliament would have propofed ways for the regulation of her court, but fhe fent them another fuch meffage, ' That fhe wondered, they being called by her
' thither to confult of public affairs, they fhould inter-
' meddle with the government of her ordinary family,
' and to think her to be fo ill an houfewife as not to be
' able to look to her own houfe herfelf.'

In another parliament there was a motion made, that the Queen fhould entail the fucceffion of the crown, and declare her next heir; but *Wentworth* who propofed it, was committed to the *Tower*, where he breathed his laft; and *Bromely* upon a lefs occafion was clapped in the *Fleet*.

Another time the houfe petitioning that fome lords might join in private committees with the commoners, fhe utterly rejected it. You know how *Stubbs* and *Page* had their hands cut off with a butcher's knife and a mallet, becaufe they wrote againft the match with the Duke of *Anjou;* and *Penry* was hanged at *Tyburn,* though *Allured* who wrote a bitter invective againft the late *Spanifh* match, was but confined for a fhort time: how Sir *John Heywood* was fhut up in the *Tower*, for an epiftle dedicatory to the Earl of *Effex,* &c.

Touching her favourites, what a monfter of a man was *Leicefter*, who firft brought the art of poifoning into *England?* How many of her maids of honour did receive claps at court? Add hereunto that privy-feals were common in her days, and preffing of men more frequent, efpecially for *Ireland,* where they were fent in handfuls, rather to continue a war, (by the cunning of the officers) than to conclude it. The three fleets fhe fent againft the *Spaniards* did hardly make the benefit of the voyages to countervail the charge. How poorly did the *Englifh* quit *Havre-de-Grace?* And how were we baffled for the arrears that were due unto *England* (by article) for the forces fent into *France?* For buildings, with all kind of braveries elfe that ufe to make a nation happy,

happy, as riches and commerce inward and outward, it was not the twentieth part fo much in the beft of her days, (as appears by the cuftom-houfe book) as it was in the reign of her fucceffors.

Touching the religion of the court, fhe feldom came to fermon, but in *Lent* time, nor did there ufe to be any fermon upon *Sundays*, unlefs they were feftivals: whereas, the fucceeding kings had two duly every morning, one for the houfhold, the other for themfelves, where they were always prefent, as alfo at private prayers in the clofet; yet it was not their fortune to gain fo much upon the affections of city or country. Therefore, my Lord, the felicity of Queen *Elizabeth* may be much imputed to the rare temper and moderation of mens minds in thofe days; for the pulfe of the common people and *Londoners*, did beat nothing fo high as it did afterwards when they grew pampered with fo long peace and plenty. Add hereunto, that neither *Hans*, *Jocky*; or *John Calvin*, had taken fuch footing here as they did g afterwards, whofe humour is to pry and peep with a kind of malice into the carriage of the court, and myfteries of ftate, as alfo to malign nobility, with the wealth and folemnities of the church.

My Lord, it is far from my meaning hereby to let drop the leaft afperfion upon the tomb of that rare tenowned Queen; but it is only to obferve the differing temper both of time and people. The fame of fome princes is like the rofe, which, as we find by experience, fmells fweeter after it is plucked: the memory of others is like the tulip and poppy, which make a gay fhew, and fair flourifh upon the ftalk, but being cut down, they give an ill-favoured fcent. It was the happinefs of that great long-lived Queen to caft a pleafing odour among her people both while fhe ftood, and after fhe was cut off by the common ftroke of mortality; and the older the world grows, the frefher her fame will be. Yet fhe is little beholden to any foreign writers, unlefs it be the *Hollanders;* and good reafon they had to fpeak well of her, for fhe was the chiefeft inftrument, who, though with

with the expence of much *English* blood and bullion, raised them to a republic, by casting that fatal bone for the *Spaniard* to gnaw upon, which shook his teeth so ill-favouredly for fourscore years together. Other writers speak bitterly of her for her carriage to her sister the Queen of *Scots*, for her ingratitude to her brother *Philip* of *Spain*; for giving advice by her Ambassador with the *Great Turk*, to expel the jesuits, who had got a college in *Pera*; as also that her Secretary *Walsingham* should project the poisoning of the waters of *Douay*; and lastly, how she suffered the festival of the nativity of the Virgin *Mary* in *September* to be turned to her own birth-day, &c. But these stains are cast upon her by her enemies; and the aspersions of an enemy use to be like the dirt of oisters, which doth rather cleanse than contaminate.

Thus my Lord, have I pointed at some remarks, to shew how various and discrepant the humours of a nation may be, and the genius of the times, from what it was; which doubtless must proceed from a high all-disposing power: a speculation that may become the greatest, and knowingest spirits, among whom your Lordship doth shine as a star of the first magnitude; for your house may be called a true academy, and your head the capitol of knowledge, or rather an exchequer, wherein there is treasure enough to give pensions to all the wits of the times. With these thoughts, I rest, my most highly honoured Lord,

Your ever obedient, and ever obliged servant,

Lond. Aug. 15.　　　　　　　　　　　J. H.

LETTER LXXXVII.

To the Right Honourable the Earl of Clare.

My LORD,

AMONG those high parts that go to make up a grandee, which I find concentred in your Lordship, one is, the exact knowledge you have of many languages,

guages, not in a superficial vapouring way, as some of
our gallants have now a-days, but in a most exact manner both in point of practice and theory. This induced
me to give your Lordship an account of a task that was
imposed lately upon me by an emergent occasion, touching the original, the growth, the changes, and present
consistence of the *French* language, which I hope may
afford your Lordship some entertainment.

There is nothing so incident to all sublunary things as
corruptions and changes: nor is it to be wondered at,
considering that the elements themselves, which are the
principles or primitive ingredients whereof they be compounded, are naturally so qualified. It were as easy a
thing for the spectator's eye to fasten a firm shape upon a
running cloud, or to cut out a garment that but for a
few days together might fit the moon, (who by privilege of her situation and neighbourhood, predominates
more over us than any other celestial body) as to find
stability in any thing here below.

Nor is this common frailty, or fatality rather, incident only to the grosser sort of elementary creatures, but
mankind, upon whom it pleased the Almighty to imprint
his own image, and make him as it were Lord paramount
of this lower world, is subject to the same lubricity of
mutation: neither is his body and blood only liable thereunto, but the ideas of his mind, and interior operation
of his soul, religion herself, with the notion of holiness,
and the formality of saving faith not excepted; nay, the
very faculty of reason (as we find it too true by late experience) is subject to the same instableness.

But to come to our present purpose, among other privileges which are peculiar to mankind, as emanations
flowing from the intellect, language is none of the least.
And languages are subject to the same fits of inconstancy
and alteration, as much as any thing else, especially the
French language: nor can it seem strange to those who
know the airy volatile humour of that nation, that their
speech should partake somewhat of the disposition of their
spirit, but will rather wonder it hath received no oftner
change,

change, especially considering what outward causes did also concur thereunto; as, that their kings should make six several voyages to conquer or preserve what was got in the *Holy-Land;* considering also how the *English* being a people of another speech, kept firm footing in the heart of *France.* Add hereunto the wars and weddings they had with their neighbours, which, by the long sojourn of their armies in other countries caused by the first, and the foreign courtiers that came in with the second, might introduce a frequent alteration: for languages are like laws or coins, which commonly receive some change at every shift of princes; or as slow rivers, by insensible alluvions take in and let out the waters that feed them, yet are they said to have the same beds; so languages, by a regardless adoption of some new words, and manumission of old, do often vary, yet the whole bulk of the speech keeps intire.

Touching the true antient and genuine language of the *Gauls,* some would have it to be a dialect of the *Dutch,* others of the *Greek,* and some of the *British* or *Welsh.* Concerning this last opinion, there be many reasons to fortify it, which are not altogether to be slighted.

The first is, that the antient *Gauls* used to come frequently to be instructed here by the *British* druids who were the divines and philosophers of those times, which they would not probably have done, unless by mutual communication they had understood one another in some vulgar language, for this was before the *Greek* or *Latin* came this side the *Alps,* or that any books were written, and there are no meaner men then *Tacitus* and *Cæsar* himself who record this.

The second reason is, that there want not good geographers who hold, that this island was tied to *Gallia* at first (as some say *Sicily* was to *Calabria,* and *Denmark* to *Germany*) by an *isthmus* or neck of land from *Calais* to *Dover;* for if one do well observe the quality of the cliffs on both shores, his eye will judge that they were but one homogeneal piece of earth at first, and that they

were

were flented and fhivered afunder by fome act of violence, as the impetuous waves of the fea.

The third reafon is, that before the *Romans* conquered the *Gauls*, the country was called *Wallia*, which the *Romans* called *Gallia*, turning *W* into *G*, as they did elfewhere: yet the *Walloon* keeps his radical letter to this day.

The fourth reafon is, that there be divers old *Gaulick* words yet remaining in the *French*, which are pure *Britifh*, both for fenfe and pronounciation, as *havre* a haven, which is the fame in *Welfh*, *derechef* again, *putaine* a whore, *arrain* brafs-money, *prou* an interjection of ftopping, or driving of a beaft; but efpecially, when one fpeaks any old word in *French* that cannot be underftood, they fay *il parle baragouin*, which is to this day in *Welfh*, white bread.

Laftly, *Paufanias* faith, that *Mark* in the celtick old *French* tongue fignifieth a horfe, and it fignifieth the fame in *Welfh*.

But though it be difputable whether the *Britifh*, *Greek*, or *Dutch* was the original language of the *Gauls*, certain it is that it was the *Walloon;* but I confine myfelf to *Gallia Celtica*, which when the *Roman* eagle had faftened his talons there, and planted twenty-three legions up and down the country, he did in tract of time utterly extinguifh: it being the ordinary ambition of *Rome*, wherefoever fhe prevailed, to bring in her language and laws with the lance; which yet fhe could not do in *Spain*, or this ifland, becaufe they had pofts and places of faftnefs to retire unto, as *Bifcay* and *Wales*, where nature hath caft up thofe mountains as propugnacles of defence, therefore the very aboriginal languages of both countries remain there to this day. Now *France* being a paffable and plain pervious continent, the *Romans* quickly diffufed and rooted themfelves in every part thereof, and fo co-planted their language, which in a fhort revolution of time came to be called *Roman;* but when the *Franco-zians*, a people of *Germany*, came afterwards to invade

Q q

and poſſeſs *Gallia*, both ſpeech and people was called *French* ever after, which is near 1300 years ſince.

Now as all other things have their degrees of growing, ſo languages have before they attain a perfection. We find that the *Latin* herſelf in the times of the *Sabines* was but rude; afterwards under *Ennius* and *Cato the* Cenſor it was refined in twelve tables; but in *Cæſar*, *Cicero*, and *Salluſt*'s time it came to the higheſt pitch of purity; and ſo dainty were the *Romans* of their language then, that they would not ſuffer any exotic or ſtrange word to be enfranchiſed among them, or enter into any of their *diplomata*, and public inſtruments of command, or juſtice. The word *emblema* having got into one, it was thruſt out by an expreſs edict of the ſenate; but *monopolium* had with much ado leave to ſtay in, yet not without a large preface and apology. A little after, the *Latin* tongue in the vulgarity thereof began to degenerate, and decline very much; out of which degeneration ſprang up the *Italian*, *Spaniſh* and *French*.

Now, the *French* language being ſet thus upon a *Latin* ſtock, hath received ſince ſundry habitudes, yet retaining to this day ſome *Latin* words intire, as *animal*, *cadaver*, *tribunal*, *non*, *plus*, *qui*, *os*, with a number of others.

Childeric, one of the firſt race of *French* kings commanded by public edict, that the four *Greek* letters Θ Χ Φ Ψ ſhould be added to the *French* alphabet to make the language more maſculine and ſtrenuous; but afterwards it was not long obſerved.

Nor is it a worthleſs obſervation, that languages uſe to comply with the humour, and to diſplay much the inclination of a people. The *French* nation is quick and ſpriteful, ſo is his pronounciation: the *Spaniard* is ſlow and grave, ſo is his pronounciation: for the *Spaniſh* and *French* languages being but branches of the *Latin* tree, the one may be called *Latin* ſhortened, and the other *Latin* drawn out at length; as *corpus*, *caput*, *tempus*, &c. are monoſyllables in *French*, as *corps*, *temps*, *caps*, or *chef*; whereas the *Spaniard* doth add to them, as *cuerpo*, *po, tiempo, cabeca*.   And indeed of any other the *Spaniard* affects long words, for he makes some thrice as long as they are in *French*, as of *levement*, arising, he makes *levantamiento;* of *compliment* he makes *complimento:* besides, the *Spaniard* doth use to pause in his pronounciation, that his tongue seldom fore-runs his wit, and his brain may very well raise a second thought before the first be uttered.   Yet is not the *French* so hasty in his utterance as he seems to be, for his quickness or volubility proceeds partly from that concatenation he useth among his syllables, by linking the syllable of the precedent word with the last of the following, so that sometimes a whole sentence is made in a manner but one word; and he who will speak the *French* roundly and well, must observe this rule.

The *French* language began first to be polished, and arrive to that delicacy she is now come unto, in the midst of the reign of *Philip de Valois*.   *Marot* did something under *Francis* I. (which King was a restorer of learning in general, as well as of language) but *Ronsard* did more under *Henry* II.   Since these kings there is little difference in the context of speech, but only in the choice of words, and softness of pronounciation, proceeding from such wanton spirits that did miniardize and make the language more dainty and feminine.

But to shew what changes the *French* hath received from what it was, I will produce these few instances in verse and prose, which I found in some antient authors: the first shall be of a gentlewoman that translated *Esop*'s fables many hundred years since out of *English* into *French*, where she concludes :

‘ Au finement de cest’ escrit
‘ Qu’en *Romans* ay tourne et dit ;
‘ Me nommer ay par remembrance,
‘ *Marie* ay nom je suis de *France ;*
‘ Per l’amour de conte *Guillaume*
‘ Le plus vaillant de ce royaume,
‘ M’ entremis de ce livre faire

' Et de *l'Anglois* en *Roman* traire,
' *Efope* appelle l'on cil livre,
' Qu'on tranflato et fit efcrire ;
' De *Griec* en *Latin* le tourna,
' Et le Roy *Alvert* qui l'ama,
' Le tranflata puis en *Angloiz*,
' Et je l'ay tourne en *Francois*.

Out of the *Roman de la Rofe* I will produce this example :

' Quand ta bouche toucha la moye,
' Ce fut dont au cœur jeus joye ;
' Sire juge, donnes fentence
' Par moy, car, la pucelle eft moye.'

Two of the moft antient and approvedeft authors in *French* are *Jeffrey de Villardovin* Marfhal of *Campagne*, and *Hugues de Berfy*, a Monk of *Clogny*, in the reign of *Philippe Augufte*, above 500 years fince : from them I will borrow thefe two enfuing examples, the firft from the Marfhal upon a *croifada* into the *Holy-Land*.

' Schachiez que l' an 1188 ans apres l'incarnation al
' temps *Innocent* III. apoftoille de *Rome*, et *Philippe*
' Roy de *France*, et *Richard* Roy *d'Engleterre* eut un
' Saint homme en *France*, qui et nom folque de nuilly, et
' il ere preftre, et tenoit le paroichre de la ville et ce
' folque commenca a parler de biex, et noftre fire fit ma-
' nits miracles par luy, *&c*.'

Hugues de Berfy who made the *Guiot* bible fo much fpoken in *France*, begins thus in verfe :

' D'oun fiecle puant et horrible
' M'e ftuet commencer une bible,
' Per poindre, et per ai guillonner
' Et per bons exemples donner,
' Ce n'ert une bible bifongere
' Ma' fine, et voire et droit uriere
' Mironer ert a toutis gens.'

If

If one would compare the *English* that was spoken in those times, which is about 560 years since, with the present, he should find a greater alteration.

But to know how much the modern *French* differs from the antient, let him read our common law, which was held good *French* in *William* the Conqueror's time.

Furthermore, among other observations, I find that there are some single words antiquated in the *French*, which seem to be more significant than those that are come in their places; as *maratre, paratre, filatre, serourge*, a step-mother, a step-father, a son or daughter-in-law, a sister-in-law, which now they express in two words, *belle mere, beau pere, belle sœur*. Moreover, I find there are some words now in *French* which are turned to a counterfense; as we use the *Dutch* word *crank* in *English* to be well-disposed, which in the original signifieth to be sick. So in *French*, *cocu* is taken for one whose wife is light, and hath made him a passive cuckold; whereas clean contrary, *cocu*, which is the cuckow, doth use to lay her eggs in another bird's nest. This word *pleiger* is also to drink after one is drunk unto; whereas the true sense of the word was, that if the party drunk unto was not disposed to drink himself, he would put another for a pledge to do it for him, else the party who began would take it ill. Besides, this word *abry* derived from the *Latin apricus* is taken in *French* for a close place or shelter, whereas in the original it signifieth an open free sun-shine. They now term in *French* a free boon companion, *roger bon temps*, whereas the original is, *rouge bon temps*, reddish and fair weather: they use also in *France*, when one hath a good bargain, to say, *Il a joue a boule veue*, whereas the original is *a bonne veue*. A beacon or watch-tower is called *beffroy*, whereas the true word is *l'effroy*: a travelling warrant is called *passeport*, whereas the original is *passe par tout*. When one is grown hoarse, they use to say, *Il a veu le loup*, he hath seen the wolf; whereas that effect of hoarseness is wrought in whom the wolf hath seen first, according to *Pliny*, and the poet,—*Lupi*

illum

illum videre priores. There is·another faying or proverb which is obfervable, whereby *France* doth confefs
herfelf to be ftill indebted to *England*, which is, when
one hath paid all his creditors, he ufeth to fay, *j' ay paye
tous mes anglois;* fo that in this, and other phrafes
anglois is taken for *craencier* or creditor; and I prefume
it had its foundation from this, that when the *French*
were bound by treaty in *Bretigny*, to pay *England* fo
much for the ranfom of King *John* then prifoner, the
contribution lay fo heavy upon the people that for many
years they could not make np the fum. The occafion
might be feconded in *Henry* VIII's time at the furrend-
ery of *Bullen*, and upon other treaties; as alfo in Queen
Elizabeth's reign, befides the monies which fhe had dif-
burfed herfelf to put the crown on *Henry* IV's head;
which makes me think on a paffage that is recorded in
Pafquier, that happened when the Duke of *Anjou* under pretence of wooing the Queen, came over into *England*, who being brought to her prefence, fhe told him,
' He was come in good time to remain a pledge for the
' monies that *France* owed her father; and other of her
' progenitors;' whereunto the Duke anfwered, ' That he
' was come not only to be a pledge, but her clofe pri-
' foner.'

There be two other fayings in *French*, which though
they be obfolete, yet are they worthy the knowledge:
the firft is, *Il a perduc fes cheveux*, he hath loft his hair,
meaning his honour: for in the firft race of kings there
was a law called, *La loy de la cheveleure*, whereby it
was lawful for the *noblefle* only to wear long hair, and if
any of them had committed fome foul and ignoble act,
they ufed to be condemned to have their long hair to be
cut off as a mark of ignominy; and it was as much as if
he had been *flouerdelized*, viz. burnt on the back or
hand, or branded in the face.

The other proverb is, *Il a quitté fa cienture*, he hath
given up his girdle, which intimated as much as if he had
become bankrupt, or had all his eftate forfeited: it being
the antient law of *France*, that when any upon fome offence

fence had that penalty of confiscation inflicted upon him, he used before the tribunal of juftice to give up his girdle, implying thereby, that the girdle held every thing that belonged to a man's eftate, as his budget of money and writings, the key of his houfe, with his fword, dagger, and gloves, &c.

I will add hereunto another proverb which had been quite loft, had not our order of the garter preferved it; which is, *Hony foit qui mal y penfe;* this we *Englifh, Ill to him who thinks ill,* though the true fenfe be, *Let him be bewrayed who thinks any ill:* being a metaphor taken from a child that hath bewrayed his clouts; and I dare fay, there is not one of a hundred in *France* who underftands this word now a-days.

Furthermore, I find in the *French* language, that the fame fate hath attended fome *French* words, as ufually attend men, among whom fome rife to preferment, others fall to decay and an undervalue. I will inftance in a few: this word *maiftre* was a word of high efteem in former times among the *French,* and appliable to noblemen, and others in high office only; but now it is fallen from the Baron to the boor, from the Count to the cobler, or any other artifan; as *Maiftre* jean *le fauvetier,* Mr. *John* the cobler; *Maiftre* jaquet *le cabaretier,* Mr. *Jammy* the tapfter.

Sire was alfo appropriate only to the King: but now, adding a name after it, it is appliable to any mean man upon the indorfement of a letter or otherwife; but this word *fouverain* hath raifed itfelf to that pitch of greatnefs, that it is applied now only to the King, whereas in times paffed, the prefident of any court, any bailiff or fenefhal, was ufed to be called *fouverain.*

Marefhal likewife was at firft the name of a fmith, farrier, or one that dreffed horfes; but it is climbed by degrees to that height, that the chiefeft commanders of the gendarmery and militia of *France* are come to be called *marfhals,* which about 100 years fince were but two in all, whereas now they are twelve.

The

The title *majesty* hath no great antiquity in *France*, for it began in *Henry* II's time. And indeed the ftyle of *France* at firft as well as of other countries, was to *tutoyer*, that is, to thou any perfon that one fpake unto, though never fo high: but when the commonwealth of *Rome* turned to an empire, and fo much power came into one man's hand, then, in regard he was able to confer honour, and offices, the courtiers began to magnify him, and treat him in the plural number by *tou*, and by degrees to deify him by tranfcending titles; as we read in *Symmachus*, in his epiftles to the Emperor *Theodofius*, and to *Valentinian*, where his ftyle to them is, *Veftra æternitas, veftrum numen, veftra perenitas, veftra clementia;* fo that *you* in the plural number, with other compliments and titles, feem to have their firft rife with the Weftern monarchy, which afterwards by degrees defcended upon particular perfons.

The *French* tongue hath divers dialeɛts, *viz.* the *Picardy*, that of *Jerfey* and *Guernfey*, appendixes once of *Normandy*; the *Provenfal*, the *Gafcon*, or the fpeech of *Languedoc*, which *Scaliger* would etymologize from *Langue d'ouy*, whereas it comes truly from *Langue de got*, in regard the *Goths* and *Saracens*, who by their incurfions and long ftay in *Aquitain*, firft corrupted the fpeech of *Gallia :* the *Walloon* is another dialeɛt, which is under the King of *Spain:* they alfo of *Liege* have a dialeɛt of the *French*, which among themfelves they call *Roman* to this day.

Touching the modern *French* that is fpoken now in the King's court, the court of parliament, and in the univerfities of *France*, there hath been lately a great competition which was the beft; but by the learnedeft, and moft indifferent perfons, it was adjudged that the ftyle of the King's court was the pureft and moft elegant, becaufe the other two did fmell, the one of pedantry, the other of chicanery. And the late Prince of *Conde*, with the Duke of *Orleans* that now is, were ufed to have a cenfor in their houfes, that if any of their family fpoke any
word

word that favoured of the palace or the schools, he should incur the penalty of an amercement.

The late Cardinal *Richlieu* made it part of his glory to advance learning, and the *French* language. Among other monuments he erected an university where the sciences should be read and disputed in *French* for the ease of his countrymen, whereby they might presently fall to the matter, and not spend time to study words only.

Thus have I presumed to send your Lordship a rambling discourse of the *French* language passed and present, humbly expecting to be corrected when you shall please to have perused it. So, I subscribe myself

‣ *Your Lordship's thrice obedient servant,*

London, Oct. 1.   J. H.

LETTER LXXXVIII.

To Sir J. Tho. *Knight.*

SIR,

THERE is no request of yours but is equivalent to a command with me; and whereas you crave my thoughts touching a late history published by one Mr. *Wilson*, which relates the life of King *James*, though I know for many years your own judgment to be strong and clear enough of itself, yet to comply with your desires, and for to oblige you that way another time to me, I will deliver you my opinion.

I cannot deny but the thing is a painful piece, and proceeds after a handsome method, in drawing on the series and head of the story; but it is easily discernable, that a partial presbyterian vein goes constantly throughout the whole work, and you know it is the genius of that people to pry more than they should into the courts and comportments of princes, and take any occasion to traduce and bespatter them: so doth this writer, who endeavours all along (among other things) to make the world believe

that

that King *James* and his fon after him were inclined to
popery, and to bring it into *England*; whereas I dare a-
vouch, that neither of them entertained the leaft thought
that way, they had as much defign to bring in *Prefter-
John* as the Pope, or *Mahomet* as foon as the mafs.
This conceit made the writer to be fubject to many grofs
miftakes and mifreprefentations, which fo fhort a circuit
as a letter cannot comprehend.

Yet I will inftance in one grofs miftake he hath in relating a paffage which concerns Sir *Elias Hicks*, a worthy
Knight, and a fellow-fervant of yours and mine. And
he doth not only mifreprefent the bufinefs, but he foully
afperfeth him with the terms of unworthinefs and infamy. The truth of that paffage is as followeth, and I
had it from very good hands.

In the year, 1621. the *French* King making a general
war againft them of the religion, beleaugered *Montauban* in perfon, while the Duke of *Efpernon* blocked up
Rochel. The King having lain a good while before the
town, a cunning report was raifed that *Rochel* was fur-
rendered: this report being blown into *Montauban*, muft
needs difhearten them of *Rochel*, being the prime and
tenableft propugnacle they had: Mr. *Hicks* happened to
be then in *Rochel*, being commended by Sir *George Goring*
to the Marquis *de la Force*, who was one of them that
commanded in chief, and treated Mr. *Hicks* with much
civility, fo far that'he took him to be one of his domeftic attendants. The *Rochellers* had fent two or
three fpecial envoys to *Montauban* to acquaint them
with their good condition, but it feems they all mifcarried; and the Marquis being troubled in his thoughts one
day, Mr. *Hicks* told him, that by God's favour he would
undertake and perform the fervice to *Montauban*: hereupon he was put accordingly in equipage; fo after ten
days journey, he came to a place called *Moyfak*, where
my Lord of *Doncafter*, afterwards Earl of *Carlifle*, was in
quality of Ambaffador from *England*, to obferve the
French King's proceedings, and to mediate a peace betwixt
him and the proteftants. At his firft arrival thither, it
was

was his good hap to meet cafually with Mr. *Peregrin Fairfax*, one of the Lórd Ambaffador's retinue, who had been a former comrade of his : among other civilities he brought Mr. *Hicks* to wait upon the Ambaffador, to whom he had credential letters from the affembly of *Rochel*, acquainting his Lordfhip with the good ftate they were in : Mr. *Hicks* told him befides that he was engaged to go to *Montauban* as an envoy from *Rochel*, to give them true information how matters ftood. The Ambaffador replied, that it was too great a truft to put upon fo young fhoulders : fo Mr. *Hicks* being upon going to the *French* army which lay before *Montauban*, Mr. *Fairfax* would needs accompany him thither to fee the trenches and works; being come thither, they met with one Mr. *Thomas Webb* that belonged to the Marfhal St. *Gerand*, who lodged them both in his own hut that night ; and having fhewed them the batteries and trenches the day after, Mr. *Hicks* took notice of one place which lay moft open for his defign, refolving with himfelf to pafs that way to the town. He had told *Fairfax* of his purpofe before, who difcovering it to *Webb*, *Webb* afked him whether he came thither to be hanged ; for divers were ufed fo a little before. The next day *Hicks* taking his leave of *Webb*, defired *Fairfax* to ftay behind, which he refufing, did ride along with him to the place which *Hicks* had pointed out the day before for his defign, and there *Fairfax* left him. So having got betwixt the *Corps de gard* and the town, he put fpurs to his horfe, and waving his piftol about his head, got in, being purfued almoft to the walls of the town by the King's party : being entered, old Marfhal *de la Force* who was then in *Montauban* having heard his relations of *Rochel*, fell on his neck and wept, faying, that he would give 1000 crowns he were as fafely got back to *Rochel* as he came thither ; and having ftaid there three weeks, he, in a fally that the town made one evening, got clear through the leaguer before *Montauban*, as he had formerly done before that of the Duke of *Efpernon*, and fo recovered *Rochel* again. But to return to Mr. *Fairfax*, after he had parted with

Mr.

Mr. *Hicks* he was taken prisoner, and threatened the rack, but whether out of the apprehension thereof, or otherwise, he died a little after of a fever at *Moysac;* though it is true that the *gazettes* in *Paris* did publish that he died of the torture, with the *French* mercury since.

Mr. *Hicks* being returned to *London*, was questioned by Sir *Ferdinando Fairfax* for his brother's death: thereupon Mr. *Webb* being also come back to *London*, who was upon the very place where these things happened in *France*, Mr. *Hicks* brought him along with him to Sir *Ferdinand*'s lodgings, who did positively affirm, that Mr. *Hicks* had communicated his design to Mr. *Peregrin Fairfax*, and that he revealed it first to him; so he did fairly vindicate Mr. *Hicks*, wherewith Sir *Ferdinand* remained fully satisfied, and all his kindred.

Whosoever will observe the carriage and circumstance of this action, will needs confess that Mr. *Hicks* (now Sir *Elias Hicks*) did comport himself like a worthy gentleman from the beginning to the end thereof: the design was generous, the conduct of it discreet, and the conclusion very prosperous, in regard it preserved both *Montauban* and *Rochel* for that time from the fury of the enemy; for the King raised his siege a little after from before the one, and *Espernon* from the other. Therefore it cannot be denied but that the said writer (who so largely intitles his book the *History of* Great Britain, though it be but the particular reign of King *James* only) was very much to blame for branding so well a deserving gentleman with infamy and unworthiness, which are the words he pleaseth to bestow upon him; and I think he would willingly recant and retract his rash censure were he now living, but death pressed him away before the press had done with his book, whereof he may be said to have died in child-bed.

So presenting herewith unto you my hearty respects and love, endeared and strengthened by so long a tract of time, I rest,

Your faithful true servant,

London, *Nov.* 9. J. H.

L E T-

L E T T E R LXXXIX.

To J. Anderson, *Esq;*

S I R,

YOU have been often at me (though I know you to be a proteftant fo in grain, that all the water of the *Tyber* is not able to make you change colour) that I fhould impart to you in writing what I obferved commendable and difcommendable in the *Roman* church, becaufe I had eaten my bread often in thofe countries where that religion is profeffed and practifed in the greateft height. Touching the fecond part of your requeft, I need not fay any thing to it, for there be authors enough of our church to inform you about the pofitions and tenets wherein we differ, and for which we blame them. Concerning the firft part, I will give you a fhort intimation what I noted to be praife worthy and imitable in point of practice.

The government of the *Roman* church is admirable, being moulded with as much policy as the wit of man can reach unto; and there muft be civil policy as well as ecclefiaftical ufed to keep fuch a world of people of feveral nations and humours in one religion: though at firft when the church extended but to one chamber, then to one houfe, after to one parifh, then to one province, fuch policy was not fo requifite. For the church of Chrift may be compared to his perfon in point of degrees of growing; and as that coat which ferved him in his childhood could not fit him in his youth, nor that of his youth when he was come to his manhood, no more would the fame government (which compared to the fundamentals of faith, that are ftill the fame, are but as outward garments) fit all ages of the church, in regard thofe millions of accidents that ufe to attend time, and the mutable humours of men: infomuch that it was a wholefome caution of an antient father, *Diftinguas inter tempora, & concordabis*

R r *cum*

cum scriptura. This government is like a great fabr
reared up with fuch exact rules of art and architectur
that the foundation, the roof, fides, and angles, wi
all the other parts, have fuch a dependance of mutu
fupport by a rare contignation, concinnity, and inden
ings one in the other, that if you take but out one fton
it hazards the downfall of the whole edifice. Th
makes me think that the church of *Rome* would be co
tent to part with, and rectify fome things, if it mig
not endanger the ruin of the whole; which puts t
world in defpair of an oecumenical council again.

The uniformity of this fabric is alfo to be admire
which is fuch as if it were but one intire continued h
mogeneous piece: for put cafe a *Spaniard* fhould go
Poland, and a *Pole* fhould travel to the furtheft part
Spain, whereas all other objects may feem ftrange-
them in point of lodging, language and diet, though t
complexion and faces, the behaviour, garb, and ga
ments of men, women and children, be differing, tog
ther with the very air and clime of the place; though
things feem ftrange unto them, and fo fomewhat u
comfortlefs, yet when they go to God's houfe in eith
country, they may fay they are there at home: for n
thing differs there either in language, worfhip, fervic
or ceremony; which muft needs be an unfpeakable co
fort to either of them.

Thirdly, it muft needs be a commendable thing th
they keep their churches fo cleanly and amiable, for th
dwellings of the Lord of hofts fhould be fo: to whic
end your greateft ladies will rife before day fometim
in their night-cloaths to fall a fweeping fome part of th
church, and decking it with flowers, as I heard Cou
Gondomar's wife ufed to do here at *Ely-houfe* chapel
befides, they keep them in conftant repair, fo that if b
a quarry of glafs chance to be broken, or the leaft ftor
be out of fquare, it is prefently mended. Moreove
their churches ftand wide open early and late, inviting
it were all comers, fo that a poor troubled foul ma
have accefs thither at all hours to breath out the pantin

of his heart, and the ejaculations of his foul either in prayer or praife : nor is there any exception of perfons in their churches, for the cobler will kneel with the Count, and the laundrefs gig by geoul with her Lady, there being no pews there to caufe pride and envy, contention and quarrels which are fo rife in our churches.

The comely proftrations of the body, with genuflection, and other acts of humility in time of divine fervice is very exemplary. Add hereunto, that the reverence they fhew to the holy function of the church is wonderful ; princes and queens will not difdain to kifs a capuchin's fleeve, or the furplice of a Prieft : befides, I have feen the greateft and beautifulleft young ladies go to hofpitals, where they not only drefs, but lick the fores of the fick.

Furthermore, the conformity of feculars, and refignment of their judgments to the governors of the church is remarkable. There are not fuch fcepticks and cavillers there as in other places ; they humbly believe that *Lazarus* was three days in the grave, without queftioning where his foul was all the while ; nor will they expoftulate how a man that was born blind from his nativity fhould prefently know the fhapes of trees, whereunto he thought the firft men he ever faw were like, after he received fight. Add hereunto, that they efteem for church preferments molt commonly a man of a pious good difpofition, of a meek fpirit, and godly life, more than a learned man, that is either a great linguift, antiquary, or philofopher ; and the firft is advanced fooner than the latter.

Laftly, they think nothing too good or too much for God's houfe or for his minifters, no place too fweet, no building too ftately for them, being of the beft profeffion. The molt curious artifts will employ the beft of their fkill to compofe hymns, and anthems for God's houfe, &c.

But, methinks I hear you fay, that you acknowledge all this to be commendable, were it not that it is accompanied with an odd opinion that they think to merit thereby, accounting them works of *fupererogation*.

Truly

Truly Sir, I have difcourfed with the greateft' mag-nifiers of meritorious works ; and the chiefeft of them, made me this comparifon, that the blood of Chrift is like a great veffel of wine, and all the merits of men whether active or paffive, were it poffible, muft be put into that great veffel, and fo muft needs be made wine ; not that the water hath any inherent virtue of itfelf to make itfelf fo, but as it receives it from the wine.

It is reported of *Cofmo de Medici*, that having built a goodly church with a monaftery thereunto annexed, and two hofpitals, with other monuments of piety, and en-dowed them with large revenues ; as one did much mag-nify him for thefe extraordinary works, for which doubt-lefe he merited a high reward in heaven, he anfwered, ' It is true, I employed much treafure that way, yet when ' I look over my leger-book of accompts, I do not find ' that God almighty is indebted to me one penny, but I' ' ftill in the arrear to him.'

Add hereunto, the fundry ways of mortification they have by frequent long faftings, and macerations of the flefh, by their retirednefs, their abandoning the world, and fequeftrations from all mundane affairs ; their notable humility in the diftribution of their alms, which they do not ufe to hurl away in a kind of fcorn as others do, but by putting it gently into the beggar's hand.

Some fhallow-pated puritan in reading this, will fhoot his bolt, and prefently cry me up to have a Pope in my belly ; but you know me otherwife, and there is none knows my intrinfecals better then you. We are come to fuch times, that if any would maintain thofe decencies, and humble poftures, thofe folemnities and rites which fhould be practifed in the holy houfe of God, (and holi-nefs becomes his houfe for ever) nay, if one paffing through a church fhould put off his hat, there is, a giddy and malignant race of people (for indeed they are the true malignants) who will give out that he is running poft to *Rome ;* notwithftanding that the religion eftablifhed by the laws of *England* did ever allow of them ever fince the reformation began, yet you know how few have run

thither.

thither. Nay, the *Lutherans* who ufe far more cere-monies fymbolizing with thofe of *Rome*, then the *Eng-ifh* proteftants ever did, keep ftill their diftance, and are as far from her now as they were at firft.

England had lately (though to me it feems a great while fince) the face and form, the government and gravity, the conftitutions and comelinefs of a church: for fhe had fomething to keep herfelf handfome; fhe had wherewith to be hofpitable, and do deeds of charity, to build *alms-houfes*, *free-fchools*, and *colleges*, which had been very few in this ifland, had there been no church-benefactors: fhe had brave degrees of promotion to induftry, and certainly the conceit of honour is a great encouragement to virtue. Now, if all profeffions have fteps of rifing, why fhould divinity the beft of all profeffions, be without them? The *apprentice* doth not think it much to wipe his mafter's fhoes, and fweep the gutters, becaufe he hopes to be an Alderman: the common foldier carrieth hopes in his knapfack to be one day a Captain, or Colonel: the ftudent in the inns of courts turns over *Ployden* with more alacrity, and tugs with that crabbed ftudy of the law; becaufe he hopes one day to be a judge; fo the fcholar thought his labour fweet, becaufe he was buoyed up with hopes that he might be one day a Bifhop, Dean, or Canon. This comely fubordination of degrees we once had, and we had a vifible confpicuous church, to whom all other reformifts gave the upper-hand; but now fhe may be faid to have crept into corners, and fallen to fuch a contempt that fhe dares fcarce fhow her face. Add hereunto, in what various kinds of confufions fhe is involved; fo that it may be not improperly faid, while fhe thought to run away fo eagerly from *Babylon*, fhe is fallen into a babel of all opinions: infomuch that they who came lately from *Italy* fay, how *Rome* gives out, that when religion is loft in *England*, fhe will be glad to come to *Rome* again to find one out, and that fhe danceth all this while in a circle.

Thus have I endeavoured to fatisfy your importunity as far as a fheet of paper could reach, to give you a

touch

touch what may be not only allowable but laudable, and consequently imitable in the *Roman* church: for

——*Fas eft et ab hofte doceri.*

But I defire you would expound all with the *fane fenfe*, wherewith I know you abound; otherwife I would not be fo free with you upon this ticklifh fubject: yet I have caufe to queftion your judgment in one thing, becaufe you magnify fo much my talent in your laft. Alas, Sir, a fmall handkerchief is enough to hold mine, whereas a large table-cloth can hardly contain that rich talent which I find God and nature hath intrufted you withal : in which opinion I reft always

Your ready and real fervant

London, July 3. **J. H.**

L E T T E R XC.

To the truly Honourable the Lady SYBILLA BROWN *at her Houfe near* Sherburn.

Madam,

WHEN I had the happinefs to wait upon you at your being in *London*, there was a difpute raifed about the ten *Sibyls* by one, who, your Ladyfhip knows, is no great friend to antiquity; and I was glad to apprehend this opportunity to perform the promife you drew from me then, to vent fomething upon this fubject for your Ladyfhip's fatisfaction.

Madam, in thefe peevifh times, which may be called the ruft of the iron age, there is a race of crofs-grained people, who are malevolent to all antiquity. If they read an old author, it is to quarrel with him, and find fome hole in his coat: they flight the fathers of the primitive times, and prefer *John Calvin*, or a *Caufaban* before them all. Among other tenets of the firft times,

they

they hold the ten *Sibyls* to be fictitious and fabulous, and no better than *Urganda*, or the Lady of the lake, or such doting beldams. They stick not to term their predictions of Christ to be mere mock oracles, and odd arrepititious frantic extravagancies. They cry out, that they were forged and obtruded to the world by some officious christians to procure credit and countenance to their religion among the *Pagans*.

For my part Madam, I am none of this incredulous perverse race of men; but what the current and concurrent testi nonies of the primitive times do hold forth, I give credit thereunto without any scruple.

Now, touching the works of the *Sibyls*, they were in high request among the fathers of the first four centuries, insomuch that they used to urge their prophecies for conversion of *Pagans*, who therefore called the christians *Sibylianists*, nor did they hold it a word of reproach. They were all virgins, and for reward of their chastity, it was thought they had the gift of prophecy; not by any endowment of nature, or inherent human quality, or ordinary ideas in the soul, but by pure divine inspirations, not depending on second causes in sight. They spake not like the ambiguous *Pagan* oracles in riddles, but so clearly, that they sometimes go beyond the *Jewish* prophets: they were called *Siobula*, that is, of the counsels of God, *Sios* in the *Eolic* dialect being *Deus*. They were preferred before all the *Chaldean* wizards, before the *Bacides*, *Branchydæ*, and others; as also before *Tyresias*, *Manto*, *Matis*, or *Caßandra*, &c.

Nor did the christians only value them at that height, but the most learned among the *Ethnicks* did so, as *Varro*, *Livi*, and *Cicero*; the first being the greatest antiquary, the second the greatest historian, and the third the greatest orator, that ever *Rome* had; who speaks so much of that famous acrostic that one of them made of the name of our Saviour, which sure could not be the work of a christian, as some would maliciously obtrude, it being so long before the incarnation.

But

But for the better difcharge of my engagement to your
Ladyfhip, I will rank all the ten before you, with fome
of their moft fignal predictions.

The *Sibyls* were ten in number, whereof there were
five born in *Europe*, to wit, *Sibylla Delphica*, *Cumæa
Samia*, *Cumana*, and *Tyburtina :* the reft were born in
Afia and *Africa*.

The firft was a *Perfian* called *Samberta*, who plainly
foretold many hundred years before in thefe words,
‘ The womb of the Virgin fhall be the falvation of the
‘ *Gentiles*, &c.’

The fecond was *Sibylla Lybica*, who among other
prophecies. hath this, ‘ The day fhall come that men
‘ fhall fee the King of all living things, and a Virgin
‘ Lady fhall hold him in her lap.’

The third was *Delphica*, who faith, ‘ A Prophet fhall
‘ be born of a Virgin.’

The fourth was *Sibylla Cumæa*, born in *Campania* in
Italy, who hath thefe words, ‘ That God fhall be born
‘ of a Virgin, and converfe with finners.’

The fifth was the famous *Erythræa*, born at *Babylon*,
who compofed that famous acroftic which St. *Auguftin*
took fo much pains to tranflate into *Latin ;* which begins, ‘ The earth fhall fweat figns of judgment, from
‘ heaven fhall come a King who fhall reign for ever, *viz.*
‘ in human flefb, to the end that by his prefence he judge
‘ the world. A river of fire and brimftone fhall fall
‘ from heaven, the fun and ftars fhall lofe their light, the
‘ firmament fhall be diffolved, and the moon fhall be
‘ darkened; a trumpet fhall found from heaven in wo-
‘ ful and terrible manner; and the opening of the earth
‘ fhall difcover confufed and dark hell; and before the
‘ judge fhall come every King, *&c.*’

The fixth was *Sibylia Samia*, who faith, ‘ He being
‘ rich, fhall be born of a poor maid : the creatures of the
‘ earth fhall adore him, and praife him for ever.’

The feventh was *Cumana*, who faith, ‘ That he fhould
‘ come from heaven, and reign here in poverty : he fhould
‘ rule in filence, and be born of a Virgin.’

The

The eighth was *Sibylla Hellespontica*, who foretells plainly, that ' A woman shall descend of the *Jews*, called *Mary*, and of her shall be born the Son of God, ' and that without carnal copulation, *&c.*'

: The ninth was *Phrygia*, who saith, ' The highest ' shall come from 'heaven, and shall confirm the counsel ' in heaven, and a Virgin shall be shewed in the valleys. ' of the desarts, *&c.*'

The tenth was *Tyburtina*, born near *Tyber*, who saith, ' The invisible world shall be born of a Virgin, he ' shall converse with sinners, and shall of them be despised, *&c.*'

. Moreover, St. *Augustin* reciteth these prophecies following of the *Sibyls:* ' Then shall he be taken by the ' wicked hands of infidels, and they shall give him buffets on his face; they shall spit upon him with their ' foul and accursed mouths, he shall turn unto them his ' shoulders, suffering them to be whipped: he also shall ' be crowned with thorns; they shall give him gall to ' eat, and vinegar to drink: then the veil of the temple ' shall rend, and at mid-day it shall be dark night, *&c.*'

Lanctantius relateth these prophecies of theirs, ' He ' shall raise the dead, the impotent and lame shall go, the ' deaf shall hear, the blind shall see, and the dumb ' speak, *&c.*'

In fine, out of the works of the *Sibyls* may be deduced a good part of the miracles and sufferings of Christ; therefore for my part I will not cavil with antiquity, or traduce the primitive church, but I think I may believe without danger, that those *Sibyls* might be select instruments to announce the dispensations of heaven to mankind. Nor do I see they do the church of God any good service or advantage at all, who question the truth of their writings, (as also *Trismegistus* his *Pymandra* and *Aristæus*, &c.) who have been handed over to posterity as incontroulable truths for so many ages.

. Thus, Madam, have I done something of that task you imposed upon me touching the ten *Sibyls;* whereunto I may well add your Ladyship for the eleventh: for

among

among other things, I remember you foretold confidently that the *Scotifh* kirk would deftroy the *Englifh*
church; and that if the hierarchy went down, monarchy
would not be of long continuance.

Your Ladyfhip I remember foretold alfo, how thofe
unhappy feparatifts the puritans would bring all things at
laft into confufion, who fince are called prefbyterians,
or *Jews* of the New Teftament; and they not improperly may be called fo, for they fympathize much with
that nation in a revengeful fanguinary humour, and thirft-
ing after blood. I could produce a cloud of examples,
but let two fuffice.

· There lived a few years before the long parliament
near *Clun-Caftle* in *Wales*, a good old widow that had
two fons grown to mens eftate, who having taken the
holy facrament on a firft *Sunday* in the month, at their
return home they entered into a difpute touching the
manner of receiving it   The eldeft brother who was an
orthodox proteftant (with the mother) held it was very
fitting, it being the higheft act of devotion, that it
fliould be taken in the humbleft pofture that could be
upon the knees: the other, being a puritan, oppofed it,
and the difpute grew high, but it ended without much
heat. The next day being both come home to dinner
from their bufinefs abroad, the eldeft brother, as it was
his cuftom, took a nap upon a cufhion at the end of the
table, that he might be the more frefh for labour. The
puritan brother, called *Enoch Evans*, fpying his opportunity fetched an ax, which he had provided it feems on
purpofe, and ftealing foftly to the table, he chopped off
his brother's head: the old mother hearing a noife, came
fuddenly from the next room, and there found the body
and head of her eldeft fon both afunder, and reaking in
hot blood: O villain, cried fhe, *Haft thou murdered*
thy brother? Yes, quoth he, *and you fhall after him;*
and fo ftriking her down, he dragged her body to the
threfhold of the door, and there chopped off her head
alfo, and put them both in a bag: but thinking to fly he
was apprehended and brought before the next Juftice of

Peace, who chanced to be Sir *Robert Howard;* ſo the murderer the next aſſizes after was condemned, and the law could but only hang him, though he had committed matricide and fraticide.

I will fetch another example of their cruelty from *Scotland.* The late Marquis of *Montroſe* being betray-ed by a Lord in whoſe houſe he lay, was brought pri-ſoner of war to *Edinburgh;* there the common hangman met him at the town's end, and firſt pulled off his hat, then he forced him up to a cart, and hurried him like a condemned perſon, though he had not yet been arraign-ed, much leſs convicted, thro' the great ſtreet, and brought him before the parliament, where being pre-ſently condemned, he was poſted away to the gallows, which was above thirty foot high: there his hand was cut off firſt, then he was lifted up by pullies to the top, and then hanged in the moſt ignominious manner that could be. Being taken down, his head was chopped off and nailed to the high croſs; his arms, thighs, and legs were ſent to be ſet up in ſeveral places, and the reſt of his body was thrown away, and deprived of chriſtian burial. Thus was this nobleman uſed, though one of the antienteſt peers of *Scotland,* and eſteemed the great-eſt honour of that country both at home and abroad. Add hereunto the mortal cruelty they uſed to their young King, with whom they would not treat unleſs he ac-knowleged his father to be a tyrant, and his mother an idolatreſs, &c.

So I moſt humbly kiſs your hands, and reſt always, Madam,

Your Ladyſhip's moſt
faithfully devoted ſervant,

London, *Aug.* 30.   J. H.

LETTER XCI.

To the incomparable Lady, the Lady M. CARY.

Madam,

I Have difcovered fo much of divinity in you, that he who would find your equal, muft feek one in the other world. I might play the oracle, and more truly pronounce you the wifeft of women, than he did *Pythagoras* the wifeft of men: for queftionlefs, that he or fhe are the wifeft of all human creatures, who are careful of preferving the nobleft part of them, I mean the foul. They who prink and pamper the body, and neglect the foul, are like one, who having a nightingale in his houfe, is more fond of the wicker cage than of the bird; or rather, like one who hath a pearl of an invaluable price, and efteems the poor box that holds it more than the jewel. The rational foul is the breath of God almighty, fhe is his very image: therefore who taints his foul may be faid to throw dirt in God's face, and make his breath ftink. The foul is a fpark of immortality, fhe is a divine light, and the body is but a focket of clay that holds it. In fome this light goes out with an ill-favoured ftench; but others have a fave-all to preferve it from making any fnuff at all. Of this number, Madam, you are one that fhine cleareft in this horizon, which makes me fo much

Your Ladyfhip's truly devoted fervant,

Lond. Nov. 3.   **J. H.**

The E N D.

INDEX

PRINCIPAL MATTERS contained
in thefe LETTERS.

S f   Breda

Elizabeth

I N D E X.

Henry

INDEX.

INDEX.

INDEX.

INDEX.

F I N I S.

Lightning Source UK Ltd.
Milton Keynes UK
UKHW030444290119
336361UK00006B/623/P